The New Politics of Strategic Resources

THE NEW POLITICS OF STRATEGIC RESOURCES

Energy and Food Security Challenges in the 21st Century

DAVID STEVEN
EMILY O'BRIEN
BRUCE JONES

Editors

BROOKINGS INSTITUTION PRESS
Washington, D.C.

Library of Congress Cataloging-in-Publication data

The new politics of strategic resources : energy and food security challenges in the 21st
century / David Steven, Emily O'Brien, and Bruce Jones, editors. —1st Edition.
   pages   cm
Includes bibliographical references and index.
   Summary: "Examines the political dimensions of strategic resource challenges at the
domestic and international levels, including energy and food markets, water scarcity, and the
roles of various actors such as the U.S., China, India, Russia, Saudi Arabia, and others"—
Provided by publisher.
   ISBN 978-0-8157-2533-6 (pbk. : alk. paper)—ISBN 978-0-8157-2534-3 (ebook) 1.
Energy policy. 2. Food security. 3. Natural resources—Management. I. Steven, David,
1968– editor.

HD9502.A2N493 2014
333.7—dc23   2014028556

Digital printing

Typeset in Adobe Garamond

Composition by Cynthia Stock
Silver Spring, Maryland

Contents

PART III. THE CRITICAL ACTOR

Acknowledgments

We wish to thank the many who provided strategic help and support along the way, enabling the publication of this edited volume, as well as its companion, *The Risk Pivot: Great Powers, International Security, and the Energy Revolution*, written by two of the editors, Bruce Jones and David Steven.

Both volumes have been made possible by the John T. and Catherine D. MacArthur Foundation, which first underwrote a key research project at Brookings investigating the geopolitics of resource scarcity. The findings of that program became the principal source of research for this book. The Skoll Global Threats Fund supported a cognate project exploring the governance of global issues—of which energy and climate are emerging as critical exemplars of the challenges facing world leaders today. We are very grateful for the support received from both organizations.

New York University's Abu Dhabi Institute also hosted a conference in November 2013 during which the findings reflected here were reviewed with scholars from the United States, Europe, and the emerging powers, as well as with officials from the United Nations, International Renewable Energy Agency, and other key institutions. We appreciate all participants' collaboration.

In addition, Shiri Avnery and Farah Hegazi of the NYU Center on International Cooperation, Matthew Kent and Jane Frewer of River Path, and Rob Keane and Katherine Elgin of the Brookings Institution all provided research efforts from which we've drawn.

A particular thanks to our contributors for the quality of their contributions and the endurance of their patience with us—edited volumes are a long and laborious process, and we appreciate their engagement and good humor throughout.

This work on the geopolitics of resource scarcity project was one part of a broader program at Brookings, the Project on International Order and Strategy.

1

Introduction: Energy Policy on the Edge

BRUCE JONES AND DAVID STEVEN

This book is about the political economy of energy. There are few more consequential topics for understanding today's global economy, for global development, or the very well-being of humankind.

Energy isn't always thought of as being essential to the fabric of the global economy, or to development—but it should be. This can be dramatized by juxtaposing three simple facts.

Energy goods account for almost one out of every five dollars traded in today's global economy. That makes it one of the largest sectors in contemporary globalization. Only finance is in the same league in terms of shares of global economy activity.

Despite the huge volumes of energy being produced and consumed, more is needed: 1.3 billion people live without access to modern energy. This is not a phenomenon primarily of the world's poorest states, but of its most dynamics ones—there are upward of 300 million without access to modern energy in India alone, a state otherwise poised to join the ranks of the top powers. Securing new supplies for the world's energy insecure is going to be among the most critical tasks of development in the coming decades.

Yet, we're already burning more fossil fuels than our climate can handle. The drive to expand energy access and security will complicate and be complicated by the mounting fight and fright over global warming. The vast majority of the world's scientists agree that to stabilize the global climate at a less than 2°C rise in average global temperatures requires keeping the quantity of carbon and other greenhouse gases in the atmosphere at around 450 parts per million. Right now, we're at

403 ppm and we're on track to hit 650 ppm—and that's *if* governments meet the climate targets they agreed to in Copenhagen in 2009. Growing demand for energy by the world's rising states and growing middle classes puts that target comprehensively out of reach even if we see something approaching the full-scale decarbonization of the economy in the West—a near-impossible challenge.

The long and the short of it is, energy is emerging as a defining feature of globalization, of global development, and, of course, of climate change. Indeed, if the first phase of modern globalization was about its geographical spread (what's been called *extensive* globalization), and the second was about the deepening of economic integration between existing markets (*intensive* globalization), there's a case for arguing that the next phase is going to be heavily about energy—its acquisition, transportation, and, most importantly, the debate over whether to constrain its use. Call it the phase of *sustainable* globalization.

It's also reshaping geopolitics. In a book published simultaneously with this one, Bruce Jones and David Steven examine the geopolitical consequences of the changing global energy landscape. *The Risk Pivot: Great Powers, International Security, and the Energy Revolution* focuses on the way energy is amplifying three already complicated problems: geopolitical competition between the great powers; the struggle over global development in the new middle powers, as well as in fragile states; and global climate change negotiations. The book highlights the critical choices facing the top powers. As we see it, these are three: whether to allow energy to continue to be a source of geopolitical tension for globalization; whether to choose deliberately to use energy as a source of additional tension, that is, to use energy as a political and economic weapon against one another; or whether to forge a "governance" approach, that is, to build the relationships, rules, and mechanisms to limit the way energy amplifies tensions and, by contrast, to find areas—and important ones do exist—where energy is a source of win-win outcomes and thus of potential cooperation.

While those outward themes echo through this book as well, our concentration here is *inward*—on the way energy plays into the internal political economy of major states, and on their search for internal and human security (though not neglecting regional security). Geopolitics and international war get a prominent mention herein too, because they cannot be wished away even from the search for more basic forms of security, like food security and internal political stability. But our emphasis here is on the search by major states for secure national "control" (if that word meaningfully applies to global energy dynamics) over the sources of their internal growth and social well-being. Energy plays vitally into that search, especially for the rapidly growing powers.

This book proceeds as follows. We look first precisely to those rapidly growing powers, to examine how it is that energy is literally fueling and simultaneously complicating their rise. These chapters cover the three most important rising powers—China, India, and Brazil. But we also include an analysis of a rising state often overlooked, Nigeria—the seventh most populous state in the world, larger than both Russia and Japan. Then we turn to various dimensions of security, between states to be sure but primarily within states—incorporating key dynamics of human security in our analysis. We examine regional security (between Asia's two giants and in Europe's backyard); the way energy-producing regimes often use energy as a weapon in regional or even global political struggles; and internal security. These chapters incorporate what we might consider status quo actors, like the European Union (EU) and Saudi Arabia—though as the chapters make clear, even these countries face serious challenges to their own status quo. This part also incorporates Russia—often considered to be a "rising" power, but for all intents and purposes really a slumping one.

Then, finally, we look at both the internal and international dimensions of the one state whose energy developments will most shape and constrain global ones: the United States. It may seem odd to treat the United States this way, given the mostly dominant narrative that it is a declining and retreating power. The realities are different. Seen through the lens of energy, the United States is part way through a stunning renaissance. These do not eradicate other sources of U.S. challenge or constraint, but they do substantially offset them. And the energy revolution in the United States is a function first and foremost of the dynamism of the American market model—a fact that has not gone unnoticed in Mumbai or Shanghai, even if it's not yet fully acknowledged in New Delhi or Beijing. Important questions remain for the United States. These are first of all internal—how will it respond to a series of U.S. political economy challenges? But they are also external—will it use its new-found energy strength to attempt to shield itself from international dynamics, retreating into a more isolationist stance? Will it seek to use its energy endowment as a "weapon" of foreign policy? Or will it use its energy strength as a lever to push for more stable markets?

Unsustainable Developments: Energy and the Rising Powers

We start by looking in depth at the internal challenges of energy in the world's most dynamic markets. China and India are obvious targets of that analysis, as the world's two most populous states, and the core of the Brazil, Russia, India, China, and South Africa, or BRICS, grouping. Brazil is not as populous as either state, but it's richer, and so has already thrust its way into the ranks of the top six economies, topping Britain; and it's done so in substantial part because of its ability to harness its own vast energy and food resources. And Nigeria: the world's seventh most populous state doesn't show up on everyone's account of rising state dynamics of the past decade, but it will in the next. At least, it will if it can overcome some deep internal challenges—Nigeria is both a rising state, and a fragile one, a dichotomy that increasingly will characterize the next set of rising states.

If one theme connects the dots between this otherwise disparate set of countries, it is energy insecurity. This is true even of the largest and most successful of them to date, China.

The simple fact is that as China grows, its demand for oil and other forms of energy grows, and so too does the complexity of its search for energy security. In "China's Search for Oil Security: A Critique," Andrew B. Kennedy analyzes the ways in which the Chinese government has sought to enhance its access to oil supplies, focusing on four policies that aim to improve access to oil supplies.

For more than a decade, the Chinese government has encouraged its national oil companies (NOCs) and other state-owned enterprises to "go out"—to invest overseas and gain greater access to foreign resources. However, the results of going out have been limited. While the Chinese NOCs' overseas equity production surpassed 1.5 million barrels a day in 2011, that's only a fraction of global crude oil production at 84.5 million barrels a day. Furthermore, the NOCs do not necessarily send the oil they produce back to China, and it is not necessarily cheaper or more available to China in a supply crisis. Lastly, there is concern that the NOCs' international expansion may actually detract from China's overall welfare and security as the expansion brings China into relationships with isolated states like Iran. (This theme of political risk increasingly flowing to the emerging Asian giants is a central theme of *Risk Pivot*.)

In addition to encouraging its own NOCs to go abroad, China has sought to diversify its energy import mix through "loan-for-oil" and "loan-for-gas" deals, as well as try to diversify the routes that its oil shipments follow. Yet, though the loan-for-oil deals will improve China's overall energy security by reducing its reliance on imports from the Middle East and Africa, the effects will likely not be large.

Also, recognizing the great percentage of its energy that travels through open waters, China has been working to improve its blue-water navy. In theory, a stronger navy would improve China's leverage in its territorial disputes in the East China and South China Seas, helping it to gain control over energy resources there. However, it remains unclear how extensive the energy resources are, and in any case it is unlikely they would dramatically reduce China's dependence on oil imports.

Last, China has been building its own strategic petroleum reserve to strengthen its energy security. This investment has the potential to make a significant contribution to the country's energy security, as it provides Beijing with new policy options in the event of a disruption to oil imports. However, it would be more effective if it were used in coordination with the reserve systems of other countries.

While Beijing has been trying to build up domestic capabilities and bilateral deals with oil-producing states, the payoff for China's energy security has been limited. Going forward, Kennedy argues, China will need to invest in stronger multilateral cooperation to truly enhance its energy security.

If anything, India faces starker challenges still. As India's economy and population grow, so too does its resources challenge. Energy, water, food, and environmental challenges will continue to present themselves globally, but India provides a powerful illustration of how complex and deep these challenges are. Domestically, inadequate infrastructure, intense political pressures, and the need to tackle poverty all constrain India's options with regard to resources.

Thus, in "Materials, Markets, Multilateralism: A Strategic Approach to India's Resource Challenges," David Steven and Arunabha Ghosh argue that while resource scarcity will play an important role in shaping India's future, it is unclear that India will be able to change the game domestically. More likely, global drivers will help frame what is possible within India's domestic policy environment: India's exposure to the breakdown in global energy markets could grow; the country's size does give it considerable power in the food market; transnational water stress issues may prove unmanageable in the medium term; the intersection between maritime and energy security could become a source of international friction; and climate change politics will become increasingly challenging.

However, the global governance regimes that deal with the issues that India most cares about are both weak and contested, and India often lacks a clear strategy for its international engagement. Both India and its allies, therefore, have an incentive to look for opportunities for international cooperation on resource and environmental issues. Greater international engagement can help increase understanding of the risks that India faces, provide India with a platform to share potential solutions with its partners, provide a basis for Indian leadership in the G-20, and help India influence the post-2015 development agenda. But to take full advantage of more decisive international engagement on resource issues, India will need to increase its capacity to engage internationally.

Brazil has had an easier time so far, as it is well endowed with domestic resources. Of the emerging powers, it's the country that most resembles the United States in terms of its providence and commitment to global norms. No surprise, then, that as energy insecurity has receded as an internal challenge for Brazil, it has turned its gaze outward. As Antonio Jorge Ramalho argues in "Brazil's Principled Pragmatism: A Viable Response to the New Geopolitics of Resource Competition?," Brazil's concern increasingly is not its internal energy issues, but its external ones. As the world population and developing economies expand, Brazil is preparing for a world with increased demand for resources and attempting to position itself to take advantage of the opportunities such a world offers.

Brazil sees a strong link between development and security. As resource scar-city grows, it sees a greater potential for international conflicts. To cope with this possibility, governments need a legitimate global response that will allow coun-tries like Brazil to enlarge their supply of biofuels. Brazilian policy emphasizes the argument that to sustainably grow, these governments must respect both human rights and the environment, suggesting that sustainable development and social inclusion need to be part of the response. Brazil, which is already in the process of reducing subsidies to Petrobras and relies on small farms to provide more than 40 percent of the country's total agriculture, believes that it can become a model of sustainable development for other developing countries, and that it can lead on the articulation of multilateral frameworks to advance these goals.

Nigeria has no such luck. Domestic demand in Nigeria is shaped primarily by two forces—a growing, urbanizing, and slowly aging population, and a grow-ing but unstable economy. Nigeria's population has more than quadrupled since 1950, and most of the population is now adult and increasingly urban, creating significant demand for food, water, land, power, and other resources. Further increasing resource demand is Nigeria's oil-dependent economy, an economy that is large for the region but still does not provide jobs for its population. Overall, consumption exceeds production, with natural resource revenues, debt, remittances from overseas, and development assistance filling the gap.

These factors combined create the possibility of a demographic disaster, cou-pled with a steep growth in domestic resource demand. Nigeria—Africa's biggest oil producer—has already failed to meet domestic energy requirements, and the gap between supply and domestic demand will continue to grow without major reforms. In addition, a growing population will put increased stress on Nigeria's land, food, and water resources, and this stress will likely be exacerbated by cli-mate change.

Looking forward, then, Mark Weston in "The Big Squeeze: Nigeria on the Brink" sees three broad scenarios ahead: the good, the bad, and the ugly. *The good*—Nigeria begins by reforming oil and gas production, reducing waste, and taking much stronger measures to limit damage to the local environment. The Nigerian government has already taken two important steps toward this out-come: investing excess profits in three funds (one for the long term, one for shorter-term investments, and one for stabilization) managed by the Nigerian Sovereign Investment Authority; and becoming more involved with the Extrac-tive Industries Transparency Initiative. In this scenario, Nigeria's international partners play a key role by allowing more Nigerians to migrate legally to find work, reducing transnational crime by legalizing narcotics, and holding their businesses in Nigeria accountable. *The bad*—If Nigeria continues with busi-ness as usual, its prospects of meeting domestic and international demand for resources will be bleak, with problems beginning at a local level likely to spread to the whole country and perhaps to the wider West Africa region. And *the ugly*—In this scenario, the country reverts to the military dictatorships of its past or descends into civil war. This would in part be caused by increased difficulty in investing in the impoverished, troubled north of the country.

The effects of the country's failure to capitalize on its human and natural resources have so far been limited to widespread and growing poverty and intermittent localized unrest, but the consequences of continued failure over the next two decades are likely to be much more serious. Nigeria does not lack resources or the human capital required to make use of them. Until now, however, it has lacked the leadership and the vision to realize its potential, and this has left it delicately balanced between feast and famine as it prepares for a more crowded, more demanding future.

Perhaps even more than India, Nigeria illustrates what's ahead as we grapple with (un)sustainable globalization.

International, Regional, and Human Insecurity: The Modern Dynamics of Energy

Nigeria and other developing states may face the toughest challenges, but even today's most established energy players can't escape the consequences of turbulent global realities. That's true for Europe, exposed to serious energy security risks through its reliance on Russian imports—a reality that Europe was exploring, but not really grappling with, before the Ukraine crisis. Energy complicates regional security, as India and China—potential partners, practical rivals—are discovering. It also complicates internal stability, as Saudi Arabia is discovering. Saudi Arabia is still the country whose oil exports will do most to affect the global price of oil, but it is now a country facing serious internal political economy constraints around energy use and domestic instability. And all developing states confront both short-term food insecurity and long-term water insecurity as a consequence of global energy and climate patterns. Most states have to tackle these issues internally; some, notably petrostates, sometimes try to export them, including by financing revolutionary politics overseas, or, in the case of Russia, positioning itself to profit from instability in global markets.

Europe's search for greater energy security has, until now, largely been a story about pipelines. As Angel Saz-Carranza and Marie Vandendriessche outline in "Routes to Energy Security: The Geopolitics of Gas Pipelines between the EU and Its Southeastern Neighbors," Europe was engaged in an exploration of alternatives to relying on Russian pipelines well before the Ukraine crisis. As the world's energy flows evolve, Europe is scrambling to respond to the new energy outlook while simultaneously confronting classical geopolitical issues with Russia.

The European Union is highly reliant on imports for energy (it imports 54 percent of its energy needs), and although Europe is working toward a low-carbon economy, it will likely remain so. The European Commission has identified three main policy tracks to improve its security of supply. First, continue exploiting and increasing indigenous energy sources such as renewable energy, domestic reserves of conventional and unconventional fossil fuels, and nuclear energy. Second, improve energy efficiency, including deploying smart grids and having all member states meet the previously agreed objective of ensuring electricity interconnections equivalent to 10 percent of their installed production capacity. Third, and most difficult, diversify supply countries and routes for imported fossil fuels. Natural gas is increasing its share of the EU's energy mix—currently at 24 percent—and forms the centerpiece of an intricate geopolitical competition to the EU's east. There is no such thing as a global natural gas market: natural gas is produced, transported, and traded through regional, fragmented markets. Its pricing also displays regional differentiation. A further particularity of natural gas as an energy source is the importance of transit countries. As demand for gas increases and production from landlocked countries grows, supply arrangements increasingly operate through transit countries. Of course, arrangements through transit countries are more prone to disruption than direct exporter-importer relations. In addition, the more intermediaries there are in the equation, the larger the set of diverging economic interests. The EU's campaign to diversify its energy imports away from Russia must take this important factor into account at all times: its efforts inevitably involve transport through additional states.

One-third of the EU's natural gas needs are met by Russia. Many have argued, through a Realpolitik lens, that Russia wields its energy policy as a foreign policy stick, but recent global gas developments may threaten Russia's power source. The EU-Russia gas relationship is currently symbiotic: while the EU relies on Russian gas to keep its houses warm, so too is Gazprom reliant on the EU—the market to which it sends over half of its exports.

As noted above, key to Europe's energy security strategy is diversification away from Russian gas and insecure transit routes. To this end, the EU's main approach has been the construction of a fourth energy corridor, the so-called Southern Gas Corridor (SGC), in order to better access supplies from Southeastern Europe and the Caspian. After much strenuous commercial and political effort, the agreed approach forward will provide Europe access to a Caspian source, but deliver just 2 percent of its future gas needs. In other words, the EU has partly achieved its policy objective of diversifying supplies, but at 2 percent the shift is far from epic. Unless sharp crises such as the 2014 Crimea one lead to rapid and creative policy reconsiderations (and beyond simple *calls* for an "energy union" to actual supranational cooperation), the EU is set to depend on Russia for gas for the foreseeable future. Europe still has a long road ahead in its quest to further diversify suppliers, increase domestic extraction, and shift to alternative energy sources.

Europe is not alone in worrying about its immediate neighborhood; so do China and India—but principally, they worry about each other.

The energy security strategies of China and India have been described as "realist" approaches that are fundamentally opposed to market-based strategies seen around the globe. And the NOCs' quest for investments in oil and gas is often perceived as the single most important energy security strategy of the two countries, portrayed as a zero-sum game for energy resources that will undermine energy security for the rest of the world, and a precursor to a more fundamental military conflict between China and India.

C. Raja Mohan and Lydia Powell examine the validity of these narratives, claiming that while policy goals such as self-reliance do contradict the market philosophy, the goals are not necessarily driven by a nationalist agenda, nor will NOCs undermine the reliability of the global oil market. Instead, as they argue in "Energy Rivalry between India and China: Less than Meets the Eye?," the policy goals are often suboptimal compromises between domestic energy challenges and international market and regulatory pressures.

The assumption that Chinese and Indian energy strategies compete with each other and may lead to larger geopolitical confrontation needs to be closely assessed. For many, China and India are seen as natural rivals and the competition between their NOCs seen as one of the many manifestations of a long-standing animosity. However, to treat the two countries' NOCs as equal is to err; the difference between Chinese and Indian NOCs is larger than the difference between the Chinese and Indian economies, and the success of Chinese NOCs over Indian NOCs illustrates the extent to which commercial logic rather than geopolitical preferences underpins the competition between Indian and Chinese NOCs.

On the whole, a combination of commercial necessity and opportunity seems to be driving the international pursuits of Chinese and Indian NOCs, while government policy seems to be driven by domestic industrial policy along with a sense of historic grievance and fear. The risk of a possible military clash between India and China over energy transport corridors cannot be entirely dismissed. India straddles the sea-lanes through which most of China's imported oil passes, and segments of the Chinese strategic and military community are concerned with the potential of the Indian navy to interdict China's maritime oil lifeline. In an atmosphere of mutual suspicion, military planners in China and India seem to be formulating strategy based on the worst-case scenario. However, it may be more appropriate to look at China's investment in maritime power to secure energy transport corridors as a response to the United States' continued command of the maritime commons and India's potential role as partner.

As the line between energy concerns and larger economic and environmental predicaments is increasingly blurred, both countries realize that their energy problem is no longer a short-term foreign policy problem, but a long-term transition to a different and more expensive mix of energy sources and unwelcome changes in the habits and institutions of their ambitious societies. However, though the state is still powerful in the realm of deciding energy policy in both countries, the high level of institutional fragmentation means that achieving consensus on policy is just as hard domestically as it is internationally. To ask them not to grow is equivalent to trapping millions of lives in poverty, yet to let them grow on fossil fuels is equivalent to trapping the world in climate change. In this context, from where and through whom India and China get their fossil fuels is far less important than the choices that India and China make regarding the types of energy they will use in the future.

While Europe, China, and India grapple with the external constraints on energy security, Saudi Arabia is grappling with its *internal* ones. "Resource Security in Saudi Arabia: Domestic Challenges and Global Implications," by Kristian Coates Ulrichsen, reveals that Saudi Arabia is facing a transformative shift in its local and global energy landscape, as domestic consumption pressures challenge the redistributive political economy of the past; Saudi responses to the Arab Spring and similar movements have exacerbated the challenge of sustaining resource scarcity; and trends in oil and gas production will shift the center of the international energy market away from the Gulf. The dilemma facing Saudi policymakers is one of balancing domestic sociopolitical stability against urgent needs to reform and diversify economic structures.

Saudi dependence on oil revenues has been intertwined with state building and economic development since the 1950s. Following the death of King Abdul Aziz Al-Saud in 1953, the processes of modern state formation were intricately connected to the receipt and redistribution of revenues generated by the export of oil—a system confronting interlinked threats to its existence. Saudi Arabia's redistributive economic model faces four major challenges in the years ahead—two internal and two external. The domestic factors are the increasingly unsustainable pattern of domestic energy consumption as well as uncertainty regarding oil reserves, while the international dimensions are, short term, the possibility of a protracted global economic downturn and, medium and longer term, the rebalancing energy landscape across the world. As domestic and regional resource constraints become more pressing, managing the processes of change will become progressively more difficult. The fact that sensitive internal reforms to the sociopolitical and economic structures of rent redistribution must now be undertaken against the backdrop of profound regional upheaval will inject major new uncertainties into the regional security landscape.

Furthermore, the rapidly rising breakeven price of oil needed to balance the budget and the impending succession dynamics within Saudi Arabia increase the likelihood of political volatility. The steady rise both in public spending and in the breakeven level leaves the Saudi government (alongside the other Gulf States) dependent on oil prices remaining high. Any significant drop would leave them economically exposed, and political leaders fear the potential unrest that could ensue from scaling back the oil-funded redistributive state, particularly if it occurs during times of hardship. Happening in parallel to these economic challenges is the imminent political transition in Saudi Arabia as King Abdullah bin Abdul Aziz Al-Saud nears 90 and his designated successor, Crown Prince Salman bin Abdul Aziz Al-Saud, stays in poor health.

A potentially rocky road thus lies ahead for Saudi Arabia, both domestically, in terms of sustainably managing trends in the production and extraction of resources, and internationally, in terms of adapting to the shifting geopolitical balance of resources. Policymakers must be able to operate between and across the two levels in order to address the interrelated issues in an integrated way. The political economy of rent redistribution and patterns of energy-intensive industrialization mean that Saudi Arabia—and the GCC as a whole—must strike a balance between shaping global response mechanisms and decisionmaking processes while simultaneously minimizing the disruptive threat to domestic interests from pressure exerted by international responses to climate change. It also is likely that the coming years and decades will see a rising tension between the need to decisively shift into a post-oil era while seeking to maintain the sociopolitical models that have underpinned regime stability thus far. Against all these domestic uncertainties, the intersection of local and regional trends across the Arab world, with global shifts, has the capacity to produce volatile, even game-changing results. With this in mind, the only certainty is that the status quo that seemingly has survived the first phase of the Arab Spring upheaval cannot be sustained for much longer, and will, eventually, be transformed.

Saudi Arabia's challenge is particularly acute, but it is not unique. Indeed, most states outside the West—and even, to a certain extent, within the West— are grappling with rapidly evolving global markets and their impacts on internal developments. Food is one of the most immediate places that those new global developments are playing out politically, almost always for the worse.

Since the global financial crisis, food price volatility has been pronounced. Indeed, Alex Evans starts "Governance for a Resilient Food System" by highlighting that in the period of 2010–12, some 852 million people in developing countries were chronically undernourished. Part of the reason is simply that the supply and demand fundamentals for food have become progressively tighter in recent years. The convergence of the world's food and energy economies is also emerging as a key factor in food price inflation and volatility as the dependence of modern agriculture on fossil fuels grows and biofuels become more attractive. Also important is the fact that as food supply chains have become more globalized and efficient, they have also become more brittle and less resilient. Above all, a more globalized food system equals a more interdependent one too—which makes the system vulnerable when governments or other key players succumb to panic or herd behaviors.

Four key areas for action against food price volatility and for food security stand out. First, making markets work better. Measures are needed to improve markets in periods of tight supply and demand, including food reserves, more effective regulation of commodity futures, and improved market transparency. Second, reducing the risk of global zero-sum games with food. Ways are needed to reduce the risk of zero-sum games such as panic buying and export bans, protectionism in agricultural trade, and the need to balance countries' right to decide their own policies with their international responsibilities to their trade partners. Third, building resilience on the ground and improving access to food. More work is needed in developing countries, in particular, to improve access to food by scaling up social protection systems. Fourth, addressing long-term supply and demand fundamentals. More investment is needed in a "twenty-first-century green revolution" that improves output, while reducing resource intensity and using land and crops more efficiently and with less waste.

Evans's chapter is neither the first nor the last time we encounter an important subtheme of the volume: the reality that there is a lack of leadership and political space for collective action on resource security, but in addition, current multilateral institutions are badly configured to support and facilitate such action. More broadly, decisionmaking bodies that focus on only one issue struggle to take account of the big picture, often because they only engage one kind of policymaker. The underlying long-term need is for much more shared awareness and interoperability between governments and international organizations.

Like food, water dynamics are similarly important. But water systems work differently than food systems. While water is a global necessity, it is also deeply specific to national and local context, especially as climate change affects various regions dissimilarly. Water use is a transnational challenge—but one that differs from others with subtly distinctive characteristics and therefore responses. "Water Security: Global Implications and Responses," by Daniel Kim Chai Yeo, frames water security as a crosscutting challenge in the context of global resource scarcity and reflects on the role of national and international policy in addressing water security challenges.

Water is one of the most basic human needs, essential for drinking, cooking, washing, and cleaning. But it is also an economic resource, vital for growing crops, keeping livestock, producing goods, and providing services. This distinction between economic and social value has been a core tension in historical attempts to fashion multilateral responses to water. Water also affects other resources, particularly the production of food and generation of energy, and this interdependency between resource issues can act as a multiplier, amplifying local issues into systemic impacts. Water challenges affect every scale of society, from the community to the nation and beyond. But responding to water challenges at one level comes with its own consequences, often unintended, at other scales.

Although there are specific areas where competing uses of water clash with physical or temporal scarcity, outside of these hot spots it is the role of water in other resources that raises the biggest global challenges. The chapter highlights some of these national dimensions through a case study of Ethiopia, a country that encapsulates many of the biggest water challenges and illustrates some water issues that have been insufficiently addressed. Ethiopia has a very difficult climate, with diverse water security concerns at subnational, national, and regional scales. Perhaps most important, the government has demonstrated the political will and leadership to address these, but has limited resources and capacity to do so. The Ministry of Water, Irrigation, and Energy has chosen to focus on three water-sector areas: hydropower, irrigation, and access.

Ethiopia's very ambitious plans will require significant monies and capacity to deliver. Although Ethiopia is willing to commit its own funds to achieve its ambitions, it currently lacks the domestic financial resources to finance them and so will require considerable international support. But this support has not been forthcoming, because international opinion and concerns over environmental and social impacts have deterred development partners from investing in dams and large-scale irrigation. In addition to underinvestment, the practical delivery of Ethiopia's bold political ambitions risks being undermined by weak implementation capacity at the regional and subnational levels. On top of the institutional and political challenges, weather and climate play a defining role in managing water. Ethiopia, as with many countries, will require more support internationally. Given that Ethiopia's water security can have global implications, there is a clear need to take a coordinated and focused multilateral approach to supporting the country in responding to the complex and crosscutting challenges of water.

The case of Ethiopia highlights some practical issues at a national level. In particular, international support is a key element of domestic ambitions. But how far can the global architecture address a local issue? The evidence to date suggests that there is a long way to go. In institutional terms, the global architecture for water lacks strategic coherence. Furthermore, the complexity of water and the range of issues involved are not currently adequately reflected in political or popular discourse. Instead, global narratives of scarcity, conflict, and drought-induced disaster dominate, pointing to economizing and efficiency as the solutions, often with a strong technological bent.

Yet, responding to the complexity of water requires a multilateral architecture that seeks to enable and facilitate national change rather than prescribe solutions. Any global agenda must frame a common set of issues that encompass the full range of water dimensions, to include providing universal access, staying within natural constraints, and sharing benefits. How could multilateralism help to support and enable these outcomes at a national level? It could set a common agenda, develop evidence-based decisionmaking, broker collaboration and implementation, resolve conflict and build trust between actors, and share technical assistance and knowledge.

So far, we've been discussing the ways in which energy and related resources amplify internal political and economic challenges, and some potential state responses to mitigating those challenges. But some states select a different path: they choose to export those risks. That is, as Jeff D. Colgan makes clear in "Oil, Domestic Politics, and International Conflict," some states choose not to try to mitigate the internal political economy challenge, but to fuel instability abroad both as a way of buying off potential domestic rivals, channeling their attention outward, but also as a way of influencing global political dynamics that otherwise constrain them. This phenomenon is particularly prevalent among petrostates.

Petrostates—any country that has an annual net oil export revenue of at least 10 percent of its GDP—have a number of characteristics in common, all of which fall under the category of "petrostate syndrome." Domestically, the syndrome includes suffering from the "resource curse" and a proclivity to provide energy subsidies. In terms of foreign policy, petrostates typically have elevated military spending, large foreign aid donations to other developing countries, funding of foreign insurgencies or terrorists or both, and checkbook diplomacy.

While petrostates share many similarities and common behaviors, they differ systematically in at least one important respect: the degree to which they engage in aggressive foreign policy. This difference is caused principally by the preferences and beliefs of the country's political leadership, which is shaped largely by how the government came to power—and particularly if it came to power by means of a domestic revolution. "Petrorevolutionary" states are roughly three and a half times as likely to instigate a militarized interstate dispute than are non-revolutionary non-petrostates.

These two factors—oil income and revolutionary government—interact in a complex way. For states in which a revolutionary government has taken power, oil increases the state's propensity to instigate international conflicts. In non-revolutionary states, oil provides incentives for aggression, but these are balanced by incentives to avoid international conflict. In other words, the opportunity costs of disrupted oil exports do not really change if the petrostate's government is revolutionary, but the domestic political costs and the calculation of political benefits do change. Thus in a non-revolutionary context, oil appears to have little net impact on a state's propensity for international conflict.

These findings can contribute to a policy framework in three ways: first, by informing intelligence estimates (the elevated conflict propensity of petro-revolutionary states should be taken seriously, perhaps more seriously than it has in the past); second, by reinforcing an existing set of reasons why it is desirable to reduce global oil dependence; and third, by providing further incentive to support institutions that avoid or mitigate the resource curse in oil-producing states.

Of course, the world's most important petrostate is Russia, and it plays what's simultaneously a more complex but also potentially destabilizing game. Pavel K. Baev, author of a chapter on Russia, uses a revealing title: "Russia Gambles on Resource Scarcity: Energy Intrigues in a Time of Political Crisis."

Though Russia is home to many varied natural resources, its economic development has slowed to a 2-3 percent crawl after the 12 percent contraction in 2008–09. This diminishing output in Russian extraction industries cannot be explained by the impact of the global financial crisis alone, but can be attributed primarily to intrusive state policies that set ambitious goals and seek to turn export strength into political influence but also exhibit predatory practices shaped by massive corruption.

Street protests in Moscow in December 2011 prompted a crisis in the legitimacy of Putin's regime, the results of which appear in political zigzags in any number of policy issues. The centrality of energy in Putin's management of state affairs has been somewhat diminished by the commitment to prioritize other urgent challenges, and decisionmaking on energy policy is more than ever shaped by conflicting demands and crisis-driven changes of direction such that short-term imperatives take priority over long-term strategic priorities. The crisis of Putin's regime increases the uncertainty and aggravates the distortions in the energy sector because political control is tightening but losing coherence.

Putin's broader economic strategy has also shifted in principle, from making the country an energy superpower in the early 2000s to moving toward a "reindustrialized" nation with substantial effects on the energy industry. Recreating giant Russian manufacturing enterprises requires a lot of cheap energy and consumes great volumes of raw materials. The demand for more energy, at a cheaper cost, has contributed to a disengagement from innovations in the global energy market, relying instead on traditional (and climate-damaging) methods of extraction and production.

At the same time, Russian gas exports to Europe have become increasingly complicated. From the early 2000s, Russia saw the main problem for expanding its European exports as transit. In oil, Moscow successfully resolved this problem by building terminals in Primorsk and Novorossiysk, while also controlling a channel for oil exports from Kazakhstan and accepting the opening of the Baku-Tbilisi-Ceyhan pipeline. More complex and less successful has been Moscow's management of gas transportation and exports to Europe in general. The execution of the ill-conceived policy of opening new export channels toward the saturated European market has brought endless complications in Russia's relations with two of its key gas partners—Ukraine and Turkey.

Facing difficulties to the west, Russia can thus look east to diversify its energy markets. However, progress in this direction has been slow, largely due to its profound unease in its relations with China.

All of this points to a Russia that places less emphasis on its long-term strategy and more on short-term gains. Russian mainstream analysis of global energy developments tends to be not only rigidly conservative but also self-serving, so that only the trends that fit the interests of the stakeholders are recognized as real. Russian energy-political strategizing has been based on the idea of a golden age of gas, but the realities of such a transition support competing sources and price fluctuations rather than a Russian resurgence. In oil, Russia faces the challenge of potentially lower prices as Saudi Arabia, the United States, and possibly Iraq increase their output. With nuclear energy as well, rigid state control keeps it on a static track instead of seeking new innovation.

The globalized world is typically seen as more brutally competitive than it really is, but this vision is not translated into readiness to invest in strengthening Russia's competitiveness. Natural resources can be a major source of strength if developed responsibly, but they can also sustain bad policies—and Russia has turned itself into a test case for this sustainability.

Decaying Power, Rising Power?
The United States and Its Global Implications

And then we encounter the United States. The U.S. has gone through its own revolution—a shale revolution, and a tight oil revolution, that have seen it re-emerge as a dominant global energy producer, outstripping both Russian gas production and Saudi oil production in 2013. Many forces within the country have treated this revolution and its impact on American foreign policy with something akin to euphoria. Reality is more complex.

We start with America's internal political economy. As Joshua Meltzer, David Steven, and Claire Langley make clear in "Challenges to Sustainable Growth after the Great Recession: How America Can Lead," post–global financial crisis America's economy has some substantial difficulties ahead.

The 2000s brought a slew of unease to the U.S. financial system, and now the United States faces a number of long-term threats: (1) competitiveness is being eroded, (2) the economy is struggling to generate sufficient new jobs, (3) many workers aren't seeing an increase in their earnings, (4) American investment in infrastructure and human capital is slackening, (5) growth has been driven by high levels of indebtedness, (6) there are growing fiscal pressures, and (7) the U.S. economy is affected by broader global imbalances. Socially, this all means that while overall Americans are richer, healthier, and better educated than they were after WWII, a number of negative trends prevail, particularly increased inequality and a decline of economic mobility. Though international trends have contributed to these problems, inadequate education, tax and transfer payments, labor regulation, and housing cost regulation have also hindered mobility and equality. And there are environmental consequences to the growing economy.

Further driving unease is a strong divide about how the country should address these long-term issues. While demographics offer a picture of a more competitive America in terms of population growth and age, age and race divides may contribute to a political realignment. And though this change suggests that the political system will drive more decisive action, the country's political system is likely to remain indecisive. While polarity is growing, so is a loss of trust in the elites and in general. The view is not totally negative, however—this grid-lock may actually create space for other actors to challenge the status quo, and the country maintains a number of absolute geopolitical strengths, including its security strength and growth potential.

The chapter identifies four potential future scenarios. "Muddle through"—this scenario envisions a business-as-usual approach, though with a slight rebalancing of growth from the richest Americans to the middle classes. The United States will emerge as a major producer of both unconventional oil and gas, but carbon emissions are only reduced slowly. "Going for growth"—this scenario assumes a singular focus on growing the economy. Unconventional oil and shale gas are rapidly exploited and often exported. While domestic demand for coal falls, low-cost coal is sold to emerging markets, boosting emissions in other countries. Consumption is a key driver of economic growth, which is rapid but unevenly distributed. American resilience to risk is strengthened, but resources are used to react to, not manage, crises. "Intelligent design"—this scenario sees strong economic growth, but with a more deliberate attempt to guide trends and risks. Administrations focus on employment through investment in education and training, and innovative approaches to regulation. In the energy sector, new opportunities are maximized through policies supporting the potential of gas to reduce emissions and some contribution from the energy sector to fiscal consolidation. And "Emergency response"—this scenario sees policy driven by a series of shocks, leading to a net negative economic impact. Other impacts are difficult to predict.

Having examined the current status of the American economy, the chapter identifies three main requirements for policies that will drive the United States toward the "intelligent design" scenario: (1) a future direction cannot rely too heavily on the federal government, (2) a new growth model is only likely to work if it generates wealth for all, and (3) policies will need to fulfill a vision of environmental sustainability based on greater resilience in the face of crisis and protection from immediate environmental impacts.

The U.S. has the opportunity to lead the international system on a number of issues, but American leadership needs to be underpinned by a robust economy. By addressing the key economic, environmental, and social challenges that the country faces, the economic base for American leadership should be strengthened.

Kevin Massy picks up on this theme in "Governance Challenges and the Role of the United States in the New Energy Landscape." We asked Kevin to think through the central questions in the international governance of energy. And, wisely, rather than turning to an account of the various formal and informal institutions that have been forged to deal with energy questions, he turned instead to the single most consequential variable: how the United States seeks to shape global energy markets. He starts, as we do, by identifying insecurities and vulnerabilities—specifically, five factors that are likely to make market failures more common in the current energy landscape: a shifting macroeconomic landscape, the increasing prominence of new state-backed actors, the increasing technical and political complexity around energy production, the globalization of technology itself, and the externalized costs of greenhouse gas emissions. He notes that the United States finds itself in a unique position to address these challenges and to promote improved market function and overall energy governance.

The energy sector is witnessing a structural and permanent shift in global consumption and production patterns. Previously, trade in global energy took place within a framework of governance established by the Organization of Petroleum Exporting Countries (OPEC) and the International Energy Agency (IEA). Today, the growth in demand from emerging-market countries—particularly in Asia—coincides with a decline in demand among countries making up the Organization for Economic Cooperation and Development (OECD) owing to increased efficiency and stable or declining populations. Another factor changing the demand-supply landscape is the widespread commercialization of technology to produce "unconventional" oil and gas resources in the United States. The implications of the changing supply-demand landscape for energy governance are profound. Because China and India not full members of the OECD, and therefore not represented in the IEA, the major drivers of demand are not part of the conversation. At the same time, the increasing dysfunction of OPEC is leading to reduced certainty with regard to production.

A direct consequence of the structural changes in the global energy market is a greater prominence of state-owned or state-controlled entities in the international energy sector, usually in the form of NOCs. The increasing prominence of state-controlled companies in energy development projects overseas presents several governance-related challenges. The first challenges address the NOCs' motivations—real and perceived—which are more likely to be seen as geopolitical instead of purely commercial. The displacement of international oil companies (IOCs) by NOCs also has implications for the stability of host countries, as NOCs are not bound by the same internationally monitored levels of operational and ethical transparency as are IOCs. The rise of NOCs also raises the possibility of complicated IOC-NOC relations and NOC–host country relations in places like the United States and Canada.

As the world's demand for oil and gas rises and production from traditional hydrocarbon regions declines, countries and companies are having to look to ever more complex and challenging frontiers for production. This push for new production opportunities comes with new technical hazards for which governance structures are absent or only partially in place. Frontier production can also combine both technical and political risk, for example, in the Arctic. New mechanisms are needed to ensure that the risks of frontier exploration and production are fully internalized. Failure to do so carries the risk of an accident that will have negative consequences for the environment and industry.

A related, but distinct, trend that is increasing the challenge of energy governance is the diffusion of energy technologies, such as civil nuclear power, to emerging and developing-market countries. The transmission of complex energy-related technologies to new markets offers significant opportunity as more countries harness advanced exploration, production, and consumption knowledge to meet demand. However, this diffusion comes with the risk that countries adopting new technologies will not absorb all the risks themselves but be content to let some of these risks flow to the broader international system. An additional governance challenge arising from the globalization of energy technology relates to the increasing interconnectedness of stakeholders and the increasing potential for widespread consequences from local events.

One of the largest market failures related to the energy sector has been the ongoing externalization of the climate-related costs associated with the burning of fossil fuels. In the absence of an overarching global mechanism for mitigating greenhouse gases, several innovative measures involving direct intervention in the Earth's biosphere or atmosphere are being considered to address global warming. While geoengineering projects (which can be divided into two major categories:

carbon dioxide reduction and solar radiation management) have traditionally been considered a "Plan B," they are now gaining prominence as serious possibilities. While the merits of each of these measures as a means of reducing greenhouse gases is a matter of debate, the possible side effects or unintended consequences of their deployment throw up a stark set of governance challenges. At the time of writing, the United States has begun to carve out a leadership role on climate issues, but it remains to be seen how far, how deep, how sustained, and, most of all, how successful this effort will be.

Changing economic, technological, and environmental factors are likely to present significant new challenges for energy governance in the coming decade. The new energy landscape will pose technical as well as political governance challenges. Fortunately, for nearly all of the obstacles outlined above, one actor above others has the ability to shape the governance agenda positively for the new energy landscape: the United States, which has the prospect of being both the world's biggest consumer and producer of oil. Using market mechanisms to correct market failures and acting to further its own economic and geopolitical interests, the United States could make meaningful progress on one of the most intractable governance challenges of the age.

The pivotal role of the United States is a conclusion also of *The Risk Pivot: Great Powers, International Security, and the Energy Revolution.* That book and this one are designed to be treated as companion volumes. *The New Politics of Strategic Resources* sets out the underlying political economy realities for several of the most consequential states and for some crosscutting global challenges like food and water. *The Risk Pivot* builds on that background and extrapolates from it the key dynamics that are likely to shape great-power tensions and those that seem certain to complicate globalization and climate change negotiations.

Both set out key choices that confront the top powers but first and foremost challenge the United States. This volume provides the deep context in which the United States must make its choices. It does not aim to be comprehensive—we could have added chapters on Indonesia and Turkey, on Venezuela and Pakistan, on Australia and Canada, and many others besides. But we hope that the selection of country studies and thematic issues discussed in the book illustrate the emerging global dynamics, without exhausting them—or the reader!

PART I

The Rising Actors

2

China's Search for Oil Security: A Critique

ANDREW B. KENNEDY

As China's economy has soared in the twenty-first century, its thirst for oil has defied gravity as well. Between 2001 and 2012, China's oil consumption more than doubled, and its share of world demand jumped from 6 to 12 percent.[1] Even in 2009, as world oil consumption sank amid the global financial crisis, China's consumption grew more than 3 percent. This growing demand, along with rising production in the United States, means that China is poised to become the world's top oil importer in 2014. More and more of China's supply will come from abroad. In recent years, China has had to import between 50 and 60 percent of its crude oil.[2] By 2035 that figure could approach 80 percent.[3]

Little wonder, then, that the topic of "energy security"—traditionally defined as the ability of a country to procure sufficient, affordable, and reliable energy supplies—has become a hot topic in China over the past decade.[4] Whereas the *People's Daily* mentioned the term "energy security" (*nengyuan anquan*) only once in 2000, the Chinese Communist Party's official newspaper published 476 articles using the term from 2009 to 2011. For many in China, the country's biggest problem in this regard is its mounting reliance on energy imports and the external vulnerability that these imports imply. Others take a less traditional view and highlight China's domestic energy challenges, especially the unreliability of its power sector and the environmental costs imposed by its heavy reliance on coal. In both cases, the concern is that energy represents a growing challenge that China must confront.[5]

This chapter focuses on China's search for energy security with respect to oil in particular. While coal remains the dominant energy source for China, oil poses a unique challenge for the country. Indeed, China remains far more dependent on the outside world for oil than for any other energy source. In 2012 China imported 25 percent of its natural gas, but 59 percent of its oil.[6] There is also no ready substitute for oil as a transport fuel, notwithstanding growing interest in alternative-fuel vehicles within China. In contrast, there are several alternatives to natural gas, which is typically used for chemical feedstock and power generation.[7] To be sure, China does possess substantial shale deposits, which hold large quantities of both oil and natural gas, but the country does not possess all of the resources that have enabled the "shale revolution" in the United States. These include not only a strong oil field services sector but also a competitive and technologically innovative industry, access to land facilitated by private ownership, deep financial markets, and a supportive fiscal and regulatory environment.[8] China hopes to increase production of unconventional oil, including "tight oil" from its shale deposits, to 1 million barrels a day by 2030.[9] Yet even if China is fortunate enough to reach this goal, the new production will hardly suffice to meet China's growing demand, which is projected to increase by 5.4 million barrels a day over that time period.[10] The search for oil security will thus remain a key aspect of China's foreign relations for years to come.

The following analysis summarizes and critiques the way in which the Chinese government has sought to enhance its access to oil supplies in recent years. As described below, China has been actively building up national capabilities and concluding bilateral deals with oil-producing states. The payoff for China's energy security, however, has been limited. China has supported the international expansion of its national oil companies (NOCs), for example, but this expansion has not greatly enhanced the country's energy security. China has also sought to diversify its portfolio of oil suppliers, but it remains heavily reliant on the Persian Gulf and Africa for oil imports. China is also investing in new naval capabilities, but whether these will improve China's energy security depends on the kinds of forces that are developed and how they are used. China's development of its own strategic petroleum reserve (SPR) will give its leaders new options in the event of supply crises, but it also means that Beijing will have to coordinate more effectively with other major oil importers. Going forward, therefore, China will need to invest in stronger multilateral cooperation to enhance its energy security more substantially.

China's Search for Oil Security

China's leaders have adopted a range of policies to improve their country's access to oil supplies in recent years. Four of these are highlighted below: supporting the international expansion of China's NOCs, diversifying China's supply port-folio, extending the reach of the People's Liberation Army Navy (PLAN), and building China's own SPR. The following discussion considers each of these initiatives in turn.

The NOCs Go Out

For more than a decade, the Chinese government has encouraged its NOCs and other state-owned enterprises to "go out"—to invest overseas and gain greater access to resources abroad.[11] The NOCs themselves were already eager to go abroad to expand their reserves and increase profits. The China National Petroleum Corporation (CNPC), for example, was looking for opportunities to invest overseas as early as the late 1980s, particularly as domestic opportunities began to look comparatively meager. The government's subsequent support for the NOCs' international expansion emerged in the late 1990s as the government sought to transform some of its state-owned enterprises into internationally competitive corporations. Government support also developed as the country was becoming increasingly dependent on imported oil: it was believed that oil produced by Chinese companies abroad would be a more secure source of supply than oil purchased on international markets.[12]

China's three major NOCs—CNPC, the China Petrochemical Corporation (Sinopec), and the China National Offshore Oil Corporation (CNOOC)—are not simply tools of the Chinese state, but autonomous organizations that have a strong sense of their own interests. As Erica Downs has argued, whereas the Chinese state's capacity for regulating the energy sector is relatively weak, the NOCs are highly capable and well-resourced organizations.[13] They enjoy strong profitability and excellent political connections, and they also possess impressive technical expertise, which makes it difficult for Chinese officials to challenge their arguments. The chief executives of China's NOCs even outrank some of the officials who are charged with regulating them. To be sure, the Chinese Communist Party retains powerful leverage over state firms through its personnel appointment system, and there was a notable reshuffling of the NOC chief executive officers in 2011.[14] If anything, however, the tight connections between the Chinese Community Party and the leadership of the NOCs reinforce the tendency to conflate the international expansion of the NOCs with the enhancement of China's national energy security.[15]

The NOCs' foreign investments over the past decade have certainly been impressive. Foreign investments have been made not only by the three major NOCs but also by smaller energy players such as Sinochem and CITIC Energy. Overall, Chinese companies were involved in forty-three separate foreign oil and gas acquisition deals between 2002 and 2010, deals that were worth roughly

US$65 billion.[16] In 2011 and 2012 the NOCs invested an additional US$52 billion in overseas oil and gas assets.[17] As a result, their overseas equity oil production has grown dramatically, from 140,000 barrels a day in 2000 to roughly 2 million barrels a day by mid-2013.[18] The latter figure was still less than a third of China's oil imports in 2012, however.[19]

The question remains: how much has the NOCs' expansion enhanced China's energy security? NOC investments have certainly supported the expansion of oil production worldwide over the past decade, which has presumably helped to ease tightening markets and to limit increases in the price of crude oil. In that sense, the investments of the NOCs have enhanced the energy security not only of China, but also of other major oil consumers. Even so, these investments have made a small contribution to global production. The NOCs' overseas equity production has reached 2 million barrels a day, but global oil production was 89.2 million barrels a day in 2012.[20]

Besides making a small contribution to the expansion of global supply, it is unclear that the "going out" strategy has improved China's energy security. For example, the NOCs do not necessarily send the oil they produce overseas back to China. Instead, they apparently prefer to let market considerations dictate where it is sold. China's equity production in Venezuela, for example, is not necessarily shipped back to China, not only because of the distance involved but also because Venezuelan heavy crude was not compatible with Chinese refining capabilities in the past. Some of CNPC's equity production in Kazakhstan is also being sold on the international market. And while oil exports from African countries to China have been considerable in recent years, it remains unclear how much of the NOCs' production in Africa is shipped back to China.[21]

Nor is it reasonable to assume that oil produced by the NOCs would somehow be cheaper or more available to China in a supply crisis. Physical disruptions that impede the flow of oil to China will affect foreign and Chinese firms alike, and the NOCs have shown little inclination to grant Chinese customers a discount when prices are high. In fact, the NOCs responded to rising crude prices prior to 2008 by *reducing* their supply of refined products to China, resulting in shortages at the pump, since price controls did not allow them to pass their rising costs on to customers.[22] The autonomy that the NOCs exhibited in this case underscores the government's limited ability to control their activities, a limitation that reflects both the privileged political status of the NOCs and the weakness of China's governance capacity in this sphere.[23] Today, some senior Chinese officials apparently believe that the NOCs are motivated more by profit than by patriotism and that the expansion of their assets overseas does not necessarily enhance China's energy security.[24]

There is even concern that the NOCs' international expansion may detract from China's welfare and security. Some analysts have charged that the NOCs routinely overpay for equity stakes in foreign oil fields, thanks to generous financial support from the Chinese government. If so, their expansion could be seen as enriching the oil companies at the expense of national welfare. Recent analyses, however, suggest that this accusation may not be well founded. The scholar Bo Kong, for example, has argued that cases of overpayment seem to have taken place only in the early stages of the NOCs' international expansion, when they were comparatively inexperienced.[25] More recent research by Julie Jiang and Jonathan Sinton has uncovered no evidence of systematic or intentional overpayment.[26]

A more compelling charge against the NOCs is that their international expansion has caused China to become entangled with "pariah" states and thereby complicated its relations with the United States and Europe. Several years ago China's close relations with Sudan—intended to support the CNPC's activities in the country—led Western critics to dub the 2008 Olympics in Beijing "the Genocide Olympics."[27] The criticism evidently stung: China subsequently made a greater effort to support international attempts to address the crisis in Sudan. More recently, the NOCs' interest and activities in Iran have raised the prospect of greater tensions with the United States. In some cases, the NOCs may calculate that they have more to gain from investing in Iran than they stand to lose from U.S. sanctions, and they may lobby the Chinese government to support them accordingly.[28] However, the NOCs' growing interest in the North American market may give them more reason to worry about U.S. sanctions, potentially reducing their interest in Iran.[29]

On balance, the NOCs' "going out" does not seem to have greatly enhanced China's energy security. While it has made a marginal contribution to the global production of crude oil, it does not guarantee greater flows of that oil to China, nor does it guarantee that oil will be more available to China in a supply crisis. In addition, while suggestions that the NOCs are impoverishing China by overpaying for assets are probably going too far, NOC investments in pariah states have complicated China's foreign relations in recent years. In short, the NOCs' expansion is a positive development for the companies themselves, but it is unclear that this is the case for China as a whole.

In Search of New Suppliers

As Winston Churchill once famously observed, "Safety and certainty in oil lie in variety and variety alone."[30] China has certainly sought to heed this advice over the past two decades. In 1995 China relied on just two regions—the Persian Gulf and the Asia-Pacific—for 88 percent of its crude oil imports. Within the Asia-Pacific, China was mainly supplied by Indonesia, which alone accounted for nearly a third of China's total imports. By 2005, when China was importing much larger quantities of oil, the country had significantly diversified its import

Figure 2-1. *China's Crude Oil Imports, by Region, 2013*

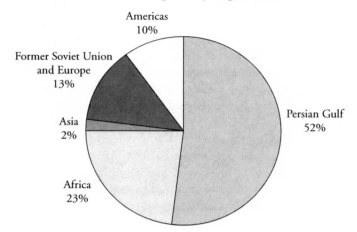

Source: Energy Information Administration, "China" (Washington: U.S. Department of Energy, February 4, 2014) (www.eia.gov/countries/cab.cfm?fips=CH).

mix. That year, African countries accounted for 31 percent of China's imports, and China also imported significant quantities from the Americas and the former Soviet Union, with Russia supplying 10 percent of China's imports. Nonetheless, China remained just as reliant on the Middle East in 2005 as it had been ten years before, with 46 percent of its imports coming from the Persian Gulf. In addition, because China was now heavily reliant on Africa as well as the Middle East, it was now more dependent on the Malacca Strait than it had been before, with more than three-quarters of its oil imports flowing through the strait.[31]

In recent years, China's import mix has altered slightly, but not necessarily for the better. In 2009 China imported nearly 48 percent of its crude from its top three suppliers (Saudi Arabia, Angola, and Iran).[32] In 2013 China imported just 42 percent from the top three—which now included Russia rather than Iran.[33] At the same time, however, China's dependence on the Persian Gulf has deepened. Whereas in 2005 China imported 46 percent of its crude from the Persian Gulf, by 2013 the figure had risen to 52 percent. As a result, China still imported three quarters of its supplies from the Persian Gulf and Africa combined in 2013 (see figure 2-1). China's growing reliance on the Persian Gulf reflects rising imports from Iraq in particular, which has helped to offset Iran's declining importance as an oil supplier for China.

It is against this backdrop that China has sought to diversify its energy import mix through a series of "loan for oil" and "loan for gas" deals in the last few years. In particular, in the midst of global financial distress, in 2009 and 2010 Chinese state-owned banks made loans worth US$77 billion to nine oil- and gas-producing countries—all of which are located outside the Middle East. In return, China's NOCs were able to conclude a series of agreements with these countries and expand their international business. The deal with Russia promised to supply China with 300,000 barrels a day over twenty years through a new pipeline system, which became operational in late 2010. The agreement with Brazil, meanwhile, promised China 150,000 barrels a day in 2009 and 200,000 to 250,000 barrels a day from 2010 to 2019. Two separate agreements reached with Venezuela appear to have arranged Chinese purchases of up to 450,000 barrels a day between 2010 and 2020. In each case, China will pay market prices for the oil it buys.[34]

These "loan for oil" deals will improve China's overall energy security to an extent by reducing its reliance on imports from the Middle East and Africa. The deal with Russia will also help to limit China's reliance on seaborne imports more generally. Nonetheless, even if the pipeline from Russia eventually operates at maximum capacity (600,000 barrels a day), it would provide only 7 percent of China's projected imports in 2020.[35] Russia is thus not going to replace the Persian Gulf as China's primary oil supplier in the foreseeable future. Russia's reliability as an energy supplier is also open to question, a point that has been noted by some Chinese analysts.[36] And while China is also reaching out to Venezuela and Brazil, it will pay a premium for oil shipped from the Americas because of the distance involved.

China's recent "loan for oil" deals thus have only limited potential to diversify its import mix away from its main suppliers today. Perhaps in recognition of this fact, Beijing has sought to diversify the route that its oil shipments take as they wend their way toward China from the Middle East and Africa. In 2009 the CNPC signed a memorandum of understanding with Myanmar to construct parallel oil and gas pipelines that would connect the Chinese province of Yunnan with the Indian Ocean. The gas pipeline was completed in 2013, and the oil pipeline will be finished sometime in 2014. The latter will allow a portion of China's crude shipments to bypass the Malacca Strait on their way to China, while also reducing the travel distance by 1,200 kilometers.[37] Yet the 440,000 barrels a day capacity of the oil pipeline could have carried only 14 percent of China's imports from Africa and the Middle East had it been operational in 2009—and that fraction is destined to shrink as China's oil imports continue to grow in the future. China also appears to be involved in developing rail and road infrastructure that will connect Pakistani ports on the Arabian Sea with western China, prompting speculation that China is developing an even closer connection to the Persian Gulf.[38] Yet as far as transporting oil is concerned, this connection will be even more constrained than the pipeline through Myanmar.[39] Estimates suggest that the rail system would only be able to carry 175,000 barrels a day, assuming it was dedicated solely to oil transport. It would also be much more costly to transport oil in this manner, making it economically uncompetitive, and the rail link will transit terrain that is vulnerable to avalanches, flooding, seismic activity, and insurgency. Building a pipeline along this route would be problematic as well, due to both economic and security considerations.[40]

In sum, while China has succeeded in diversifying its supply portfolio to some degree, the country will continue to rely on the Persian Gulf and Africa for a high percentage of its oil imports for years to come. Most of these imports, in turn, will travel to China entirely by sea, given the paucity of alternative options. In this context, it is not surprising that China is thinking more and more about ways to secure its seaborne shipments of oil.

Expanding Naval Power

China's rising dependence on energy imports, as well as its growing maritime trade more generally, have helped to motivate China's interest in developing its own blue-water navy in recent years. While to date the modernization of the PLAN has focused on submarine capabilities and area denial missions around China's periphery, attention has shifted in recent years to operations farther afield. In an indication of this emerging interest, China has recently launched its first aircraft carrier, the *Liaoning*—a refurbished Soviet carrier purchased in 1998 from Ukraine. Analysts now project that the PLAN could be operating multiple aircraft carriers by 2020, a development for which there is widespread popular support within China.[41] Chinese military officials and analysts are also actively discussing the kind of overseas support network that the PLAN would need to support operations far from China's shores.[42] Military and security officials have also become more directly involved in energy policymaking in China in recent years. The twenty-one members of China's National Energy Commission, for example, include both the deputy chairman of the military's joint chiefs of staff and the minister of state security.[43]

Chinese naval officials have seized the opportunity to serve as guardians of China's seaborne trade and the national economy more generally. Naval officers cite China's growing dependence on seaborne energy imports to call for greater investments in "far sea defense" (*yuanhai fangwei*) and to assert their service's importance. As Yao Wenhuai, the PLAN's deputy political commissar, wrote in 2007,

> Maritime transport and strategic passageways for energy resources have already become lifelines for the development of the national economy and society. Particularly for oil and other key strategic supplies, our dependence on sea transport is very great, and ensuring the security of strategic seaways

is extremely important. We must fully recognize the actual requirements of protecting our country's developmental interests at sea, fully recognize the security threats our country faces at sea, and fully recognize the special status and utility of our navy in preparing for military conflict.[44]

Yao went so far as to argue that it is time for China's army to receive a smaller proportion of defense spending and that China's navy should "bear the brunt" of the burden of national defense.

To what degree would the development of a blue-water navy enhance China's energy security? It would presumably improve China's leverage in its territorial disputes in the East China and South China Seas, helping it to gain control over energy resources in these areas. Yet even if China were to gain exclusive access to these resources, it remains unclear how extensive they are, and it is unlikely that they would dramatically reduce China's dependence on oil imports in years to come. The U.S. Energy Information Administration estimates that the East China Sea has between 60 million and 100 million barrels of oil in proven and probable reserves—a negligible amount in the context of China's overall consumption.[45] While Chinese sources claim that undiscovered resources in the East China Sea may run as high as 70 billion to 160 billion barrels, such estimates do not take into account the economic conditions that are needed to bring such reserves into production. The Energy Information Administration estimates that 11 billion barrels of proven and probable oil reserves exist in the South China Sea. But the Spratly and Paracel islands—the focus of territorial contention—are quite barren in this regard. While the Spratlys may have undiscovered reserves, it remains unclear how extensive they might be and whether extraction would be economically viable. In short, greater control over oil resources in the East China and South China Seas is not the answer to China's oil security challenge.[46]

China's growing navy may prove more useful for protecting the sea lines of communication through which its oil shipments flow. Oil tankers may become targets for pirates or terrorists, particularly when forced to transit narrow choke-points. In addition, Chinese analysts worry that the U.S. navy, in conjunction with the navies of American allies, could cut off seaborne oil shipments to China in the event of a military conflict. There is particular concern about China's imports from the Middle East and Africa, given the country's heavy reliance on these regions and the fact that shipments from them must traverse the narrow Malacca Strait. The phrase "the Malacca Dilemma" has emerged to connote both China's heavy reliance on the strait and the fact that this reliance poses distinct security challenges for China.

A robust force that would allow China to challenge the United States for sea control would provide the country with the means to counter an American-led blockade. Such capabilities would take decades to develop, however, and they would be quite costly as well. Nor would it be money well spent, since an American blockade of China is unlikely. The United States would be reluctant to attempt such a blockade, since the ensuing disruption of the Chinese economy would inevitably have repercussions for the global economy and the American economy as well. The United States would not be pressuring China so much as engaging in "mutually assured economic destruction," given the growing inter-dependence of the two economies. Even if the United States were to attempt a blockade of China, it would probably not be very successful. If the blockade were implemented far from China's shores—around the Malacca Strait, for instance—it would be extremely difficult to differentiate oil bound for China from that bound for other countries, including Japan and South Korea. A given tanker may carry oil bound for several countries, and ownership of the oil within a tanker can easily change during the course of its journey. If the blockade operations were undertaken close to China, in contrast, blockading vessels would be vulner-able to attacks from Chinese submarines and land-based forces. China also has a growing strategic reserve of petroleum with which it could counter any attempt to cut off its oil. Taking these points together, the likelihood that the United States and its allies would attempt to impose an oil blockade against China—and that such an endeavor would succeed—is rather low.[47]

In contrast, a more modest naval force focused on more limited missions would arguably be more useful from the standpoint of China's energy security.[48] Although it would not allow the PLAN to compete with the U.S. navy, it would allow China to support international efforts to combat piracy and terrorism around major shipping lanes. In fact, the PLAN has already begun to support such efforts, notably by participating in the multinational initiative to combat piracy off the coast of Somalia since late 2008. As of December 2013, China claimed that its vessels had escorted more than 5,000 ships and rescued or sal-vaged another fifty ships.[49] With this experience as a positive precedent, there is an opportunity for China to play a greater role in such multinational efforts in the future.

In short, the extent to which China's emerging naval capabilities will augment the country's energy security remains unclear. On the one hand, it is unlikely that greater leverage in territorial disputes in the East China and South China Seas would greatly improve China's energy security, given the limited oil resources available in those areas. On the other hand, greater ability to patrol sea-lanes could enhance China's energy security, depending on the approach that China takes. Developing a fleet that could challenge the United States for sea control would be quite costly, alienate other Asian countries, and not address a threat that is likely to materialize. Focusing on more limited capabilities, in contrast, would allow China to build on its recent support for multinational antipiracy efforts and address a real challenge facing both China and the international community today.

If All Else Fails: The Strategic Reserve

China is building its own strategic petroleum reserve to strengthen its energy security.[50] The construction, which began in 2004, is proceeding in three phases.[51] The first phase has been completed and holds 103 million barrels, enough for about twenty-one days of net import requirements at 2011 levels.[52] The second phase is being filled and will reportedly expand China's capacity by at least 169 million barrels by 2015. The third phase, which is scheduled to be completed by 2020, will expand China's SPR to approximately 500 million barrels. That would cover ninety-eight days of net oil imports at 2011 levels, but only sixty days of net imports at levels projected for 2020.[53] In addition, China possesses substantial commercial reserves of crude oil, with capacity estimates ranging from 250 million to 400 million barrels, although the distinction between the national reserve system and commercial reserves remains unclear.[54] China also has storage capacity for 400 million barrels of refined oil products, and the government has considered creating a strategic reserve for these as well.[55]

China's investment in its SPR system has the potential to make a significant contribution to the country's energy security. In particular, the SPR will provide Beijing with new policy options in the event that its supply of oil imports is disrupted in the future. This would appear to be a real danger: the world has seen eleven major oil supply disruptions since the mid-1950s, and five of these have occurred since 2000.[56] In short, while the cost of constructing a reserve system is considerable, China's SPR is a worthwhile investment.

Nonetheless, China's SPR will be a much more effective instrument if it is used in coordination with the reserve systems of other countries. Since the 1970s, the International Energy Agency (IEA) has enabled major oil importers to coordinate their responses to supply disruptions. In the event of a crisis, the organization allows member countries to coordinate efforts to restrain demand and to bring additional supplies to the market through the release of reserve stocks.[57] IEA members are required to maintain stocks that can meet at least ninety days of net import demand, and at the end of 2011 total stocks in the organization's members stood at 4.1 billion barrels.[58] In the event of future supply crises, Beijing is likely to find itself drawing on its own reserves at the same time that other major importers are drawing on their own, since supply disruptions are far more likely to affect many countries at once than just China alone. Should China's actions fail to be coordinated with those of other countries, or should China's response be insufficiently transparent, oil traders are more likely to be confused than reassured, and instability in the markets will persist. It is thus important that Beijing develop more robust cooperation with other major oil importers, a point considered in more detail next.

The Need for Greater Multilateralism

It is time for China to think anew about oil security. To date, China has focused primarily on unilateral and bilateral measures in this regard: it has encouraged its oil companies to invest overseas, developed relationships with new suppliers, looked to develop a blue-water navy, and begun to build its own SPR. The preceding discussion makes clear that these measures—by themselves—have limited potential to enhance China's oil security. In the future, China should develop a more well-rounded approach by making greater investments in multilateral cooperation with other countries.

China has already taken a few steps to develop this aspect of its approach to oil security. China is, for example, a member of the International Energy Forum. However, this remains a weak institution that serves mainly to promote dialogue among its eighty-nine members. More important is China's engagement with the IEA. Several attributes of the IEA would make it difficult for China to join the organization, including China's lack of membership in the Organization for Economic Cooperation and Development—normally a prerequisite for IEA membership.[59] Nonetheless, the United States has signaled that it is prepared to open the door to China in the interest of maintaining the institution's relevance: in late 2008 the Bush administration expressed its support for China joining the IEA, and the Obama administration has made it clear that it would welcome Chinese membership as well.[60]

Indeed, the most fundamental obstacle to China becoming an IEA member is Beijing's own hesitation to join the organization. To be sure, some Chinese observers have called for closer ties with the IEA. These writers maintain that closer cooperation would reassure other countries about China's rise, provide China with a stronger voice in international energy governance, and offer China greater access to the IEA's expertise and experience.[61] Yet there are also worries that joining the IEA would not be in China's interest. Chinese officials reportedly worry that joining the IEA would undermine its freedom to use the SPR as it sees fit, and there is also concern about the degree of transparency that the IEA would require.[62] More basically, some Chinese observers distrust the IEA, which they see as dominated by the United States.[63]

In early 2012, Chinese Premier Wen Jiabao proposed creating a new multilateral energy body to address international energy security issues. More specifically, Wen proposed creating an "administrative mechanism" for the global energy market under the G-20. The grouping would include energy-exporting countries, energy-importing countries, and transit countries. Wen explained that the group would develop "binding international rules through consultation and dialogue" and "build multilateral coordination mechanisms covering forecast and early warning, price coordination, financial regulation, and emergency response."[64]

It remains unclear whether Wen's proposal will attract much support internationally or where it might lead. Chinese energy experts have since indicated that Wen's proposal is but one of several options for global energy governance under discussion in China—and that these include reforming and expanding the IEA.[65] Going forward, therefore, it would seem prudent to deepen the dialogue between China and the IEA in order to develop as constructive a relationship as possible between the two. The recent decision to develop a cooperative "association" between the IEA and China, India, Russia, Brazil, Indonesia, and South Africa is a welcome step in this direction.[66] As of this writing, the details of how this voluntary and nonbinding arrangement will work are still being negotiated. The extent to which the IEA will include China and other association members in its internal deliberations remains a key question. The willingness of association members to share sensitive information with the IEA is another. Under the circumstances, one should not expect too much of this initiative immediately. Over time, however, it is to be hoped that modest collaboration in the short term will lead to more extensive cooperation down the road.

Conclusions

China's policies to address its oil security in recent years have ranged from the largely ineffective to the insufficiently developed. Beijing's support for the international expansion of China's NOCs is perhaps the least productive of its policies: it may be good for the companies themselves, but it is unclear that it enhances national energy security. China's attempts to diversify the regional sources of its oil imports represent a more effective means of pursuing energy security, and Beijing has had some success in this regard. Even so, the country will remain highly dependent on imports from the Middle East and Africa for years to come. This raises the question of how these shipments will be protected. China's efforts to develop blue-water naval capabilities could enable it to protect its oil shipments against threats such as piracy and terrorism more effectively. For the moment, however, it remains unclear whether and how China will work with other countries as it undertakes such efforts. Lastly, China's development of its own SPR system is an important and necessary step, one that will give it new options in the event of future supply crises. Yet Beijing will need to coordinate more effectively with other major oil importers in the future if it is to use its reserve system effectively.

This last point raises a broader question concerning how China pursues energy security. As argued in the preceding pages, China has traditionally emphasized unilateral and bilateral measures to ensure its access to oil supplies. Pursuing greater coordination with other oil importers—in particular, with the IEA—will allow China to develop the multilateral side of its approach to energy security. In the short term, China could deepen its level of consultation with the IEA and make its energy sector more transparent, particularly as the aforementioned association takes shape. In the longer term, China could seek membership in the IEA. Such multilateral engagement would provide Beijing with more information and greater influence in the event of future supply shocks, a danger that appears all too real. More broadly, greater multilateral engagement would demonstrate that Beijing is looking for ways to cooperate with the international community as China's rise continues.

Notes

1. British Petroleum (BP), "BP Statistical Review of World Energy 2013" (June 2013) (www.bp.com/sectionbodycopy.do?categoryId=7500&contentId=7068481), p. 9.

2. BP, "BP Statistical Review of World Energy 2013," pp. 8–9.

3. International Energy Agency (IEA), *World Energy Outlook 2013* (Paris: OECD, 2013), pp. 481, 505.

4. For a traditional definition, see IEA, *World Energy Outlook 2007* (Paris: OECD, 2007), p. 160.

5. On the emergence of these competing perspectives on China's energy security challenge, see Andrew Kennedy, "China's New Energy-Security Debate," *Survival: Global Politics and Strategy* 52, no. 3 (June-July 2010): 137–58.

6. BP, "BP Statistical Review of World Energy 2012," pp. 8, 9, 24, 25.

7. On this point, see Mikkal Herberg, "The Geopolitics of China's LNG Development," in *China's Energy Strategy: The Impact of Beijing's Maritime Policies,* edited by Gabriel B. Collins, Andrew W. Erickson, Lyle J. Goldstein, and William S. Murray (Annapolis, Md.: Naval Institute Press, 2008), p. 74.

8. BP, "BP Energy Outlook 2030" (January 2013), (www.bp.com/sectionbodycopy. do?categoryId=7500&contentId=7068481), p. 25.

9. Kate Rosow Chrisman, "China's Ambitions to Double Output by 2030 Rely on Unconventional Sources," *Breaking Energy,* February 4, 2014 (breakingenergy.com/2014/02/04/chinas-ambitions-to-double-output-by-2030-rely-on-unconventional-sources/).

10. IEA, *World Energy Outlook 2013,* p. 505.

11. The following discussion draws on Andrew Kennedy, "China's Petroleum Predicament: Challenges and Opportunities in Beijing's Search for Energy Security," in *Rising China: Challenges and Opportunities,* edited by Jane Golley and Ligang Song (Canberra: Australian National University E-Press, 2011), pp. 124–26.

12. Erica Downs, "China," *Brookings Institution Foreign Policy Studies Energy Security Series* (December 2006): 35–39.

13. Ibid., pp. 21–24.

14. Erica Downs and Michal Meidan, "Business and Politics in China: The Oil Executive Reshuffle of 2011," *China Security* 19 (2011): 3–21.

15. But the NOCs themselves have not always agreed that their investments abroad enhance China's energy security. See Downs, "China," p. 38.

16. Julie Jiang and Jonathan Sinton, "Overseas Investments by Chinese National Oil Companies: Assessing the Drivers and Impacts," Paper prepared for the Standing Group for Global Energy Dialogue (Paris: IEA, February 2011), pp. 39–40.

17. Energy Information Administration, "China" (Washington: U.S. Department of Energy, April 22, 2013, and February 4, 2014) (www.eia.gov/countries/cab.cfm?fips=CH).

18. IEA, *World Energy Outlook 2013*, p. 494.

19. BP, "BP Statistical Review of World Energy 2012," pp. 8, 9.

20. IEA, *World Energy Outlook 2013*, p. 458.

21. Jiang and Sinton, "Overseas Investments by Chinese National Oil Companies," pp. 18–19.

22. Erica Downs, "China's Energy Rise," in *China's Rise in Historical Perspective,* edited by Brantly Womack (Lanham, Md.: Rowman and Littlefield, 2010), p. 184.

23. Downs, "China," pp. 16–24.

24. Keith Bradsher, "Security Tops the Environment in China's Energy Plan," *New York Times,* June 17, 2010 (www.nytimes.com/2010/06/18/business/global/18yuan.html).

25. Bo Kong, *China's International Petroleum Policy* (Santa Barbara, Calif.: Praeger Security International, 2010), p. 92.

26. Jiang and Sinton, "Overseas Investments by Chinese National Oil Companies," p. 17.

27. For example, see Elizabeth Economy and Adam Segal, "China's Olympic Nightmare: What the Games Mean for Beijing's Future," *Foreign Affairs* 87, no. 4 (July-August 2008): 47–56.

28. Erica Downs and Suzanne Maloney, "Getting China to Sanction Iran: The Chinese-Iranian Oil Connection," *Foreign Affairs* 90, no. 2 (March-April 2011): 15–21.

29. Erica Downs, "China, Iran, and the Nexen Deal," *Policy Options* (October 2012): 26–27. "Getting China to Turn on Iran," *National Interest,* July 19 2012 (http://nationalinterest.org/commentary/getting-china-turn-iran-7215).

30. Quoted in Daniel Yergin, "Ensuring Energy Security," *Foreign Affairs* 85, no. 2 (March-April 2006): 69. The following discussion draws on Kennedy, "China's Petroleum Predicament," pp. 126–28.

31. For the data in this paragraph, see Downs, "China," p. 31.

32. Li Xiaohui, "China's Net Oil Imports Hit New Record High of 218.4 Mln Tonnes in 2009," *Xinhua China Oil, Gas, and Petrochemicals,* February 7, 2010.

33. Energy Information Administration, "China."

34. For a summary of these deals, see Jiang and Sinton, "Overseas Investments by Chinese National Oil Companies," p. 41. On the deal with Venezuela, in particular, see Erica Downs, "Inside China, Inc.: China Development Bank's Cross-Border Energy Deals," John L. Thornton China Center Monograph Series 3 (Brookings Institution, March 2011), pp. 49–53.

35. IEA, *World Energy Outlook 2013*, pp. 481, 505.

36. Zhao Hongtu, "Maliujia Kunju yu Zhongguo Nengyuan Anquan Zai Sikao [Rethinking the Malacca Dilemma and China's Energy Security]," *Xiandai Guoji Guanxi [Contemporary International Relations]* 6 (2007): 41.

37. Jiang and Sinton, "Overseas Investments by Chinese National Oil Companies," p. 34.

38. Selig Harrison, "China's Discreet Hold on Pakistan's Northern Borderlands," *International Herald Tribune,* August 26, 2010.

39. Andrew Erickson, "Still a Pipedream: A Pakistan-to-China Rail Corridor Is Not a Substitute for Maritime Transport," *China Signpost* 13 (December 22, 2010).

40. Andrew S. Erickson and Gabriel B. Collins, "China's Oil Security Pipe Dream: The Reality, and Strategic Consequences, of Seaborne Imports," *Naval War College Review* 63, no. 2 (Spring 2010): 101–03.

41. On this point, see Robert Ross, "China's Naval Nationalism: Sources, Prospects, and the U.S. Response," *International Security* 34, no. 2 (Fall 2009): 60–65.

42. Michael S. Chase and Andrew S. Erickson, "Changes in Beijing's Approach to Overseas Basing?" *China Brief* 9, no. 19 (September 24, 2009): 8–11.

43. Bradsher, "Security Tops the Environment."

44. Yao Wenhuai, "Jianshe Qiangda Haijun Weihu Woguo Haiyang Zhanlue Liyi [Build a Powerful Navy to Protect Our Nation's Strategic Maritime Interests]," *Guofang [National Defense]* 7 (2007): 1–7.

45. Energy Information Administration, "East China Sea" (Washington: U.S. Department of Energy, September 25, 2012) (www.eia.gov/countries/regions-topics.cfm?fips=ECS).

46. Natural gas reserves in the East China and South China Seas appear more substantial than oil reserves. As noted at the outset of this chapter, however, China's energy security challenge is greater with respect to oil than with respect to natural gas, whether the question is the extent of import dependence or the availability of substitute fuels.

47. On the difficulties that the United States would have imposing an oil blockade on China, see Gabriel B. Collins and William S. Murray, "No Oil for the Lamps of China?" in *China's Energy Strategy,* edited by Collins and others, pp. 387–407. Some Chinese analysts appreciate the difficulties that the United States would have. See Zhao, "Maliujia Kunju yu Zhongguo Nengyuan Anquan Zai Sikao [Rethinking the Malacca Dilemma and China's Energy Security]," pp. 36–38.

48. On the possibility of China developing a more limited force, see Michael A. Glosny and Phillip C. Saunders, "Debating China's Naval Nationalism," *International Security* 35, no. 2 (Fall 2010): 166–68.

49. "16th Chinese Naval Escort Taskforce Sets Sail from Qingdao," *People's Daily,* December 3, 2013 (http://english.peopledaily.com.cn/90786/8472951.html).

50. The following discussion draws on Kennedy, "China's Petroleum Predicament," pp. 130–32.

51. For a summary, see Energy Information Administration, "China."

52. IEA, *World Energy Outlook 2012*, pp. 85, 107.

53. Ibid.

54. Energy Information Administration, "China."

55. Ibid.

56. IEA, *IEA Response System for Oil Supply Emergencies 2012* (Paris: OECD, 2012), p. 11.

57. The IEA also allows for the coordination of fuel-switching and surge production in the event of a crisis, but these mechanisms are less viable now than in the past. See IEA, *IEA Response System,* p. 6.

58. Ibid., p. 7.

59. For a more extended discussion of the barriers to Chinese membership, see Kennedy, "China's Petroleum Predicament," p. 131.

60. "Joint U.S.-China Fact Sheet: Fifth U.S.-China Strategic Economic Dialogue," *U.S. Fed News,* December 5, 2008. "Hearing of the Senate Foreign Relations Committee; Subject: The Nomination of Kurt Campbell to Be Assistant Secretary of State for East Asian and Pacific Affairs," *Federal News Service,* June 9, 2010.

61. Wang Lianhe, "Zhongguo yu Guoji Nengyuan Jjgou—Yi Xiang Guifan Yanjiu [China and the International Energy Agency—A Normative Analysis]," *Guoji Guancha* [*International Survey*] 4 (2009): 11–17. Zhao Hongtu, "Guoji Nengyuan Zuzhi Yu Duobian Nengyuan Waijiao [International Energy Organizations and Multilateral Energy Diplomacy]," *Guoji Shiyou Jingji* [*International Petroleum Economics*] 10 (2008): 12–17.

62. Interviews with energy specialists at Chinese state-owned think tanks, Beijing, March 2009.

63. Andrew Kennedy, "China and the Free Rider Problem: Exploring the Case of Energy Security," forthcoming in *Political Science Quarterly.*

64. State Council of the People's Republic of China, "Wen Jiabao Chuxi Diwujie Shijie Weilai Nengyuan Fenghui Kaimushi Bing Zhici [Wen Jiabao Attends the Fifth World Future Energy Summit Opening Ceremony and Makes a Speech]," January 16, 2012 (www.gov.cn/ldhd/2012-01/16/content_2045649.htm).

65. Han Wenke and Yang Yufeng, "China Energy Outlook 2012: Embracing Changes, Reshaping the Future," presentation at the Center for Strategic and International Studies, Washington, March 12, 2013 (csis.org/event/chinas-energy-outlook).

66. Michel Rose, "IEA and Emerging Countries to Collaborate More Closely," *Reuters,* November 20, 2013.

3

Materials, Markets, Multilateralism: A Strategic Approach to India's Resource Challenges

DAVID STEVEN AND ARUNABHA GHOSH

In recent years, higher and more volatile energy and food prices have pushed natural resources toward the top of the international agenda, while climate change remains the most complex and intractable global challenge, and water scarcity is a growing threat to industry, agriculture, and energy generation.

In the coming decades, the world must confront three interlocking challenges with regard to the economic, social, and environmental pillars of sustainable development:

—Securing the energy, water, and other minerals needed to support economic growth

—Meeting basic needs for food, fuel, and water for a growing global population

—Managing the environmental constraints and consequences of increased resource use.

Why Resource Security Matters for India

India provides a powerful illustration of the depth and complexity of these challenges. Sometime soon after 2020, it will become the world's most populous country, as China's population begins to decline. By 2050, there will be as many Indians—around 1.7 billion—as the population of the whole world at the beginning of the twentieth century.[1] Given current trends, this larger population will be considerably richer than it is today. By some projections, the Indian economy will have grown by a factor of ten by mid-century.[2]

However, growth depends on securing access to energy and other strategic resources. India is already struggling to meet domestic demand for energy, food, and water and has 14 percent of the global population living without electricity and nearly a third of those cooking with traditional biofuels.[3] It has little spare land or water and is one of the world's most vulnerable countries to the impacts of climate change.[4] Over the coming decades, these challenges will intensify.

The 2012 electricity crisis illustrated the fragility of the Indian energy sector, as hundreds of millions of consumers and businesses were hit by the largest power cut in history as large parts of the national grid collapsed.[5] The power cuts demonstrated the impact of coal scarcity on the electricity sector, with new generation capacity lying idle;[6] the links between water and energy scarcity, as a weak monsoon hit hydroelectricity and saw farmers pumping more water for irrigation;[7] conflict between states to draw additional power from the national grid;[8] and the lack of a market for electricity, a result of competition between politicians to provide subsidized power to rural areas.[9] Drought also led to a slight fall in cereal production, at a time when a heat wave in the United States was putting further pressure on global food prices.[10] Food price inflation was in double figures in 2012, with the government of Manmohan Singh facing simultaneous pressure on both energy and food.[11]

Given the speed of both its population and economic growth, India faces some hard resource limits in the years ahead, but its major problems are a product of the intersection between dysfunctional markets and governance systems for natural resources. Long-term planning is bedeviled by short-term political pressures and a substantial deficit in infrastructure investment. Energy and food subsidies are increasingly fiscally unsustainable,[12] but are protected by vested interests, on the one hand, and by the need to tackle poverty, on the other. Many solutions can only be delivered through complex cooperation among provinces and between provinces and the center. Political gridlock continues to reduce the prospects of an effective domestic response to resource pressures.[13]

India is, of course, only partially in control of its destiny in this area, especially during periods when commodity prices are high and volatile. It is already exposed to global energy markets and will have increasing exposure to international food systems.[14] Climate and water risk is shared with Pakistan, Bangladesh, and other neighbors. Given its status as the world's third largest economy (in purchasing power terms), India also has an important, and growing, role in climate stabilization as a global public good.[15] International drivers will therefore frame India's options at home, while effective domestic policy will make it easier for the Indian government to assert its interests on the international stage.

Conversely, an increasingly competitive international dynamic—on resource nationalism, export bans, trade in commodities, or policy toward major energy exporters such as Iran—could create a growing and dangerous sense of isolation and constriction within India.

For these reasons, India is the most important international "swing voter" on strategic resources. Within the G-20, the United States is a major food producer and is enjoying a significant energy boom, with higher prices boosting its ability to produce both oil and gas.[16] The European Union has declining demand for resources, making it easier for it to manage energy and food insecurity. China faces many of the same challenges as its neighbor, but has more effective policies to enhance its resource security through investment at home and abroad and somewhat stronger governance. Meanwhile, Brazil and Russia both have a rich resource endowment and benefit from high commodity prices.

India therefore has an *especially* strong national interest in well-functioning commodity markets. As it becomes an increasingly assertive international actor, its willingness, or otherwise, to work with other major powers on energy, food, water, and climate could significantly improve the prospects for effective management of these issues. Its growing presence as a "rule shaper" and its willingness to engage on a multilateral, rather than solely a bilateral, basis offer it potential to influence both the design of robust international regimes for resource security and the provision of global environmental public goods. It will find, however, that existing regimes and their underlying rules often offer contradictory policy signals. Thus India could play an important role in developing governance frameworks that increase the coherence of rules across institutional regimes relating to resources, the environment, trade, and security.[17] However, if it takes a short-term view of its national interest or if it fails to address domestic contradictions in its policy environment, it is likely to find that resource and environmental threats place increasing pressure on its development.

In this chapter, we review the resource and environmental challenges facing India over the next twenty years, focusing in particular on their political and geopolitical dimensions. We then discuss drivers of change and possible trajectories for India's domestic and international policy on these issues. Finally, we discuss options for future Indian engagement on strategic resources and climate change, offering concrete opportunities for the Indian government to deepen its engagement and build stronger partnerships and governance arrangements with other countries.

Understanding India's Resource and Environmental Challenge

Because India is an emerging economy, its quest for resources in all the key productive sectors is expected to grow. Industry, agriculture, and commercial services will demand more energy resources along with water, land, and non-fuel minerals. Disruptions in access to resources would undermine expectations that India will be able to sustain moderate to high rates of economic growth. Equally India's per capita consumption of many resources remains low, even by world average benchmarks, and far less than in the developed world. The demand for basic needs in the form of food, fuel, and water will remain an important consideration for boosting human development overall and responding to political pressures, particularly in some of India's most populous states. Local environmental challenges and global atmospheric constraints, thanks to climate change, will further complicate the options for resource security that India can exploit.

Resources for Growth

Energy security is, and will continue to be, a defining challenge for India. The country is a second-tier energy consumer, sitting alongside Japan and Russia, but is far behind the United States, China, and the European Union. Between now and 2030, however, Indian demand is projected to increase more quickly than that of any other country in the G-20. Across eight scenarios from the International Energy Agency (IEA) and the U.S. Energy Information Administration (EIA), Indian consumption will grow 80–125 percent between 2009 and 2030, with reference scenarios projecting growth of 88–97 percent.[18] Even under an aggressive, and politically infeasible, scenario of global climate stabilization, India will consume around 60 percent more energy in twenty years than it does now.

India may struggle to acquire this additional energy at a reasonable price or to minimize interruptions in supply caused by market volatility, failure of infrastructure, or the impact of adverse weather and other disasters. It already has much higher levels of import dependence than the United States and China, with 37 percent of its energy and 76 percent of its oil coming from overseas. The Indian government expects this dependence to increase over the next five years.[19] Moreover, the Indian energy sector is already showing signs of strain, with a consistent pattern of tight supply, lack of investment, and policy and market failures across all major energy sources. Coal, oil, and natural gas account for 54 percent of India's final energy consumption.[20]

Biofuels, biomass, and waste still take in a large share of consumption (33 percent) thanks to the lack of access to modern cooking fuels for 772 million people or electricity for 293 million people.[21] As more households demand modern sources of energy, the need for fossil fuels will rise, possibly at a more rapid rate than expected if middle-class lifestyles continue to proliferate.

COAL. India is the world's third largest producer of coal and has the world's fourth largest reserves.[22] Demand for coal has, on average, been increasing by approximately 7 percent a year since 2005, up from 5 percent between 2000 and 2005, with power generation and manufacturing driving the increase.[23]

Development of the domestic coal sector, however, is beset by a lack of investment, disputes over land acquisition, and environmental concerns.[24] The industry is mostly government controlled, with Coal India, a state-owned company, producing 80 percent of the country's coal, and production is both inefficient and riddled with corruption.[25] There are also links between India's sometimes fragile internal security and its coal industry. Within the coal belt, large numbers of mafia groups are thought to be active, some of which are then "taxed" by Naxalite insurgents, producing revenue for rebel groups.[26]

In addition, a lack of port and transportation infrastructure, combined with dysfunctional markets, has hindered imports of coal.[27] Only four major ports handle coal imports, providing a capacity of just 63 million tons, leaving minor ports to pick up the slack. The major coal ports are located along the eastern coast, which made sense historically because most power plants were located in the east (closer to the coal fields). However, a series of so-called ultra-mega power projects are being constructed in the western states, with an industrial corridor also planned between Delhi and Mumbai. New infrastructure for transporting coal is, therefore, badly needed inland and along the western coast.[28]

As a result of these deficits, coal scarcity is a growing problem for India, with an estimated 15 percent gap between supply and demand in 2012.[29] The problem is especially acute in the power sector, which expects to receive only half the coal needed for new electricity generation envisaged in India's twelfth Five-Year Plan (2012–17).[30] Imports are growing rapidly, with 15 percent of coal now coming from overseas, but this is still not enough to keep up with domestic demand. Import dependence is projected to reach 40 percent by 2030, based on current trends and assuming that infrastructure is developed to bring more coal into the country.[31] More recent government estimates suggest that this level of import dependence would be reached by 2016 if the gap between supply and demand in the power sector were closed.[32]

As a result, coal, which has obvious environmental drawbacks, is making a steadily increasing contribution to energy insecurity, rather than fulfilling its traditional role as a bulwark against the vagaries of world markets. For consumers, electricity shortages and interruptions are where they perceive instability in the coal market.

OIL. India's oil sector is beset by many of the same problems as the coal sector, although India has a relatively modest domestic endowment, importing about three times more oil than it produces.[33] Production has remained almost flat over the past decade, with import dependence certain to increase, given that demand is projected almost to double by 2030.[34] As with coal, public sector enterprises control around 80 percent of production in the oil and gas sector, hampering foreign investment in the sector and leading to what the government accepts are "disappointing" increases in production.[35]

In response, the government has encouraged national oil companies to "aggressively pursue equity oil and gas opportunities overseas," with international production now equivalent to around 10 percent of domestic production.[36] This has dragged India into some of the world's most risky places, including politically fragile states such as Iran, Iraq, Kazakhstan, Libya, Nigeria, South Sudan, and Venezuela.[37] Investments have proved problematic in many of these countries and also in the South China Sea, where energy cooperation with Vietnam has created tensions with China.[38] Moreover, little "equity oil" makes its way back to India; most is sold in global markets. The net impact on Indian energy security is therefore limited and, to the extent that national oil companies are responding to political rather than commercial imperatives, their investment probably represents a poor use of scarce capital.[39] In fact, equity oil does not have consensus support across government. In the past, the Cabinet's Empowered Committee of Secretaries has disapproved of price wars to win foreign acreage in oil fields.[40] Even the Planning Commission views equity oil primarily as a "commercial decision."

In any case, dependence on imported oil will grow. According to a 2006 report by an expert committee constituted by the Indian Planning Commission, even with a massive increase in the use of coal, India's oil imports will increase four to sixfold by 2030.[41] As a result, India is exposed to both supply risks (war, strikes, or political upheavals in oil exporters and deliberate blockades of supplies to India) and market risks (higher prices, but in particular price volatility). For India, oil will increasingly become one of its most important sources of exposure to broader geopolitical volatility.

On the demand side, markets are heavily distorted, although there have been recent attempts to cut the subsidy bill. More than US$30 billion was spent on oil subsidies in 2011, equivalent to 1.9 percent of gross domestic product (GDP) and almost double the level in 2010.[42] According to the Planning Commission, "The massive underpricing of kerosene is leading to large-scale diversion for adulteration with diesel and petrol, generating a huge volume of black money. Only half of subsidized kerosene reaches its intended consumer. The LPG [liquefied petroleum gas] subsidy is completely untargeted and for the most part benefits people in the middle and upper income classes."[43] By May 2012, under-recoveries (that is, the gap between subsidized and market revenues) of oil marketing companies amounted to US$25 billion.[44]

Some progress has been made to reduce the subsidy bill. Petrol subsidies were cut in 2010, saving around US$16 billion a year.[45] The government has now begun to reform the market for diesel, which until recently was selling at 20 percent below global prices.[46] In September 2012, it increased prices by around 12 percent, a record rise that is highly politically contentious, but that will only stabilize the diesel subsidy bill given a fall in the value of the rupee against the dollar.[47] Subsidies remain unchanged for kerosene (70 percent below global market prices) and for LPG (half the global price),[48] although subsidized LPG cylinders have been restricted to six per household a year.

NATURAL GAS. In the 1990s, there was considerable enthusiasm for prospects in India's gas sector. New domestic discoveries, however, have reached only 40 percent of the level projected for 2012, again due to a lack of investment and infrastructure and to pricing decisions that saw gas being sold to the power sector at below-market rates.[49] As a result, demand for gas is estimated to outstrip supply by around a third and is projected to increase at more than 5 percent each year between now and 2030.[50] There is little immediate prospect, however, that this demand will be met by domestic production, as the sector continues to underperform. India will therefore become more reliant on imports,[51] with substantial investment needed in liquefied natural gas (LNG) terminals and, potentially, in transnational pipelines, although they would have to pass through states such as Afghanistan and Pakistan and would increase competition with China for pipeline gas.[52]

In the medium term, India has considerable potential to increase domestic production, with only 20 percent of its gas basins classified as well explored.[53] Given its size and geological diversity, it seems likely that India possesses significant shale reserves, although estimates of potential reserves are highly unreliable due to a lack of exploration.[54] The discovery of shale in West Bengal in 2011 has yet to translate into significant production, however.[55] The Indian government started a process of opening up bidding to companies for exploration, but previous auctions have repeatedly been delayed and it remains to be seen whether the gas sector will continue to perform well below its potential.[56]

OTHER ENERGY SOURCES. Nuclear and renewables are likely to continue to play only a niche role in India, at least in the medium term.

While the International Atomic Energy Agency expects to see significant growth in nuclear capacity in India and the government remains committed to increasing investment, nuclear expansion has been slower than expected, with the Fukushima disaster, civil society protest, opposition from state governments, and cost overruns limiting the sector's potential.[57] Even under the government's optimistic projections, nuclear power will provide only 1.2 percent of India's energy in 2016–17.[58] The government aims to increase its nuclear capacity to 20 gigawatts (up from 5 gigawatts currently) by 2020 and to 63 gigawatts by 2032.[59]

Renewables, particularly wind and solar power, have seen rising investments in grid-connected projects in recent years. Wind now accounts for more than 16 gigawatts of installed electricity generation capacity (about 8 percent of the total). Grid-connected solar has received a boost under the two-year-old Jawaharlal Nehru National Solar Mission. More than 2 gigawatts of capacity have been commissioned already, up from 17.8 megawatts in 2010. The aim is to reach

20 gigawatts by 2022, but meeting this target will require strategic interventions in the financing ecosystem for renewable energy, boosting domestic manufacturing and research and development capacity and resolving issues related to land acquisition, power evacuation, storage technologies, and water-efficient technologies (the latter two particularly for concentrated solar power).[60]

Renewables have a more important role in tackling energy poverty, but they are not expected to make a major contribution to broader energy security unless there is a significant improvement in the competitiveness of a distributed technology such as solar power.[61]

Economic Impact of Energy Scarcity

As this review of major energy sources has shown, India faces a tough challenge if it is to find the resources needed to meet its current target of 9 percent annual GDP growth. Energy scarcity is *already* hampering India's economy, with the government estimating that the country runs a 7.9 percent energy deficit (which rises to 13.8 percent at peak times).[62] At its current stage of development Indian growth is relatively energy intensive, increasing its vulnerability to high prices, although its energy efficiency is projected to continue to improve.[63] Energy intensity has gradually eased in manufacturing, falling by about 55 percent during 1992–2007. This fall should continue, but aggregate demand will still increase rapidly.

In recent years, subsidies have been used partially to mask this vulnerability, but at the cost of an unsustainable fiscal burden, with one estimate suggesting that fiscal profligacy has four times the long-term impact on Indian GDP growth as an oil price shock.[64] Sudden interruptions of supply, meanwhile, continue to have an especially damaging effect on the economy. In 2001 the direct costs for companies of a major power grid collapse were estimated at US$107.5 million.[65] The blackout on July 30–31, 2012, which affected more than half the population and twenty-two of India's twenty-eight states, seems certain to have made an important contribution to the economic downturn India experienced in 2012, when GDP growth fell to 4.5 percent, while also raising questions about the sustainability of the Indian economy.[66]

In the short term, at least, the economic impacts of energy scarcity seem likely to worsen, as growing numbers of middle-class consumers compete with industrial users for resources. The energy consumption of households outstripped that of agriculture for the first time during the last decade and now accounts for a third of all energy use.[67] Coal imports grew 80 percent in 2011–12 and oil imports grew 75 percent, but this is not enough to keep up with rising demand.[68] Market and governance failures, meanwhile, will take time to resolve, requiring deep-seated and politically costly reforms to natural resource ownership and allocation, pricing, environmental management, and regulatory oversight.

The picture is not wholly bleak, of course. High energy prices and technological innovation are bringing new sources of supply to market.[69] There is a global gas glut, and solar panels are also oversupplied, offering India opportunities to increase imports in a way that will improve the diversity of its energy sector.[70] Nuclear power may be in crisis, but it is possible that China will achieve a breakthrough on price and standardization, with benefits for other emerging markets. Discovery and successful exploitation of shale reserves could moderate India's growing dependency on imported energy, while slowing the growth in carbon emissions. A regional electricity grid, meanwhile, could give India access to about 100 gigawatts of electricity capacity.[71]

Global trends, however, will often exacerbate the problems facing India. The age of cheap oil is over, with future prices likely to be determined by the cost of bringing reserves to market that are expensive to extract, geopolitically risky, or both. It seems probable that China's and India's economies will rise (or fall) together, ensuring intensifying competition between the world's two largest countries for imported energy. India is one of the few major economies that has limited resources of its own and is not geographically contiguous with major sources of supply. Its vulnerability to geopolitical and geo-economic shocks through global commodity markets will therefore remain high.

Fuel, Food, and Water to Meet Basic Needs

Despite robust economic growth in recent years, India remains a poor country. By 2015, it is projected to have 288 million people who are still living in absolute poverty, more than a quarter of the global total.[72]

Resources, or the lack of them, play a critical role in the lives of India's poor. Diets have failed to improve at the same rate as the economy, with average caloric intake falling and, by some estimate, it is the lowest in the G-20.[73] Overall, nutrition standards remain among the worst in the world, especially among children; they have failed to rise as quickly as in other comparable countries and, by some measures, have not improved at all since the beginning of the century.[74] An estimated 217 million Indians are malnourished, a quarter of the world's total,[75] while half of Indian children are thought to be stunted, around a third of the global total.[76] Even before the food crisis, more than a quarter of the population stated that they did not have enough money to buy food, while a fifth said that they regularly suffered from hunger.[77] In 2012, 14 percent of people stated that they did not have enough money for food.[78]

Energy poverty is projected to be far from solved by 2030. By that date, Indians are expected to consume only between a third and half of average global per capita energy use (and only around 10 percent of the average American and 20 percent of the average Chinese consumption in the EIA reference scenario).

An estimated 144 million people will still be without electricity,[79] almost all of whom will live in rural areas, while most urban areas are likely to experience intermittent and unreliable supply.[80] Without a rapid acceleration in progress, around 40 percent of the population will lack clean cooking facilities by 2030, again mostly in rural areas.[81]

Other resource pressures have a great effect on the poor. More than half of India's population lives in areas that are water stressed, while only 72 percent of the population has access to safe drinking water.[82] Arable land per capita has halved over the past forty years, and farm size is shrinking.[83] In twenty out of India's twenty-eight states, current irrigation infrastructure now exceeds the potential left to be developed.[84] As a result, farmers are turning to groundwater to maintain productivity, with 61 percent of land now irrigated by groundwater.[85] In northern India, groundwater is disappearing according to observations made by National Aeronautical and Space Administration satellites, raising the risk of a "collapse of agricultural output and severe shortages of potable water."[86] There is also feedback between energy and other resource domains. Subsidized electricity allows farmers to overextract water, for example, while subsidies are also used to control the price of agricultural inputs (fertilizers and energy, with 42 percent of the latter derived from oil).[87]

Many of India's internal security threats have a resource dimension. The Naxalite insurgency is funded by "levies" on coal, iron, forestry, and business interests.[88] Land disputes have also fueled the insurgency.[89] Levels of corruption and criminality are high across the energy sector and in relation to subsidies for food, fuel, and water.[90] This has inevitable impacts on poverty, with an estimated 46 percent of the poor living in 125 of India's 640 districts that are affected by insurgency, while corruption has an obvious impact in diverting resources away from the poor.[91]

Resources can also play a potentially vital role in poverty reduction, both by fueling growth and by creating jobs, but more narrowly by increasing rural incomes for net sellers of food. India still has less than a third of its population living in towns and cities and will not be majority urban until 2030. (China has already crossed this threshold and is expected to have less than a quarter of its population living in rural areas by mid-century.)[92] Between 1993 and 2010 rural poverty fell 2.5 percent, as agricultural wages increased 2.9 percent.[93] In contrast to China, however, higher yields have been relatively slow to feed through to poverty reduction, due to relatively unequal distribution of land.[94] It remains to be seen the extent to which urbanization will lead to growing pressure on rural land, higher demand for food, and corresponding increases in rural incomes.

In recent years, the Indian government has continued to explore ways to address the nexus between resources, social protection, and employment generation, as it attempts to accelerate poverty reduction. The Mahatma Gandhi National Rural Employment Guarantee Act, for example, provided up to 100 days of guaranteed work to 55 million households in 2010–11 through public works focused primarily on improving natural resource management in rural areas.[95] Currently, the government is attempting to introduce a food security bill, which aims to provide subsidized grain to around three quarters of the rural and half of the urban population.[96] The government estimates that the bill will bring the cost of subsidies to around US$16 billion a year, from US$14.5 billion in 2011–12, while the Food and Agriculture Organization (FAO) projects costs as high as US$67 billion.[97] It will require up to 64 million tons of grain, with the public sector purchasing around a quarter of the total crop of food grains.[98] The bill has been reviewed and accepted by the Food Ministry and was ratified by Parliament in August 2013.[99]

Subsidies have also played an important role in limiting the transmission of global food prices to Indian consumers. During the 2008 price shock, the Indian wheat price rose by only 11 percent of the global average and rice by just 4 percent.[100] As a result, and due to the impact of rapid economic growth, self-reported levels of food insecurity and hunger actually *fell* slightly during the food crisis.[101] Indian production has also grown strongly since the crisis, with cereals forecast to be 10 percent higher in 2012 than the average for 2008–10.[102] Subsidies, however, for both food and energy, create a heavy fiscal burden and are not well targeted on the poorest.[103] Total central government subsidies have doubled in real terms over the past five years, and this has had a significant impact on a deficit that is four times the average for emerging economies.[104] The overall distributional impact of this expenditure is hard to quantify, but for LPG, 40 percent of the total subsidy goes to the richest 7 percent of the population, while only a quarter goes to the 68 percent of Indians who live in rural areas.[105]

As poverty in China and South Africa continues to fall, India will increasingly be the only country in the G-20 with a significant proportion of its citizens living in absolute poverty and suffering from hunger. This will provide it with an incentive to ensure ongoing emphasis at a global level on the links between access to resources and poverty reduction. However, it will also have incentives to act in ways that protect the poor at home but may have adverse consequences internationally. During the 2008 food crisis, Indian price stabilization and export controls played an important role in driving food prices higher for other countries, especially for rice.[106] It now plays a critical role in rice markets and is likely soon to be the world's third largest exporter. The country's reemergence as a rice exporter has helped to drive the rice price down, but continues to leave global markets vulnerable to any future resort to export bans.[107]

India could therefore play a role that is highly positive for other developing countries, especially for those poorer than itself, if it adopts a leadership position in the G-20 and other global forums on basic needs commodities. However, its actions could also have unintended negative consequences for these countries, especially during times of crisis. The balance between these forces is discussed in more detail in the concluding section.

The Environmental Constraints of Resource Demand

India has made significant progress on the first generation of "dirty" environmental problems, such as tackling indoor air pollution and providing access to clean water and modern sanitation, although these problems still have a pronounced impact on the lives of its poorer citizens. Many of the same people are also highly vulnerable to floods, drought, and other natural disasters.

Household air pollution, mainly caused by the use of solid fuels without adequate ventilation, is estimated to be the most important risk factor for the loss of healthy life years across South Asia, although it is quickly being caught up by smoking.[108] As a comparison with other health hazards, lead pollution ranks twenty-four, workplace pollution ranks twenty-five, and unimproved water ranks thirty-four.[109] In India, the share of modern fuels in total household consumption is only 14 percent, with particulate concentrations close to stoves and fires more than 100 times greater than safe levels.[110] In 2005 12 percent of households relied on an unimproved source of water (mostly unprotected wells), while only half had access to water within their own premises.[111] Moreover, 71 percent of households did not have access to improved sanitation, with 55 percent not having access to any toilet at all.

India faces similarly urgent challenges in the face of extreme weather events and other environmental disasters. Between 2000 and 2009, an average of around 30 million people were affected by flooding each year, leading to the loss of 17,830 lives,[112] while large parts of the country are also vulnerable to earthquakes and tsunamis. Around 750,000 square kilometers of the country are covered by the Drought Prone Area Programme,[113] with western and northern districts experiencing their worst drought in decades.[114] However, despite this vulnerability to drought, India has not experienced a famine since independence in 1947.

Given the scale of these impacts, addressing long-standing environmental threats will clearly remain a priority for the Indian government. However, it must also tackle new threats:

—*The environmental impact of rapid urbanization.* India's urban population is growing by around 10 million people each year,[115] with the Planning Commission describing the speed of urbanization as an "an unprecedented managerial and policy challenge."[116] While it is 30–50 percent cheaper to provide basic services to urban than to rural populations, at current rates of infrastructure development, the gap between supply and demand is projected to triple for water and to double for sewage.[117] The McKinsey Global Institute estimates that investment in urban infrastructure must grow from current levels of 0.5 percent of GDP to 2 percent of GDP each year for the next two decades if these deficits are to be addressed. Patterns of urban development are also likely to increase vulnerability to disasters, especially floods and earthquakes, while also degrading natural buffer systems, such as mangrove swamps.[118]

—*Increased land degradation and growing water scarcity.* Given the shortage of land, India is vulnerable to any deterioration in the quality of that land. Land affected by soil erosion ranges from 0.1 percent in Goa to 21.6 percent in Rajasthan, with erosion rates ranging from 5 to 20 tons of soil per hectare.[119] By 2050, India will need to support more than 18 percent of the global population on just 2 percent of the world's land, while the growing wealth of that population will continue to demand intensification of land use.[120] Demand for water is another growing problem, with India expected to be "water stressed" by 2025 and "water scarce" by 2050.[121] Water quality is also poor and will deteriorate without investment as cities grow. At present only 31 percent of municipal wastewater receives treatment, while the rest is discharged into rivers, lakes, and groundwater.[122]

—*Climate change.* India is one of the most vulnerable countries in the world to climate change, coming second on an index of vulnerability to Bangladesh.[123] A global temperature increase of 2°C–4°C is expected to increase average annual precipitation by 7–20 percent a year, with average annual monsoon precipitation increasing 10–15 percent. Central India and other semiarid regions in the country are expected to receive 5–25 percent less precipitation.[124] India's infrastructure, agriculture, and biodiversity are all susceptible to the impacts of climate change, as is its public health.[125] The Himalayan and Karakoram regions are significant sources of water for nearly 800 million people who live in the catchment areas of the Indus, Ganges, and Brahmaputra. Scientific knowledge about the current state of these glaciers is highly uncertain, and the impact of climate change on them is even more so, with controversy further fueled by inaccuracies in the Intergovernmental Panel on Climate Change's fourth assessment report.[126] However, any shift in their extent could have dramatic impacts on well-being.

Changes in India's climate are inevitable due to existing increases in atmospheric concentrations of greenhouse gases, but there is scope to adapt to these changes. Other environmental threats can be mitigated or avoided, through better land use or greater energy efficiency, for example.[127] There is also potential for cooperation on regional environmental issues, such as management of water basins or development of a South Asian "water grid" capable of transferring 174 billion cubic meters of water a year between countries.[128]

However, India faces significant constraints to increasing environmental sustainability, due to market failures and distortions, weak institutions, lobbies that protect business-as-usual interests, and lack of political will. These problems are compounded at regional and international levels, where environmental public goods are significantly undersupplied. As with energy, food, water, and other resources, the political economy dimensions of India's environmental challenge will be the key determinant in whether it is able to manage these threats effectively.

How Strategic Resources and Environmental Challenges Will Shape India's Future

Without energy, there can be no economic growth, while food and water are essential to sustaining life. Extreme weather events and environmental disasters destroy lives, property, and infrastructure, with the most serious rendering previously productive land uninhabitable. Natural resources are therefore a central policy concern in any country, while environmental shocks and long-term environmental threats such as climate change will become frontline issues whenever the number of citizens affected is significant.

This is even more the case for a country whose population and economy are growing as rapidly as India's. More, and increasingly wealthy, people create greater demand for resources, while a growing middle class tends to be less than tolerant of interruptions to supply, while also valuing a relatively clean and stable environment. New industries need a different mix of resources, change the spatial distribution of demand, and generate new environmental costs.

Given trends reviewed earlier in this chapter, it seems inevitable that strategic resources and the environment will play an increasingly important role in shaping India's future. Over the next twenty years,

—*Energy security will be a defining challenge for India.* Rapidly growing demand, energy poverty, high import dependence, and weak institutions guarantee that this issue will remain at, or close to, the top of India's political priorities. Governments will be judged on how successful they are in tackling energy scarcity, which affects both households and industry, and in maintaining secure supplies when global resource markets are volatile.

—*India is not on track to secure the energy it needs.* India fails to meet current demand for coal, oil, and electricity and faces a huge task if it is to respond to higher demand from business and consumers. It experiences profound market failures in all energy sectors, while higher, more volatile energy prices have compounded the challenge it faces. It seems unlikely that India's aspirations for rapid economic growth can be met given current energy policies.

—*Poverty will remain a key driver of policy on resources.* India's population is not expected to stabilize until the middle of this century, while it is projected to have significant levels of energy and food poverty for at least the next twenty

years. Those who escape poverty and enter the middle class will be vulnerable
to their living standards being eroded by food and energy price inflation. No
democratic government can afford to neglect these concerns, with the result that
India is likely to continue to favor an interventionist policy, at least in domestic
resource markets. At the same time, it will be constrained in global markets for
critical resources, where India's market-influencing power will often be limited.

—*India's environmental vulnerabilities are increasing*. The poor already face
serious threats from indoor air pollution, extreme weather events, and water scarcity. Climate change is an immediate and pressing danger to India, perhaps more
so than in any other G-20 country. Given its growing population and residual
poverty, India will continue to demand that the rest of the world provide it with
"space to grow." However, this will not reduce the dangers it faces if the world as
a whole continues to pursue unsustainable patterns of growth.

—*The interactions between India's resource and environmental challenges will
become more complex*. Hydroelectricity links the energy sector with water, causing
electricity shortages during times of drought. Agriculture is heavily dependent on
oil in India, which accounts for 42 percent of all agricultural energy, with energy
prices driving food inflation.[129] Subsidized energy allows farmers to overextract
water to irrigate their land, leading to both water and energy shortages and land
degradation. Climate change multiplies the risks across all sectors, with energy
infrastructure and agriculture vulnerable to extreme weather events, rising temperatures, and changes in the distribution and extent of rainfall.

The National and Global Policy Environment

Although energy, food, water, and climate all have obvious transboundary dimensions, domestic risks are both more pressing and more likely to play a decisive role
in determining India's success in rising to these challenges. More effective management of the country's dysfunctional resource markets is the most pressing priority.
Reform, however, is blocked by a lack of consensus about future direction, by vested
interests, and by the need to meet the basic resource requirements of the poor.

This has made the domestic politics of natural resources extremely contentious. Recent attempts to reduce subsidies have proved politically costly, for
example, while increased government intervention in food markets has the
potential to reduce levels of hunger and malnutrition, but at the risk of further
distorting markets and creating an unsustainable fiscal burden. There is some
evidence that the "social contract" on resources will continue to fray and widen
existing fissures. It is likely that demographic, economic, and social fault lines
will play an increasingly important role in complicating the political dimensions of key resource questions, opening divides between rural and urban areas,
for example, or between states with different patterns of demand and levels of

resource poverty. Even within states, inefficient and exclusionary management of natural resources will likely create new demands for autonomy for subregions. Intergenerational tensions over climate change are also possible, as young people are confronted by the extent of the environmental changes they will see during their lifetimes.

In the worst case, natural resources and the environment could emerge as a significant threat to India's internal security. In rural areas, there is already a resource dimension to the Naxalite insurgency, while urban areas could see unrest related to food and energy shortages. Across all resource industries, corruption and organized crime have a corrosive impact on legitimate political institutions. Given the scale of projected climate impacts, it seems likely that climate change will steadily increase the risks of competition between states or between ethnic groups, which, if unchecked, could lead to increased conflict.

Societies are often strengthened by their response to fundamental challenges, of course. It is quite possible that a crisis will drive badly needed reforms. High resource prices have placed the Indian government under increasing fiscal pressure and have already provided new impetus to reduce subsidies.[130] The power cuts of 2012 created fresh awareness of the need to invest in energy infrastructure, including off-grid systems that might have better solutions for improving energy access for the poor. In the future, dramatic evidence of the impact of land degradation, water scarcity, or climate change could make it possible for hard political decisions to be taken.

Global drivers will help to frame what is possible within India's domestic policy environment. The following trends are evident, and many have the potential to make progress at home harder to achieve:

—*India's exposure to breakdown in global energy markets will continue to increase.* India is already heavily dependent on imported oil and is increasingly dependent on imported coal. It has little immediate prospect of improving domestic governance, given governance failures, lack of investment, and limited proven reserves. Some of the measures it has taken to reduce its exposure to international markets, such as investments in equity oil, have had limited impact, while its dependence on Iranian oil has already proved problematic. Moreover, India has, to date, been slow to engage in regimes designed to manage resource dependencies, remaining outside all major multilateral and plurilateral energy regimes.

—*On food, India's size gives it considerable market power.* India is a dominant actor in the global rice market and plays an important role in other commodity markets. Its use of export bans has already had significant consequences for other market participants, shielding its own citizens from price rises in a way that has intensified the food crisis in other markets. However, India will also have a growing incentive to guarantee supply as import dependence grows, which is likely to encourage it to play an active role in shaping food regimes and responding to supply interruptions and price volatility.

—*Transnational water stress will prove manageable in the short term*. It is plausible that water scarcity will create increased tensions with India's neighbors, especially if there are other causes of friction. However, it is more likely that water will provide a focus for cooperation rather than conflict, given the interest of all countries in managing shared water resources. (The India-Pakistan Indus Waters Treaty, signed in 1960, has survived three wars and many other troughs in the relations between the two countries.) However, in the longer term (2050 and onward), climate change could complicate matters, especially in the Indus and Brahmaputra river basins.[131]

—*The intersection between maritime and energy security is a potentially serious source of friction with India's neighbors*. A large majority (95 percent) of India's trade by volume depends on maritime routes (70 percent by value), making it highly sensitive to any risk of interruption.[132] These concerns feed into a potentially adversarial relationship with China, which is playing an increasingly assertive role in the Indian Ocean.[133] However, in the short term at least, China's ability to project naval power in the Indian Ocean is limited.[134] It is therefore possible that nontraditional security threats (from rising sea levels, pollution, the decline of fisheries) could play a stronger role. These—and the need for all countries in the region to secure energy imports—have the potential to act as a focus for cooperative action.

—*Climate change politics will be increasingly challenging for India*. As its emissions grow and "atmospheric space for emissions" shrinks, India will face international pressure to change the way it engages on climate. For twenty years, international climate politics have been strongly influenced by a steadfast alliance between India and China at the heart of the G-77 negotiating bloc. Indian per capita emissions are now far below China's, however, potentially leading to what could be a highly significant realignment. India will also have a growing incentive to shape international policy on climate adaptation, given its vulnerability to a changing climate and that of its neighbors.

India will find that global governance regimes are both weak and contested for the issues that matter most to it. Energy governance is highly fragmented, with neither India nor China members of the International Energy Agency.[135] The trade regime for food is better equipped to ensure market access than to prevent export bans when markets are threatened by collapse.[136] Thirty years of negotiations on climate change have failed to restrain the rapid growth in emissions of greenhouse gases.[137] The Indian government will therefore need to play a skilled hand if it is to meet its objectives in these sectors and, by doing so, reinforce its ability to implement reforms at home.

The Role of International Cooperation: Multilateralism and Other Options

India has long been an active participant in the processes and institutions of global governance.[138] Its contributions to United Nations peacekeeping and peacebuilding operations, its (original) espousal of a nuclear weapons–free world, its endorsement of universal values in the promotion of human rights, and its engagement with the multilateral trade regime are only a few examples of India's long-standing interest in global governance and commitment to multilateralism. Despite its growing economic and political power, India's engagement with the world will continue to be contingent on how such engagement could offer outcomes that improve the human condition of her citizens. This principle will remain at the core of its diplomacy.

However, Indian diplomacy also confronts several questions in a changing global order.

On the question of whether India should be principled or pragmatic, recent developments have suggested that India does not necessarily see the two as being opposed. From India's perspective, the India-U.S. civil nuclear deal was in its national interest, but also partially corrected an "arbitrary inequity in the global non-proliferation regime."[139]

At the same time, Indian diplomats recognize that, with economic growth and resulting power, its demands from global institutions have changed. New or different international rules are needed on a range of issues, spanning economic, social, political, and security concerns.

However, there remains a concern about what kind of responsibility India will have to bear under new international regimes and, more important, whether international institutions will be used to subordinate Indian interests to those of countries that dominate the international system. There is little appetite to participate in forums to develop rules to freeze the status quo and limit India's room for maneuver.

As a result, India often lacks a clear strategy in its international engagement. This is compounded by the lack of capacity within the Indian system for contending with an increasingly crowded international portfolio. As the Indian economy grows, its interests become more complex. Often the government lacks the resources or the time to identify and further them effectively.

These problems become more pronounced for international issues that can no longer be handled within existing policy silos. Energy, food, water, and climate change are policy domains that are enmeshed in a global economy that does not respect national or sectoral borders. Energy drives climate change, while climate limits energy options. Food and energy markets are tightly interlinked, while water is essential to food and energy production and is directly affected by a changing climate. All of these issues touch on other contentious international policy challenges such as trade, finance, and technology transfer.

India seeks strategic autonomy in each of these areas, but is highly unlikely to find it, given the number and power of other actors who are involved. At home, given its size and the nature of its political system, it is equally implausible that it will develop and implement a strategic, comprehensive, and integrated response to its resource and environmental challenges. It is much more likely that it will continue to muddle through, responding to the most pressing problems in a reactive fashion, gradually building increased institutional capacity, better-functioning markets, and more resilient communities. At best, international cooperation will support this process. At worse, it will make difficult domestic decisions even harder to take.

Domestically, a series of "mini bargains" will likely have the greatest potential to strengthen resource security, with each containing sufficient incentives for relevant interest groups to support—or avoid blocking—them. These mini bargains could include, but not be limited to, reforming the most egregious of fossil fuel subsidies that have a negative impact on fiscal balances, public health, the environment, and social welfare (by being poorly targeted); reviewing critical food stocks to ensure that sudden supply shocks do not result in purely unilateral measures to secure them; and steadily strengthening the governance of energy and food markets, in order to increase supply while reducing vulnerabilities in supply chains.

While some countries might see resources as an attractive source of strategic pressure on India, on the whole, the international community has a considerable interest in supporting these developments. India will soon be the world's largest country, and the vast majority of its population either still lives in poverty or is part of an insecure middle class that hovers just above the poverty line. A stable, and increasingly prosperous, India can make an important contribution to the twenty-first century. A stagnant, or failing, India would substantially weaken the security of Asia and have clear global implications. The international community would be foolish to underestimate the risks that India faces from energy and other resources over the coming decades, especially as its middle class becomes more assertive in the pursuit of its aspirations.

Both India and its allies, therefore, have an incentive to look for opportunities for international cooperation on resource and environmental issues that will strengthen global regimes, while making India's search for domestic solutions more fruitful. Greater international engagement can help to accomplish the following:

—*Increase understanding of the risks that India faces*. As this review has demonstrated, resource and environmental issues are highly complex, interacting with each other and with all aspects of India's society and economy. They also naturally cross borders, making a purely national perspective of little value. It is therefore important for India to build a shared analysis across countries in the region and internationally as well as with the private sector and other nongovernmental actors. This will provide the foundation for developing new policies, while reducing misunderstandings and miscalculations. This work should stretch across resource challenges (food, land, water, climate, and other strategic commodities) to create a joint analysis of the stresses, risks, and opportunities facing countries across the region.

—Provide India with a platform to share potential solutions with its partners. Other countries in the region, as well as those in the G-20 such as Brazil and China, have important experience tackling resource poverty and resource challenges during a period of rapid growth. Equally, India has its own successful models, which are relevant to both emerging and poorer economies. Areas that could be explored include infrastructure development, given the sheer quantity of infrastructure needed as Asia's urban boom continues, and innovative forms of finance, given that many of the most-needed investments are too big for the public sector and too risky for private financiers to undertake on their own.

—Provide a basis for Indian leadership in the G-20. The G-20 turned its attention to energy in 2009 at the Pittsburgh Summit, focusing on energy poverty, the need to phase out subsidies, and energy and climate security, while the 2009 L'Aquila Summit laid the basis for international cooperation on food security. As pointed out in this chapter, India has an especially strong incentive to keep the G-20 focused on both issues, ensuring that it does more to implement existing commitments, while exploring new areas for international cooperation. It is surely time for India to assume the G-20 presidency, possibly after Turkey in 2015. Energy and food would provide a natural theme for India to build its presidency around, while the intersection between maritime and energy security is another promising area for cooperation within the G-20.

—Influence the post-2015 development agenda. Debate is currently under way about what should replace the Millennium Development Goals after 2015, with the new framework likely to focus both on poverty eradication and on sustainable development.[140] Given that new goals will play an important role in shaping the international agenda for the next fifteen years or more, India has a powerful incentive to ensure that food, water, and energy poverty are at the heart of the new agenda and that progress is made on sustainable development and green growth, but not at the expense of countries such as India with consumption rates well below the global per capita average.

Preparing the Ground at Home

More decisive international engagement on resource issues will only be possible if the Indian government is prepared to enhance significantly its capacity to engage internationally.

Indian diplomats increasingly recognize that, as an emerging power, India has to navigate four transitions in global governance: from rule taking to rule shaping; from framing rules to designing regimes; from singular issue-specific institutions to complex regimes; and from diplomacy through formal forums to understanding the role of informal networks and groups of countries.[141] India will need increased capacity if it is to exploit the full potential that each of these transitions provides, while using them to construct an overarching strategic posture.

The first step is to invest in resource and environmental diplomacy and the data and evidence needed to underpin this diplomacy. Indian diplomats often view foreign assessments of its economy and patterns of resource consumption with a degree of suspicion. They therefore need to generate their own answers from sources they trust, while ensuring better information flows between resource-related departments, researchers outside government, and foreign policymakers.

India's diplomats then need to survey the full range of multilateral, plurilateral, and bilateral options, while assessing what markets can be expected to deliver without any government intervention. This will allow them to develop the basis for solutions and collaborations with foreign partners on specific problems and, thereby, lay the foundations for more robust international resource governance.

The National Security Council Secretariat is the natural focus for this iterative process of analysis and design of international engagement, but many others will need to be involved. Resource ministers and others are needed jointly to monitor vulnerabilities in resource supply lines. Officials from all responsible ministries, including external affairs, need to be involved in the broader dialogue, creating a wider perspective on changing resource needs, markets, rules, and potential areas of tension. This will help to build a cadre of more strategically focused officers. Finally, the skills and knowledge of external actors must also be drawn on, including former diplomats, academics and think tanks, and industry representatives, providing a range of alternative perspectives on India's resource and environmental needs.

A strategic approach to India's resource challenges will not emerge overnight, but neither can the government afford to wait any longer. The pressure from energy, food, water, and climate is growing. It is time to engage on these issues with new vision, foresight, and determination, before signs of trouble turn into a crisis that threatens the country's prosperity, security, and international status.

Notes

1. United Nations Department of Economic and Social Affairs (UNDESA), *World Population Prospects: The 2010 Revision* (New York, 2011).

2. Knight Frank and Citi Private Bank, *The Wealth Report 2012: A Global Perspective on Prime Property and Wealth* (London: Knight Frank Research, 2012).

3. International Energy Agency (IEA), *World Energy Outlook 2011* (Paris, 2011).

4. Maplecroft, "Climate Change Vulnerability Index 2012" (Bath, 2011).

5. Charles K. Ebinger and Govinda Avasarala, "Emerging Power Crisis," *Foreign Policy* (August 1, 2012) (http://www.foreignpolicy.com/articles/2012/08/01/emerging_power_crisis).

6. Jim Yardley and Gardiner Harris, "2nd Day of Power Failures Cripples Wide Swath of India," *New York Times*, July 31, 2012 (www.nytimes.com/2012/08/01/world/asia/power-outages-hit-600-million-in-india.html?pagewanted=all). "Coal Shortages to Hit Power Generation, Brace up for More Blackouts," *India Today,* June 7, 2012 (http://indiatoday.intoday.in/story/coal-shortage-to-hit-power-generation-coal-india-ntpc/1/199551.html). Federation of Indian Chambers of Commerce and Industry, "A Wake up Call," Press Release, July 31, 2012 (www.ficci.com/press-releases-month.asp?eDate=07/2012).

7. Biman Mukherji, Saurabh Chaturvedi, and Santanu Choudhury, "In India, Weak Monsoon Adds to Power Crisis," *Wall Street Journal,* August 2, 2012 (http://online.wsj.com/article/SB10000872396390443545504577564900963094424.html).

8. Debjoy Sengupta and Mitul Thakkar, "States Seek Legislative Changes to Punish Those Drawing Excess Power from Grid," *Economic Times,* August 3, 2012 (http://articles.economictimes.indiatimes.com/2012-08-03/news/33020111_1_northern-grid-northern-states-nrpc). "Don't Make Light of It," *Hindustantimes,* August 5, 2012 (www.hindustantimes.com/News-Feed/Chanakya/Don-t-make-light-of-it/Article1-908427.aspx).

9. Milan Vaishnav, "India's Very Political Power Crisis," CNN World, August 3, 2012 (http://globalpublicsquare.blogs.cnn.com/2012/08/03/indias-very-political-power-crisis/).

10. Food and Agriculture Organization (FAO), "Crop Prospects and Food Situation" (Rome, December 2012) (www.fao.org/docrep/017/al995e/al995e00.htm). Niharika Mandhana, "Sluggish Monsoon Threatens India's Growth," *New York Times India,* August 10, 2012 (http://india.blogs.nytimes.com/2012/08/10/sluggish-monsoon-threatens-indias-growth/). James Hansen, Makiko Sato, and Reto Ruedy, "Perceptions of Climate Change: The New Climate Dice" (Columbia University, 2012) (www.columbia.edu/~jeh1/mailings/2012/20120105_PerceptionsAndDice.pdf). U.S. Department of Agriculture, Economic Research Service, *U.S. Drought 2012: Farm and Food Impacts* (Washington, 2012) (www.ers.usda.gov/newsroom/us-drought-2012-farm-and-food-impacts.aspx).

11. James Fontanella-Khan, "Indian Inflation Rises as Food Prices Jump," *Financial Times,* June 14, 2012 (www.ft.com/intl/cms/s/0/77718118-b5f8-11e1-a511-00144feabdc0.html#axzz2JHcK2VJ3). "Indian Inflation Slows in July," BBC News, August 14, 2012 (www.bbc.co.uk/news/business-19252730). "Despite Inflation Slowing, Government Is Still Unable to Rein in Food Prices," *Times of India,* January 16, 2013 (http://articles.timesofindia.indiatimes.com/2013-01-16/edit-page/36353703_1_food-prices-grain-prices-wholesale-price-increases).

12. Grant Danise, Marc Lanteigne, and Indra Overland, "Reducing Energy Subsidies in China, India, and Russia: Dilemmas for Decision Makers," *Sustainability* 2, no. 2 (2010): 475–93.

13. "Indian Power Failure Shows Growing Political Gridlock," *Bloomberg*, August 3, 2012 (www.bloomberg.com/news/2012-08-02/indian-power-failure-highlights-growing-political-gridlock-view.html). "Now Finish the Job," *Economist*, April 15, 2012 (www.economist.com/blogs/banyan/2012/04/indias-economic-reforms?zid=309&ah=80dcf28 8b8561b012f603b9fd9577f0e).

14. Indian Planning Commission, *Faster, Sustainable, and More Inclusive Growth: An Approach to the Twelfth Five-Year Plan* (New Delhi, 2011), p. 29.

15. McKinsey and Company, *Charting Our Water Future: Economic Frameworks to Inform Decision Making* (New York, 2009).

16. IEA, *Worldwide Trends in Energy Use and Efficiency* (Paris, 2008). U.S. Energy Information Administration (EIA), "Global Natural Gas Prices Vary Considerably," *Today in Energy*, September 30, 2011 (www.eia.gov/todayinenergy/detail.cfm?id=3310).

17. Arunabha Ghosh and others, *Understanding Complexity, Anticipating Change: From Interests to Strategy on Global Governance,* Report of the Working Group on India and Global Governance (New Delhi: Council on Energy, Environment, and Water, December 2011) (ceew.in/pdf/CEEW_WGIGG_Report.pdf).

18. IEA, *World Energy Outlook 2011*. EIA, *International Energy Outlook 2011* (Washington, 2011).

19. Indian Planning Commission, *Faster, Sustainable, and More Inclusive Growth*, p. 29.

20. Indian Central Statistics Office, *Energy Statistics 2012* (New Delhi, 2012).

21. IEA, *World Energy Outlook 2012* (Paris, 2012).

22. IEA, *Energy Technology Perspectives: Scenarios and Strategies to 2050* (Paris, 2010). World Coal Institute, *The Coal Resource: A Comprehensive Overview of Coal* (Paris, 2009).

23. IEA, *World Energy Outlook 2011*.

24. Saurabh Chaturvedi and Rakesh Sharma, "Coal India Trims Outlook on Environmental Issues," *Wall Street Journal*, December 21, 2010 (http://online.wsj.com/article/SB10001424052748703581204576033112469285354.html). "Coal India Mines Face Closure over Environmental Concerns in Jharkhand," *Economic Times*, August 24, 2011 (http://economictimes.indiatimes.com/news/news-by-industry/indl-goods/svs/metals-mining/coal-india-mines-face-closure-over-environmental-concerns-in-jharkhand/articleshow/9720497.cms). H. B. Sahu and Er. S. Dash, "Land Degradation due to Mining in India and Its Mitigation Measures," Paper presented at the Second International Conference on Environmental Science and Technology, Singapore, February 26–28, 2011. Shiv Pratap Raghuvanshi, Avinash Chandra, and Ashok Kumar Raghav, "Carbon Dioxide Emissions from Coal-Based Power Generation in India," *Energy Conversion and Management* 47, no. 4 (March 2006): 427–41.

25. IEA, *World Energy Outlook 2011*. Comptroller and Auditor General of India, *Performance Audit: Allocation of Coal Blocks and Augmentation of Coal Production* (http://saiindia.gov.in/english/home/Our_Products/Audit_Report/Government_Wise/union_audit/recent_reports/union_performance/2012_2013/Commercial/Report_No_7/Report_No_7.html). "PM's Response to Report," Wall Street Journal blog, August 27, 2012 (http://blogs.wsj.com/indiarealtime/2012/08/27/transcript-prime-minister-singh-counters-coalgate-allegations/). Vikas Bajaj and Jim Yeardley, "Scandal Poses a Riddle:

Will India Ever Be Able to Tackle Corruption?" *New York Times,* September 15, 2012 (www.nytimes.com/2012/09/16/world/asia/scandal-bares-corruption-hampering-indias-growth.html?pagewanted=all&_r=0). "India Story Alive and Kicking: Jyoti-raditya Scindia," NDTV, January 28, 2013 (http://profit.ndtv.com/news/economy/article-india-story-alive-and-kicking-jyotiraditya-scindia-316819).

26. William Magioncalda, *A Modern Insurgency: India's Evolving Naxalite Problem* (Washington: Center for Strategic and International Studies, 2010) (http://csis.org/files/publication/SAM_140_0.pdf).

27. "New Pricing May See Cut in Higher Grade Coal Imports," *Economic Times of India,* February 2, 2012 (http://bit.ly/xsRzpp).

28. Arunabha Ghosh, "Industrial Demand and Energy Supply Management: A Delicate Balance," in *Empowering Growth: Perspectives on India's Energy Future* (London: Economist Intelligence Unit, October 2012), pp. 29–30 (www.managementthinking.eiu.com/empowering-growth.html).

29. Ajoy K. Das, "Coal Shortage Causes India's Electricity Generation to Slump," *Mining Weekly,* May 17, 2011 (www.miningweekly.com/article/coal-shortage-causes-indias-electricity-generation-to-slump-2011-05-17).

30. Sujay Mehdudia, "Coal Shortage to Hit Power Capacity Plans," *Hindu,* February 23, 2012 (www.thehindu.com/business/Economy/article2924660.ece). Sudheer Pal Singh, "Govt Expects Coal Shortage to Touch 15% by 2012," *Business Standard,* February 11, 2010 (www.business-standard.com/india/news/govt-expects-coal-shortage-to-touch-15-by-2012/385289/).

31. McKinsey and Company, *Environmental and Energy Sustainability: An Approach for India* (Mumbai, 2009).

32. Indian Ministry of Power, *Report of the Working Group on Power for Twelfth Five-Year Plan (2012–17)* (New Delhi, January 2012), ch. 7, p. 5 (http://planningcommission.nic.in/aboutus/committee/wrkgrp12/wg_power1904.pdf).

33. EIA, *International Energy Statistics* (Washington, 2012) (www.eia.gov/cfapps/ipdbproject/IEDIndex3.cfm).

34. IEA, *World Energy Outlook 2011.*

35. Indian Planning Commission, *Faster, Sustainable, and More Inclusive Growth,* p. 33.

36. Indian Ministry of Finance, *Economic Survey 2011–12* (New Delhi, 2012) (www.indiabudget.nic.in/survey.asp).

37. Lydia Powell, "Do India's Equity Oil Investments Make Sense?" *Energy News Monitor* 8, no. 43 (April 10, 2012) (www.observerindia.com/cms/sites/orfonline/modules/enm-analysis/ENM-ANALYSISDetail.html?cmaid=35815&mmacmaid=35813).

38. Anilesh S. Mahajan, "World Wide Woe: ONGC Videsh's Overseas Woes: Could the Problems Have Been Avoided?" *Business Today,* August 19, 2012 (http://businesstoday.intoday.in/story/overseas-problems-of-ongc-videsh-other-oil-companies/1/186797.html). "ONGC to Continue Exploration in South China Sea," *Wall Street Journal,* July 19, 2012 (http://online.wsj.com/article/SB10000872396390444464304577536182763155666.html).

39. Powell, "Do India's Equity Oil Investments Make Sense?"

40. Ricardo Soares De Oliveira, "India's Rise and the Global Politics of Energy Supply: Challenges for the Next Decade," Eleventh Vasant J. Sheth Memorial Lecture, Vasant J. Sheth Memorial Foundation, December 2008, p. 18.

41. Indian Planning Commission, *Integrated Energy Policy: Report of the Expert Committee* (New Delhi, 2006).

42. IEA, "Fossil-Fuel Consumption Subsidy Rates as a Proportion of the Full Cost of Supply, 2011" (www.iea.org/subsidy/index.html).

43. Indian Planning Commission, *Faster, Sustainable, and More Inclusive Growth*, p. 32.

44. "Grasp the Nettle," *Times of India*, May 25, 2012 (http://articles.timesofindia. indiatimes.com/2012-05-25/edit-page/31850590_1_diesel-prices-kerosene-and-lpg-prices-hike-in-petrol-prices).

45. Vikas Bajaj, "India Cuts Subsidies for Fossil Fuels," *New York Times*, June 25, 2010 (www.nytimes.com/2010/06/26/business/global/26rupee.html). Amy Kazmin, "India Cuts Petrol Subsidies," *Financial Times*, June 25, 2010 (www.ft.com/cms/s/0/68a87eec-804a-11df-8b9e-00144feabdc0.html#axzz1px6YeTBq).

46. Indian Planning Commission, *Faster, Sustainable, and More Inclusive Growth*, p. 31.

47. Victor Mallet and Amy Kazmin, "India Cuts Fuel Subsidies to Curb Deficit," *Financial Times*, September 13, 2012 (www.ft.com/intl/cms/s/0/15e495a0-fdbc-11e1-9901-00144feabdc0.html#axzz2J6rLxzal).

48. Indian Planning Commission, *Faster, Sustainable, and More Inclusive Growth*, p. 31.

49. Observer Research Foundation, "Dash for Gas: Opportunities and Challenges," Policy Brief 13 (New Delhi, 2012), p. 3.

50. Ibid. Anne-Sophie Corbeau, *Natural Gas in India* (Paris: IEA, 2010).

51. EIA, *International Energy Statistics*.

52. Anil Jain and Anupama Sen, "Natural Gas in India: An Analysis of Policy" (Oxford Institute for Energy Studies, April 2010).

53. Ibid.

54. B. S. Negi, M. S. Pahwa, and Surbhi Arora, "Shale Gas Revolution: Is India Ready?" paper prepared for the International Conference on Energy and Infrastructure, School of Petroleum Management, Pandit Deendayal Petroleum University, Gandhinagar, India, January 3–4, 2012. EIA, *World Shale Gas Resources: An Initial Assessment of 14 Regions outside the United States* (Washington, 2011) (www.eia.gov/analysis/studies/worldshalegas/?src=email). Economist Intelligence Unit, "Breaking New Ground: A Special Report on Global Shale Gas Developments" (London, 2011), p. 22.

55. Economist Intelligence Unit, "Breaking New Ground."

56. "India Plans Shale Gas Blocks Auction by 2013 End," *Economic Times*, July 31, 2012 (http://articles.economictimes.indiatimes.com/2012-07-31/news/32961539_1_shale-gas-gas-blocks-dgh). "India's 1st Ever Shale Gas Exploration Bidding by 2013-end, Says PM," *Economic Times*, March 23, 2012 (http://articles.economictimes. indiatimes.com/2012-03-23/news/31230446_1_shale-gas-conventional-oil-and-gas-coal-bed-methane). "India to Offer Shale Gas Blocks by End of 2011," *Economic*

Times, October 18, 2010 (http://articles.economictimes.indiatimes.com/2010-10-18/news/27570138_1_shale-gas-gas-blocks-onland-blocks).

57. Govindasamy Agoramoorthy, "Nuclear Power: India Should Exploit Renewable Energy [correspondence]," *Nature* 481 (2012): 145.

58. Indian Planning Commission, *Faster, Sustainable, and More Inclusive Growth,* p. 29.

59. IEA, *World Energy Outlook 2011.*

60. Council on Energy, Environment, and Water and the Natural Resources Defense Council, *Laying the Foundation for a Bright Future: Assessing Progress under Phase 1 of India's National Solar Mission,* Interim Report (New Delhi, April 2012) (http://ceew.in/solar). Council on Energy, Environment, and Water and the Natural Resources Defense Council, "Concentrated Solar Power: Heating up India's Solar Thermal Market under the National Solar Mission" (New Delhi, September 2012) (http://ceew.in/solar).

61. Asian Development Bank, "Proposed Guarantee Facility Solar Power Generation (India)" (Mandaluyong City, 2011), p. 3. Jawaharlal Nehru National Solar Mission, "Towards Building SOLAR INDIA" (New Delhi, n.d.) (http://india.gov.in/allimpfrms/alldocs/15657.pdf).

62. Indian Planning Commission, *Eleventh Five-Year Plan 2007–2012,* vol. III: *Agriculture, Rural Development, Industry, Services, and Physical Infrastructure.* Oxford University Press.

63. IEA, *World Energy Outlook 2011.*

64. B. B. Bhattacharya and Sabyasachi Kar, *Shocks, Economic Growth, and the Indian Economy* (Washington: IMF, 2005) (www.imf.org/external/np/res/seminars/2005/macro/pdf/bhatta.pdf).

65. Andrew MacAskill and Kartikay Mehrota, "Singh Answers Sought as Worst Power Crisis May Hurt Growth," Bloomberg, August 1, 2012 (www.bloomberg.com/news/2012-07-31/india-power-grid-collapses-for-second-time-in-two-days.html).

66. International Monetary Fund (IMF), "World Economic Outlook Update: Gradual Upturn in Global Growth during 2013" (Washington, January 13, 2013) (www.imf.org/external/pubs/ft/weo/2013/update/01/).

67. Arunabha Ghosh, "Industrial Demand and Energy Supply Management: A Delicate Balance," in *Empowering Growth: Perspectives on India's Energy Future* (London: Economist Intelligence Unit, October 2012), pp. 26, 29 (www.managementthinking.eiu.com/empowering-growth.html).

68. Amol Sharma and Megha Bahree, "Grinding Energy Shortage Takes Toll on India's Growth," *Wall Street Journal,* July 1, 2012 (http://online.wsj.com/article/SB10001424052702304331204577352232515290226.html).

69. Ashwani Kumar, Kapil Kumar, Naresh Kaushik, Satyawati Sharma, and Saroj Mishra, "Renewable Energy in India: Current Status and Future Potentials," *Renewable and Sustainable Energy Reviews* 14, no. 8 (2010): 2434–42.

70. Subhes C. Bhattacharyya, "Shaping a Sustainable Energy Future for India: Management Challenges," *Energy Policy* 38, no. 8 (2010): 4173–85. Ramchandra Pode, "Addressing India's Energy Security and Options for Decreasing Energy Dependency," *Renewable and Sustainable Energy Reviews* 14, no. 9 (2010): 3014–22. Anil Razdan, "The Future of Energy in India," *Siemens Living Energy* 3 (2010): 62–66.

71. "India Sees 100,000 MW on Tap in Saarc Grid," *Times of India,* April 28, 2011 (http://articles.timesofindia.indiatimes.com/2011-04-28/india/29482244_1_grid-mw-india-and-pakistan).

72. United Nations, *The Millennium Development Goals Report 2011* (New York, 2011), p. 7.

73. Praduman Kumar, Anjani Kumar, Shinoj Parappurathu, and S. S. Raju, "Estimation of Demand Elasticity for Food Commodities in India," *Agricultural Economics Research Review* 24 (2011): 1–14.

74. Angus Deaton and Jean Drèze, "Food and Nutrition in India: Facts and Interpretations," *Economic and Political Weekly* 44, no. 7 (2009): 42–65.

75. Food and Agriculture Organization (FAO), *State of Food Insecurity* (Rome, 2012) (www.fao.org/docrep/016/i3027e/i3027e.pdf).

76. Robert E. Black, Lindsay H. Allen, Zulfiqar A. Bhutta, Laura E. Caulfield, Mercedes de Onis, Majid Ezzati, Colin Mathers, and Juan Rivera, for the Maternal and Child Undernutrition Study Group, "Maternal and Child Undernutrition: Global and Regional Exposures and Health Consequences," *Lancet* 371, no. 9608 (January 19, 2008): 243–60 (www.thelancet.com/journals/lancet/article/PIIS0140-6736(07)61690-0/fulltext#article_upsell).

77. Julie Ray and Cynthia English, "Even before Crisis, Affording Food a Challenge for Many," Gallup, April 25, 2008 (www.gallup.com/poll/106807/Even-Before-Crisis-Affording-Food-Challenge-Many.aspx).

78. Gallup WorldView 2012 data (https://worldview.gallup.com/default.aspx).

79. IEA, "World Energy Outlook: Energy Access Projections to 2030, Table 1" (Paris, 2012) (www.worldenergyoutlook.org/resources/energydevelopment/energyaccess projectionsto2030/).

80. IEA, *World Energy Outlook 2011,* p. 469.

81. IEA, "World Energy Outlook: Energy access Projections to 2030, Table 1." Population of the United States in 2012 from U.S. Census Bureau, "Population Estimates: National Totals; Vintage 2012" (Washington, 2013) (www.census.gov/popest/data/national/totals/2012/index.html).

82. Günther Fischer, Harrij van Velthuizen, Mahendra Shah, and Freddy Nachtergaele, *Global Agro-Ecological Assessment for Agriculture in the 21st Century* (Laxenburg: International Institute for Applied Systems Analysis, 2001). Indian Ministry of Finance, *Economic Survey 2011–12: Human Development* (New Delhi, 2012) (www.indiabudget.nic.in/es2011-12/echap-13.pdf).

83. World Bank, World Databank calculations based on FAO data, "Arable Land (Hectares per Person)" (Washington, 2012). U.S. Department of Agriculture, Foreign Agricultural Service, "India Agricultural Economy and Policy Report" (Washington, 2009).

84. Martin A. Burton and others, *National Water Resources Framework Study,* Research Report submitted to the Planning Commission for the Twelfth Five-Year Plan (New Delhi: Council on Energy, Environment, and Water and 2030 Water Resources Group, September 2011), p. 152 (http://ceew.in/water).

85. Ibid., p. 219.

86. Matthew Rodell, Isabella Velicogna, and James S. Famiglietti, "Satellite-Based Estimates of Groundwater Depletion in India [letter]," *Nature* 460 (2009): 999–1002. Gretchen Cook-Anderson, "NASA Satellites Unlock Secret to Northern India's Vanishing Water," NASA Earth Science News Team, August 12, 2009 (www.nasa.gov/topics/earth/features/india_water.html).

87. Derek Headey and Shenggen Fan, "Reflections on the Global Food Crisis: How Did It Happen? How Has It Hurt? And How Can We Prevent the Next One?" (Washington: International Food Policy Research Institute, 2010).

88. Nandini Sundar, "At War with Oneself: Constructing Naxalism as India's Biggest Security Threat," in *India's Contemporary Security Challenges,* edited by Michael Kugelman (Washington: Woodrow Wilson International Center for Scholars, 2011) (www.wilsoncenter.org/sites/default/files/ASIA_100423_IndiaSecurityFINAL.pdf).

89. Shrey Verma, *Far-Reaching Consequences of the Naxalite Problem in India: Understanding the Maoist Problem* (Santa Clara, Calif.: Rakshak Foundation, 2011) (www.rakshakfoundation.org/wp-content/uploads/2011/08/White-Paper-on-Naxalite-Movement-in-India.pdf). Raman Dixit, "Naxalite Movement in India: The State's Response," *Journal of Defence Studies* 4, no. 2 (April 2010) (www.idsa.in/system/files/jds_4_2_rdixit.pdf). Jairam Ramesh, "From Tirupati to Pushupati: Some Reflection on the Maoist Issue," speech given at the Sardar Patel Memorial Lecture organized by Prasar Bharati, New Delhi, October 11, 2011 (http://pib.nic.in/newsite/erelease.aspx?relid=76575).

90. Vikas Bajaj, "As Grain Piles up, India's Poor Still Go Hungry," *New York Times,* June 8, 2012 (www.nytimes.com/2012/06/08/business/global/a-failed-food-system-in-india-prompts-an-intense-review.html?_r=1&pagewanted=all).

91. Verma, *Far-Reaching Consequences of the Naxalite Problem.*

92. UNDESA, *World Urbanization Prospects: The 2011 Revision* (New York, 2012).

93. Anjani Kumar, Sant Kumar, Dhiraj K. Singh, and Shivjee, "Rural Employment Diversification in India: Trends, Determinants, and Implications on Poverty," *Agricultural Economics Research Review* 24 (2011): 361–72 (http://mahider.ilri.org/bitstream/handle/10568/12418/AERR_rural.pdf?sequence=1).

94. FAO, *State of Food Insecurity.*

95. Indian Ministry of Finance, *Economic Survey 2011–12: India and the Global Economy* (New Delhi, 2012) (www.indiabudget.nic.in/es2011-12/echap-14.pdf).

96. See Sunil Prabhu, "Parliamentary Panel Clears Food Security Bill," NDTV, January 11, 2013 (www.ndtv.com/article/india/parliamentary-panel-clears-food-security-bill-316322).

97. Indian Ministry of Finance, *Economic Survey 2011–12: Agriculture and Food* (New Delhi, 2012) (www.indiabudget.nic.in/es2011-12/echap-08.pdf). FAO, "Food Outlook: Global Market Analysis, May 2012" (Rome, 2012) (www.fao.org/fileadmin/user_upload/newsroom/docs/Final%20web%20version%202%20May%20(2).pdf).

98. FAO, "Food Outlook: May 2012." Centre for Budget and Governance Accountability, "Unfulfilled Promises? Response to Union Budget 2012–13" (New Delhi, 2012), p. 54.

99. *Gazette of India,* "The National Food Security Act, 2013" (New Delhi: Ministrty of Law and Justice, September 10, 2013) (indiacode.nic.in/acts-in-pdf/202013.pdf).

100. FAO, "Food Outlook: Global Market Analysis, November 2011" (Rome, 2011), p. 26.

101. Derek Headey, "Was the Global Food Crisis Really a Crisis? Simulation Versus Self-Reporting," IFPRI Discussion Paper 01087 (Washington: International Food Policy Research Institute, 2011) (www.ifpri.org/sites/default/files/publications/ifpridp01087.pdf).

102. FAO, "Food Outlook: May 2012."

103. James Lamont and Amy Kazmin, "Singh Aide Urges India to End Energy Subsidies," *Financial Times,* June 14, 2011 (www.ft.com/cms/s/0/7f48e1f8-96b7-11e0-baca-00144feab49a.html#axzz1pfwZAcMj).

104. Indian Ministry of Petroleum and Natural Gas, "Basic Statistics on Indian Petroleum and Natural Gas 2010–11" (New Delhi, 2011), p. 36. IMF, "Nurturing Credibility While Managing Risks to Growth," *Fiscal Monitor,* July 16, 2012 (www.imf.org/external/pubs/ft/fm/2012/update/02/pdf/0712.pdf). IMF, "India: 2012 Article IV Consultation—Staff Report; Staff Statement and Supplements; Public Information Notice on the Executive Board Discussion; and Statement by the Executive Director for India" (Washington, April 2012) (www.imf.org/external/pubs/ft/scr/2012/cr1296.pdf).

105. Energy Resources Institute and the International Institute for Sustainable Development's Global Subsidies Initiative, *A Citizens' Guide to Energy Subsidies in India* (Geneva, 2012). UNDESA, *World Population Prospects: The 2010 Revision.*

106. David Dawe and Tom Slayton, "The World Rice Market in 2007–08," in *Safeguarding Food Security in Volatile Global Markets,* edited by Adam Prakesh (Rome: FAO, 2011) (www.fao.org/docrep/013/i2107e/i2107e13.pdf).

107. FAO, "Food Outlook: May 2012."

108. Institute for Health Metrics and Evaluation (IHME), "BD 2010 Change in Leading Causes and Risks between 1990 and 2010" (Seattle, 2012) (www.healthmetrics andevaluation.org/gbd/visualizations/gbd-2010-change-leading-causes-and-risks-between-1990-and-2010?cr=risk&metric=DALY).

109. C. J. L. Murray and others, "Disability-Adjusted Life Years (DALYs) for 291 Diseases and Injuries in 21 Regions, 1990–2010: A Systematic Analysis for the Global Burden of Disease Study 2010," *Lancet* 380, no. 9859 (December 2012): 2197–23 (www.thelancet.com/journals/lancet/article/PIIS0140-6736(12)61689-4/fulltext). IHME, "Visualizations" (Seattle, 2012) (www.healthmetricsandevaluation.org/gbd/visualizations/regional). National Commission on Macroeconomics and Health, "Burden of Disease in India" (New Delhi, 2005).

110. IEA, Energy Development Index database (www.iea.org/media/weowebsite/energydevelopment/2012updates/WEO2012EDIdatabase_WEB.xlsx). Esther Duflo, Michael Greenstone, and Rema Hanna, "Indoor Air Pollution, Health and Economic Well-Being, " Surveys and Perspectives Integrating Environment and Society (SAPIENS) (http://sapiens.revues.org/130).

111. Indian Ministry of Health and Family Welfare, *National Family Health Survey,* vol. 1 (New Delhi, 2007) (www.measuredhs.com/pubs/pdf/FRIND3/FRIND3-Vol1And Vol2.pdf).

112. Indian Ministry of Statistics and Programme Implementation, *Compendium on Environment Statistics India* (New Delhi, 2011) (http://mospi.nic.in/mospi_new/upload/compendium_2011_30dec11.htm).

113. Ibid.

114. Ibid. R. S. Eshelman and ClimateWire, "India's Drought Highlights Challenges of Climate Change Adaptation," *Scientific American,* August 3, 2012 (www.scientificamerican. com/article.cfm?id=indias-drought-highlights-challenges-climate-change-adaptation).

115. UNDESA, "On-Line Data: Urban and Rural Population" (New York, 2010) (http://esa.un.org/unpd/wup/unup/index_panel1.html).

116. Indian Planning Commission, "The Challenges of Urbanization in India" (New Delhi, n.d.) (*12thplan*.gov.in/12fyp_docs/17.pdf).

117. McKinsey Global Institute, "India's Urban Awakening: Building Inclusive Cities, Sustaining Economic Growth" (New York, 2010) (www.mckinsey.com/~/media/ McKinsey/dotcom/Insights%20and%20pubs/MGI/Research/Urbanization/Indias%20 urban%20awakening%20Building%20inclusive%20cities/MGI_Indias_urban_ awakening_full_report.ashx).

118. Energy and Resources Institute, "Climate Resilient and Sustainable Urban Development" (London: Department for International Development, n.d.) (http://blogs. dfid.gov.uk/wp-content/uploads/2010/09/sustainable-urban-development-background-paper.pdf).

119. Indian Planning Commission, *Eleventh Five-Year Plan 2007–12,* vol. III: *Agriculture, Rural Development, Industry, Services, and Physical Infrastructure* (New Delhi, 2008) (http://planningcommission.nic.in/plans/planrel/fiveyr/11th/11_v3/11th_vol3.pdf). Indian Ministry of Environment and Forests, *State of Environment Report: India 2009* (New Delhi, 2009), p. 13 (http://envfor.nic.in/downloads/home/home-SoE-Report-2009.pdf).

120. Indian Ministry of Environment and Forests, *State of Environment Report.*

121. Institute for Defence Studies and Analyses, *Water Security for India: The External Dynamics: IDSA Task Force Report* (New Delhi, 2010).

122. FAO AQUASTAT data for 2012 (www.fao.org/nr/water/aquastat/data/query/ index.html?lang=en).

123. Maplecroft, "Big Economies of the Future—Bangladesh, India, Philippines, Vietnam, and Pakistan—Most at Risk from Climate Change" (Bath, October 21, 2010) (http://maplecroft.com/about/news/ccvi.html).

124. Divya Sharma and Sanjay Tomar, "Mainstreaming Climate Change Adaptation in Indian Cities," *Environment and Urbanization* 22 (2010): 451 (http://eau.sagepub. com/content/22/2/451.full.pdf).

125. Prakriti Naswa and Amit Garg, "Managing Climate-Induced Risks on Indian Infrastructure Assets," *Current Science* 101, no. 3 (August 10, 2011) (www.currentscience. ac.in/Volumes/101/03/0395.pdf). Indian Network for Climate Change Assessment, *Climate Change and India: A 4x4 Assessment; a Sectoral and Regional Analysis for 2030s* (New Delhi: Ministry of Environment and Forests, 2010).

126. T. Bolch, A. Kulkarni, A. Kääb, C. Huggel, F. Paul, J. G. Cogley, H. Frey, J. S. Kargel, K. Fujita, M. Scheel, S. Bajracharya, and M. Stoffel, "The State and Fate of Himalayan Glaciers," *Science* 336, no. 6079 (April 20, 2012): 310–14. Intergovernmental Panel on Climate Change, *IPCC Statement on the Melting of Himalayan Glaciers* (Geneva, January 20, 2010) (www.ipcc.ch/pdf/presentations/himalaya-statement-20 january2010.pdf).

127. Indian Ministry of Environment and Forests, *State of Environment Report.* McKinsey and Company, *Environmental and Energy Sustainability.*

128. International Water Management Institute, *Strategic Analyses of the National River Linking Project (NRLP) of India Series 5. Proceedings of the Second National Workshop on Strategic Issues in Indian Irrigation, New Delhi, India, 8–9 April 2009* (Colombo, 2009), p. 29. Rathinasamy Maria Saleth, "Water Scarcity and Climatic Change in India: The Need for Water Demand and Supply Management," *Hydrological Sciences Journal* 56, no. 4 (2010): 671–86. Tushaar Shah, U. A. Amarasinghe, and P. G. McCornick, "India's River Linking Project: The State of the Debate," in *Strategic Analyses of the National River Linking Project (NRLP) of India Series 2. Proceedings of the Workshop on Analyses of Hydrological, Social, and Ecological Issues of the NRLP,* edited by U. A. Amarasinghe and B. R. Sharma (Colombo: International Water Management Institute, 2008) (www.iwmi.cgiar. org/publications/Other/PDF/NRLP_Proceedin-2.pdf).

129. Headey and Fan, "Reflections on the Global Food Crisis."

130. IMF, *World Economic Outlook, April 2012: Growth Resuming, Dangers Remain* (Washington, 2012) (www.imf.org/external/pubs/ft/weo/2012/01/index.htm).

131. Walter W. Immerzeel, L. P. Van Beek, and M. F. Bierkens, "Climate Change Will Affect the Asian Water Towers," *Science* 328, no. 5984 (June 11, 2010): 1382–85.

132. "National Level Infrastructure: Maritime Transport," business.gov.in (http:// business.gov.in/infrastructure/maritime_transport.php).

133. National Maritime Foundation, "Maritime Security Challenges in the Indian Ocean Region: A Workshop Report" (Washington: Center for the National Interest, 2011).

134. Michael J. Green and Andrew Shearer, "Defining U.S. Indian Ocean Strategy," *Washington Quarterly* 35, no. 2 (Spring 2012): 175–89 (csis.org/files/publication/ twq12springgreenshearer.pdf).

135. Ann Florini, "The International Energy Agency in Global Energy Governance," *Global Policy* 2, no. 1 (September 2011): 40–50

136. Alex Evans, *The Feeding of Nine Billion: Global Food Security for the 21st Century* (London: Chatham House, 2009).

137. Alex Evans and David Steven, *Hitting Reboot: Where Next for Climate after Copenhagen* (Brookings, 2010)

138. Parts of this section draw extensively on the first report on India and global governance. See Ghosh and others, *Understanding Complexity, Anticipating Change.*

139. Ibid., p. 23.

140. Alex Evans and David Steven, *Beyond the MDGs: Agreeing a Post-2015 Development Framework* (Brookings; New York University, Center on International Cooperation, 2012). See also David Steven, *Goals in a Post-2015 Development Framework: Options and Strategic Choices* (New York University, Center on International Cooperation, 2013).

141. Ghosh and others, *Understanding Complexity, Anticipating Change,* pp. 6–8.

4

Brazil's Principled Pragmatism: A Viable Response to the New Geopolitics of Resource Competition?

ANTONIO JORGE RAMALHO

Brazil is approaching the challenges posed by the changing patterns in the supply of and demand for strategic resources based on three premises: (1) world population will grow in an increasingly complex and conflictive world; (2) geopolitical rearrangements in current international relations[1] make room for middle powers; and (3) Brazil has an opportunity to play a strategic role in responding to those challenges.

Brazil is responding to these challenges by addressing domestic challenges, by seeking to strengthen ties within South America, and by attempting to improve multilateral institutions. By solving its own problems through means that are replicable in other developing countries (an experience that it willingly shares with others), it is consolidating its position as a leader in the international community of nations. Brazil takes a pragmatic approach to international affairs that is based on principles and a long-term perspective.

In a world of deeper and growing interdependence, the political networks inherent in international organizations have become a necessary complement to agent-to-agent relations. But no institution can effectively manage global governance without fully representing its own constituents. Indeed, international organizations need reform if they are to continue to be meaningful players in the international realm. They need to make room for emerging leaders, including Brazil, in international affairs.

Overview

Brazil is seeking to improve global governance through a complex, multilayered process, which involves global initiatives to provide the international community with services in different sectors, regional cooperation to integrate and develop South America, and domestic policies to foster sustainable socioeconomic development. Brazilian policy starts with a focus on the role that expectations play in political processes and presumes that in politics perceptions and the management of expectations are at least as important as evolving realities.

Potential scarcities in the sectors of food, water, and energy increase the probability of conflicts, both within and among states, highlighting the link between security and development. Historically, sovereigns have tackled famine, thirst, and other perceived threats to their survival through conquest and war. This implies a zero-sum view of world affairs, in which social groups construct enemies and rivals by attributing their main problems to others.

Interdependence has changed this. Sovereigns can no longer attribute their failures exclusively to others. Not only are citizens better informed and capable of understanding the ruptures frequently associated with conflicts; they also know that they will suffer most should conflicts occur. Because connections between social phenomena have become more transparent, zero-sum approaches to social conflicts are no longer politically viable. Most people understand that instability in one part of the world has repercussions elsewhere and that some level of cooperation between states is necessary.[2]

Brazil's policy thus has two broad objectives, which integrate more specific goals: (1) to strengthen multilateral institutions to accommodate the emerging multipolarity in world affairs and (2) to increase the supply of scarce resources. Brazil's efforts focus on five specific goals: (1) improve the global governance architecture and stabilize international markets, favoring longer-term planning and inviting new investments; (2) reduce competition and conflict between sovereigns; (3) expand commodities markets, tackling the risks of shortages inherent in industries heavily affected by environmental forces; (4) promote the integration of South America, consolidating the region as a zone of peace and cooperation; and (5) offer technical cooperation to less developed countries. Only the combination of these processes will provide greater stability in the long run, reduce the probability of conflicts, and enhance the appropriate management of expectations. This implies changing the traditional zero-sum approaches to international politics and fostering greater levels of trust between states. This, in turn, requires dialogue and diplomacy. Brazil's approach has been effective at the regional level, which suggests that it could be effective worldwide in sectors such as food security, trade, and climate change. Brazil organizes its initiatives for the purpose of influencing the long-term substance and form of this cooperation. It does so inspired by moral concerns and by national interests. The premises on which it builds this approach are the focus of this chapter.

Premise One: Growing Scarcities and the Supply Side

The world population is expected to reach 9.6 billion by 2050, with the highest rates of growth in developing countries.[3] Life expectancy is rising steadily, as are average levels of education. Demographic pressures will increase for the next fifty years.[4] In late 2011, the seventh billion newborn confirmed the trend evident since the 1960s: 1 billion people will be added to the human population every thirteen to fourteen years. If median fertility prevails, the world's population will stabilize at 10 billion around 2070; if the expected replacement level of the 2010–15 period prevails, it will be 9.9 billion in 2100.[5]

Thus demand for food, water, and energy—and their prices—will rise steadily. Between 1990 and 2012, the price of food rose more than 80 percent in real terms.[6] Increases in world electricity generation averaged 3.6 percent a year between 1971 and 2009, greater than the 2.1 percent growth in total primary energy supply. From 1990 to 2009, electricity generation rose from 11.8 terrawatt-hours to more than 20 terawatt-hours per year. Still, nowadays roughly 2.5 billion people have unreliable or no access to electricity.[7]

Undernutrition currently affects more than 12.5 percent of the world's population.[8] As climate change affects production patterns, the world will need more food. Even worse, the kind of food on demand will require a greater amount of water to grow. United Nations (UN) projections forecast a 50 percent increase in demand for food and for energy by 2030. Global meat consumption per capita is expected to reach 52 kilograms, 15 kilograms more than average consumption in 2000. Since each kilogram of beef consumes roughly 15,000 liters of water to produce (compared with about 3,500 liters for each kilogram of rice),[9] tensions related to the control of water resources are also on the rise.

Meanwhile, more than 2.8 billion people live in areas of water stress. Already under unprecedented pressure, energy and water resources face growing competition from people, industries, ecosystems, and economies. At 9 billion, the world's population will require a 50 percent increase in agricultural production and another 15 percent increase in water withdrawals. By 2035, the world's energy consumption will grow 35 percent, increasing water use for power generation 15 percent and its consumption 85 percent—mainly due to the patterns of agricultural production.[10]

These trends constrain states' choices, particularly as people's lifestyles across the globe have changed. International markets for food, water, and energy are dynamic, and greater scarcity will increase the probability of conflicts. Despite the economic downturn initiated in 2008, economic recovery will eventually take place, and the long-term restructuring of world politics will continue.

To cope with this challenge in a sustainable way, governments need to articulate a legitimate global response. This process may create opportunities for countries like Brazil, whose low-cost agriculture may expand significantly, feeding people and supplying biofuels. To grow, these countries must satisfy people's expectations and respect the environment, which means that sustainable development and social inclusion need to be part of the equation.

Brazil is responding pragmatically to the growing competition for scarce resources. It acknowledges that subsidies may not be dismantled overnight, but suggests that they should be discussed. "Virtually all of the world's economies provide energy subsidies of some kind when measured on a tax-inclusive basis, including thirty-four advanced economies … In 2011, global pre-tax subsidies reached US$480 billion (0.7 percent of global GDP or 2 percent of total government revenues)."[11] Realistically, we will not build a green-energy future by subsidizing fossil fuels, particularly when subsidies for renewable energy were only about US$66 billion in 2010.

Brazil is in the process of reducing the subsidies to Petrobras (a state-owned oil company), while transforming ethanol, among other products, into an international commodity, expanding and stabilizing the supply of energy.[12] Biofuels make sense: they capture carbon and reduce negative externalities associated with energy production, without necessarily competing with food crops.[13]

Food issues are more challenging, as the unrest in 2008 in more than 30 countries[14] and the Arab Spring in 2010–11 illustrated. There are different ways to deal with them. The G-8, for instance, launched the New Alliance for Food Security and Nutrition, recognizing that "food security is critical to economic growth and poverty alleviation" as well as that sustainable development cannot occur without "country ownership." The New Alliance for Food Security and Nutrition works through public-private partnerships to attain both objectives.[15] In contrast, Brazil emphasizes improving global governance frameworks to expand the supply of food, water, and energy and relying on small farmers to assure food security, through international technical cooperation provided by the United Nations Food and Agriculture Organization (FAO). Brazil's successful campaign to head the FAO reflects this focus. The kind of cooperation that the FAO aspires to achieve can help to stabilize supplies, spread knowledge, strengthen green industries, and empower the poor. Responding to the 2008–09 food crisis and Haiti's recent dependence on imported food and based on its own experience in reducing hunger domestically through the Zero Hunger Program, Brazil has actively engaged with other developing countries in reforming the Committee on World

Food Security.[16] Such actions help to translate into reality "the future we want" along the lines proposed by the Rio+20 Conference final document.[17]

Premise Two: Brazil's Opportunity

Brazil is an important source of water, food, and energy. It is home to roughly 12 percent of the global sources of freshwater.[18] In the last fourteen years, Brazilian grain harvests have almost doubled, increasing from 100.3 million tons in 2000–01 to an estimated 195.9 million tons in 2013–14.[19] As a producer, Brazil ranks first in coffee, processed beef, and orange juice worldwide; second in white sugar, chicken, tobacco, soybeans, and beans; and third in corn.[20] Brazil is the second global supplier of soybeans and the third of corn. Brazil intensively uses ethanol and biodiesel in its car market, which is the fourth largest in the world.[21] Brazil also has one of the cleanest energy mixes in the world[22] and will become a large exporter of oil once the Pre-Salt reserves, an oil field of roughly 1,000 square miles with more than 8 billion barrels of oil, become fully productive.[23]

Despite its abundant domestic resources, Brazil urgently needs additional sources of energy, for its economy has remained relatively stable since the mid-1990s as a result of a long period without appropriate investments in infrastructure. Indeed, poor transportation networks and limits on its capacity to generate power are among the main factors preventing the country's economy from growing at higher rates. Hence the government and the private sector are struggling to overcome short-term difficulties. The Pre-Salt reserves may help to reduce constraints regarding the supply of energy, but they require huge investments in cutting-edge technologies and will take several years to become fully productive—if everything goes right. This tempers expectations regarding self-sufficiency and raises questions regarding the opportunity costs of those investments. As a result, expectations regarding the exploration of these reserves focus on the long term. Between 2011 and 2013, Congress and the Presidency clashed over the purpose of this endeavor. The final decision was to export the bulk of the oil to be taken from the Pre-Salt reserves and invest most of the royalties in the public systems of education and health.

Meanwhile, Brazil is seeking to assure its supply of energy by further integrating with South America. Since the 1970s it has bought energy from Paraguay; in the 1990s, it built a pipeline to receive natural gas from Bolivia, and in the 2000s it embraced Venezuela as an important trade partner. Greener sources of energy (mainly wind and solar) will become increasingly larger parts of Brazil's energy mix as Brazilian society comes to accept their benefits.

In the last decade, Brazil's agribusiness focused on exports, while family farmers enhanced their productivity. More than 40 percent of the country's total agricultural production and 60 percent of internal food consumption now come from small farms, who have also become suppliers of renewable energy.[24]

So Brazil does not seek just to supply food, water, and energy to world markets; it also aims to become a model of sustainable development for other developing countries.

Sustainable Exports and Self-Reliance

Ranking seventh among the largest economies in the world in 2012, Brazil is now focused on improving its social infrastructure. Having added more than 42 million people to its middle class in the last twenty years (approximately the population of Argentina), Brazil shares with other developing countries its expertise in implementing social policies.

Since the mid-1990s, stability has brought long-term investments, which may engender a virtuous cycle. Coping with social inequalities has become a political priority.[25] Increases in the minimum wage and social policies have expanded the demand for goods and services. Roughly 60 percent of the population—120 million citizens—are now middle class, bringing gross domestic product (GDP) per capita to more than US$13,000 in 2012, up from US$3,000 in 2002.[26] As a result, Brazil's Index of Human Development rose from 0.522 in 1980 to 0.73 in 2012,[27] and its Gini coefficient fell from 0.639 in 2001 to 0.567 in 2012.[28] Among the BRICS (Brazil, Russia, India, China, and South Africa), it alone has been able to maintain economic growth while reducing social inequalities.

The focus on reducing inequalities serves moral, political, and economic purposes. From a macroeconomic standpoint, doing so fosters growth. In 2012, having achieved investment grade, with net public debt at 37 percent of GDP (down from roughly 62 percent in 2002), Brazil received the fourth largest flow of foreign direct investment in the world (behind the United States, China, and Hong Kong).

Several industries are poised to grow more. Among them, oil is paramount: the Pre-Salt reserves may turn Brazil into one of the top dozen oil producers by 2025. Petrobras plans to invest more than US$73 billion in the reserves between 2011 and 2015 and US$237 billion through 2017, expecting to extract more than 1.8 million barrels of oil a day in 2020. Its goal is to double oil production to approximately 4 million barrels a day by 2020.

Achievements in the fields of research and development and innovation, in tandem with the plethora of services necessary to consolidate this segment of the oil industry, require capacities that will spill over to other economic sectors. Infrastructure has become a priority due to the need to reduce inefficiencies and attract investments to other sectors and to global events such as the World Cup and the upcoming Olympics.[29]

Simply put, Brazil is working to create the political and macroeconomic conditions for prosperity. Political elites understand the need to reduce social inequalities and prioritize investments in education, health, innovation, and infrastructure. If it achieves success, Brazil may become a model for other countries that need to bridge the gap between expectations and possibilities.

The way ahead is not free from perils, though. The gap between expectations and possibilities has widened in Brazilian society, as people no longer have to struggle merely to survive every passing day. As the 2013 demonstrations made evident, Brazilians are not satisfied with the quality of public services or with the ineffectiveness of institutions. To some extent, the authoritarian period disincentivized the involvement of young entrepreneurs in politics, and the 1988 Constitution set up a framework that overprotects representatives, while empowering them in their relations with the executive branch. In this context, the need to reform the political system emerges as the sole consensus among analysts. However, those who have the power to reform benefit from its shortcomings and face no incentives to render Brazilian politics more prone to promote the public good. In a society whose political culture values nonconfrontational approaches, improvements are modest and irregular. It remains to be seen whether Brazilian society will patiently wait one or two generations to modernize the political system.

Political Empowerment and Scarcity

Another clear trend in the next decades is political. Governments will have to manage increased scarcity in a context of an empowered citizenry. With cheap information, people tend to increase their surveillance and control over their governors, who are under rising pressure to deliver better public services.

New technologies also empower firms. Shortened life cycles of products and plants impose the challenge of attracting investments while raising funds to provide public services. This equation threatens nation-states in their ability to manage the global order. Indeed, popular demonstrations in all continents and future scenarios create a high probability of increasingly tense political relations between citizens and governments.[30] Where the ability to provide citizens with the range of public services they expect is absent, political tensions rise. And where access to basic goods, such as food and shelter, are unreliable, the risks of unrest are even greater.

According to the World Economic Forum, this trend is affecting "social stability within countries and threatening security on a global scale."[31] Oxfam also notes the unsustainability of processes that increase the concentration of wealth in a world where 1 percent of the families own almost half (46 percent) of total wealth. The fact that the richest 85 people own more than the bottom half of the world's population is no longer secret, and those who are in the bottom half are not content with this situation.[32]

Governments that value peaceful solutions to conflicts and global governance—and Brazil's government sees itself as one of those—attempt to expand the supply of basic goods, while enhancing political arrangements, both domestically and internationally, to satisfy citizens' legitimate expectations worldwide.

Regional cooperation thus is a key strategy to promote international stability, sustainable economic growth, and social justice.[33] Integrating South America has become a crucial part of Brazilian efforts to promote its own development while contributing to global governance. It is also a reasonable response to the new geopolitics of resource competition and is consistent with the self-interested desire to live in a world that is minimally managed and manageable.

Premise Three: Geopolitical Rearrangements

Geopolitical rearrangements in current international relations would merit a whole chapter. In short, the changes include the redefinition of the U.S. role in world affairs, the rise of China, and the attempt by Russia and Europe to be perceived as great powers, assuming that Europe will overcome its democratic deficits and find a way to deal with its new Germany-on-the-top configuration. In addition, the growing influence of middle powers, such as Indonesia, Iran, South Africa, and Brazil, affirms the consolidation of a multipolar world that is not reflected in the current governance of multilateral institutions.

Few doubt that institutions have to adapt in order to provide adequate frameworks for global governance. The problem is how to adjust them. Indeed, reforms would have to accommodate countries, such as India, Japan, France, and the United Kingdom, that see themselves between the two major powers and the emergent powers.

Tensions have risen in the Middle East and other parts of the world for various reasons. Social unrest in countries as distinct as Ukraine and Venezuela illustrate the limits under which governments now operate. Pirate assaults along African coasts threaten international trade in ways unexpected ten or fifteen years ago. Fears of "short and sharp wars" in the East China and South China Seas raise concerns around the world.[34] Meanwhile, the UN Security Council systematically fails to address the violations of human rights in Syria (although it has, of course, continued to respond to other crises in Africa and beyond).

In this context and considering its limited military capacity, Brazil's central policy orientation is to keep South America stable and prosperous. It also contributes to peacekeeping operations in Haiti, Lebanon, and the Democratic Republic of Congo, while cooperating, within the framework of the Zone of

Peace and Cooperation of the South Atlantic, with developing countries on the western coast of Africa. Oriented by the principles of nonintervention in internal affairs and tolerance, while practicing self-restraint, Brazil aims to earn the confidence of other states and gradually reposition itself in international institutions.[35]

In fact, it has achieved some results already. At the FAO, at the UN Security Council, and at the World Trade Organization, to name the most important settings, it tries to be a useful partner in an interdependent world. Sooner or later, it bets, sovereigns will value leaders who provide global public goods without threatening others.

This perception is obviously disputable. Although Brazilian diplomats are skeptical that it will be possible to reform these institutions in the medium term, they are also confident in their capacity to operate within them. Whether their self-confidence is on solid ground remains to be seen—so far, Brazilian diplomats have built a reputation of professionalism and effectiveness. But there is no doubt that they consider the best bet for Brazil as being to improve global institutions by strengthening a rules-based system and for Brazil to become more effective—hence more important—as a political operator at these institutions.

Regional Approaches

Brazil is a peaceful country. The last conflict it fought in South America ended in 1870. Since then, it has negotiated its borders with ten neighbors and brokered solutions to regional disputes, such as those involving Peru and Ecuador (Cenepa in 1995) and Ecuador and Colombia (Reyes crisis in 2008). In 2007 Brazil settled with Bolivia the occupation of Petrobras facilities, and in 2010 it negotiated a new contract with Paraguay for purchasing energy produced at the Itaipu dam, showing its determination to avoid regional confrontations. With experience in arbitration, Brazil has worked to prevent conflicts either bilaterally or through the Union of South American Nations and its South American Defense Council. It is no coincidence that South America records the lowest military expenditure of any region, most of which goes to maintaining military personnel.[36] With roughly half of South American resources in terms of territory, population, GDP, and military expenses, Brazil bears disproportionate responsibility for managing these regional processes.[37]

With three of the largest river basins in the world (the Amazon, Orinoco, and Rio de la Plata) and the Guarani aquifer,[38] South America is home to 28 percent of the world's freshwater resources and 12 percent of the world's land, most of which is arable, but only 6 percent of the world's population. Rich in oil, gas, coal, and strategic minerals, the region is crucial to stabilizing the global supply of food, water, and energy.

At least since the mid-1990s, integrating the region has been Brazil's top foreign policy priority. Successive governments have reaffirmed their intention to integrate the region and promote socioeconomic development. Brazil's thirty-fifth and thirty-sixth presidents, Luiz Inácio Lula da Silva and Dilma Rousseff, repeatedly visited all South American countries. The National Economic and Social Development Bank has invested heavily in infrastructure, aiming to integrate South American countries and to enable Brazilian exports to exit through the Pacific Ocean. Created in 2008, the Union of South American Nations adopted the former Initiative for the Integration of Infrastructure in South America, which expects to invest more than US$75 billion in more than 500 projects in the coming years.

Regional integration is seen as a reasonable way both to promote socioeconomic development and to deter external threats. Deeper cooperation among South American countries may also lead to more effective dissuasive power. For this reason, Brazil's defense policy sees a close association between defense, cooperation, and development.[39]

Brazil's National Defense Strategy

With significant reserves of natural resources to protect and important vulnerabilities in its defense system, Brazil considers diplomacy a deterrent. The investments called for by the National Defense Strategy (NDS) for the next thirty years are intended to update, not expand, Brazil's defense capacities.[40] Meanwhile, Brazil shows in diplomatic skills what it lacks in military might. To the same extent that Brazil often abstains from interfering in its neighbors' internal affairs, it also seeks to prevent foreign interventions in its own problems. Brazil's military lacks equipment and combat experience precisely because the country has historically managed to solve its conflicts through peaceful negotiations. It follows that a world governed by rules suits Brazil's interests better than power politics. The country's diplomatic narrative simultaneously defends treating sovereigns equally before international law and strengthening global governance.[41]

This principled attitude toward international affairs is consistent both with Brazil's desire to improve the supply of essential commodities to the growing world population and with its role as a provider of food, water, energy, and peace.[42] Brazil's NDS deserves special attention because it is the most detailed document in the field of defense and development and because it takes a long-term view of public policies dealing with the geopolitics of resource competition.[43]

The NDS is the closest Brazil has come to spelling out a grand strategy. On the one hand, Brazil has adopted a blend of tolerance and diplomatic engagement as the first option to address international conflicts; on the other, it has sought cooperation in its efforts to respond to the collective challenges posed by the new geopolitics of resource competition. However, it acknowledges that international affairs are often decided on the basis of force; hence the document stresses the need to prepare the military and to provide it with adequate equipment to resist possible aggression in the future.

As a logical corollary to this approach, national security is defined in terms of reducing vulnerabilities. Such an approach not only is legitimate in the international realm but also targets no one in particular: it establishes priorities to strengthen Brazil's capacity to dissuade—and, if this is unsuccessful, respond to—aggression.

Brazil's NDS thus avoids dichotomies (friends-enemies or allies-rivals) and highlights problems to solve and challenges to face. It does not name potential enemies, instead concentrating efforts on concrete actions and pragmatic definitions of cooperation. It also avoids prejudices in defining the country's relations with other nation-states. Finally, it acknowledges the accelerated pace of transformations in world affairs and seeks long-run solutions to specific problems.

Brazil's Quest for Leadership

Huge inequalities in international relations are unsustainable both on moral and on political grounds. For this reason, Brazil equates sustainable socioeconomic development with dissuasive defense policies. This does not imply the *securitization* of socioeconomic policies or processes. It merely asserts that national security depends on socioeconomic stability—and perhaps on positive expectations regarding prosperity.

Indeed, governments will be more successful in enhancing their defense capabilities if they simultaneously promote economic growth and social justice, as doing so helps to create internal cohesion and supports a positive domestic political agenda, which may be extended to the international arena. More stable and prosperous societies tend to have fewer reasons to behave aggressively toward other states, particularly if they are self-reliant and fully integrated in global production chains. Creating a virtuous cycle at home helps to engender economic growth, with positive externalities that may spill over to the international realm. Historically, this has happened at the regional level in other parts of the world, and it seems to be occurring in South America today. Interdependence may spread those processes to the rest of the world.

To support structural sustainable development, Brazil stresses the Rio+20 Agenda, which articulates a common understanding of how to reconcile the social, economic, and environmental agendas of different countries.[44] By confronting collective challenges coherently and treating them in the appropriate international settings, states will engage in a positive-sum process, reducing the risks of misunderstanding between them and their citizens' anxieties regarding social inclusion and economic prosperity.

This agenda complements and balances the equally necessary collective efforts to sustain stability in the realm of international security. Due to interdependence, local instabilities rapidly spill over to the international sphere. Security problems in Afghanistan and in Guinea-Bissau illustrate the problems of failing to engage the international community in resolving conflicts.

By addressing its own socioeconomic problems while respecting democratic institutions of governance, Brazil hopes to set an example for other developing countries and to play a more important role in international institutions, brokering deals that will serve the international community as a whole.

In Brazil, the Ministry of External Relations (Itamaraty) filters demands from different areas and articulates them into an encompassing long-term strategy informed by a realistic assessment of the country's possibilities in the international realm and by the principles that influence its foreign policy.[45] This process forms the basis of Brazil's integrated approach to global governance, as reflected in its participation in various international forums.

Brazil is using its tenure as the FAO's director to commit other governments to domestic legislation that will increase the production of food and achieve food security for all. By the same token, it is pushing for enhanced international cooperation, mainly South-South, to address the four pillars of food security (availability, access, use, and stability). According to the Global Strategic Framework for Food Security and Nutrition, "The institutional model and programmes established by the Zero Hunger Strategy are inspiring similar initiatives by several countries in Africa, Asia, and Latin America."[46]

Brazil is taking a similar approach at the World Trade Organization. At the ninth ministerial conference held in Bali in 2013, the former U.S. ambassador to Brazil acknowledged that Brazil maintained its tradition to "get the best deal possible," simultaneously acting "as a leader of a particular group of countries, while at the same time brokering" a deal and using "the event as a way to assert leadership."[47] Most important, Brazil was committed to brokering a deal in Bali and remains interested in deepening the Doha Round, seeing trade as a strategic tool to enhance economic growth on an environmentally sustainable basis, increase the supply of food and energy, and create opportunities to reduce social inequalities. Brazil's initiatives in the international forums in which it participates reflect these three principles, conferring consistency and predictability on its contributions to global governance. This also explains why Brazil put such an enormous effort into and took significant political risk in calling for the Rio+20 Conference: it seeks to lead the effort to make global governance more legitimate and effective.

Conclusions

The new geopolitics of resource competition is challenging for countries like Brazil. To respond to these challenges, Brazil has five goals: (1) improve the global governance architecture and stabilize international markets, favoring longer-term planning and inviting new investments; (2) reduce competition and conflict between sovereigns; (3) expand commodities markets, tackling the risks of shortages inherent in industries heavily affected by environmental forces; (4) promote the integration of South America, attempting to consolidate the region as a zone of peace and cooperation; and (5) provide technical cooperation to less developed countries.

However, sovereigns can attain these goals only within the framework of a global agenda for sustainable socioeconomic development. This explains Brazil's support for the Sustainable Development Goals envisaged at the Rio+20 Conference and its concern with the post-2015 agenda. Brazil engages in efforts on three levels.

At the global level, it fosters cooperation and pushes for more representative and effective regimes to promote food security, sustainable and inclusive development, and freer trade in commodities markets. This also favors universalizing the production of specific crops, such as corn and sugarcane, as a means to develop biofuels as a commodity traded worldwide. Brazil expects to benefit from larger and more resilient markets for these goods: as a supplier, it has comparative advantages in these industries. The growing world population completes the effort, expanding the markets for food and water. Expectations of stable prices and large investments will encourage governments to adopt biofuels as a new source of energy, further developing those markets.

At the regional level, Brazil seeks to integrate South American energy infrastructure and markets, both to assure the supply of energy for its growing economy and to facilitate regional development, which favors social inclusion and reduces political tensions within and among countries.

At the domestic level, Brazil pursues regulatory reforms and stimulates new investment to prevent shortages of food and energy, trying to control inflationary pressures and to universalize access to energy, food, and clean water for its population.

Brazil implements these pragmatic approaches while embracing the core principles of tolerance, nonintervention, self-determination, and equal treatment before the law. Within a generation, this principled pragmatism may advance Brazil in its quest for leadership, while helping to stabilize world markets and improve global governance.

Notes

1. Especially the redefinition of the role played by the United States internationally, the emergence of multipolarity, and the prospects of greater turbulence in Eurasia, Africa, and the Middle East.

2. As a result, theories have shifted from explaining the continuities to understanding the changes in world affairs.

3. See United Nations, "World Population Prospects: The 2012 Revision; Key Findings and Advance Tables" (http://esa.un.org/wpp/Documentation/pdf/WPP2012_Press_Release.pdf).

4. The United Nations Population Reference Bureau expects the ninth billion newborn around 2044.

5. United Nations, Department of Economic and Social Affairs, Population Division, *World Population Prospects: The 2010 Revision* (New York, 2011) (http://esa.un.org/unpd/wpp/Analytical-Figures/htm/fig_11.htm).

6. See the Food and Agriculture Organization (FAO) website (www.fao.org/worldfoodsituation/wfs-home/foodpricesindex/en/).

7. Organization for Economic Cooperation and Development, *OECD Factbook 2011–2012* (Paris, 2011) (www.oecd-ilibrary.org/docserver/download/fulltext/3011041ec049.pdf?expires=1325531300&id=id&accname=freeContent&checksum=B0267BA78E86DC5E9A38314C7689984F).

8. See FAO, *The State of Food Insecurity in the World* (Rome, 2012).

9. "UN Water Day 2013: Facts and Figures" (www.unwater.org/water-cooperation-2013/water-cooperation/facts-and-figures/en/).

10. World Bank, "Will Water Constrain Our Energy Future?" (Washington, January 16, 2014) (www.worldbank.org/en/news/feature/2014/01/16/will-water-constrain-our-energy-future).

11. Post-tax energy subsidies "are much larger than pre-tax subsidies, amounting to US$1.9 trillion in 2011—about 2.5 percent of global GDP or 8 percent of total government revenue." See Arunabha Ghosh and Himani Gangania, "Governing Clean Energy Subsidies: What, Why, and How Legal?" (Geneva: International Centre for Trade and Sustainable Development, 2012) (www.ictsd.org).

12. See Christof Ruehl, *BP Energy Outlook 2030* (London: British Petroleum, January 2012).

13. The consensus is that the expansion of biofuels tends to compete with the production of food. This view is partially right: roughly one third of the harvested areas recently destined for biofuels, mainly in developed countries, is taken from food crops, while the other two thirds result from adding new arable land. Of the 532 million hectares of the world's arable land, 187 million hectares (more than 37 percent) are in Brazil and 85 percent are in Africa and South America (see the International Institute for Applied Systems Analysis world food system simulations, scenario FAO-REF-00, May 2009, available in Günther Fisher, "World Food and Agriculture to 2030/50: How Do Climate Change and Bioenergy Alter the Long-Term Outlook for Food, Agriculture, and Resource Availability?" presentation at the FAO Expert Meeting on How to Feed the World in 2050, June 24–26, 2009 (ftp://ftp.fao.org/docrep/fao/012/ak542e/ak542e07.pdf), pp.126–45. This considers neither the technological improvements in agriculture that have consistently helped Brazil to increase its production without either necessarily having to occupy new agricultural frontiers (70 million hectares are cultivated today) or to reclaim degraded area, which only recently has become an object of public policy. An independent study prepared by the World Wildlife Fund–Brasil for the Allianz Group in 2009 points to the same conclusion. See World Wildlife Fund, "O impacto do mercado

mundial de biocombustíveis na expansão da agricultura brasileira e suas consequências para as mudanças climáticas" (Brasília, 2009).

14. See Paul Collier, "The Politics of Hunger: How Illusion and Greed Fan the Food Crisis," *Foreign Affairs* 87, no. 6 (November-December 2008): 67–68 (www.foreign affairs.com/articles/64607/paul-collier/the-politics-of-hunger).

15. Jonathan White, "The New Alliance for Food Security and Nutrition: Pushing the Frontier of Enlightened Capitalism," Economic Policy Paper (Washington: German Marshall Fund of the United States, April 2013).

16. Created in 1974, the Committee on World Food Security reports annually to the United Nations Economic and Social Council, but it is open to the participation of civil society, international agricultural research networks, and the private sector. Among the reforms initiated since 2008, two have been instrumental in promoting food security and fostering South-South cooperation: (1) creation of the Voluntary Guidelines on the Responsible Governance of Tenure of Land, Fisheries, and Forests in the Context of National Food Security, endorsed by member states in their 144th session, held in Rome in June 2012, and (2) publication of the Global Strategic Framework for Food Security and Nutrition, updated in 2013, which articulates the efforts of governments, nongovernmental organizations, and the private sector at all levels (local, subregional, national, regional, and global) to promote food security. The Voluntary Guidelines are the result of a Brazilian initiative to organize, in partnership with the FAO, the Sixth International Conference on Agrarian Reform and Rural Development, held in Porto Alegre in 2006, reinserting agrarian reform in the international agenda, which had not been addressed by governments at that setting since 1979. This is obviously a long-term process, which Brazil intends to promote during its tenure as FAO director.

17. See www.uncsd2012.org/content/documents/727The%20Future%20We%20 Want%2019%20June%201230pm.pdf. At the end of the Rio+20 Conference, in 2012, member states agreed on the need to create a set of global goals to replace the Millennium Development Goals, which target 2015. The consensus reached in Rio stressed the need to establish post-2015 goals that simultaneously contemplate social, economic, and environmental objectives. Known as "The Future We Want," the conference's final document is far from precise in spelling out how to balance these goals, but its principled approach committed states to negotiating further joint endeavors. Amid the climate that has prevailed since the 2008 crisis and challenging the preference of the United States and Germany (whose president and chancellor, respectively, did not attend the conference), this was nevertheless an achievement, which may pave the road to relaunching the Doha Round of the World Trade Organization, even if with modest expectations.

18. Brazil ranks first in total water resources, with 8,233 cubic kilometers a year, almost the double those of Russia, ranking second, with 4,507 cubic kilometers a year. See FAO, "World Water Resources by Country" (www.fao.org/docrep/005/y4473e/ y4473e0g.gif). Brazil ranks seventh among large water consumers, with less than 3 percent, behind India (13 percent), China (11 percent), the United States (9 percent), Russia and Indonesia (4 percent each), and Nigeria (3 percent).

19. Brazilian Ministry of Livestock and Food Supply; Ministry of Finance, "Brazil's Economic Outlook and Infrastructure: Investment Opportunities" (Brasília, 2014)

(www.fazenda.gov.br/divulgacao/publicacoes/infraestrutura-no-brasil/brazils_economic_outlook_and_infrasctructure_investment_opportunities).

20. See FAO, *State of Food Insecurity in the World.*

21. After China, the United States, and Japan. See http://focus2move.com/item/1011-world%E2%80%99s-car-market-statistics-top-50-countries-ranking. More than 60 percent of the almost 36 million vehicles in Brazil can run on either ethanol or gasoline. By 2022 more than three fourths of the 60 million vehicles will have this ability. See Plano de Desenvolvimento Energético 2022, p. 40 (www.cogen.com.br/mwg-internal/de5fs23hu73ds/progress?id=uvihRyY5aO).

22. Power generation in Brazil comes mainly from renewables: hydro constitutes 68 percent; natural gas, 11 percent; biomass, 9 percent; oil, 6 percent; coal, 3 percent; wind, almost 2 percent; and nuclear, about 1.5 percent. The 2030 Strategic Plan highlights major investments in biomass and wind power. See www.aneel.gov.br/aplicacoes/capacidadebrasil/operacaocapacidadebrasil.asp.

23. The Pre-Salt reserves, which are only partially known, are situated below the Salt layer (from 3.2 to 4.4 miles deep) in the Atlantic, up to 190 miles off the Brazilian coast. Their exploration is a major technological challenge, which will demand approximately US$1.4 trillion in investments (US$700 billion to explore and develop and another US$700 billion to operate) for the next thirty years. See Instituto Brasileiro de Petróleo (www.ibp.org.br/main.asp?View={70411687-443D-4072-BB40-C1A0E66F1AFB}). Besides the positive externalities, these investments promise a great amount of oil: Libra, the first Pre-Salt oil field submitted to auction, corresponds to 80 percent of Brazilian proven reserves (of 15.7 billion barrels). A consortium of five major oil companies (Petrobras, Royal Dutch Shell, Total, China National Petroleum Corporation, and Chinese National Offshore Oil Corporation) paid an entrance fee of US$6.8 billion for the right to explore it; 42 percent of the output will be handed over to the Brazilian state.

24. See www.conab.gov.br/conteudos.php?a=1125&t=2. The larger is the share of small farms in domestic food production, the more stable are local markets, improving food security. This renders local markets less influenced by the ups and downs of international markets.

25. Economic policies combine inflation targets, a flexible exchange rate regime, fiscal discipline, and controlled public debt.

26. Fluctuations in exchange rates affect those figures.

27. United Nations Development Program, *Human Development Report, 2014* (New York, 2014).

28. Comisión Económica para América Latina y el Caribe, "CEPALSTAT estadísticas de América Latina y el Caribe" (Santiago, 2014) (http://estadisticas.cepal.org/cepalstat/WEB_CEPALSTAT/Portada.asp).

29. Brazil's financial system ranks second (behind Germany) measured by the Basel Index of Capital Adequacy (17) and fifth in international reserves (behind China, Japan, Saudi Arabia, and Russia).

30. See Álvaro de Vasconcelos, ed., "Global Trends 2030: Citizens in an Interconnected and Polycentric World," ESPAS Report (Paris: European Union Institute for Security Studies, 2012) (www.iss.europa.eu/mwg-internal/de5fs23hu73ds/progress?id=km5jKxxfOn).

31. World Economic Forum, "Outlook on the Global Agenda 2014" (Geneva, 2013).

32. See Oxfam, "Working for the Few," Oxfam Briefing Paper 178 (Oxford, 2014) (www.oxfam.org/mwg-internal/de5fs23hu73ds/progress?id=9XFwHq7q0h).

33. This process is unique in contemporary international relations. Unlike other major historic shifts, at the end of the cold war the victorious powers did not have the opportunity to reorganize the rules and institutions for managing the new world order.

34. See Geoff Dyer, "China Training for 'Short, Sharp War,' Says Senior US Naval Officer," *Financial Times*, February 20, 2014 (www.ft.com/intl/cms/s/0/687e31a2-99e4-11e3-91cd-00144feab7de.html#axzz2trjNNuyH).

35. Brazilian foreign policy has traditionally asserted the principles of respect, equal treatment under international law, and nonintervention. Lacking significant military capabilities, Brazil has always felt vulnerable and defends those principles for pragmatic reasons. A rules-based international society is safer for countries lacking military might but having diplomatic skills.

36. The whole of Latin America accounts for 4 percent of the world's military expenditure, according to the Stockholm International Peace Research Institute. See www.sipri.org/research/armaments/milex/milex-graphs-for-data-launch-2013/World-military-expenditure-by-region-in-2012.png.

37. All South American countries spent almost US$21.86 trillion on defense alone in 2012; Brazil spent US$35.5 billion. See Atlas Resdal (www.resdal.org/atlas/atlas12-00-region.pdf).

38. One of the world's largest groundwater bodies, covering more than 11.2 million square kilometers.

39. See the National Defense Strategy (www.defesa.gov.br/arquivos/2012/mes07/end.pdf).

40. This is stated in the first Brazilian National Defense White Paper, published in 2013, which is available in Portuguese at www.defesa.gov.br/projetosweb/livrobranco/lbdndigital/livrobranco.pdf and may be translated into English by the end of 2014.

41. The argument is far from new. Ruy Barbosa, the main author of Brazil's 1891 Constitution (proclaimed when the country became a republic), voiced it more than a century ago, at the Second Hague Peace Conference in 1907.

42. This follows what March and Olsen call the logic of appropriateness and the traditional utility calculations. See James G. March and Johan P. Olsen, *Rediscovering Institutions: The Organizational Basis of Politics* (New York: Free Press, 1989).

43. The Brazilian Ministry of External Relations traditionally publishes only speeches and formal agreements. Therefore, understanding Brazil's foreign policy is useful because it develops concepts at length and articulates ideas on how the Brazilian government conducts its international relations.

44. See www.uncsd2012.org/content/documents/727The%20Future%20We%20Want%2019%20June%201230pm.pdf.

45. Many reasons explain this broad perspective on international affairs, starting with the country's size and its huge domestic problems, which command people's attention and energy. But its autarchic orientation, its tradition of tolerance and diplomatic engagement, and Itamaraty's bureaucratic competence also explain the country's capacity to articulate political processes conducted in different international arenas.

46. See Committee on World Food Security, "Global Strategic Framework for Food Security and Nutrition" (Rome: FAO, October 2013), p. 40 (www.fao.org/fileadmin/templates/cfs/Docs1213/gsf/GSF_Version_2_EN.pdf).

47. See "Shaping U.S.-Brazil Relationship after the Snowden Affair: A Conversation with Ambassador Thomas Shannon" (Washington: Wilson Center, February 2014) (www.wilsoncenter.org/sites/default/files/AmbassadorThomas%20Shannon%20-%20 Final.pdf).

5

The Big Squeeze: Nigeria on the Brink

MARK WESTON

"Looking at faces of people, one gets the feeling there's a lot of work to be done."

—Wole Soyinka

Nigeria has spent much of its five and a half decades as an independent nation wasting opportunities. The country has resources, land, and labor in abundance, but more than half of its people languish in poverty. Vast oil reserves have led not to increased prosperity but to environmental devastation, rampant corruption, and violent unrest in the oil-producing south. In the middle belt and the north, a swelling young workforce has turned not to productive activities but to bitter sectarian conflict. Despite rapid economic growth in the past decade, with cities such as Lagos demonstrating the potential to become engines of economic growth for the entire West African region, hunger remains widespread, life expectancy is just fifty-three years, and jobs are few and far between.

And although it seldom makes the headlines overseas, Nigeria matters globally. Africa's biggest economy and by far its most populous nation, Nigeria is an economic and political heavyweight. Half of West Africans are Nigerian, as is almost three-quarters of the region's economic output. By the end of the century the country will have the third largest population in the world—the United Nations projects a population of 913 million in 2100, fourteen times that of South Africa, which is currently its closest rival for the title of Africa's economic heavyweight and whose population is currently just under one third the size of

Nigeria's. Even the most conservative projections put Nigeria's population in 2100 at 644 million people.[1]

The country is also one of the world's top ten oil exporters. Nigerian oil accounted for 3 percent of U.S. oil imports in 2013, making it the eighth most important supplier to the United States.[2] It is also the sixth largest member of the Group of 77 bloc of developing countries at the United Nations, and the Nigerian army is often called on to keep the peace in its volatile neighbors.

Politics at home, therefore, not only affect Nigeria's inhabitants; they ripple outward, first to the rest of Africa and then across the oceans. If Nigeria fails to meet domestic demand for its resources, or if it fails to distribute limited resources fairly, popular pressure on the country's institutions will ratchet up, and the strain will render them less able to maintain stability at home and to respond to the needs of international partners. The key domestic dynamics of demographic change and a growing and modernizing economy will combine with resource scarcity and the effects of climate change to heighten the burden on Nigerian policymakers. While the former increase optimism that the country will be able to overcome its challenges and thrive in the coming decades, the latter reduce confidence and suggest that chaos may be as likely as calm.

This chapter examines the interaction between politics and the supply of and demand for resources in Nigeria and discusses how the mismatch between supply and demand at home has growing repercussions abroad. The first part outlines the key drivers of and trends in demand for strategic resources domestically and asks whether the country's resource needs are being met. The second discusses the international effects of these domestic pressures by mapping out three possible scenarios for the future, and highlights the key areas on which national and international policymakers should focus if they are to secure positive outcomes.

The Big Squeeze

This section begins by describing the domestic demand for strategic resources and then asks whether supply is meeting demand.

Domestic Demand

Domestic demand in Nigeria is shaped primarily by two forces—a growing, urbanizing, and slowly aging population and a growing but unstable economy.

BIGGER, OLDER, MORE URBAN. Nigeria's population has more than quadrupled—to 178 million people—since 1950. Census data in the country are contested, and disputes over today's figures make future projections hazardous (between 2006 and 2010 the United Nations added 30 million people to its projection for 2030),[3] but current estimates suggest that Nigeria will be home to 261 million people by 2030.[4]

Demand for resources will intensify not only because there will be nearly 100 million more Nigerians to feed, house, and employ, but also because the shape and geographic distribution of the population are changing. With fertility slowly declining and life expectancy rising, the proportion of working-age adults (15–64 years of age) in the population is edging upward and is projected to grow from 53 percent today to 55–57 percent by 2030.[5] The *number* of adults is forecast to rise from 97 million to 150 million. Since adults consume more than children, this will increase the demand for food, water, land, power, and other resources.

Most of Nigeria's population growth will take place in cities. In 1950 only 10 percent of Nigerians lived in urban areas; by 2030 this proportion is projected to rise to 60 percent. The country's rural population—currently half of the total—is expected to increase by only 20 million between 2010 and 2030, meaning that towns and cities will have to absorb 80 million additional people over that period.[6]

Urbanization has long been thought to be associated with increased economic growth and social advance. Rapid economic expansion in East Asia in the second half of the twentieth century, for example, went hand in hand with urbanization. In Africa, however, this link has proved less robust. As the World Bank has found, not all African countries that experienced rapid urbanization between 1985 and 2010 saw a concomitant growth in per capita incomes.[7] Some experienced economic decline, while even those that grew did so much later in the urbanization process than their East Asian counterparts. Nigeria is one of the countries where urbanization has not always been matched by income growth; although cities such as Lagos and Abuja have experienced rapid economic improvements in recent years, others, particularly in the north, have been unable to provide their burgeoning populations with productive income, and many of their new inhabitants are stagnating in poverty. Data on slum populations are unreliable, but the United Nations estimates that 60 percent of urban Nigerians live in slums, meaning that they lack access to improved sanitation facilities, treated water, sufficient living area (fewer than three people per habitable room), non-hazardous locations, and secure tenure.[8] If such a situation persists or worsens as cities grow, urban unrest may escalate, setting off vicious spirals where public funds are diverted from supporting productive activities to maintaining security and containing epidemics, foreign investors and tourists are scared off, and local economies suffer as crime and violence spread. In such a scenario urban poverty will become more widespread, and the risks of unrest still greater.

As well as rapid growth, urban areas—and in particular Lagos—will also experience the fastest changes in population structure. Research by the Next Generation Nigeria Task Force, an independent study group convened in 2009 by the British Council and chaired by the current Nigerian finance minister, Ngozi Okonjo-Iweala, found that while in 1991 most regions had similar shares of working-age adults in the population, by 2006 Lagos had almost two working-age adults for every dependent child or elderly person, double the number in the northern state of Kaduna. This disparity is a mixed blessing for Nigeria. On the one hand, worker-heavy populations such as in Lagos and other cities—provided that they have access to jobs and do not turn instead to crime and violence—could experience rapid economic growth. On the other hand, states where children continue to predominate are likely to languish in poverty. Many of these states are in the north, where resentment toward the south is already growing, and a widening demographic and economic gulf threatens to add to the strain on national cohesion.[9]

JOBLESS GROWTH. The second key force shaping domestic demand is the economy. Nigeria's economy is the biggest in Africa, although its per capita gross domestic product (GDP) of US$2,689 is only slightly above the average for sub-Saharan Africa.[10] Having stagnated during the three decades following independence, the past ten years have seen rapid GDP growth, exceeding 6 percent in each of 2011, 2012, and 2013.[11] Robust oil prices have assisted this growth, but although oil accounts for 95 percent of Nigeria's exports, it makes up only 15–20 percent of GDP; the burgeoning telecommunications sector, construction, retail, and hotel and restaurant businesses have also helped to drive recent economic expansion.[12]

Diversification away from oil is urgently needed, for oil production is a capital- rather than a labor-intensive industry and creates few jobs. Official figures do not exist, but estimates from 2003 suggest that the oil sector, which accounts for 95 percent of exports and 65 percent of government revenues, employs less than 0.2 percent of the labor force.[13] The benefits of the industry are therefore poorly distributed—although the industry helps to boost overall GDP, the majority of the population sees little or no benefit from it. The recent economic growth, moreover, has had little impact on unemployment, which stands at 23 percent and has increased since 2010.[14] Poverty also remains widespread, although the recalculation of the country's GDP in April 2014—which saw the size of the economy reassessed at almost double what was previously thought—suggests that reported increases in the poverty rate from 54 percent in 2004 to 61 percent in 2011 are likely to be, at best, overly pessimistic.[15] Although new poverty data are urgently needed in light of the new GDP estimate, there is little doubt that some parts of the country have huge numbers of people languishing in penury. In some northern states, it is estimated that more than four in five people live on less than US$1 a day.[16]

Although in the short term only a minority of people are profiting from Nigeria's economic growth, in the next two decades there is potential for the cake to be shared more widely. The country's demographic structure, wherein a large and growing population of working-age adults supports a smaller population of dependents, could allow it to collect a "demographic dividend" as the productive capacity of the economy increases and adults' income is freed up for investing in businesses and saving for the future. If the rates of economic growth seen since 2000 continue until 2030, the average Nigerian's income will more than double, and if the country can capitalize on its demographic advantages by creating jobs and strengthening human capital through investments in health and education, incomes could triple.[17]

At present, however, such economic growth is rendered more difficult to achieve by a continued failure to invest in human capital, which leaves Nigerians ill equipped to reach their full productive potential. Life expectancy, an indicator of the quality and quantity of health care and nutrition, lags behind the sub-Saharan African average at fifty-three years.[18] In education, while primary enrollment stands at 95 percent, more than half of primary school children in urban areas and four-fifths in rural areas are unable to read a simple sentence. Less than one-third of secondary school-age children, moreover, are in school.[19] The recent growth in the construction, retail, and other service industries offers hope that jobs can be found for increasing numbers of young people without high levels of education, but for the continued expansion of the telecommunications and other sectors that demand skilled workers, a reversal of the country's historic underinvestment in human capital will be required.

SUMMARY. These economic bottlenecks raise the possibility that Nigeria will fail to maximize the potential of its huge number of young people. According to calculations by the Next Generation Nigeria Task Force, at least 50 million new jobs—a doubling in the size of the labor market—will be needed by 2030 if new entrants to the labor market are to be absorbed and unemployment is to be reduced to 7 percent.[20] If this does not happen, the struggle for resources will heat up as their numbers swell.

Population growth has begun to slow in recent years, but a fertility rate of 5.5 children per woman is still high by global standards.[21] If current forecasts prove accurate, Nigeria is likely to face a future characterized by a burgeoning population that continues to urbanize as it ages and some of its members grow wealthier. Demand for jobs, food and water, land and housing, power, transportation, health care, and education will increase not only because of population growth, but also because of the increase in the proportion of adults in the population and potentially also because of growing wealth. Towns and cities in particular will have to find ways of accommodating millions of new residents, and the heightened demand for resources is likely to ratchet up competition between urban and rural areas, between north and south, and between and within cities.

The chapter turns next to the question of whether the country is meeting these challenges and whether supply is keeping up with domestic demand.

Domestic Supply

Increased domestic demand for resources is likely to put pressure on the supply of energy, land, food, and water. This section looks at each of these areas in turn.

ENERGY. Nigeria has failed to meet domestic energy requirements, and without drastic reforms the gap between supply and demand will become a chasm as the population grows, urbanizes, and becomes wealthier. Nigerian citizens are keenly aware of this problem. Asked which of a series of issues (including job creation, education, water, and corruption) was most important for the government to deal with over the following twelve months, 23 percent of respondents to a 2007 Gallup poll ranked electricity first, a larger proportion than for all other issues.[22]

Nigeria is Africa's biggest oil producer. Shell and British Petroleum first struck oil in the swamps of the Niger Delta on the Atlantic coast in 1956. It did not take long for the industry to cause trouble. The Biafran war, which broke out in the southeast in 1967, was in part a battle for oil.[23] The Igbo majority population of that region did not feel that they were receiving a fair share of revenues from oil production, which was centered in their territory, and this was one of several factors behind their bid for independence and behind the central government's successful attempt to quash the rebellion. The industry has been plagued by corruption and violence ever since. Nationalization in 1971 allowed political parties and leaders to plunder oil profits and use them to entrench themselves in power. The country was ruled by a series of dictators and military juntas through the 1970s and 1980s, all of whom grew wealthy on the back of oil exports. As the industry was slowly opened up to private sector partners (Shell, Mobil, Agip, Elf, Texaco, and Chevron are among the foreign companies currently sharing production with the Nigerian National Petroleum Corporation), violence continued as inhabitants of oil-producing areas agitated for a greater share of revenues. A low-level rebellion has continued in the Niger Delta for decades, with armed groups such as the Movement for the Emancipation of the Niger Delta (MEND) alleged to have carried out kidnappings, attacks on oil facilities, sabotage of pipelines, and theft. Between 2000 and 2008, the estimated value of oil stolen in the delta was US$38.4 billion, with the value of production lost due to interruptions amounting to a further US$77 billion.[24] The government has responded firmly, sometimes excessively. In 1995 it sparked international protests by hanging the nonviolent environmental activist Ken Saro-Wiwa, and its heavy-handed actions have often fanned the anger of local groups.

Nigeria is currently the world's eleventh largest producer of oil, yielding 2.5 million barrels a day in 2012.[25] A member of the Organization of Petroleum Exporting Countries (OPEC) since 1971, the country is estimated to have

37.2 billion barrels of proven reserves, enough to last for up to thirty-six years at current rates of production.[26] Almost all of the oil produced is exported (86 percent in 2009),[27] as is nearly all of the natural gas (83 percent in 2011).[28] This means that Nigerians face serious and sustained energy shortages. Total primary energy supply is only 40 percent of the world average and only slightly above the sub-Saharan African average. Approximately 80 percent of fuel is imported, and more than two thirds of households use wood for cooking.[29]

In 2011, electricity consumption was 149 kilowatt-hours per capita, compared with an average of 536 and 3,044 kilowatt-hours per capita for sub-Saharan Africa and the world, respectively.[30] Half of Nigerian households have some access to electricity (85 percent in urban areas, 31 percent in rural areas),[31] but electricity supply is prone to frequent planned outages (known as load shedding) as well as unplanned outages. Nine in ten industrial consumers—and as many private consumers as can afford to—generate their own electricity,[32] with a total of almost one third of electricity generated privately.[33]

Government subsidies of petroleum products, which cost US$16 billion in 2011,[34] have not had the desired effect on availability. The gasoline subsidy is over 40 percent, making gasoline acquired in Nigeria the cheapest in West Africa.[35] The subsidy for both electricity and household kerosene is over 60 percent.[36]

Fossil fuel subsidies are an inefficient means of improving national well-being. They divert public funds from more productive activities such as education and health care; they encourage excess fuel consumption and waste, thereby increasing pollution and carbon emissions; they foster corruption (subsidized kerosene, for example, often disappears into the black market, which then charges much higher prices to consumers); they lead to smuggling of fuel to neighboring countries; and they benefit the wealthier segments of society at the expense of the poor (an International Monetary Fund study of developing countries found that, on average, the wealthiest quintile of the population captures six times more in subsidies than the poorest).[37] For an oil producer such as Nigeria, subsidies also mean that less oil is available for export, which has harmful consequences for the entire economy.[38]

Despite the many negative impacts, however, removing subsidies is politically difficult. The World Bank, an enthusiastic supporter of subsidy removal, has acknowledged that such measures are likely to have negative social effects, at least in the short term, as inflation rises, unrest spreads, and poorer families are unable to buy fuel for basic needs.[39] There is a widespread feeling among Nigerians that cheap fuel is the only benefit they receive from the oil industry, and when the government attempted to remove the subsidy early in 2012, violent protests erupted across the country as prices soared.[40]

The World Bank recommends mitigating the negative impacts of subsidy removal by directing a proportion of the money saved toward social programs for

the worst off and by making concerted efforts to communicate the wider benefits of removing the subsidy. The reduction of fuel subsidies in Ghana in 2005,
for example, was accompanied by the immediate removal of fees for attending
primary and secondary school, thereby softening the blow of a 50 percent spike
in the cost of fuel.[41] Iran, which until 2010 had spent more than US$60 billion
a year on fuel subsidies, prepared citizens for the removal of subsidies by giving
families cash transfers in the months leading up to the reform. These transfers
have continued since and have helped families that apply for them to cope with
the sharp rise in prices. As the *Economist* has reported, "Iranians have rapidly got
used both to paying a lot more for some things and to having more money to
spend as they wish. A family of five now pockets monthly sums [in cash transfers]
close to Iran's minimum wage, enough to pull a big proportion of the 10 percent
of Iranians who live on less than US$2 a day above that bar."[42]

As well as having very little impact on fulfilling Nigeria's domestic energy
needs and failing to employ more than a handful of Nigerians, the oil industry
has also reduced the availability of other strategic resources. Communities in the
Niger Delta have been displaced from their homes and forced to compete with
others for land. Government investment has been diverted from agriculture to
oil, and food production has suffered as a consequence—where Nigeria was once
an exporter of food it is now a net importer. The attractiveness of agriculture has
declined further because oil exports have kept the exchange rate high, rendering
food exports expensive relative to those from non-oil-producing countries.

The environmental damage created by the oil industry in the Niger Delta has
affected fish stocks and arable land. Between 1976 and 1996 more than 2 million
barrels of oil were spilt in the delta, with 1.8 million of those lost to the environment. Between 1997 and 2001 there were a further 2,000 oil spill events, and
incidents continue to this day.[43] According to a report by the World Bank and
the Department for International Development, "Mismanagement of the country's oil resources resulted in significant environmental degradation and contributed to persisting social conflict. Oil spills, leakages through old and corrosive
pipelines, dumping of oil into the waterways, [and] burning of excess gases have
all been extensive, often poisoning drinking water, polluting the air, destroy-
ing vegetation, fisheries, [and] land quality, and undermining the livelihoods of
local people. Weak enforcement of environmental laws, which draws support
from past political leadership, has exacerbated the problems."[44] The effects on
soil fertility of oil pollution are not yet well documented, but water pollution's
detrimental effects on fish stocks have both reduced the quantity of food available for those living in the delta and, by depriving fishermen of their livelihoods,
forced many to resort to illegal activities, a subject discussed in the second part
of this chapter.[45]

LAND, FOOD, AND WATER. Growth in population will obviously decrease the availability of land per capita. Population density in Nigeria stands at approximately 180 persons per square kilometer today and will reach 295 by 2030 if current projections are borne out.[46]

At present, 61 percent of Nigerian households own agricultural land (including one third of those living in urban areas),[47] but the quantity of arable land per capita fell from 0.57 to 0.25 hectare between 1960 and 2007 and is projected to fall to 0.14 hectare by 2025.[48] But while it poses challenges, it is not inevitable that an increase in population density will overstretch the land. A projected density of 295 persons per square kilometer is not excessive by world standards (forty-eight countries are more crowded today), and much of the growth will be absorbed by cities rather than rural areas. However, farming in Nigeria is unproductive: although it occupies 70 percent of the labor force either full or part time, and despite some improvements in food production in the past half-decade, agriculture has failed to provide enough food for domestic needs. More than one quarter of children below five years of age are malnourished; in the northeast and northwest regions, the proportion is 40 percent.[49] Imports of food, including staples such as sugar, wheat, and fish, outweigh exports, accounting for 12 percent (US$8 billion) of annual imports. The country is the world's second largest rice importer.[50]

The Nigerian government has announced plans to reduce dependency on food imports, and there is scope for significant improvements in agricultural productivity.[51] As cities such as Lagos grow and gain in economic strength, rural areas—particularly those in the vicinity of large cities—stand to benefit from increased urban demand for food. If international food prices continue to rise, as seems likely given the emergence of China and India as economic powers and the threats posed by climate change to food production, Nigerian food exports could revive.

For this to happen, major changes will be needed. The World Bank has identified priorities for reform of agriculture, including investing in rural infrastructure and improving market access (transport and storage problems and the absence of effective links between producer and seller result in 20–40 percent of food being lost post-harvest).[52] Efforts by the Nigerian government to encourage young people to take up farming may also be required—many young Nigerians see rural areas and agriculture as the antithesis of the modernization they desire, and high food prices alone will not be enough to lure them back to or keep them in the fields.[53] To relieve the pressure on cities and bolster the food supply by encouraging productive young people to reengage in farming, it will be important to increase investment in modern technologies, to reform land tenure laws in ways that strengthen security of title and thereby help farmers to access credit, and to bolster investment in training and education programs that inform farmers about new and more sustainable techniques.

As well as demand for land and food, demand for water is also likely to increase in the coming decades. Few households receive an adequate supply, and as the population grows, the risk of water-related conflict is likely to increase unless action is taken to redress the deficit. Thirty-nine percent of Nigerians lack access to an improved source of drinking water, and 69 percent lack access to improved sanitation.[54] Twenty-three percent of the water supply is imported, nearly all of it via rivers that enter the country from Niger and Cameroon, and while all three countries are members of both the Lake Chad Basic Commission and the Niger Basin Authority, there are no treaties governing the water provided to Nigeria by its neighbors. Although perhaps unlikely given Nigeria's relative political and economic clout, it is possible that water could be used as a political bargaining chip or threat or that Niger or Cameroon could be forced to cut off supply or overuse their rivers if experiencing future water shortages of their own.

Climate change exacerbates the latter threat, as well as increasing the pressure on farmland and food production. Carbon dioxide emissions by Nigerians are very low, measuring 0.5 metric ton per capita in 2010 compared with a global average of 4.9 tons,[55] but the country is likely to suffer from climate change caused elsewhere. Large swathes of Nigeria are already afflicted by extreme weather events. In the arid north, droughts and food shortages are common; in the tropical and coastal south, flooding poses an annual threat. Across West Africa, rainfall is highly variable, with frequent deviations of 40–80 percent from the annual average.[56] Average precipitation in the northern Nigerian Sahel has declined 25 percent in the past thirty years, while flooding has increased significantly in the Niger Delta in the south.[57]

Climate change is likely to lead to an increase in droughts and floods, with the Sahel region forecast by the International Panel on Climate Change (IPCC) to be one of the world's hardest-hit regions. In West Africa as a whole, the IPCC has warned of reduced crop yields, damage to coastal settlements as a result of rising sea levels and flooding, and threats to fisheries because of environmental degradation in coastal areas. In Nigeria, average annual rainfall in the period between 2020 and 2039 is expected to be 2 percent higher than the average in the period between 1980 and 1999, while the average annual temperature is expected to be 1°C higher.[58] Changes in precipitation will be distributed unevenly across the country, with the already impoverished and drought-prone northeast likely to see less rainfall and more drought and desertification and the flood-prone southeast likely to see more rainfall accompanied by sea level rises, which could threaten coastal agriculture. The southwest may be less vulnerable to changes in precipitation.[59]

The effects of climate change on Nigeria's economy and on land, pasture, and water availability may heighten the threat of internal conflict. The link between climate change and conflict is not firmly established, since it is often difficult to disaggregate climate change from the many other causes of violence. Climate-induced conflict, moreover, may be more likely in some countries than in others—those with a history of violence, for example, or weak or corrupt institutions that fail to keep a lid on discontent, or those with mushrooming, poor populations that have limited ability to cope with shocks may be more vulnerable than their more stable, wealthier counterparts.

Africa is characterized by many of these and other potential risk factors. Burke and co-authors concluded that temperature changes are linked to civil war in Africa.[60] An annual increase in temperature of 1°C, the study found, is associated with a 4.5 percent increase in the incidence of civil war. If projections of future temperature changes are borne out, this would lead to a 54 percent increase in civil war in Africa by 2030. In another study, the economists Raymond Fisman and Eduardo Miguel found that in Africa "the risk of armed civil conflict is much more likely the year after a large drop in rainfall than in normal years" and that with climate change expected to reduce average annual precipitation in the Sahel as a whole by 24 percent by 2080, the risk of civil conflict in the region will increase 15 percent, meaning that some countries will face a one in three chance of civil war each year.[61]

Evidence from Nigeria is so far limited to specific examples of conflicts that appear to be related to climate or resource scarcity. More than half of rural northerners polled in a 2003/04 survey reported that local conflicts had arisen because of competition for natural resources between pastoralists and sedentary farmers.[62] In October 2012, more than fifty people were killed in two separate clashes between herders and farmers in Kaduna and Benue states.[63] Violence in the middle belt area around Jos, which has plagued the city and its surroundings since 2001, also appears to be linked to disputes over resources between different ethnic groups.[64]

SUMMARY. Nigeria is doing a bad job of meeting domestic demand. The country's huge reserves of oil have not only failed to provide sufficient energy for Nigerians' day-to-day use; they have also wreaked havoc on agriculture and the environment and reduced the ability and will of the political classes to drive forward the country's development and maintain stability. As the population grows in the coming decades and as demand for oil, land, food, and water intensifies, this status quo is likely to prove unsustainable. Unless the supply of strategic resources increases to meet rising demand, the country may implode.

Fortunately, there is an escape valve from this big squeeze. Nigeria does not lack resources, but it has so far lacked the ability or will to exploit and distribute them effectively. The country has more than enough oil and gas to power its cities and villages, and there is scope for huge advances in food production. Some of the demand-side pressures create an opportunity for suppliers: booming urban populations will provide a hungry and potentially wealthy market for farmers; the burgeoning young adult population could be a magnet for foreign investors and a wellspring of domestic entrepreneurship and job creation.

All of this will require a radical shift in how the country is governed. Without dramatic change, prosperity and peace will characterize only one of three possible futures awaiting Nigerians over the next two decades. As discussed in the next section, the other scenarios are much less rosy.

The Good, the Bad, and the Ugly

The uncertainty over Nigeria's ability to meet demand for its resources has not gone unnoticed by its international partners. Petroleum products account for 95 percent of the country's exports,[65] with the United States the biggest buyer. Between 2011 and 2013, however, the United States reduced by two thirds its purchases of Nigerian crude.[66] This occurred both because of advances in U.S. technology, which enable the refining of heavier grades of crude (Nigerian crude is highly valued for its lightness), and also because of instability and crime in the Niger Delta region. Enormous quantities of oil have been stolen in recent years, with some reports estimating that up to 10 percent of the oil produced each year (250,000 barrels a day) is lost to theft.[67] Royal Dutch Shell, the dominant foreign oil producer in the country, declared in 2012 that because of sabotage it would be unable to meet its promised supply of two types of crude,[68] and the company has sold off some of its Nigerian leases.[69]

But although U.S. demand is weakening, the worldwide appetite for Nigerian oil is unlikely to abate in the coming decades. Economic and population growth in Asia, particularly in China and India, should compensate for losses elsewhere, while Nigeria itself may become a more significant market if the economy continues to expand. In assessing whether the country will be able to meet domestic and international demand, three broad possible scenarios present themselves, the first good, the second bad, the third very ugly.

The Good

Under this scenario, Nigeria would begin by reforming oil and gas production, reducing waste so that more oil and gas come on stream—the country flares more natural gas than any other except Russia, with more than 21 percent of production dissipated in this way in 2011[70]—and taking much stronger measures to limit damage to the local environment so that the fishing and farming capacity of local communities will recover. The current National Petroleum Act does not include penalties against polluters, although a step toward remedying this was taken in July 2012 with the National Oil Spill Detection and Response Agency recommending that parliament impose a US$5 billion fine on Shell for a 2011 spill.[71]

If more concerted action on limiting waste and pollution were accompanied by investment of oil revenues in improving the lives of people living in the Niger Delta, oil production would proceed more peacefully and with fewer interruptions. The heartland of the oil industry has the highest infant and child mortality rates in the south, the lowest proportion of vaccinated children, and the lowest child literacy rates.[72] These figures reflect historical underinvestment in the region. Given that it produces so much of the country's wealth, it is perhaps not surprising that armed groups such as MEND have agitated, often violently, for a greater share of oil revenues.

Linked to cleaning up the oil industry and sharing oil wealth more widely is the need to reduce corruption. If Nigeria's leaders can tackle this blight, they will go a long way toward defusing the resentment felt by the many citizens who see no benefit from oil. As well as large-scale corruption in the oil industry—exemplified by the US$6.8 billion lost between 2010 and 2012 in a subsidy scam involving fuel imports—a 2012 report by the Petroleum Revenue Special Task Force showed that US$29 billion had been stolen in the past decade in a fraud involving natural gas price fixing.[73] Mineral resources in Africa are often linked to corruption, as narrow elites scramble to control them and, freed by mineral wealth from the need to tax and therefore answer to their subjects, use their fruits to enrich those closest to them.[74] Nigeria is no exception. The Next Generation Nigeria Task Force found corruption to be a key factor fomenting the anger of the nation's young people and recommended involving youth in policymaking and monitoring of anticorruption efforts as a key step in reducing tension and promoting transparency, honesty, and meritocracy in business and politics.[75]

The government has recently taken two important steps to clear the path from oil production to prosperity. A sovereign wealth fund began investing excess profits from oil and gas in 2013, starting with US$1 billion accrued from the difference between budgeted and actual oil prices. The state-owned Nigerian Sovereign Investment Authority (SIA) will manage three funds—a Future Generations Fund, intended to build up savings for the long term; a Nigerian Infrastructure Fund, whose profits will be directed toward much-needed shorter-term investments; and a Stabilization Fund, designed to protect government revenues and spending against oil price volatility.[76] An earlier Excess Crude Account, which the SIA has replaced, was beset by accusations of corruption, and the SIA's success will depend crucially on transparency over the amounts held and the investments made. At US$1 billion, moreover, Nigeria's fund is small compared with its export revenues from oil (which amounted to US$50 billion in 2011)[77] and with other oil-producing countries (Angola began its own fund in 2012 with US$5 billion). This still leaves significant revenues available for less constructive purposes, and there is a case for increasing the share of oil profits invested in the fund as the global economy revives.

The second step is the country's involvement with the Extractive Industries Transparency Initiative (EITI). Nigeria achieved EITI-compliant status in 2011, having committed, among other measures, to conduct regular audits of the oil sector and to enshrine in law the reporting of payments by oil and gas companies and revenues received by government.[78] Although transparency has improved, however, grave concerns remain, as the aforementioned reports of fraud show, about corruption in the oil and gas industries. The 2013 Nigeria EITI report found that the state oil firm, Nigerian National Petroleum Company (NNPC), owed the government more than US$8 billion in unpaid revenues from crude oil earnings between 2009 and 2011 and that private sector oil and gas firms owed US$5.8 billion in unpaid taxes and royalties.[79] While EITI compliance is a promising step, it will need to be accompanied by a stronger commitment, not just to identify where corrupt practices have occurred but to call to account those behind them. That it was a Dutch court and not a Nigerian one that in January 2013 found Shell Petroleum Development Company of Nigeria Ltd. guilty of failing to prevent an oil spill in the Niger Delta is an indication of how much clean-up work, including the cleaning up of international oil companies, remains to be done.[80]

That oil production often leads to corruption is a further argument in favor of diversifying away from it. The positive scenario for Nigeria would see oil revenues used to tackle the problems not just of the Niger Delta but of the country as a whole. Three areas in particular demand urgent attention.

First, the SIA's Infrastructure Fund offers an opportunity to strengthen rural infrastructure—rural roads, irrigation systems, and markets are all inadequate— so that farmers can take advantage of rising food prices and higher domestic demand from cities. Investing in human capital via training rural communities in new farming technologies and in climate change adaptation strategies would improve the efficiency of land use and food production and potentially slow the exodus from rural to urban areas. This would help Nigerian agriculture to capitalize on its competitive advantage of inexpensive labor as well as to relieve the pressures on cities that are struggling to accommodate rapid growth.

Second, providing a reliable supply of power to cities is a priority. Lagos and other cities have the potential to pull the rest of the country toward prosperity as industries such as telecommunications and textiles blossom, but without electricity the businesses that are the motors of job creation will continue to be hobbled. Facing down the generator industry lobby, which benefits from an ineffective national grid, is an important starting point for reform, although foreign investors might be attracted by the possibility of helping Nigeria to leapfrog to solar power, bypassing the traditional grid in the same way that cell phone companies across Africa have bypassed the fixed-line network.

Third, significant investment is required in the north of the country, where resentment and instability are building as the north-south divide grows. Neighboring Niger has launched a five-year, US$2.5 billion Strategy for Development and Security to address the needs of its northern population, and Nigeria would benefit from a similar scheme, with specific funding commitments for northern security and development projects.[81] Forums that involve young people in drawing up such plans will be essential, since satisfying the demands of the young will be key to determining whether the region follows a road toward stability or chaos. Closing the gap between north and south will both promote national unity and allow the north's fast-growing youth population to contribute positively to social and economic development.

Nigeria's international partners would play a key role in securing the positive scenario. They could benefit both themselves and Nigerians by allowing more of the latter to migrate legally to find work. This would ease the pressure on resources caused by overcrowding in Nigeria, reduce illegal trafficking of humans, and fill gaps in the aging labor markets of wealthy countries. Wealthy countries could also work to reduce transnational crime by legalizing the narcotics that, as they pass through the region on the way to Europe or North America, increase instability in Nigeria and West Africa as a whole. And they could help to curtail corruption by holding their businesses to account for bad behavior in Nigeria—Western oil and gas companies have been convicted of bribing officials and have been accused by the Nigerian government of failing to pay tax.[82]

Under the good scenario, if Nigeria could attend to these problems, the rewards would be immense. If the country can capitalize on its potentially favorable population structure, which if fertility continues to decline will see the number of workers per dependent almost double by 2050, its economy will mushroom, with 30 million people lifted out of poverty and average incomes tripling by 2030.[83] Acting as a motor for development in West Africa as a whole, its people, healthy and well educated and a magnet both for foreign investors and for aging Western and Asian societies, would benefit from an uninterrupted flow of oil revenues and a diversified economy that creates rather than stifles employment. Most countries that have experienced baby booms have emerged from them, often after a great deal of turbulence on the way, much better off than before they started.[84] Nigeria has an opportunity to tread a similar path.

The Bad

If Nigeria continues with business as usual, its prospects of meeting domestic and international demand for resources will be bleak, with problems beginning at a local level likely to spread to the whole country and perhaps to the wider West Africa region.

In the Niger Delta, population growth will lead to increased competition over land, food, and fisheries. If oil companies are allowed to continue to pollute and to displace local people from their homes, the current lull in the unrest in the region is unlikely to last. An amnesty signed by the government and MEND in 2009 will not withstand many more years of government neglect, and renewed violence could interrupt oil production on a scale not previously seen, potentially pushing foreign oil companies out of the country and leaving Nigeria ill placed to supply international and domestic needs.

As well as damaging the southern states' development prospects, unrest in the delta and excess demand for its resources may push more residents offshore and into piracy. Piracy attacks off the Nigerian coast, including hijackings of oil tankers, have increased sharply in recent years, with forty attacks reported in the first nine months of 2012 and many more assumed to have been hushed up.[85] The International Maritime Bureau's warnings about Nigeria may prove insufficiently cautious if conditions in the delta do not improve:

> Pirates/robbers are often violent and have attacked, hijacked, and robbed vessels/kidnapped crews along the coast, rivers, anchorages, ports, and surrounding waters. Attacks reported up to 120nm [nautical miles] from coast . . . A number of crew members were injured in past attacks. Generally all waters in Nigeria remain risky. Vessels are advised to be vigilant as many attacks may have gone unreported.[86]

Population growth also threatens to heighten the risk of conflict in the rest of the country. High unemployment, inhumane living conditions made worse by the contest for electricity and other services in burgeoning urban slums, competition in rural areas for land and water, and the absence of opportunities for young Nigerians to express themselves and influence policy could be an explosive cocktail. Such a combination of frustrations could lead to widespread protests along the lines of those seen in recent years in North Africa. Some of these protests are likely to turn violent, and the absence of alternatives for young people could see Nigeria exporting not oil and food but terrorists, criminals, mercenaries, drugs,[87] and angry, uneducated migrants.

Simmering nationwide unrest would render continued policy failures more likely. It is possible that Nigeria's governing institutions will prove sufficiently robust and effective to work as shock absorbers, keeping a lid on trouble by assuaging domestic demand for resources—even as resources become scarcer as a result of population growth and climate change, discontent will be contained more easily if the country's rulers are seen to be making efforts to distribute limited resources fairly.

The current trajectory of institutions, however, offers little encouragement. The political classes are widely regarded as corrupt and as keener to feather their own nests than to promote the national interest. Overreliance on one resource, oil, has hollowed out government institutions and left them ill-equipped to deal with shocks. Nigeria ranks 144 out of 175 countries on Transparency International's 2013 Corruption Perceptions Index,[88] down from 121 in 2008, while a 2011 Gallup poll of 1,000 adults found that 94 percent of Nigerians believe their government is corrupt, even though they gave the current president, Goodluck Jonathan, high personal popularity ratings (this points to a perception of entrenched institutional corruption that goes beyond the role of individuals).[89]

Continued corruption would not only fuel popular resentment but also weaken the capacity of government to perform the roles for which it is designed—the education and health systems, for example, are already failing to adapt to increased demand, and the state energy provider is a laughingstock.[90] The country's security forces are another example of institutional weakness. The police and army have been unable to quell violence in the north and in the middle belt around Jos or to prevent terrorist attacks in the capital, Abuja, while the December 2012 kidnapping in Delta State of the mother of the country's finance minister, Ngozi Okonjo-Iweala, is a further indicator that the turmoil may be spiraling out of control. Like the political classes, the security forces are viewed with suspicion by many Nigerians. As Human Rights Watch has argued, "The long-term failure of the authorities to address police bribery, extortion, and wholesale embezzlement threatens the basic rights of all Nigerians."[91] Such behavior is more liable to provoke than to prevent further violence, adding to the strains on the security forces' capacity.

The Ugly

The "bad" scenario, where underdevelopment in the south disrupts oil production and a government that relies excessively on oil revenues becomes steadily less capable of maintaining national stability and promoting development, would see Nigeria waste its potential and stagnate, as it has for much of the post-independence period. There is, however, a much worse scenario, which could see the country revert to the military dictatorships of the 1980s and 1990s or even descend into civil war.

Reductions in government revenues from lost oil production and the need to divert public funds to policing the delta and the seas would make investing in the impoverished, increasingly troubled north of the country more difficult. The northern states lag behind the south in terms of wealth and other measures of human development. All ten of Nigeria's poorest states are in the north, and the north has the lowest school attendance rates, the lowest vaccination rates, the highest infant and child mortality rates, and the highest maternal mortality rate in the country.[92] On some indicators, the north-south differences are stark. Vaccination rates are seven times higher in the southeast region than in the northeast, and child mortality in the northwest is double that in the southeast. This divide is evidence of the neglect of the north in recent decades, and if inequality with the south continues to grow alongside the pressures brought about by climate change and population growth, so will the resentment that northerners feel toward the rest of the country and the government.

Northern Nigeria is already dangerously volatile. Conflict between pastoralists and settled farmers is becoming more frequent as resources dwindle, and the rise of the Muslim fundamentalist terrorist group Boko Haram is likely to be linked to the growing anger felt by young northerners at the absence of opportunities in the region. Boko Haram is thought to have killed up to 1,000 people in 2011 and 2012 in shootings, bombings, and suicide attacks, and heavy-handed responses by the army and police risk pushing more recruits into the group's arms.[93] The United Nations estimates that the group was responsible for 1,224 deaths between May and December 2013 after a state of emergency was declared in the northeastern states of Adamawa, Borno and Yobe.[94]

Boko Haram has not hitherto branched out beyond Nigeria, but its bombing of the United Nations headquarters in Abuja in 2011 hinted at international ambitions, and a splinter group named Ansaru, which stepped up its kidnappings of foreigners in 2012, may have a more explicit international agenda.[95] With the rise of al Qaeda in the Islamic Maghreb in Mali and other parts of the Sahel and Sahara, where along with kidnappings of Westerners its activities have included an assault on the Malian state and the capture of hundreds of employees at a large, internationally run natural gas plant in Algeria, the U.S. government is not alone in worrying about the emergence of a pan–West African Islamic terrorist movement.[96]

Although that scenario is perturbing, there may be worse to come if the northern problem remains unresolved. The Nigerian Nobel Prize–winning writer Wole Soyinka has warned that the country is on course for civil war between north and south, and there have been demonstrations against Boko Haram in southern cities, including by self-styled "Yoruba militia" groups, as southerners become frustrated with the group's expansion.[97]

Such a conflict would have significant international repercussions. First, there would be security impacts. Wars in Africa tend to spill across borders, and a war in a country as big as Nigeria could draw in neighbors from across the continent. The United States and United Kingdom would probably be forced to intervene in such a conflict, either in peacekeeping or in fighting (while France intervened to repel al Qaeda's advance in Mali in 2013, it would be unlikely to play more than a supporting role in Nigeria). The United Kingdom's intervention to help to end Sierra Leone's civil war in 2002 was a success, but Nigeria would likely prove much more intractable: continued British military assistance to the government side did not prevent the Biafran civil war of the 1960s from continuing for three years.

Second, there would be economic impacts. Global oil production has struggled to keep up with demand in recent years, and the loss of a major producer such as Nigeria would push up prices and hurt economies worldwide. Some observers believe that violence in the Niger Delta has already contributed to oil price spikes in the past decade, but these disruptions would pale in comparison with what might happen if civil war broke out.[98]

Third, there would be developmental impacts. A civil war would cripple efforts to eradicate poverty, with setbacks in such a populous country rendering internationally agreed post-2015 development goals elusive. Serious domestic unrest could spark a vicious spiral, bringing oil production to a halt, obstructing food production (leaving the country ever more vulnerable to shocks that affect food imports), and spreading hunger and poverty by making it yet more difficult to access resources. Even the threat of war may reverse development gains—Nigeria (along with West Africa as a whole) has a history of military coups, and it is not inconceivable that the army could muscle its way back into politics if it perceives a threat to the nation's integrity. Previous military governments have proved economically disastrous, and even if it does not degenerate into outright war, northern unrest could be an indirect trigger for a developmental downturn.[99]

Conclusions

Only one of the three scenarios outlined above would see Nigeria enjoying a prosperous, peaceful future. While it clearly has the potential to become Africa's economic and political powerhouse, recent decades have largely been a story of opportunities lost rather than seized.

The effects of the country's failure to capitalize on its human and natural resources have so far been limited to widespread poverty and intermittent localized unrest, but the consequences of continued failure over the next two decades are likely to be much more serious. As the population—and especially the youth population—mushrooms, and as the big squeeze on resources grows ever tighter, muddling through will no longer be an option. Muddling through will lead at best to nationwide, violent disorder and a failure to capture the one-off chance of a demographic dividend. At worst, it will pose an existential threat to the country, with serious repercussions across West Africa and for the United States and other international stakeholders.

The country's current trajectory is highly volatile—while the Niger Delta is enjoying a period of relative peace and the national economy, led by cities such as Lagos and Abuja, is growing, the north is increasingly chaotic and poverty remains widespread. Nigeria does not lack resources or the human capital required to make use of them; indeed it abounds in minerals, land, and young, energetic working-age adults. Until now, however, it has lacked the leadership and the vision to realize its potential, and this has left it delicately balanced between feast and famine as it prepares for a more crowded, more demanding future.

Notes

1. United Nations Population Division, "World Population Prospects: The 2012 Revision" (New York: United Nations Secretariat, Department of Economic and Social Affairs, 2012) (http://esa.un.org/unpd/wpp/index.htm).

2. Energy Information and Administration, "Petroleum and Other Liquids: U.S. Imports by Country of Origin" (Washington, 2013) (www.eia.gov/dnav/pet/pet_move_impcus_a2_nus_ep00_im0_mbbl_a.htm).

3. Next Generation Nigeria Task Force, "Nigeria: The Next Generation Report," PGDA Working Paper 62 (London: British Council, Program on the Global Demography of Aging, and Harvard School of Public Health, 2010).

4. United Nations Population Division, "World Population Prospects: The 2012 Revision" (New York: United Nations Secretariat, Department of Economic and Social Affairs, 2012) (http://esa.un.org/unpd/wpp/index.htm).

5. Ibid.

6. Ibid. United Nations Population Division, "World Urbanization Prospects: The 2011 Revision" (New York: United Nations Secretariat, Department of Economic and Social Affairs, 2010).

7. World Bank, *World Development Report 2013: Jobs* (Oxford University Press, 2012).

8. United Nations 2012 data: Slum Population in Urban Areas (http://data.un.org/Data.aspx?d=MDG&f=seriesRowID%3A711).

9. Next Generation Nigeria Task Force, "Nigeria: The Next Generation Report."

10. "Nigeria's GDP Recalculation: The Hidden Costs," *Financial Times,* April 14, 2014.

11. Ibid.

12. "Nigeria Economy Picks up on Non-Oil Sector Growth," Reuters, March 13, 2012.

13. Sola Fajana, "Industrial Relations in the Oil Industry in Nigeria," Working Paper 237 (Geneva: International Labor Office, 2005).

14. African Development Bank, "African Economic Outlook: Nigeria" (Tunis-Belvedère, 2012).

15. "Nigerians Living in Poverty Rise to Nearly 61 Percent," BBC News, February 13, 2012.

16. World Bank, "World Development Indicators: Nigeria" (Washington, 2012).

17. Next Generation Nigeria Task Force, "Nigeria: The Next Generation Report."

18. CIA, *World Factbook.*

19. Next Generation Nigeria Task Force, "Nigeria: The Next Generation Report."

20. Next Generation Nigeria Task Force, "Nigeria: The Next Generation Report."

21. World Bank, "World Development Indicators: Nigeria" (Washington, 2012).

22. NOI Polls and Gallup Organization, "Second National Opinion Poll" (Abuja, November 2007).

23. Daniel Yergin, *The Prize: The Epic Quest for Oil, Money, and Power* (London: Simon and Schuster, 2009).

24. United States Institute of Peace, "Blood Oil in the Niger Delta" (Washington, 2009) (www.usip.org/files/resources/blood_oil_nigerdelta.pdf).

25. U.S. Energy Information Administration (EIA), "Country Analysis Brief: Nigeria" (Washington, December 13, 2013).

26. International Energy Agency (IEA), "Oil Market Report 2010" (Paris, 2010).

27. Global Trade Information Services, *Global Trade Atlas 2010* (Columbia, S.C., 2010).

28. CIA, *World Factbook.*

29. Nigeria National Population Commission, *Nigeria Demographic and Health Survey 2008* (Abuja, 2009).

30. World Bank, "World Development Indicators: Nigeria."

31. Nigeria National Population Commission, *Nigeria Demographic and Health Survey 2008* (Abuja, 2009).

32. African Development Bank Group, "Nigeria Economic and Power Sector Reform Program (EPSERP): Appraisal Report" (Tunis-Belvedère, 2009).

33. Fikerte Solomon, Esther Petrilli, and Carmen Pineda, "Strategic Gas Plan for Nigeria" (Washington: World Bank–Netherlands Partnership Program, 2004).

34. "Nigeria's Oil: A Desperate Need for Reform," *Economist,* October 20, 2012.

35. International Institute for Sustainable Development (IISD), "A Citizen's Guide to Energy Subsidies in Nigeria" (Winnipeg, Canada, September 2012).

36. Ibid.

37. Javier Arze del Granado, David Coady, and Robert Gillingham, "The Unequal Benefits of Fuel Subsidies: A Review of Evidence for Developing Countries," IMF Working Paper 202 (Washington: International Monetary Fund, 2010).

38. IISD, "Untold Billions: Fossil Fuel Subsidies, Their Impacts, and the Paths to Reform" (Winnipeg, Canada, March 2010).

39. IISD, "A Citizen's Guide to Energy Subsidies in Nigeria."

40. "Nigeria Faces $4bn Fuel Subsidy Gap," *Financial Times,* June 18, 2012.

41. Arze del Granado, Coady, and Gillingham, "The Unequal Benefits of Fuel Subsidies."

42. "Economic Jihad," *Economist,* June 23, 2011.

43. Fatai Egberongbe, Peter Nwilo, and Olusegun Badejo, "Oil Spill Disaster Monitoring along Nigerian Coastline," Paper prepared for the fifth FIG Regional Conference, Accra, Ghana, March 8–11, 2006.

44. World Bank and Department for International Development, "Country Partnership Strategy for the Federal Republic of Nigeria" (Washington and London, June 2, 2005).

45. Leo Osuji and Augustine Uwakwe, "Petroleum Industry Effluents and Other Oxygen-Demanding Wastes in Niger Delta, Nigeria," *Chemistry and Biodiversity* 3, no. 7 (2006): 705–17.

46. World Bank, "World Development Indicators: Nigeria."

47. CIA, *World Factbook*.

48. Birte Junge, Robert Abaidoo, David Chikoye, and Karl Stahr, "Soil Conservation in Nigeria: Past and Present On-Station and On-Farm Initiatives" (Ankeny, Iowa: Soil and Water Conservation Society, 2008).

49. World Health Organization, "Malnutrition Database: Nigeria" (Geneva, 2012) (www.who.int/nutgrowthdb/database/countries/who_standards/nga.pdf).

50. CIA, *World Factbook*. "Nigeria Tries to Curb Appetite for Imported Food," *Global Post*, April 27, 2012 (www.globalpost.com/dispatch/news/regions/africa/nigeria/120423/decrease-food-imports-increase-food-security).

51. "Nigeria Tries to Curb Appetite for Imported Food."

52. Food and Agriculture Organization of the United Nations (FAO), "Global Forest Resources Assessment 2005: Progress towards Sustainable Forest Management" (Rome, 2005) (www.fao.org/docrep/008/a0400e/a0400e00.htm). World Bank, "Nigeria Employment and Growth Study," Report 51564-NG (Washington, November 13, 2009).

53. Mark Weston, "Nigeria, In Its Own Words" (London: Next Generation Nigeria Project, 2009). Next Generation Nigeria Task Force, "Nigeria: The Next Generation Report."

54. Nigeria National Population Commission, *Nigeria Demographic and Health Survey 2008;* World Bank, "World Development Indicators: Nigeria." Weston, "Nigeria, In Its Own Words"; Next Generation Nigeria Task Force, "Nigeria: The Next Generation Report."

55. World Bank, "World Development Indicators: Nigeria."

56. Mirjam de Bruijn and Han van Dijk, "Climate Change and Climatic Variability in West Africa" (Leiden, the Netherlands: African Studies Centre, 2006).

57. J. C. Nkomo, A. O. Nyong, and K. Kulindwa, "The Impacts of Climate Change in Africa," Final draft submitted to the *Stern Review on the Economics of Climate Change* (London, 2006).

58. World Bank, "Nigeria Profile," Climate Change Knowledge Portal, 2013. United Nations Development Program, "Nigeria Country Profile: Adaptation Learning Mechanism" (Geneva, 2013).

59. Federal Ministry of the Environment, "National Environmental, Economic, and Development Study (NEEDS) for Climate Change in Nigeria" (Abuja, September 2010).

60. Marshall Burke, Edward Miguel, Shanker Satyanath, John Dykema, and David Lobell, "Warming Increases the Risk of Civil War in Africa," *Proceedings of the National Academy of Sciences of the United States of America* 106, no. 49 (December 8, 2009): 20670–74.

61. Raymond Fisman and Edward Miguel, *Economic Gangsters: Corruption, Violence, and the Poverty of Nations* (Princeton University Press, 2008).

62. Anthony Nyong, "Climate-Related Conflicts in West Africa," in *Environmental Change and Security Program Report 12 2006–2007* (Washington: Woodrow Wilson International Center, 2007).

63. John Campbell, "A Bloody Week for Nigeria," Council on Foreign Relations blog, October 18, 2012 (http://blogs.cfr.org/campbell/2012/10/18/a-bloody-week-for-nigeria).

64. Crisis Group, "Curbing Violence in Nigeria (1): The Jos Crisis," Crisis Group Africa Report 196 (Brussels, December 17, 2012).

65. CIA, *World Factbook.*

66. U.S. Energy Information and Administration (EIA), "Petroleum and Other Liquids: U.S. Imports by Country of Origin"; "U.S. Oil Boom Upends Nigerian Exports," *Wall Street Journal,* October 18, 2012 (http://online.wsj.com/article/SB10000872396390444473480457806421171489 5152.html).

67. "Nigeria: Oil-Gas Sector Mismanagement Costs Billions," BBC News, October 25, 2012 (www.bbc.co.uk/news/world-africa-20081268).

68. "Royal Dutch Shell Makes Nigeria Production Warning," Associated Press, October 23, 2012 (http://finance.yahoo.com/news/royal-dutch-shell-makes-nigeria-production-warning-103154801--finance.html).

69. "Shell Has No Plan to Pull out of Nigeria, Says MD," Business Day Online, August 1, 2012 (www.businessdayonline.com/NG/index.php/news/76-hot-topic/42114-shell-has-no-plan-to-pull-out-of-nigeria-says-md).

70. EIA, "Country Analysis Brief: Nigeria" (Washington, December 13, 2013).

71. "Shell Urged to Pay Nigeria $5bn over Bonga Oil Spill," BBC News, July 17, 2012.

72. Next Generation Nigeria Task Force, "Nigeria: The Next Generation Report" and "Nigeria: The Next Generation Literature Review."

73. "Nigeria's Oil: A Desperate Need for Reform," *Economist,* October 20, 2012. "Nigeria: Oil-Gas Sector Mismanagement Costs Billions," BBC News, October 25, 2012.

74. Mark Weston, *The Ringtone and the Drum: Travels in the World's Poorest Countries* (London: Zero Books, 2012), pp. 145–48.

75. Next Generation Nigeria Task Force, "Nigeria: The Next Generation Report."

76. SWF Institute, "Nigerian Sovereign Investment Authority" (Las Vegas, Nev., 2013) (www.swfinstitute.org/swfs/excess-crude-account/).

77. Revenue Watch Institute, "The 2013 Resource Governance Index: Nigeria" (New York, 2013).

78. Extractive Industries Transparency Initiative (EITI), "Nigeria EITI: Making Transparency Count, Uncovering Billions," Case Study (Oslo, Norway, January 20, 2012).

79. "Nigeria Oil Firm Owes Billions to Government: Audit," Reuters, January, 31, 2013.

80. "Dutch Court Says Shell Responsible for Nigeria Spills," Reuters, January 30, 2013.

81. Mark Weston, "An Agenda for the North, or How to Avert Civil War in Nigeria," Global Dashboard, January 27, 2012 (www.globaldashboard.org/2012/01/27/an-agenda-for-the-north-or-how-to-avert-civil-war-in-nigeria/).

82. "Shell to Pay $48m Nigerian Bribe Fine," *Daily Telegraph* (London), November 4, 2010. "NEITI: Oil Companies Owe FG N1.3tn in Taxes," Nigeria Energy Intelligence, September 24, 2012 (http://nigeriaenergyintelliegence.blogspot.com.es/2012/09/neiti-oil-companies-owe-fg-n13tn-in.html).

83. Next Generation Nigeria Task Force, "Nigeria: The Next Generation Report."

84. Bo Malmberg, *Global Population Ageing, Migration, and European External Policies,* Final Report (Stockholm: Institutet för Framtidsstudier).

85. "Surviving the Pirates off the Coast of Nigeria," BBC News, September 11, 2012. International Maritime Bureau, "Live Piracy and Armed Robbery Map 2012" (London, 2012) (www.icc-ccs.org.uk/piracy-reporting-centre/live-piracy-map).

86. International Maritime Bureau, "Piracy and Armed Robbery Prone Areas and Warnings" (London, 2012) (www.icc-ccs.org.uk/piracy-reporting-centre/prone-areas-and-warnings).

87. The United Nations Office on Drugs and Crime has described the country as "a transit point for heroin and cocaine [from Asia and South America] intended for European, East Asian, and North American markets." United Nations Office on Drugs and Crime, "Nigeria: Drugs, Organized Crime, and Terrorism" (Abuja, 2012) (www.unodc.org/nigeria/en/drug-prevention.html).

88. Transparency International, Corruption Perceptions Index (http://cpi.transparency.org/cpi2013/results/).

89. "Almost All Nigerians Say Government Is Corrupt," Gallup World, January 16, 2012 (www.gallup.com/poll/152057/almost-nigerians-say-gov-corrupt.aspx).

90. Mark Weston, "Nigeria, In Its Own Words."

91. Human Rights Watch, "Everyone's in on the Game: Corruption and Human Rights Abuses by the Nigeria Police Force" (New York, August 17).

92. Next Generation Nigeria Task Force, "Nigeria: The Next Generation Report" and "Nigeria: The Next Generation Literature Review."

93. Police mistreatment of the group's then-leader is thought to have been the trigger that persuaded it to resort to terror attacks, with members subsequently citing the army and police as their principal enemies. Abuses have continued as the fight to contain the new threat has intensified. "In Nigeria, a Deadly Group's Rage Has Local Roots," *New York Times,* February 25, 2012. Human Rights Watch, "World Report 2012: Nigeria" (New York, 2012).

94. "UN: Over 1,000 Killed in Boko Haram Attacks," Al Jazeera, December 16, 2013 (www.aljazeera.com/news/africa/2013/12/un-1224-killed-boko-haram-attacks-2013 1216175810115265.html).

95. "Islamists Ansaru Claim Attack on Mali-Bound Nigeria Troops," Reuters, January 20, 2013 (www.reuters.com/article/2013/01/20/us-nigeria-violence-idUS-BRE90J0B520130120). "Nigeria: What Do We Know about Ansaru?" Think Africa Press, January 22, 2014 (http://thinkafricapress.com/nigeria/who-are-ansaru).

96. "Africa's Islamist Militants 'Coordinate Efforts.'" BBC News, June 26, 2012.

97. "Wole Soyinka on Religion's Role in Nigeria's Turmoil," BBC News, January 10, 2012.

98. Tomas Malina, "Militancy in the Niger Delta" (University of Pittsburgh, Mathew B. Ridgway Center for International Security Studies, 2010).

99. The unwritten tradition of alternating the presidency between northerners and southerners was broken when the southerner Goodluck Jonathan, who had assumed power after Umaru Yar'Adua died in office in 2010, won the 2011 election. Many northerners felt that Yar'Adua should have been succeeded by another northerner until the 2015 election.

PART **II**

Facets of Resource Security

6

Routes to Energy Security: The Geopolitics of Gas Pipelines between the EU and Its Southeastern Neighbors

ANGEL SAZ-CARRANZA AND MARIE VANDENDRIESSCHE

The world's energy flows are in constant evolution. Recent years have brought a shift from debates on peak oil to a flood of unconventional gas flowing from previously import-dependent states. Energy demand, meanwhile, is also moving across the globe: by estimates from the International Energy Agency, emerging economies will account for 90 percent of net energy demand growth through 2035. In the realm of geopolitics, resource fluctuations bring about power changes. It is these dynamics that this chapter examines, with a special focus on natural gas and its flows between the European Union and its southeastern neighbors.

The European Union (EU), whose very origins lie in the quest for energy supply and security, finds itself among those scrambling to respond to the new energy outlook, while simultaneously confronting classical geopolitical issues with Russia, its giant energy-producing neighbor to the east. While the United States is experiencing a domestic energy revolution, the EU has not experienced dramatic changes in indigenous production: overall trends—declining domestic production, strong and growing import dependence (in the case of petroleum and other liquid fuels, but spectacularly so for natural gas), and overall, an increasing reliance on natural gas in the energy mix—remain steady. Meanwhile, and as the current Ukraine crisis shows, its interdependent hydrocarbon relation with gas giant Russia has grown ever more tense since the mid-2000s, remaining paramount in almost all of the foreign policy dealings between Brussels and Moscow.

The EU's chosen route to external energy security—which can be translated to security of supply—is chiefly through source diversification for natural gas and a careful choice of transit routes. Here we will examine the gas pipelines making up the so-called Southern Corridor, a chief component of the EU's strategy in supply diversification. These projects have been at the heart of an intricate geostrategic game for many years. Geopolitics, geo-economics, and commercial interests intersect in the decisions on the various pipeline proposals, ranging from Nabucco, Trans Adriatic Pipeline (TAP), and Trans Anatolian Pipeline (TANAP) to South East Europe Pipeline (SEEP) and Interconnector Turkey-Greece-Italy (ITGI), as well as Russia's South Stream. States, the EU, and firms meet at these crossroads, each defending its interests, whether from the perspective of suppliers, transit countries, or consumers.

We first offer a general outline of the current global energy scenario and the energy panorama in the EU, including its energy policy. Thereafter, we zero in on natural gas in the region: after some insights into the particularities of the natural gas market, this part examines the demand and supply dynamics in Europe and their evolution, as well as the EU's natural gas policy. In the following parts, the chapter turns to the Southern Corridor as the prime example of the EU's energy security efforts through diversification. Four of the proposed southeast European gas pipelines—Nabucco, South Stream, TANAP, and TAP—are examined in turn. In each case, the relevant actors, their interests, and their power bases are scrutinized. The final geopolitical and geo-economic analysis of the region's gas pipeline dynamics makes sense of the recent results of the pipeline competition, framing them in the current regional geopolitical context.

Energy in the EU: A Bird's-Eye View

For Europe, energy has always been at the top of the agenda: the EU's origins in the European Coal and Steel Community (ECSC) are more than mere coincidence. In June 1955 the six ministers of foreign affairs of the ECSC gathered at the Messina Conference, where they asked Henri Spaak to prepare a report on a future customs union—which would later develop into the European Economic Community. At the same meeting, the six declared there could be no future European community without cheap and abundant energy.

The EU's energy situation is one of import reliance: lacking the indigenous energy endowments required for self-sufficiency, the EU depends on its energy-rich neighbors to the North, the South, and the East to ensure its supply. In 2011 the then-twenty-seven member states imported more than half of their energy (54 percent), with Russia and Norway as their main petroleum and gas suppliers. Moreover, this dependence continues to rise steadily, especially for natural gas, where imports stand at 154 percent in comparison with 1995 levels.

While the United States has in recent years experienced a resurgence of energy production through its so-called shale revolution, the EU is unlikely to stumble on such riches in the immediate future. Significant obstacles stand in the way of a European non-conventional hydrocarbon production boom: on the one hand, Europe's geology and geography are less forgiving than the American easy-to-access shales; on the other, social and institutional factors such as population density, citizen concerns, and property rights complicate the prospects for such techniques as hydraulic fracking. Exploration projects are under way in some eastern EU member states, but the European Commission (EC), which shares competences with the member states in setting energy policy (that is, the states exercise their competence in energy policy to the extent that the EU has not done so), itself in 2012 recognized that Europe could not be self-sufficient with regard to natural gas: in the best case, domestic shale gas production would simply replace conventional gas production—that is, natural gas extracted from traditional, well-defined reservoirs and using traditional techniques, keeping import dependence around 60 percent.[1]

According to Eurostat, the EU-27's energy mix in 2011 was split as follows: petroleum products and natural gas made up over half of the whole (providing 35 percent and 23 percent of needs, respectively), with solid fuels (17 percent), nuclear heat (14 percent), and renewables (10 percent) delivering the rest.[2] This mix is forecast to shift gradually, with natural gas increasing its share of the pie.

A conglomeration of factors conspire in this increase. First, in the quest for cleaner energy—where the EU has repeatedly asserted its will to play a leading role—and in the absence of effective and widespread carbon capture and storage (CCS), energy production through coal and liquids must decline. Natural gas, relatively abundant and easily transportable through an extensive and established pipeline network, is seen as a stable route to lowering greenhouse gas emissions. Moreover, in electricity provision, natural gas is fungible in its ability to fill the supply gaps left by newly installed intermittent renewable sources. Second, natural gas may again serve to seal electricity gaps in a number of EU member states that have revised their nuclear policies post-Fukushima (recall that in 2011, nearly 28 percent of the EU's electricity was produced by nuclear power).

The EU's Energy for the Future: The New 2030 Energy Policy

The EU's Europe 2020 Strategy, set out in 2010, included three main energy and climate change targets for the union, often referred to as 20-20-20. According to the EC, the EU is "well on track" to meet these goals: greenhouse gas emissions decreased by 18 percent relative to emissions in 1990 (the 2020 target is 20 percent), 13 percent of final energy consumed comes from renewable sources (target: 20 percent), and the energy efficiency target (20 percent reduction in energy intensity of the EU economy by 2020) has been met, through a reduction of 24 percent between 1995 and 2011.[3]

Early in 2014 the European Commission established an energy policy for the period 2020 to 2030,[4] now pending approval by the European Council and Parliament. The document highlights the EU's current difficulties and those it will face in the midterm. These include the financial crisis, a malfunctioning Emissions Trading System (ETS), high fossil fuel prices, and the EU's dependence on foreign fossil fuels (the EU's oil and gas import bill amounted to more than €400 billion in 2012, 3.1 percent of the union's GDP). Additionally, member states have not always ensured market integration and undistorted competition.

The EU's general aims for 2030 are to progress toward a low-carbon economy, while guaranteeing affordable energy for all consumers as well as regulatory certainty. Some of the main points are a greenhouse gas emission reduction target for domestic EU emissions of 40 percent in 2030 relative to emissions in 1990, as well as a new renewables goal: increasing the share of renewable energy to at least 27 percent by 2030.

A Common Energy Market for Europe

Ever since the mid-nineties, the European Commission's main policy goal in the realm of energy has been the creation of a common market. In order to integrate the distinct national scenes, first markets had to be created, since most member states governed energy through public monopolies.

Two European directives were approved in the late 1990s: one on electricity (1996)[5] and the other on gas (1998),[6] with the aim to liberalize these markets and promote integration of a European energy market. In order to liberalize the markets, the directives advocated for vertically separating (unbundling) gas and electricity providers from the transport and supply organizations (TSOs). The goal was thus to desegregate the vertically integrated state-owned energy companies of the past in order to allow for EU-wide integration. Unbundling initiatives first focused on legal and functional aspects, with ownership unbundling added later in the EU's Third Energy Package, adopted in 2009.

Furthermore, the original directives obliged national governments to set up independent regulatory authorities to settle disputes related to contracts and access to electricity grids and gas pipelines. In 1998 and 1999 two forums were set up by the regulatory authorities—and by initiative of the EC—as platforms for discussing energy cross-border trade and the management of interconnection: the Florence Forum for Electricity and the European Gas Regulatory Forum of Madrid. These annual forums gathered national regulatory authorities, national ministerial representatives, EC officials, electricity and gas producers, distributors, traders, consumers, network users, and power and gas exchange operators.

A central broker of all European national regulators, the Agency for the Cooperation of Energy Regulators (ACER),[7] was finally established in 2009 as a result of a third round of integration initiated by the EC in early 2007.[8]

The External Dimension: Securing Supply

As the EU currently relies on imports for 54 percent of its energy needs,[9] securing supply is of vital interest. The EC proposes three main policy tracks to improve its security of supply. First, continue exploiting and increasing indigenous energy sources such as renewable energy sources, domestic reserves of conventional and unconventional fossil fuels, and nuclear energy. Second, diversify supply countries and routes for imported fossil fuels. Third, improve energy efficiency, including deploying smart grids and having all member states meet the previously agreed objective of ensuring electricity interconnections equivalent to 10 percent of installed production capacity.

Throughout the rest of this chapter, we will focus primarily on the second policy, namely the diversification of sources and supply routes, particularly in the case of natural gas.

Natural Gas in Europe

Natural gas, an increasingly important energy source worldwide, is increasing its share in the EU energy mix and forms the centerpiece of an intricate geopolitical competition to the union's east. Natural gas markets display a number of unique traits, which set this market apart from other energy markets such as those for oil or coal. These characteristics include a regional scope, a historical tendency to long-term contracting (especially in Europe) and government regulation, and the importance of pipeline infrastructure and transit countries.

The Particularities of Natural Gas as a Traded Good

There is no such thing as a global natural gas market: natural gas is produced, transported, and traded through regional, fragmented markets. Its pricing also displays regional differentiation. Outside of North America, where deregulated hub pricing reigns, the majority of natural gas pricing in the world is long term and linked to oil prices. In Europe, in particular, the latter type of pricing was introduced after the discovery of gas in the Netherlands (the Groningen gas field). These long-term, oil-indexed contracts, which typically include take-or-pay clauses (specifying a minimum, pre-set volume of gas per year that the buyer will pay for at the contract price, regardless of whether the volume is taken or not), provide a boost to immature markets, because their reliability ensures the infrastructure investments required for natural gas trade.

When markets grow more mature, however, the arguments for other pricing mechanisms gain ground. Alternatives include government-regulated pricing, or spot pricing based on hub prices, reflecting the market's natural competition. Indeed, a number of recent developments in the world energy scene are leading to more competitive, global natural gas markets. First, it is likely that the supply increase due to the flood of unconventional gas will foster growth of regional gas trading hubs, and thus competition between said hubs. Second, global liquid natural gas (LNG) trade, which doubled over the last decade, facilitates spot market trading.

As stated above, Europe's gas has traditionally been traded in the form of long-term, oil-indexed contracts. However, this scheme has severe downsides. These were clearly uncovered in 2008–10 when oil prices spiraled upward and clung close to the $100/barrel limit and when the gas price spread with the United States widened due to America's sudden gas bounty. Over the past few years, there have been signs of change in Europe's pricing policies.

On the outbreak of the global economic crisis, gas demand dropped and a number of EU member states ultimately managed to negotiate modifications of their long-term contracts with their main supplier, Russian Gazprom. In early 2012 Gazprom made further concessions to a number of its customers, including rebates in the case of excessive gaps between the contract price and the spot price.[10] Overall, it is estimated that 45 percent of gas sold in Europe in 2012 was based on hub prices rather than oil-linked prices,[11] a trend set to increase, especially given the gradual movement toward a more hub-based, competitive global market.

A further particularity of natural gas as an energy source is the importance of transit countries. As demand for gas increases and production from landlocked countries grows, supply arrangements increasingly operate through transit countries. Of course, arrangements through transit countries are more prone to disruption than direct exporter-importer relations. In addition, the more middlemen there are in the equation, the larger the set of diverging economic interests. The EU's campaign to diversify its energy imports away from Russia must take this important factor into account at all times: its efforts inevitably involve transport through additional states.

Current Natural Gas Demand and Supply in the EU

In the EU, natural gas currently makes up 23.4 percent of the energy mix and 22.2 percent of electricity needs. These proportions are similar to global trends, where the respective figures stand at 21.3 percent and 21.9 percent. Nearly three-quarters of the world's proven reserves lie in the Middle East and Eurasia.[12] Generally speaking, the world's reserves of natural gas are ample, and increasing: it is estimated that they have grown by 39 percent over the past twenty years.[13]

Together, Europe and Eurasia produce 31 percent of the world's natural gas. However, the EU countries' share in that percentage is low and decreasing. The Netherlands and the United Kingdom are the EU's main indigenous producers; the latter, in particular, has seen its production drop over the last decade—from 108.4 bcm (billion cubic meters) in 2003 to 57.1 bcm in 2013, while Dutch production is essentially flat. Gas therefore flows into the union from abroad, mainly from Russia and Norway: a member of the European Economic Area (EEA) and the European Free Trade Area (EFTA), Norway continues to increase its production, flirting with Russia for the top spot in EU imports.[14] Meanwhile, the EU's import dependency is expected to increase, from 67 percent in 2011 to 80 percent or more in 2030.

Given this equation of supply and demand, natural gas trade in the region is very intense. In 2011 Europe and Eurasia accounted for the trade of 469.7 bcm of the total 694.6 bcm of international pipeline-supplied natural gas. The infrastructure matches the trend: two-thirds of the world's international natural gas pipelines operate in Europe. The EU already holds some €500 billion of sunk costs in natural gas infrastructure; the EC estimates some €70 billion more will be necessary in the period up to 2020.[15]

Key Gas Infrastructure

With regard to this critical infrastructure, the EC at the end of 2013 published its strategy for long-term energy infrastructure in Europe,[16] defining the following priorities for gas: first, diversify the gas infrastructure; second, expand the Southern Gas Corridor (see below) in order to import about 10 percent of European demand from the Caspian region and the Middle East; third, increase flexibility by developing more LNG terminals and storage facilities; finally, increase indigenous production from the Eastern Mediterranean, from biogas or unconventional sources (see figure 6-1).

The strategy identifies as key the following gas infrastructure:

—North-South gas interconnections in Western Europe ("NSI West Gas"):

—North-South gas interconnections in Central Eastern and Southeastern Europe ("NSI East Gas"): gas infrastructure for regional connections between and in the Baltic Sea region, the Adriatic and Aegean Seas, the Eastern Mediterranean Sea, and the Black Sea.

—Southern Gas Corridor ("SGC"): infrastructure for the transmission of gas from the Caspian Basin, Central Asia, the Middle East, and the Eastern Mediterranean Basin to the EU to enhance diversification of gas supply.

—Baltic Energy Market Interconnection Plan in gas ("BEMIP Gas"): gas infrastructure to end the isolation of the three Baltic states and Finland and their dependency on a single supplier.

Figure 6-1. *Energy Infrastructure—Natural Gas*

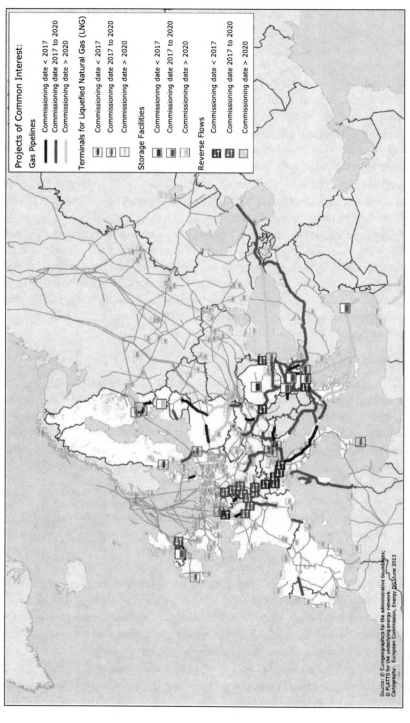

Source: European Commission.

Spotlight on Relations with Russia

One-third of the union's natural gas needs are met by one single supplier: Russia. This tight relationship is precarious, especially for EU members such as Lithuania, Bulgaria, and Estonia, which depend on the Russian giant for 100 percent of their gas needs. Recent power struggles over the nations sandwiched between Russia and western Europe, reminiscent of the cold war, have not eased the minds of policymakers and citizens in Europe's energy-dependent nations.

The long-standing EU-Russian gas relation is symbiotic and delicate: the EU relies on Russian gas to keep its households warm, yet Russia's Gazprom too is dependent on the EU as the market for more than half of its exports (see table 6-1). Throughout the 1960s to 1990s, these relations, rooted in standard long-term contracts, were relatively stable, but the new millennium brought a number of severe supply shocks. The Ukraine gas cutoffs in 2006 and 2009, culminations of Ukraine-Russia (Gazprom) disputes on issues such as payments and pricing, as well as the supply glitches during the 2012 cold snap, heightened the unease about Russia's energy policy.

Many have argued, through a Realpolitik lens, that Russia wields its energy policy as a foreign policy stick. After the end of the cold war, the dissolution of the Soviet Union, and subsequent events such as Russia's economic crisis and NATO's succession of enlargements (in 2004 three ex-Soviet Baltic states joined NATO), Russia's material power was reduced to its energy reserves. Moreover, energy and the Russian state are tightly interwoven: Gazprom is state-controlled, and Moscow depends on energy revenue for half or more of its budget. For Gazprom, in turn, maintaining exports is vital, especially given the low prices it fetches for gas domestically because of government price regulation.In addition, recent global gas developments may threaten Russia's power source. The shale revolution in the United States has upped the ante. Until very recently, Russia's focus has been on conventional sources with few or no plans for shale development. The country is stuck in an old model of production, and the global panorama might just leave Russia stranded. If the United States continues on its path of approval for LNG exports, Russia will face new competition from LNG trade and may see its power to set the conditions for gas export diminish. Moreover, the recent changes and innovation in the global gas markets may indeed expose some of the country's technological backwardness: though a few exploration deals have been inked of late, the development of indigenous unconventional resources is still a distant prospect. All in all, the global gas revolution only adds to Russia's fear of loss of leverage over the EU.

The two parties are very conscious of their natural gas symbiosis. Institutionally, at least, this interdependence was formally recognized in 2013 when the

Table 6-1. *Dependence on Russian Gas among the EU-28 Member States*
Percent

Country	Share of natural gas imported from Russia, 2012
Austria	52
Belgium	43
Bulgaria	100
Croatia	37
Cyprus	0
Czech Republic	81
Denmark	0
Estonia	100
Finland	100
France	17
Germany	40
Greece	55
Hungary	50
Ireland	0
Italy	20
Latvia	100
Lithuania	100
Luxembourg	28
Malta	0
Netherlands	6
Poland	54
Portugal	0
Romania	24
Slovakia	63
Slovenia	57
Spain	0
Sweden	100
United Kingdom	0

Sources: BP, *BP Statistical Review of World Energy 2013;* Eurostat; U.S. Energy Information Administration, as cited in Michael Ratner and others, *Europe's Energy Security: Options and Challenges to Natural Gas Supply Diversification;* CRS Reports for Congress, R42405 (Washington: Congressional Research Service, August 20, 2013).

Roadmap for Energy Cooperation to 2050 was signed by EU Energy Commissioner Guenther Oettinger and Russian Energy Minister Alexander Novak.[17] The EU and Russia, however, uphold very different paradigms with regard to energy policy. As described earlier here, EU policy is mainly focused on market liberalization and a campaign of vertical unbundling, while in Russia, Gazprom still serves very much as a state instrument—this despite stipulations in the aforementioned road map that the Russian gas market be liberalized.

The Southern Gas Corridor

The EU's quest for energy security and for a unionwide energy policy has been lengthy. Supply diversification and secure transit routes are key ingredients. In particular, adding a fourth external supplier to the three established sources—the North Sea, Algeria, and Russia—is a priority. Seeking alternative supplies of gas, away from Russia, as well as more secure supply routes (avoiding the unstable transit country of Ukraine, for example), the EU aims to construct a fourth energy corridor, the so-called Southern Gas Corridor (SGC), in order to better access supplies from southeastern Europe and the Caspian.

This corridor, a network of gas pipelines reaching from the gas lands of the southeast (the Caspian, Central Asia, and even potentially the Middle East) to the EU's power plants and homes, has no pre-established route. Instead, over the course of the past dozen years, a number of competing and interconnecting pipelines have been proposed to form the corridor: Nabucco, TAP, TANAP, as well as Russia's South Stream (see figure 6-2). While Nabucco has stalled, TAP has just recently secured the gas supply and investment it needs, and is now starting construction. Meanwhile, TANAP is also under construction and Russia has initiated work on its end of South Stream.

Geopolitics, geo-economics, and commercial interests all converge in matters concerning these pipelines. Each represents a crossroads where states, the EU, and business meet, with each entity defending its interests from a variety of perspectives—supplier, transit country, or consumer.

The geopolitical competition over the Southern Corridor essentially played out in a recent episode between two EU-sponsored pipelines—TAP and Nabucco West—and intensified with a Russian counterproject, South Stream. TAP is the more modest proposal, which essentially involves connecting existing Italian and Turkish pipelines to pipe gas from Turkey's western border to Austria via Italy and Greece. Nabucco West, a much more ambitious project, would connect Turkey and Austria via Bulgaria, Romania, and Hungary.

We now trace this competition, beginning with the original Nabucco project, started in 2002, through to the counterproposals of South Stream and rival

Figure 6-2. *The Southern Gas Corridor—Competing Pipelines*

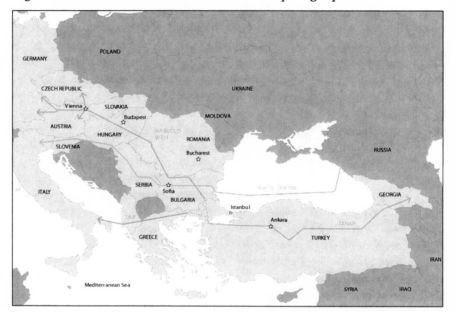

TANAP and the final struggle between TAP and Nabucco West. Last, we will summarize the underlying rationale for the ultimate pipeline decisions in more detail.

Nabucco, the Original

In 2002, before signing a protocol of intention to construct the pipeline Nabucco, the five partners (from Austria, Turkey, Hungary, Romania, and Bulgaria) attended a performance of Verdi's famous opera of the same name. The project was one of the first to be proposed in the Southern Gas Corridor (see figure 6-3). Austria's OMV and Turkey's BOTAŞ initially discussed the pipeline in early 2002, with MOL (Hungary), Bulgargaz (Bulgaria), Transgaz (Romania), and RWE (Germany) signing on later.[18] Each partner held one-sixth of the venture.

The European Commission threw its weight behind the project, financing feasibility studies for Nabucco—as well as for ITGI (Interconnector Turkey-Greece-Italy) and White Stream—through the European Energy Program for Recovery (EEPR).[19] The project was likewise backed by the United States. In 2009, for instance, Special Envoy Richard Morningstar represented the United States at the signing of the intergovernmental agreement among the five states along Nabucco's route: Turkey, Romania, Bulgaria, Hungary, and Austria.

The project envisioned for Nabucco was grand: a 3,300–3,900 km pipeline, running from Erzurum in eastern Turkey to the central European gas hub in

Figure 6-3. *Nabucco*

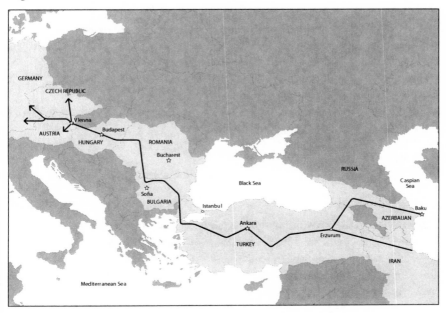

Austria's Baumgarten an der March. The sheer length of the pipeline would allow some EU states most dependent on Russian gas to be hooked up directly to sources from the Caspian and beyond: in Erzurum, Nabucco would connect to the South Caucasus Pipeline.[20] The pipeline's initial capacity was estimated at some 13 bcm, with predictions for an increase to approximately 31 bcm in later years.

The Search for Supply

Ambitious plans for Nabucco envisioned its eastern starting point as an access point not only for Caspian gas, but also for resources from the Middle East and possibly even North Africa (Egypt, in particular). However, from the very beginning, obtaining firm commitments from suppliers in order to ensure diversified sourcing (one of the main goals in the project) was problematic. The Middle East proved unworkable as a source for gas to run through Nabucco: northern Iraq's attractive gas fields were not yet ripe for picking, due to the uncertainty regarding their governance.[21] Infrastructure was a further inhibitor: accessing Iraq's gas would require construction of an extra connector to hook up to existing pipelines heading toward Europe. And Iran, bordering the Caspian, still had its resources locked away because of sanctions related to its nuclear program. (See table 6-2.)

The remaining Caspian nations found—and find—themselves in the middle of a tug-of-war. Turkmenistan holds the largest reserves of natural gas in the

Table 6-2. *Nabucco's Possible Sources of Gas, 2013*

Country	Natural gas proven reserves, end 2013	
	In trillion cubic meters	*Share of world total*
Iran	33.8	18.2
Russia	31.3	16.8
Turkmenistan	17.5	9.4
Iraq	3.6	1.9
Kazakhstan	1.5	0.8
Uzbekistan	1.1	0.6
Azerbaijan	0.9	0.5

Source: BP, *BP Statistical Review of World Energy 2014.*

Caspian, is investing in a number of recently reassessed fields (such as the South Yolotan-Osman field), and already exports to Russia and, since 2009, to China.[22] In its efforts to diversify its export markets, nevertheless, it has looked northwest. In order to transport gas to Europe, it would have to cross the Caspian Sea, and plans for a Trans-Caspian Gas Pipeline have been discussed at various junctures. However, political and legal disputes with the Caspian littoral states—chiefly muscular Russia, as well as Iran—have prevented any true progress up to now. In the meantime, China has edged in, offering investment and loans for Turkmen gas field development and pipeline construction.

With Turkmenistan's supplies unattainable and Kazakhstan still more concentrated on oil than gas production, the Nabucco partners turned to Azerbaijan, whose giant offshore Shah Deniz gas field lies just 70 km from the capital, Baku, on the South Caspian Sea (see box 6-1). More important, however, Shah Deniz gas could easily be transported directly to Europe (via Turkey) without having to traverse countries such as Russia or Iran. Both the European Commission and the United States, therefore, pushed hard to secure Azeri gas supplies for the EU and Nabucco—all of this while Russia's Gazprom eyed the same final markets.

The Competition

As the Nabucco partners developed detailed engineering plans for the pipeline and attempted to secure diversified supply, Russia launched in 2007 a pipeline project of its own: South Stream (see box 6-2). This pipeline was designed, depending on interpretation, either to bypass troublesome transit states along its transport route, such as Ukraine or Belarus, or to thwart the EU's attempts to diversify its gas imports away from Russian dominance.

Box 6-1. *The Shah Deniz Gas Field and Its Consortium: Source and Judge*

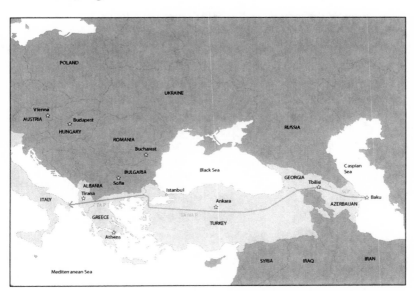

Azerbaijan's Shah Deniz field is estimated to hold reserves of up to 1,200 bcm of gas and 3 billion barrels of oil equivalent. Discovered in 1999, the field began operating in 2006. It currently produces 9 bcm of gas per year, but is expected to increase by another 16 bcm/year from 2018 as part of its stage 2 development. The field is operated by BP, with a 25.5 percent share in the Shah Deniz Consortium (SDC), which is furthermore composed of Statoil (25.5 percent, Norway), SOCAR (10 percent, Azerbaijan), Total S.A. (10 percent, France), LUKoil (10 percent, Russia), NIOC (10 percent, Iran), and TPAO (9 percent, Turkey).[a]

The SDC connects into the South Caucasus Pipeline (SCP, in darker color above),[b] which is operated by BP and carries 7 bcm/year from Baku (Azerbaijan) to Erzurum (Turkey) through Georgia. It is 692 km long, running along the same corridor as the much smaller Baku–Tbilisi–Ceyhan (BTC) crude oil pipeline. The SCP is currently under expansion, as part of the stage 2 development of the Shah Deniz Consortium, and will triple its capacity once enlarged.

a. SOCAR = State Oil Company of Azerbaijan Republic; NIOC = National Iranian Oil Company; TPAO = Türkiye Petrolleri Anonim Ortaklığı, Turkey's national oil and gas company.

b. Also known as Baku-Tbilisi-Erzurum (BTE) Pipeline or Shah Deniz Pipeline.

Box 6-2. *The South Stream Pipeline*

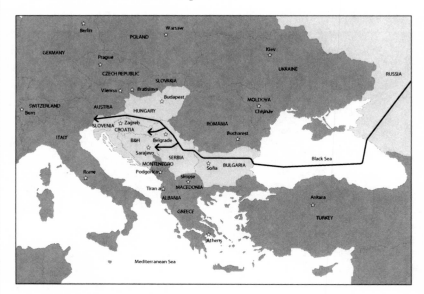

South Stream is the grandest pipeline presently proposed in the Southern Corridor, stretching for 2,380 km. Announced in 2007 and under construction at this writing, Russian officials have estimated South Stream will be operational by 2015. It will transport 28 bcm/year initially, though it is planned to be enlarged fourfold to 63 bcm/year by 2018. Costs have been estimated as €16 billion.

Shareholders of South Stream's offshore component are Gazprom (50 percent, Russia), Eni (20 percent, Italy), and EdF (Électricité de France S.A.) and Wintershall (France and Germany, 15 percent each). The offshore tract will connect Russia with Bulgaria. From there on the pipeline will travel over land to Serbia, Hungary, and Slovenia, finally connecting with northeastern Italy.

Impressively, during 2008–10, Russia signed agreements with all European transit countries committing them to South Stream and even signed memorandums of understanding with Greece and Austria.

After much speculation and fierce competition with other pipeline projects, Nabucco suffered a second blow in the form of the Trans Anatolian Pipeline (TANAP), running from Georgia to Greece (see box 6-3). This route would essentially make Nabucco's eastern section unviable.

When SOCAR (Azerbaijan's state oil company), BOTAŞ, and TPAO (Turkey) agreed to construct TANAP, the Nabucco project started to unravel. In

Box 6-3. *The Trans Anatolian Pipeline*

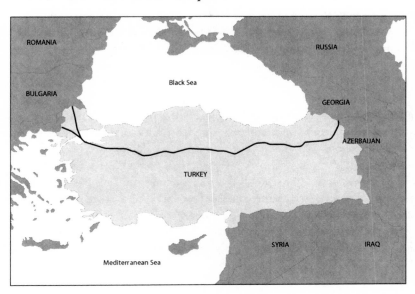

The Trans Anatolian Pipeline (TANAP), announced in 2011, will start construction in 2014 and cost €10 billion. It runs across Turkey, spanning 1,900 km from Georgia to Greece and will at first carry 6 bcm/year on initial operation in 2018. It may be expanded to 24 bcm/year. Founded and owned originally by SOCAR (80 percent, Azerbaijan), BOTAŞ (15 percent, Turkey), and TPAO (5 percent, Turkey), BP is expected to join in the ownership soon.

From its starting point on the Turkish-Georgian border, connections to the Eastern Mediterranean, Iran, and Iraq are possible and planned. However, so far TANAP is only fed by Shah Deniz, through the South Caucasus Pipeline.

committing their support to TANAP, the Turkish and Azeri governments effectively killed Nabucco: TANAP stole away the first two-thirds of Nabucco's planned route, as well as its direct feed-in from the Azeri Shah Deniz field.

One of the chief reasons for TANAP's victory over Nabucco was its ownership structure. The earlier proposals for pipelines across Turkey, notably the eastern section of the initial Nabucco design ("Nabucco East"), would have been predominantly owned by international companies from downstream, consuming countries. TANAP, on the other hand, was founded and owned by Azeri SOCAR and Turkish TPAO, members of the consortium developing the Shah Deniz field, which will provide the initial gas.[23] Turkey and Azerbaijan thus preferred TANAP to Nabucco's eastern tract.

Struggling Forward: Nabucco West

Nevertheless, the Nabucco consortium did not surrender, proposing in May 2012 a severely shortened version of its original route. This proposal, dubbed Nabucco West, would span the 1,300 km from TANAP's end at the Turkey-Bulgaria border to Baumgarten in Austria (Nabucco's original target). However, the proposal faced stiff competition from three other pipelines: TAP (see box 6-4), SEEP, and ITGI.[24]

Though the Shah Deniz field holds enough gas resources to supply both TAP and Nabucco West, this capacity is not yet available: such volumes would require further development to be completed, and this is not estimated for another decade at least. Therefore, SDC had to elect which one of the two pipelines to supply.

Important to note is that for either of the two EU-sponsored pipelines (Nabucco West or TAP) to be constructed, each must prove a business case. This, in essence, comes down to the construction and maintenance costs, on the one hand, and the demand and supply of gas on the other. Thus, the pipelines' viability depends crucially on having guarantees that they would have sufficient supplies. The decision on whom to supply, in turn, resides exclusively with the SDC.

And the Winner Is . . .

In June 2013 the Shah Deniz Consortium announced it had chosen the Trans Adriatic Pipeline (TAP) over Nabucco West. Here we offer a set of reasons to explain why TAP was the chosen route.

A first key issue, though perhaps not the central one, was economic viability. Nabucco West was four times more expensive than TAP, making the latter a much more viable and realistic option. However, it was the combination of cost and supply and demand uncertainty that exacerbated the doubts over Nabucco West's viability (see table 6-3).

As for supply, the only source available for Nabucco West in the short and mid-term was Azerbaijan's Shah Deniz field, because Iran remains under sanctions, northern Iraq's export rights are far from being settled, prospect of a pipeline crossing Syria from north to south remains highly dubious, and Turkmenistan's gas is a sea away, lacking the Trans-Caspian Pipeline required for transport. However, the Nabucco consortium found itself in a serious bind regarding supply: banks and customers were unwilling to commit to the project before supplies were guaranteed, while Azerbaijan refused to sign any delivery contract before being certain of the pipeline's viability.

In terms of demand, Russia's South Stream project introduced uncertainty regarding the actual demand for gas from southeastern European countries. Although the pipeline's viability remains doubtful, South Stream's target

Box 6-4. *The Trans Adriatic Pipeline*

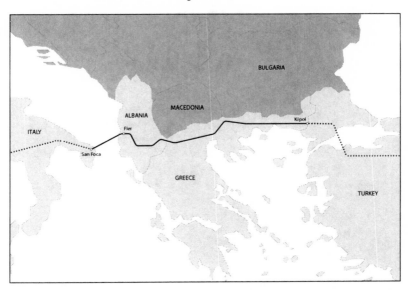

The Trans Adriatic Pipeline (TAP) will connect Italy with the Trans Anatolian Pipeline (TANAP) near the Turkish-Greek border. Promoted initially by Axpo of Switzerland, Norway's Statoil, and E.ON of Germany, it now also includes as shareholders BP (United Kingdom), Total (France), SOCAR (Azerbaijan), and Fluxys (Belgium).

Running for 870 km, TAP will be capable of transporting 10 bcm of gas per year, expandable to 20.[a] The pipeline would also be capable of supplying the Balkans through the proposed Ionian Adriatic Pipeline (IAP), which would run 516 km through Albania, Montenegro, Bosnia and Herzegovina, and Croatia, and have a capacity of 5 bcm/year.

Additionally, if the Greece Bulgaria Interconnector (IGB) is built (the rights to which are owned 25 percent by the Greek DEPA, 25 percent by the private Italian company Edison, and 50 percent by the Bulgarian state energy holding company EAD), TAP could provide gas to Bulgaria, one of the EU states most dependent on imports from Russia.

a. The 10 bcm it will initially carry to Europe represents only around 2 percent of the EU's gas consumption.

countries have already signed a long list of deals commiting them to Russian gas. Even if Nabucco had been built, then, Balkan states might have continued to buy Russian gas.

Second, the distribution of shareholders over the different projects also played a role. Interestingly, Nabucco West did not include a single entity from a supply country—in particular Azerbaijan's SOCAR. In contrast, SOCAR holds

Table 6-3. *Comparing the Pipeline Bids*

	TANAP	Nabucco West	TAP	South Stream
Capacity (bcm/year)	6–24	10–23	10–20	16–63
Cost (billions of euros)	10	7.9	1.5	28
Length (km)	1,900	1,329	870	2,380
Shareholders (shares in percent)	SOCAR: 80 BOTAŞ: 15 TPAO: 5 (BP will join project soon)	BOTAŞ: 16.67 BEH: 16.67 GDF Suez: 9 MOL: 16.67 OMV: 24.34 Transgaz: 16.67	BP: 20 SOCAR: 20 Statoil: 20 Fluxys: 16 Total S.A.: 10 E.ON: 9 Axpo: 5	Gazprom: 50 Eni: 20 EdF: 15 Wintershall: 15*
Transit	Turkey Georgia	Turkey Bulgaria Romania Hungary Austria	Italy Albania Greece Turkey	Russia Bulgaria Serbia Hungary Slovenia Italy
Announced	2011	2002	2003	2007
Construction	2014		2015	2012
Operational	2018		2018	2015

*Note: Shares here apply to the offshore section.

20 percent in TAP. Moreover, SOCAR recently acquired Greece's privatized natural gas distribution company, DESFA, a necessary piece to connect TAP to the Balkans.[25]

Third, the shadow of confronting Russia was also part of the equation. Nabucco West directly competes with South Stream. TAP, on the other hand, is less of a competitor given that the planned interconnections to the Baltic and the southeastern countries—through the Ionian Adriatic Pipeline, which will go from Albania to Croatia, and the Interconnection Greece-Bulgaria, respectively—will hold half the capacity of Nabucco West (5 bcm/year each as opposed to 10). It seems reasonable to think that both Azerbaijan and (to a lesser extent) Turkey opted for TAP to avoid direct competition with Russia.

The Shah Deniz Consortium partners may have reasoned in a similar vein. According to some estimates, the majority of BP's growth over the coming decades will take place in Russia, through its participation in Rosneft. In particular, Arctic reserves, to which Rosneft has rights, are considered BP's central

Table 6-4. *Country Interests per Pipeline*

	Nabucco West	TAP	South Stream
Key countries			
Russia	(blank)	(blank)	(dark)
Turkey	(light gray)	(gray)	(blank)
Azerbaijan	(gray)	(gray)	(blank)
EU	(gray)	(light gray)	(blank)
Other suppliers			
Turkmenistan	(gray)	(light gray)	(blank)
Iran	(gray)	(blank)	(blank)
Iraq	(gray)	(blank)	(blank)
Major transit countries			
Italy	(blank)	(gray)	(light gray)
Bulgaria	(gray)	(light gray)	(gray)
Austria	(gray)	(light gray)	(blank)
Greece	(blank)	(gray)	(blank)
Other transit countries			
Romania	(gray)	(blank)	(blank)
Serbia	(blank)	(blank)	(gray)
Hungary	(gray)	(blank)	(gray)
Slovenia	(gray)	(blank)	(gray)
Croatia	(gray)	(light gray)	(gray)
Albania	(blank)	(gray)	(blank)
Montenegro	(blank)	(gray)	(blank)
Georgia	(light gray)	(gray)	(blank)

Note: Darker tint indicates greater interest in a pipeline by that country.

growth driver for the future. It is thus reasonable to argue that BP was hesitant to confront Russia directly.

Moreover, the countries that would have benefited most from a potential Nabucco West pipeline did not put their full weight into the project, given that South Stream represented an equal substitute. And in this respect, Russia was extremely quick to sign supply agreements with most of these countries.

Table 6-4 shows schematically the countries favoring each project (the darker the shade, the stronger the preference). The only key player who favored Nabucco was the EU as a whole. Nabucco was not backed by a single realistic supplier, though disconnected second-order suppliers—such as Turkmenistan, Iran, and Iraq—did favor Nabucco due to its larger capacity in the Balkans and southeast Europe. However, these countries had little influence on the decision.

Conclusion

Today, the EU imports 67 percent of its natural gas. However, the EC expects that in just twenty years, the EU-28 (that is, including its newest member, Croatia) could end up relying on imports for more than four-fifths of its needs. This degree of reliance on outside sources is precarious, especially when much of the supply is concentrated in the hands of a small selection of big suppliers. One of the EU's main concerns is its reliance on Russia for one-third of its supply of natural gas. Numerous episodes over the past decade, including the Ukraine disputes in 2006 and 2009, as well as the Crimea crisis in 2014, significantly heighten anxiety over Russia's foreign and energy policy objectives.

The EU thus aims to increase its energy security, including options such as increasing natural gas storage facilities to weather supply shocks, increasing energy efficiency, and redoubling efforts to construct regasification plants. However, the analysis presented here has zoomed in on the policy option of diversification of supply and transit routes, namely through the establishment of a fourth external source of gas—through a network of pipelines called the Southern Corridor.

The geo-economic and geopolitical quest to establish this corridor has revealed the interests and direct, and indirect, tools of all actors involved. More than a decade ago, an ambitious suggestion for a pipeline stretching over 3,000 km, and capable of importing gas from Iraq, Iran, Turkmenistan, Azerbaijan, and Egypt (Nabucco), led to various proposals, which were presented and discarded until a compromise was ultimately found: the TANAP and TAP combination. This pipeline will supply Europe with Azeri gas through Italy, which is capable of distributing it to central Europe, the Balkans and Southeast Europe but without completely antagonizing Europe's main gas supplier, Russia.

Nabucco is dead; the final list of key infrastructure published by the EC by the end of 2013 endorsed TAP, TANAP, IAP, and IGB, but does not include Nabucco. All in all, Europe has gained access to a Caspian source (Azerbaijan), although it is important to recall that the new 10 bcm/year that TAP will introduce into Europe only represents 2 percent of its future gas needs. Moreover, access to Turkmenistan's huge gas reserves (which eclipse Azeri estimates) will be extremely difficult given Iran's and Russia's opposition to an offshore pipeline across the Caspian.

In other words, the EU has partly achieved its policy objective of diversifying supplies, but at 2 percent, the shift is far from epic. Unless sharp crises such as the 2014 events in Crimea lead to rapid and creative policy reconsiderations (and beyond simple *calls* for an "energy union" to actual supranational cooperation), the EU is set to depend on Russia for gas for the foreseeable future. Europe still has a long road ahead in its quest to further diversify suppliers, increase domestic extraction, and shift to alternative energy sources.

Figure 6-4. *Key European Commission Projects of Common Interest Relative to the Southern Gas Corridor*

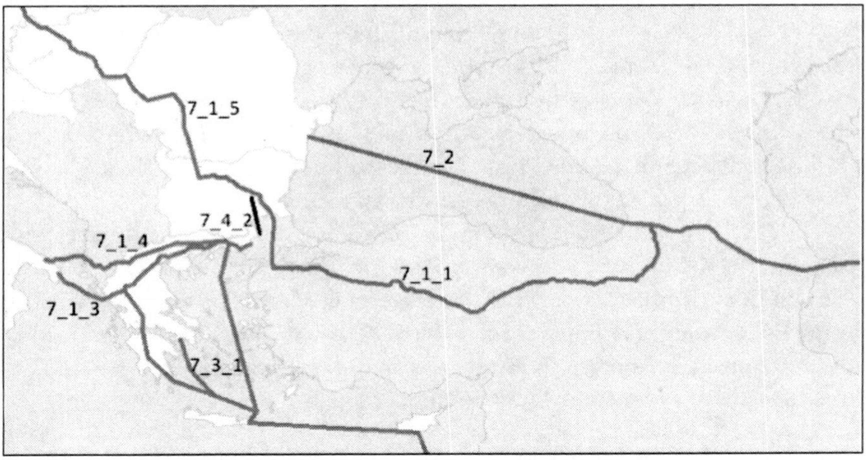

Source: DG Energy, European Commission; interactive map, labeling by the authors.

Appendix

The European Commission's list of key infrastructure relative to the Southern Gas Corridor (and the related North-South Interconnections in Eastern Europe) is spelled out in the document *Technical Information on Projects of Common Interest* (COM 2013).[26] Being included in this list is key, since it allows the selected projects to vie for official EU financing via EC grants, the Connecting Europe Facility, or the European Investment Bank.

The following projects are all, at a minimum, in the feasibility study stage and have a set commissioning date (see figure 6-4; numbers below correspond to those in the figure). Projects of Common Interest (PCIs) related to the priority Southern Gas Corridor include:

—(7.2)—The easternmost sections of this project include TCP & SCP: Trans-Caspian Pipeline (TCP): Offshore pipeline in the Caspian sea with a length of 300 km and a capacity of 32 bcm/year. Will connect Turkmenistan with the San-gachal terminal in Azerbaijan. South Caucasus Pipeline (SCP): Upgrade of the existing pipeline system between Azerbaijan and Turkey via Georgia, with capacity upgrades of 16 bcm/year (or 5 bcm/year depending on the tranche) by 2019.

—(7.1.1)—TANAP: New onshore and offshore pipeline between the eastern and western borders of Turkey with a length of 1,900 km and a capacity of 16 bcm/year.

—(7.1.3)—TAP: New onshore and offshore pipeline between Greece, Turkey, and Italy with a total length of 871 km and a normal capacity of 27.1 mcm/day (initial throughput capacity of 10 bcm/year).

—(7.1.4)—ITGI: New onshore and offshore pipeline between Greece and Italy with a total length of 823 km and a capacity of 10 bcm/year.

—(7.1.5)—Gas pipeline from Bulgaria to Austria via Romania and Hungary, with a length of 1,318 km and capacity of 23 bcm/year. White Stream (7.2.3): Onshore and offshore pipeline from Georgia to Romania via the Black Sea with a total length of 1,250 km and a capacity of 46 mcm/day.

—(7.3.1)—Pipeline from offshore Cyprus to Greece mainland via Crete with a length of 1,500 km and a capacity of 24.5 mcm/day.

In addition to the above, the list of Projects of Common Interest identified by the EC as being very important for the SGC also includes the construction of LNG terminals and storage facilities, as well as the remodeling of existing pipelines to facilitate bidirectional functioning.

List of Abbreviations and Acronyms

Acronym	In full	Country, in cases of companies
bcm	billion cubic meters	
BOTAŞ	BOTAŞ Petroleum Pipeline Corporation	Turkey
DEPA	Dimosia Epichirisi Paroxis Aeriou (Greek government's natural gas contracting company)	Greece
DESFA	DESFA The National Natural Gas System Operator	Greece
EAD	Bulgarian Energy Holding EAD (BEH EAD)	Bulgaria
EC	European Commission	
EdF	Électricité de France S.A.	France
IAP	Ionian Adriatic Pipeline	
IGB	Greece Bulgaria Interconnector	
ITGI	Interconnector Turkey-Greece-Italy	
MOL	Magyar Olaj- és Gázipari Nyilvánosan működő Részvénytársaság, or Hungarian Oil and Gas Public Limited Company	Hungary
mcm	million cubic meters	
RWE	Rheinisch-Westfälisches Elektrizitätswerk AG (until 1990)	Germany
SDC	Shah Deniz Consortium	
SEEP	South East Europe Pipeline	
SOCAR	State Oil Company of Azerbaijan Republic	Azerbaijan
TANAP	Trans Anatolian Pipeline	
TAP	Trans Adriatic Pipeline	
tcm	trillion cubic meters	
TPAO	Türkiye Petrolleri Anonim Ortaklığı (Turkey's national oil and gas company)	Turkey

Notes

1. European Commission Joint Research Centre, *Unconventional Gas: Potential Energy Market Impacts in the European Union* (JRC 70481). Luxembourg: Publications Office of the European Union, 2012 (http://ec.europa.eu/dgs/jrc/downloads/jrc_report_2012_09_unconventional_gas.pdf).

2. European Commission, Eurostat data for 2011, published in April 2013. Figures are rounded.

3. European Commission, *Communication from the Commission to the European Parliament, the Council, the European Economic and Social Committee and the Committee of the Regions: A Policy Framework for Climate and Energy in the Period from 2020 to 2030* (COM/2014/015), 2014 (http://eur-lex.europa.eu/legal-content/EN/TXT/HTML/?uri=CELEX:52014DC0015&from=EN).

4. Ibid.

5. Directive 96/92/EC of the European Parliament and of the Council of December 19, 1996, concerning common rules for the internal market in electricity.

6. Directive 98/30/EC of the European Parliament and of the Council of June 22, 1998, concerning common rules for the internal market in natural gas.

7. ACER was created by the ERGEG (European Regulators' Group for Electricity and Gas), which was established in 2003 and acted as an official advisory body to the EC in relation to the integration of European gas and power markets, by both assessing the implementation of current regulation and proposing future regulation.

8. See European Commission, *Communication from the Commission to the European Council and the European Parliament: An Energy Policy for Europe* (COM/2007/0001) (http://eur-lex.europa.eu/legal-content/EN/TXT/HTML/?uri=CELEX:52007DC0001&from=EN).

9. European Commission, *EU Energy in Figures: Statistical Pocketbook 2013* (Luxembourg: Publications Office of the European Union, 2013) (http://ec.europa.eu/energy/publications/doc/2013_pocketbook.pdf).

10. Jonathan Stern, "International Gas Pricing in Europe and Asia: A Crisis of Fundamentals," *Energy Policy* 64 (2014): 43–48.

11. International Gas Union, *Wholesale Gas Price Survey—2013 Edition. A Global Review of Price Formation Mechanisms 2005–2012* (Fornebu, Norway, 2013) (www.igu.org/sites/default/files/node-page-field_file/IGU%20-%20Wholesale%20Gas%20Price%20Survey%20-%202013%20Edition.pdf).

12. U.S. Energy Information Administration (EIA), *International Energy Outlook 2013* (DOE/EIA-0484(2013)) (Washington, 2013).

13. "Worldwide Look at Reserves and Production," *Oil and Gas Journal* 110, no. 12 (2012): 28–31.

14. Ibid. Norway's production increased by more than 12 percent in 2012, according to BP data.

15. European Commission, *Proposal for a Regulation of the European Parliament and of the Council on Guidelines for Trans-European Energy Infrastructure and Repealing Decision No 1364/2006/EC.* (COM(2011) 658), 2011.

16. European Commission, *Communication from the Commission to the European Parliament, the Council, the European Economic and Social Committee and the Committee of the Regions: Long-Term Infrastructure Vision for Europe and Beyond* (COM/2013/0711), 2013 (http://eur-lex.europa.eu/legal-content/EN/TXT/HTML/?uri=CELEX:52013DC 0711&from=EN).

17. EU-Russia Energy Dialogue, *Roadmap EU-Russia Energy Cooperation until 2050,* 2013 (http://ec.europa.eu/energy/international/russia/doc/2013_03_eu_russia_road map_2050_signed.pdf).

18. Austria: Österreichischen Mineralölverwaltung Aktiengesellschaft (OMV); Turkey: BOTAŞ Petroleum Pipeline Corporation; Germany: until 1990, Rheinisch-Westfälisches Elektrizitätswerk (RWE); Hungary: Magyar Olaj-és Gázipari Nyilvánosan működő Részvénytársaság (MOL), or Hungarian Oil and Gas Public Limited Company. In early 2013, RWE sold its shares (16.67 percent) to OMV, which in May 2013 sold 9 percent of the shares to GdF Suez.

19. White Stream was proposed to begin in Georgia, cross the Black Sea, and land in either Romania or the Crimean Peninsula.

20. This pipeline runs 692 km from Baku (Azerbaijan) to Erzurum (Turkey) through Georgia, along the same corridor as the Baku-Tbilisi-Ceyhan (BTC) crude oil pipeline.

21. Perspectives have improved of late, thanks to the Kurdish government's newly found maneuvering room, which has widened as the main players grow more preoccupied with other sources of turmoil in the region.

22. According to the EIA, 52 percent of Turkmenistan's natural gas exports currently are destined for China.

23. This was part of a strategy, as energy security specialist John Roberts puts it, "in which the [pipeline] owners would control both intake and offtake and thus be able to ensure contractual commitments were met" (Caspian Research Institute: http://69.195.1 24.211/~caspian7/2012/11/30/tanap-ratification-seals-the-southern-corridor-in-place//).

24. SEEP, the South East Europe Pipeline, was a BP-backed project that would extend from Bulgaria to central Europe.

25. At first, it seemed Greece's entire natural gas trading system was set for a Russian takeover: Gazprom made a lone bid for DEPA (the Greek government's natural gas contracting company) when the Greek government sought to privatize its energy sector, while Sintez (a Russian firm apparently under indirect Gazprom control) simultaneously bid to acquire DESFA's domestic gas pipelines. However, the European Commission intervened indirectly shortly before the SDC decision on TAP versus Nabucco West. By insisting that the market liberalization directives of its Third Energy Package would be applied, the EC blocked Gazprom from controlling a monopoly in the operation of Greece's national gas grid. After the EC's intervention, Gazprom and Sintez withdrew, and Azerbaijan's SOCAR stepped in to acquire DESFA.

26. European Commission. *Technical Information on Projects of Common Interest Accompanying the Commission Delegated Regulation (EU) No 1391/2013 of 14 October 2013 amending Regulation (EU) 347/2013 of the European Parliament and of the Council on Guidelines for Trans-European Energy Infrastructure as Regards the Union List of Projects of Common Interest,* 2013(http://ec.europa.eu/energy/infrastructure/pci/doc/com_2013_0711_technical_en.pdf).

7

Energy Rivalry between India and China: Less than Meets the Eye?

C. RAJA MOHAN AND LYDIA POWELL

Today, China and, to a lesser extent, India are the most dynamic and rapidly changing factors in the energy market. In the next two decades, their importance will grow even further. By 2035 China and India are expected to consolidate their respective positions as the world's largest and third largest energy consumers.[1] China's energy demand is likely to grow to become 77 percent larger than that of the United States, the second largest, while India's energy demand is expected to be 69 percent of the energy demand in the United States.[2] The unprecedented energy demand from India and China is expected to unsettle the global energy order hitherto dominated by the United States. Until the early 2000s, the United States was a large and growing oil market, the ultimate dream of producers in the Organization of Petroleum Exporting Countries (OPEC). Oil imports of the United States were equal to the total imports of China and Japan.[3] The United States was the only player others needed to interact with as it had sufficient market and military power to induce change in the energy system if necessary.[4]

China and India could not be more different. Their demand is growing at a time of perceived resource scarcity and constrained resource use and is therefore seen to be "challenging" rather than "driving" the global market. China and India do not participate in organizations such as the International Energy Agency (IEA) that coordinate cooperation among oil importers. The new energy silk road between oil producers in the Middle East and oil consumers in Asia has generated concerns over an unwelcome nexus in the industrial world.[5]

While China's and India's aggregate levels of energy consumption are stagger-ing and comparable to those of rich economies, their qualitative or per capita levels of consumption are comparable to those of some of the poorer develop-ing economies. China's energy consumption per capita is about three times that of India, but it is well below average levels for the Organization for Economic Cooperation and Development (OECD).[6] India's per capita levels of energy con-sumption are comparable to those of sub-Saharan Africa. This inherent contra-diction between the international and domestic dimensions of energy security in China and India is influencing the narratives on energy security and leading to some interpretations that are largely speculative.

One of the presumptions in these narratives is that both China and India dis-regard the market mechanism as a means to energy security. Given that the mar-ket has proved to be the most successful instrument in ensuring the energy secu-rity of industrial nations, China's and India's failure to embrace markets is seen as a deliberate choice. The increasing presence of Chinese and Indian national oil companies (NOCs) is read as a hedge against the market, and the competition between Chinese and Indian oil companies for hydrocarbon assets is interpreted as a geopolitical conflict between nations rather than as a commercial competi-tion between companies. This, in turn, is feeding the fear of military conflict between the two nations, particularly over energy transport corridors.

This chapter examines the validity of these narratives and, if necessary, con-tests them. While policy goals such as self-reliance that go against the philoso-phy of the market do persist in both nations, they are not necessarily driven by nationalist agendas. Nor is there any evidence to confirm the belief that Indian and Chinese NOCs undermine the reliability of the global oil market. China's and, more important, India's key energy challenges are domestic in nature but subject to international market and regulatory pressures. Their responses are often suboptimal compromises between these competing demands.

Energy Rivalry: In the Eyes of the Beholder?

The Pulitzer Prize–winning author Daniel Yergin's observation that some views on China's energy security come perilously close to "shortages equal security threat" scenarios of the 1970s aptly captures prevailing opinions on India as well.[7] The energy security strategies of China and India are described as state-driven or "realist" approaches that are fundamentally opposed to the predominantly market-based strategies of the industrial world.[8] India and China are also said to have a preference for regimes and empires rather than markets and institu-tions, and this preference is seen to be enabling them to obtain energy resources without participating in any international mechanism. Their state-driven energy systems are said to guarantee national strategic interests more effectively than market-driven systems and to enable them to postpone indefinitely far-reaching political, judicial, social, and economic reforms.[9]

Some observations take the "whole" for the "part" or the "part" for the "whole." The large volumes of energy demand from these countries are projected as unjustified or irresponsible consumption and are described with captions such as "Asia's insatiable appetite for oil"[10] and "big appetites take seats at the oil table,"[11] despite the fact that even in 2035 China's energy consumption will only be 52 percent of that in the United States on a per capita basis. Indian per capita energy consumption will be much lower and will touch the level of 1 ton oil-equivalent per capita, which is considered to be the bare minimum required for a decent quality of life, only in 2035.[12]

The relentless quest of Chinese and Indian NOCs for equity investments in oil and gas assets around the world is often perceived as the single most important energy security "strategy" of China and India and is portrayed as a zero-sum competition for energy resources that will, among other things, lock up energy supplies and undermine energy security for the rest of the world.[13] China's and India's attempt to deliver energy security through bilateral arrangements and equity investments in oil-producing countries is often interpreted as evidence of their strategic approach to energy security as opposed to a more market-oriented approach.[14]

Greater import dependence and long transport routes from producers are seen to be creating vulnerabilities for China and India similar to those of Japan in the 1970s, and these, in turn are seen to be driving their nationalist energy strategies.[15] Japan (and France) pursued a "go it alone" energy strategy to mitigate vulnerabilities following the oil crises of the 1970s, but it was a partner in the global system led by the United States and a member of the IEA safety net. The fear now is that China and India will "go it alone," free riding on the energy security safety nets of the OECD nations and undermining the international arrangements of Japan and South Korea through bilateral energy deals with common suppliers.[16]

Furthermore, India and China are seen to be competing with each other to secure access to energy resources, and this is seen as a precursor to a more fundamental military conflict.[17] Although the NOCs of China and India have jointly bid for hydrocarbon assets in South America, Africa, and the Persian Gulf and signed various memoranda of understanding, the competition between the same NOCs in Africa, South America, and Central Asia is seen to be far more significant and enduring.[18] As oil equity investments are seen primarily as state-driven policy moves toward energy security, Chinese NOCs outbidding Indian NOCs to secure oil and gas assets is often projected as a devastating setback for Indian energy security.[19]

One common mistake made in assessing China's and India's energy security is that the focus is disproportionately on the external expression of their energy strategies, which overlooks serious domestic energy crises such as inadequate electricity supplies and energy poverty, particularly in India. This is partly because their energy moves are scrutinized under the traditional framework, which is state centric, supply oriented, and focused on oil.[20] Under the traditional approach, the energy problem of a country is seen primarily as an oil import problem, and ownership of key oil resources and control of their transport routes are seen as the dominant response. Although the influence of the traditional approach cannot be denied in India's and China's early energy policies, its relevance to the goal of "self-reliance was central to both India and China.

The Pursuit of Self-Reliance

Self-reliance is among the most important and consistent common values that are reiterated in the energy policy documents of both countries. Self-reliance as a broad goal was important in Chinese policy during imperial rule and continued under the Maoist regime.[21] But its importance was reemphasized in the context of energy during the Sino-Soviet split in the 1960s, when China lost around 50 percent of its oil supplies imported from the Soviet Union as well as the support of Soviet specialists who were helping to develop the oil industry in China, illustrating the risks in dependence.[22]

The eventual discovery of the Daqing, Shengli, and Liahe oil fields in China not only led to self-reliance with regard to oil supplies but also made China a net exporter, which validated the power of energy "independence."[23] The inability of these three giant fields to meet the growing oil needs of China along with the failure in its efforts to make new oil discoveries after it became a net importer of oil in 1993 brought energy security to the forefront of China's policymaking.[24] China's return to dependence on imported oil went against the Maoist doctrine of self-reliance, which was the key theme for economic development in the 1960s and 1970s.[25]

This brought China close to the traditional interpretation, which was strongly "oil supply" oriented.[26] Policy advisers encouraged the Chinese government to use the experience of Russia, the United States, and Japan and to adopt an energy security policy that was "grounded in national security and strategic vision, encourage overseas activities of Chinese NOCs, and increase Government bilateral intervention on behalf of these enterprises."[27]

Toward this end, China started advocating the use of foreign direct investment through its NOCs to secure oil.[28] China's oil strategy highlighted diversification of supply sources, co-developing oil and gas wells with other countries, cutting out unreliable marine oil transportation routes, and developing a single dedicated destination for oil produced by Chinese companies.[29] In 2002 when Hu Jintao became general secretary of the Communist Party, China adopted the "go-out" strategy to meet its growing oil demand.[30] Oil equity investments, which offered a degree of control but not independence, fitted well with China's interpretation of self-reliance, which meant the ability to control initiatives, not total independence.[31]

For India, the importance of self-reliance became apparent following independence from British rule and the separation of Pakistan, which removed access to water for irrigation from the Indus canal system. India, with 82 percent of the population of undivided British India, got only half the canal system, carrying 400,000 cubic feet of water per second, and less than half of 24 million acres of land irrigated by state-owned canals.[32] The first and third Five-Year Plan documents (1947–60) were therefore preoccupied with strategies for increasing "self-reliance" in food production.

Newly independent India was also eager to consolidate its hold over the oil and gas industry, which was, until then, dominated by a few Anglo-American companies.[33] This was in line with India's industrial policy resolution of 1948 and 1956, which clearly stated the government's aspiration and future plans for core industries like petroleum, with all future development reserved for public sector undertakings.[34]

India's third Five-Year Plan projected nuclear energy as an option for generating power and a means for improving India's self-reliance in the context of energy.[35] Following the oil shocks of the 1970s, the sixth Five-Year Plan advocated self-reliance through the development of domestic resources and pricing reforms to conserve energy.[36] The refusal of international oil companies (IOCs) operating in India to comply with the Indian government's request to control the price of oil products during the 1970s oil embargoes reinforced the desire for "self-reliance" among policymakers and pushed India toward nationalization of these companies.[37]

Investments in equity oil seen as a means to self-reliance were emphasized in a series of policy documents in the 2000s. In 2000 the Hydrocarbon Vision 2025 commissioned by the prime minister of India to address the issue of energy security recommended "intensification of exploration efforts and securing acreages in countries having high attractiveness for ensuring sustainable long-term supplies" such as Russia, Iran, Iraq, and North Africa.[38] The Integrated Energy Policy Report released in 2006 commented that "obtaining equity oil, coal, and gas abroad only contribute toward diversifying supply sources and not toward energy security," but it also recommended "investing in equity oil" to enhance energy security in subsequent sections.[39] The new division on energy security created within India's Ministry of External Affairs in 2011 and designated as "the nodal point for energy security related matters involving coordination with line ministries, the Planning Commission, Indian missions and posts abroad, international organizations, and foreign missions" also emphasized facilitation of energy equity investment and bilateral energy deals in energy-exporting countries in Africa, Latin America, Central Asia, and Southeast Asia.[40]

The quest for a degree of self-reliance through oil equity investments is evident from China's and India's policy approaches, but they were not original approaches devised to pursue realist interests. China and India were merely adopting "classic moves" deployed by industrial nations when their share of imported oil was growing.[41] India's policies toward oil equity investments as stated in its Five-Year Plans show a lag, with China's similar policies betraying a "me too" approach to policymaking.

Competition or Conflict?

For many observers, China and India are natural rivals, and the competition between the China National Petroleum Corporation (CNPC), the China Petrochemical Corporation (Sinopec), and the China National Offshore Oil Corporation (CNOOC)[42] in China and the Oil and Natural Gas Corporation Videsh Limited (OVL)[43] and Gas Authority of India Limited (GAIL) in India is one of the many manifestations of their long-standing animosity.[44]

The success of Chinese NOCs in outbidding Indian NOCs over equity oil assets supports the Sino-Indian rivalry thesis. The 2009 decision of Myanmar to award an important gas project to China's CNPC rather than India's GAIL, which was the original favored bidder in 2004, is among the most recent examples cited.[45] In July 2009 Myanmar's Ministry of Energy and China's CNPC signed a memorandum of understanding that would allow CNPC to construct parallel oil and gas pipelines that will carry 440,000 barrels of oil a day and 12 billion cubic meters of gas into China from Myanmar's gas fields at an investment of more than US$2.5 billion.[46] While this may be a commercial loss to GAIL, the decision to award the contract to CNPC was a shrewd and economically rational choice by Myanmar.[47] For Myanmar, the quick execution capabilities of CNPC combined with a longer pipeline route that offered greater potential advantages to the domestic economy were enough to tip the balance in favor of CNPC.[48]

The US$2 billion offer by Sinopec for a 50 percent stake in an Angolan asset against US$600 million offered by India's OVL is another example cited in the rivalry thesis.[49] Once again this was a commercial victory for Sinopec, which is much larger and far more experienced in overseas deals than OVL. Whether or not this is a commercial loss to OVL in the long run is uncertain, as Chinese companies are said to have a history of overpaying for equity positions.[50] In 2009 the total premium paid by the Chinese NOCs is said to have been 40 percent above the base case valuation of acquired assets.[51] Some analysts have blamed intermediaries such as investment banks who facilitate these deals for driving up the premium on hydrocarbon assets.[52] On the whole there seems to be no conclusive evidence for systematic or intentional overpayment by Chinese NOCs, which implies that political or financial pressure is not being used to move the deals against commercial judgment.[53]

Although Chinese and Indian NOCs are often compared as equals, the difference between them is larger than the difference between the Chinese and Indian economies. The largest Indian upstream company, ONGC, the parent of OVL, was ranked 357 in the list of Fortune 500 companies in 2012, while the largest Chinese NOCs, Sinopec and CNPC, were ranked 5 and 6, respectively. Total overseas investments of OVL stood at US$14.35 billion, which is less than one third of what Chinese NOCs spend in a year.[54]

OVL's equity oil and gas production in the year ending in March 2012 was about 4 percent of India's total oil consumption and 5 percent of oil imports.[55] The equity oil production by Chinese NOCs was roughly ten times that of Indian NOCs and accounted for 15 percent of oil consumption and more than 27 percent of imports.[56]

There are also significant differences in the level of empowerment of Indian and Chinese companies when it comes to decisionmaking on overseas investments. The board of directors of OVL is empowered to approve investments of up to US$75 million,[57] which is a significant limitation for an international upstream exploration and production company. Investments above that require approval from a committee of cabinet ministers.[58] More than 73 percent of OVL's investments so far were financed through internal accruals, and external loans accounted for less than 5 percent of its investments.[59] In contrast, China's NOCs received generous funding from the China Development Bank as well as the China Export-Import Bank for their investments aboard.[60]

If the idea of competition between Indian and Chinese NOCs for energy assets is revisited in light of the significant quantitative and qualitative differences between them, it should not be surprising that Chinese NOCs outbid Indian NOCs. In fact, the success of Chinese NOCs over Indian NOCs illustrates the extent to which commercial logic rather than geopolitical preferences underpins the competition between Indian and Chinese NOCs.

Chinese and Indian NOCs often find themselves competing against each other because they share the "latecomer's dilemma" in the global upstream oil industry where most of the low-hanging fruit is already taken by international oil companies. The Asian NOCs settle for the few assets in politically and economically difficult regions that Western companies shun. These assets often have little upside profitability and thus are of minimal interest to IOCs. China was particularly disappointed that CNOOC's bid to acquire Unocal, an American oil company, and to gain a stake in the Kashagan field dominated by IOCs was treated with "undue hostility."[61] Yishan observed that Chinese companies were subjected to "unfair and discriminatory" policies so as to force them out of prime assets.[62] Chinese NOCs are now so large that they are increasingly in competition with IOCs for higher-quality assets. China's NOCs were the largest single group of winning bidders in postwar Iraq's oil development projects, where IOCs were their main competitors.[63]

Chinese and Indian NOCs are products of their industrial policies, which prioritize state involvement in most sectors. These policies precede energy security policies by at least three decades, and state involvement is much stronger in domestic sectors such as food, fertilizer, and electricity generation and distribution. In this context, it would be an aberration in policy if the oil and gas sector were excluded from state involvement.

Unlike powerful NOCs such as Saudi Aramco that are based in oil-exporting countries whose primary objective is to protect domestic resources, NOCs based in oil-importing large economies such as China and India have to serve broader commercial and national goals.[64] They need to invest abroad if they are to survive and grow as commercial entities because oil reserves in their own countries are declining in production. New discoveries have not been made in either country despite persistent efforts. Investments in the upstream sector best meet the objective of commercial profitability as downstream investments have low or no margins, especially because downstream pricing is under the control of the government in both India and China. Expansion abroad also increases their international competitiveness through the development of new capabilities in areas such as shale oil and gas or ultra-deepwater drilling. In domestic markets, NOCs are subject to pressure from their governments to serve social goals such as job creation and infrastructure development that cannot be justified on commercial grounds. Abroad, Asian NOCs are much freer to operate along commercial lines.

There are other more prudent economic reasons for overseas equity oil investments, especially for China. Chinese equity investments in Western financial firms plunged after the financial crisis, and this was seen by China as a plot against it.[65] Investing in commodities such as oil through equity stakes and energy-backed loans offered a way of diversifying China's foreign exchange reserves, as it shifted them away from low-yielding financial instruments such as U.S. Treasury bonds.[66] Although this opportunity also exists for India, the extent of investment is not significant enough to make a difference. Investments in oil and minerals are a good hedge against a declining dollar and rising commodity prices given China's soaring oil demand and the consequent increase in oil prices.[67]

The motivation for Chinese agencies such as China Development Bank and China Export-Import Bank to lend to NOCs' overseas activities is thus not merely the government's "go-out" policy, but rather the prospect of profits.[68] Chinese banks are said to be offering credit to the NOCs at good rates, but they are not seen to be compromising on their commercial interests.[69] Essentially Chinese lending agencies seem to be using the opportunity that government policy provides to position themselves as a bridge between the strategic objectives of the government and the commercial activities of Chinese NOCs.[70]

The recent global financial crisis proved to be an unexpected opportunity for Asian NOCs. Upstream capital costs fell by about 12 percent, and upstream spending was around 15 percent lower following the crisis.[71] This made assets cheaper for Asian NOCs, and they encountered less competition from Western oil majors. For China this proved to be a particular opportunity, as the appreciation of its currency made buying assets abroad cheaper. Moreover, Chinese NOCs also enjoyed a competitive advantage through their access to the country's approximately US$3 trillion in foreign exchange reserves.

Some fears are more specific to Chinese NOCs. One is that they are managed by members of the Communist Party,[72] but recent research by the IEA found no evidence of the Chinese government imposing any restrictions on NOC operations. It also found that the Chinese government did not impose a quota on how much equity oil should be shipped back to China and that decisions over marketing equity oil were dominated by commercial concerns.[73]

However, there does seem to be some evidence of the "tail is wagging the dog,"[74] as Chinese oil companies are said to be routinely consulted by the government on policy matters.[75] This is not necessarily negative. Commercial knowledge of the NOCs is more internationally oriented and is more aware of energy sector dynamics than state-held institutional knowledge. The government's increasing fiscal dependence on NOCs gives them a degree of political clout. Top positions in Chinese NOCs are appointed by the Central Committee of the Chinese Communist Party, which gives them direct access to the Chinese leadership.[76]

Indian NOCs are largely professionally managed, but they do use government support in accessing overseas assets. Indian NOCs advocate oil equity investment policies for energy security partly because they contribute to their commercial advancement.[77] Government diplomatic support reduces transaction costs in accessing resources overseas, and it also increases the possibility of success. It is very likely that NOCs of both nations understand quite well that their equity oil supplies are no more secure from political or logistical disruptions than long-term contract supplies or market purchases. As history has clearly shown, the ill-defined ideas of "national security" and "energy security" offer an excellent allegory for using state power to protect narrow commercial interests.

On the whole, a combination of commercial necessity and opportunity seem to be driving the international pursuits of Chinese and Indian NOCs, while government policy seems to be driven by domestic industrial policy along with a sense of historic grievance and fear.[78] The shared presumption of market failure among policymakers in India and China is a factor behind equity investments. Both India and China use state power to promote NOCs as the means to retain economic and social relevance in their rapidly modernizing economic contexts. Both governments do use foreign policy to support energy policy and energy policy to support foreign policy, but today's oil market is far too large and far too liquid to be threatened by these moves.[79]

The fear that Asian NOCs' investment in equity oil is "locking up" resources and therefore contributing to global energy insecurity is not backed by economic logic. The presumption is that equity oil produced outside the country is equivalent to oil produced domestically and therefore is secure and available at lower prices. But oil is priced on world markets according to its opportunity cost, and so even if every drop of oil used by China or India is produced domestically or obtained through equity oil, the opportunity cost of oil is the same as that of globally traded oil.

As equity oil of China and India is mostly sold into the global oil market, it may be presumed that profits from the sale of oil will insulate the respective economy from high world oil prices.[80] If foreign oil assets are priced fairly at the time of purchase, China or India would benefit as countries only when the purchase helps to smooth its income—that is, it increases income when the economy is depressed and vice versa—but for large oil-importing countries like China and India oil prices are likely to be high when their economies are growing and using plenty of oil and not the other way around.[81] In other words, equity oil will add to economic income when it is least needed by China or India and subtract from it when it is most needed. In a globally integrated world, "energy security" broadly interpreted as the "availability of energy" is a public good. When any nation, be it a democracy or a dictatorship, invests in increasing the supply of energy, it contributes to global energy security.

The Real Energy Crisis

The "threat" narrative that characterizes India's and China's energy security moves conceals and distracts attention from the qualitative dimension of energy security, which includes, but is not limited to, energy poverty and energy shortage, which are far more acute in India than in China.[82]

The per capita consumption of India in 2010 at 566 kilogram oil-equivalent was lower than that of sub-Saharan Africa (683), one third that of China (1,807) and one twelfth that of North America (7,185).[83] Per capita energy consumption is not a perfect indicator of energy poverty, but it is a fairly accurate indicator of relative lack of access to modern energy services.[84] India ranks lower than sub-Saharan Africa in per capita energy consumption, and an overwhelming majority of households accounting for more than 750 million people use biomass as fuel for cooking.[85] In energy-equivalent terms, this is more than the energy derived from oil in India and almost equal to the total energy consumption of Australia,[86] but in reality it provides very little useful energy to the poor. More than 70 percent of the energy content is wasted as biomass is burnt in inefficient cookstoves. The opportunity cost of human labor used in collecting and processing biomass does not feature in any energy balance sheet. The result is that the poorest segment of the population uses the most inefficient and consequently the most expensive form of energy.[87]

The fact that many millions use little or no commercial forms of energy[88] makes the Indian per capita energy consumption figure a statistical artifact rather than a representation of majority energy consumption levels. Roughly one fifth of the Indian population live in households that are officially unelectrified, and another two fifths live in households that are under-electrified.[89] In terms of absolute numbers, India has the largest population in the world without access to electricity as well as the largest population using biomass energy sources for cooking.[90] Obviously there is colossal biophysical "need" for modern forms of energy, but this need is often misinterpreted as unmet "market demand" for energy or a form of "supply-induced scarcity" of energy that India is seeking to address by augmenting supplies from all over the world. Energy poverty is the result of entrenched structural inequalities in the society, which can only be addressed through a complex set of political and socioeconomic solutions and not by the mere augmentation of supplies at the aggregate level or through the introduction of alternative-energy sources or technologies.[91]

An array of political and administrative policy interventions such as subsidies on energy prices, rural electrification schemes, and decentralized energy programs based on renewable energy sources implemented by the government of India over the last several decades to address the issue of energy poverty have not made a difference to the extent desired.[92] The government is financially stretched to capacity, and private investment is not expected to flow into the sector, as there is little or no profit potential. This is the human face of India's energy security challenge, which most external observers miss. Whether or not the millions of energy-poor households eventually gain access to modern sources of energy and whether their source of energy will be green or brown are an open question, but the path that they eventually take will make a significant difference to both India and the rest of the world in the context of economic growth and climate change.[93]

The well-intended but poorly designed and implemented policy interventions to increase energy access to the poor have led to price distortions in the sector that have stifled investment. This is most visible in the Indian electricity sector, which is characterized by chronic shortages even in affluent industrial and urban areas. At the national level, 10 percent or more of peak electricity demand has routinely not been met by the Indian power sector in the last several decades.[94] If availability of primary fuels is the only determinant of energy security, India should not face a shortage in the power sector, as it is well endowed with cheap coal that generates most of the electricity. India has the fourth largest coal reserves in the world, equal to 7 percent of global reserves, and in theory domestic reserves are adequate to meet demand.[95]

India's electricity shortages are the result not of the unavailability of coal but of the inability of India to produce and use domestic coal efficiently.[96] Coal accounts for 66 and 41 percent, respectively, of China's and India's primary energy basket and generates more than 80 and 70 percent of their respective electricity.[97] In comparison, oil accounts for only 17 and 24 percent, respectively, of China's and India's energy baskets, and equity oil accounts for only 15 and 4 percent of their respective oil consumption.[98]

Reforming the coal sector has been on the agenda for at least two decades, but making even incremental changes has not been possible, as it entails significant social and political costs. Imported coal that is bridging the gap between supply and demand has increased the pressure on India's fragile external trade balance.[99] Coal imports are adding about 8 percent to India's trade deficit, which is stressed by an oil trade deficit that accounts for 54 percent of India's total trade deficit.[100] A reduction in imports of oil and coal on account of increased domestic production or increased efficiency in the use of oil or coal will substantially reduce the pressure on India's balance of payments position. Once again, this is an issue of economic security rather than supply security and can only be addressed through deep structural reforms in the domestic economy.

The Security Dynamic

A critical subdynamic in the narrative of energy conflict between India and China is the possible military clash between them over energy transport corridors. This serious allegation cannot be dismissed as mere perception, as military documents from both India and China refer to the threat of disruption to energy supply lines and make the case for strengthening their respective maritime forces.

India's first Maritime Doctrine published in 2004 explicitly highlighted energy security of the country as a context requiring the application of maritime power in both offensive and defensive operations to protect the country's maritime trade.[101] The doctrine also highlighted the importance of the Persian Gulf region and Central Asia for India's energy security and specifically mentioned safeguarding Indian energy assets outside territorial India and preserving international sea lines of communication through the Indian Ocean on a permanent basis, envisioning several scenarios of conflict in which the Indian navy may have to be involved in the future.[102]

India straddles the sea-lanes though which most of China's imported oil passes, and segments of the Chinese strategic and military community are concerned with the potential of the Indian navy to interdict China's maritime oil lifeline.[103] The oil security strategy outlined by the National Development and Reform Commission and the State Economic and Trade Commission in 2002[104] called for measures aimed at increasing China's control over its energy supplies, including the construction of strategic petroleum reserves in western China for emergency use and the development of Chinese naval and air forces to protect China's energy supplies.[105] China is also concerned that in the event of a Sino-U.S. military conflict over Taiwan, the United States could interrupt China's seaborne oil imports.[106]

In an atmosphere of mutual suspicion, military planners in China and India seem to be formulating strategy based on the worst-case scenario. This is perceived by the other as a potential threat to its national security that forces it to adopt an even more stringent precautionary approach in its own decisionmaking. This could potentially escalate into a spiral of insecurity not unlike the cold war, with maritime force replacing nuclear weapons.[107] This is an unwarranted development, especially in the light of significant changes in the volume and direction of oil flows that are most likely in the future.

An increase in the flow of traded oil has the virtue of consolidating global interdependence, but it brings the risk of short-term supply interruptions, particularly because concentration in geographic supply is likely to increase the significance of a few strategic supply routes. Oil transportation is likely to increase from about 18 million barrels a day in 2010, or 42 percent of global trade in oil, to almost 25 million barrels a day in 2035, or 50 percent of projected trade through the Strait of Hormuz, the world's most important maritime oil-shipping route.[108] As more oil flows eastward from the Middle East to meet rising demand in Asia, there is also growing reliance on the Strait of Malacca, where oil transit volumes as a share of global trade are expected to rise from 32 percent in 2010 to 45 percent in 2035.[109]

However, U.S. dependence on supplies that transit the Strait of Hormuz is expected to fall dramatically in the next two decades, partly on account of an increase in domestic production and partly on account of stagnation in demand. As new discoveries in the North American continent come on-stream, the United States is likely to source most of its imported oil closer to home. Overall total oil imports of the United States are expected to fall from 9.5 million barrels a day in 2011 to about 4.5 million barrels a day by 2035.[110] If the United States implements policies for increasing fuel efficiency and reducing emissions, imports are likely to fall to 3.4 million barrels a day.[111] U.S. imports from the Middle East have already declined from around 2.8 million barrels a day in 2000 to 2 million barrels a day in 2011. In the next ten years, this is expected to fall to just 0.3 million barrels a day.[112]

In contrast, China's oil imports are expected to increase from 4.9 million barrels a day in 2012 to more than 12.3 million barrels a day by 2035, and India's oil imports are expected to increase from 2.5 million to more than 6.9 million barrels a day by 2035.[113] Given that almost 80 percent of the oil imports of China and India originate in the Middle East, most of the oil moving through the Strait of Hormuz will be heading toward Asia, particularly India and China. As of now, the United States is the net provider of security in the region. The overwhelming power of American maritime forces not only underwrites the stability of oil production in the region but also ensures the security of the Hormuz Strait. The provision of security and stability to oil-producing regions subsidizes the global oil market, as it reduces the overall cost of oil production and supply. Effectively, it is a global public good on which the rest of the world free rides. As oil imports to the United States from the region fall, the rationale for a U.S. presence in the region will come under scrutiny. Questions will arise as to why the so-called "rising powers" of China and India are allowed to free ride on the security provided by the United States, when they are the biggest oil importers from the region.

Despite the strengthening of their respective maritime forces toward ensuring the security of oil supplies, there is no evidence that China or India will replace the United States as a net provider of security in the region. The maritime security documents of India and China betray a mercantilist approach to security that presumes that they can unilaterally secure their oil supplies.[114] The energy security strategy documents of India and China state that diversifying their oil supply sources to include a greater number of "secure sources" will provide additional insurance against future supply disruptions.[115] These twin economic fallacies are likely to increase rather than decrease security in the oil-producing region and along oil supply routes.

In the event of a major military conflict, it will be almost impossible unilaterally to ensure the safety of oil shipments. Even if it is possible, the oil market will price oil thus transported so high that it will be unaffordable. When there is a threat of disruption or instability in the Middle East, the price of oil would rise sharply well before the crisis unfolds, and the oil market would make no distinction between oil from the Middle East and oil from supposedly secure places such as Norway. A disruption somewhere is a disruption everywhere as far as the oil market is concerned, and this will be reflected in the global price of oil. China and India, even with oil from "secure" regions and secure supply lines, cannot beat the oil market, as they will be in no better position than a country that sources all of its imports through the Hormuz as far as access and price are concerned.

It may be more appropriate to look at China's investment in maritime power to secure energy transport corridors as a response to the United States' continued command of the maritime commons and India's potential role as partner. In this context, it could be argued that although the rest of the world benefits from the security provided by the United States, its "command of the commons" strategy is driving insecurity in the region. The growing stakes that India and China have in the stability of the global oil market imply that they must be given the opportunity to act as global stakeholders in maintaining the existing order and be invited to participate in a cooperative rather than a competitive mechanism to protect the global maritime commons. As John Mitchell has observed, the extent to which China and India are willing to pursue expensive but ineffective moves to reduce dependence on energy trade depends on the extent to which they expect to be permanently in conflict with the world's major powers.[116]

While there is much mutual mistrust between Delhi and Beijing on maritime issues, in 2012 they agreed to initiate a dialogue on maritime security issues. The United States has indeed offered to develop a trilateral dialogue with India and China. For the moment, though, Beijing seems hesitant. In the long run, the financially constrained and ecologically threatened world will be better off with a multilateral approach to protecting the maritime commons.

Conclusions

The rapid ascent of economic growth and material prosperity as primary goals of policy in the last decade and the growing importance of global trade as a means to both of these goals have led to a revision of how energy is perceived in China and India. Rather than being merely a means to national security concentrated in oil, energy is increasingly seen as a means to material prosperity that can be derived from sources including, but not limited to, oil. As the line between energy concerns and larger economic and environmental predicaments is increasingly blurred, both countries realize that their energy problem is no longer a short-term foreign policy problem, but a long-term transition to a different and more expensive mix of energy sources and unwelcome changes in the habits and institutions of their ambitious societies.

For China, growing oil insecurity, despite measures taken in the 1990s, the electricity crisis in 2003, and the environmental impact of energy production and consumption have revealed dimensions of energy security that cannot be addressed through an oil supply–centered energy security policy.[117] For India, the inability of policy to change key dimensions of its energy insecurity, such as high dependency on oil imports, inefficient coal production, and persistent, extreme energy poverty despite efforts made over the last sixty-five years, has exposed the inadequacy of its oil supply–centric approach.[118]

For both India and China, economic adjustment to higher oil prices in the last decade has caused problems that are both broader and more profound as they interact with other long-term and cyclical economic problems. Inflation fueled by high oil prices is now seen as a far more potent threat to the economy.[119] In the long run this can only be addressed by increasing the oil and energy efficiency of the economy, which means radical structural and economic reform in the domestic economy.

The extent of India's energy imports is a national macroeconomic problem rather than a global security problem. India imports around 36 percent of its primary energy needs but spends more than 3–4 percent of its gross domestic product (GDP) on energy imports in net terms. In comparison Japan, which imports more than 90 percent of its energy needs, spends less than 2 percent of GDP on imports. Any improvement in terms of trade for India can be achieved only through deep and sustained structural and economic reforms.[120]

Although the state is still powerful in the realm of deciding energy policy in both countries, the high level of institutional fragmentation means that consensus on policy is just as hard domestically as it is internationally. The need to reconcile economic transition with ideological, political, and social factors means that energy security strategies and energy sector reform policies must also serve distributional objectives with contradictory effects. Although energy prices in India are among the highest in the world in terms of purchasing power parity, they are inflexible, which means that they cannot meaningfully reflect changes in the global and domestic energy market. For large segments of the population in India, flexible market prices for energy have become simply unacceptable, as elections are typically fought on which political party can retain the status quo on prices.

There is international pressure on India and China to reduce "subsidies" on energy partly to improve conditions for greener sources of energy and partly to improve China's and India's responses to changes in the global energy market. While China has managed to introduce a phased program for linking domestic energy prices with international prices, the task is proving to be complex for India, and this is not just because it is a democracy. India's energy subsidies are not straightforward "underpricing" of energy but rather a complex system of taxes and cross-subsidies that ultimately increase the average price of energy. To rationalize the price of energy in India, a broad range of structural and fiscal reforms have to be undertaken. This is not easy when a majority of the population does not have even the most basic economic capabilities to adapt to dramatic changes in the external environment.

Finally, there is the inconvenient issue of social and economic justice that India and China raise in the context of efforts to reduce global carbon emissions. India and China together are expected to account for more than 75 percent of the global net increase in carbon dioxide emissions by 2035, primarily because their economic growth is likely to be fueled by fossil fuels.[121] To ask them not to grow is equivalent to trapping millions of lives in poverty, yet to let them grow on fossil fuels is equivalent to trapping the world in climate change. The low-carbon growth path that is supposed to deliver growth and contain carbon emissions has not materialized, and even if it has, as the technology optimists claim, the economic, social, and political costs of taking the road are uncertain. In this context, from where and through whom India and China get their fossil fuels is far less important than the choices that India and China make regarding the types of energy they will use in the future.

Notes

1. International Energy Agency (IEA), *World Energy Outlook 2012* (Paris: OECD, 2012).

2. Ibid.

3. British Petroleum (BP), "BP Statistical Review of World Energy 2009" (www.bp.com/liveassets/bp_internet/globalbp/globalbp_uk_english/reports_and_publications/statistical_energy_review_2008/STAGING/local_assets/2009_downloads/statistical_review_of_world_energy_full_report_2009.pdf).

4. E. L. Morse, "USA and the Changing Geopolitics of Asian Energy," paper prepared for the Conference on Asian Security and Implications for USA, National Bureau of Asian Research and the Pacific Northwest Centre for Global Security, 2004.

5. Philip Andrews-Speed, "China's Energy Role in the Middle East and Prospects for the Future," in *The New Energy Silk Road: The Growing Asia–Middle East Energy Nexus*, edited by Philip Andrews-Speed, Sumit Ganguly, Manjeet S. Pardesi, Mikkal E. Herberg, Hormoz Naficy, and Jean-François Seznec, pp. 13–27 (Seattle, Wash.: National Bureau of Energy Research, 2009).

6. World Bank Database (http://data.worldbank.org/topic/energy-and-mining).

7. Daniel Yergin, Dennis Eklof, and Jefferson Edwards, "Fueling Asia's Recovery," *Foreign Affairs* 77, no. 2 (1998): 34–50.

8. Advisory Council on International Affairs, *Energised Foreign Policy* (The Hague, December 2005).

9. Ibid.

10. "Asia's insatiable appetite for oil coupled with tight supplies has triggered the start of a global bidding war for oil from the Middle East," according to the head of Chevron-Texaco Corporation, quoted in the *Boston Globe*, February 17, 2005.

11. "Two Big Appetites Take Seats at the Oil Table," *New York Times*, February 18, 2005. The article goes on to say, "India, sharing a ravenous thirst for oil, has joined China in an increasingly naked grab at oil and natural gas fields that has the world's two most populous nations bidding up energy prices and racing against each other and global energy companies."

12. IEA, *World Energy Outlook 2012*.

13. In testimony to the Foreign Relations Committee of the Government of the United States on June 22, 2006, Senator Larry E. Craig quoted the administration's own National Security Strategy Paper as saying, "China was expanding trade but acting as if it can somehow lock up energy supplies around the world or seek to direct markets rather than opening them up" (http://lugar.senate.gov/energy/hearings/pdf/060622/Craig_Testimony.pdf). An article titled "China and India Ratchet up Battle over Foreign Oil," *Baltimore Sun*, September 15, 2005, described how China's national oil company CNPC outbid India's OVL to acquire oil and pipeline interests in Ecuador owned by Encana, a Canadian oil company, and commented that this US$1.4 billion deal was part of China's bid to lock up oil supplies (http://articles.baltimoresun.com/2005-09-15/business/0509150029_1_china-and-india-state-oil-oil-analyst).

14. John Lee, "China's Geostrategic Search for Oil," *Washington Quarterly* 35, no. 2 (2012): 75–92.

15. Morse, "USA and the Changing Geopolitics of Asian Energy."

16. Ibid.

17. Lee, "China's Geostrategic Search for Oil."

18. Vibhuti Hate, "India's Energy Dilemma," *South Asia Monitor* 98 (Washington: Centre for Strategic and International Studies, 2006).

19. Christopher Griffin, "Containment with Chinese Charateristics," *Asian Outlook*, September 7, 2006.

20. Yergin, Eklof, and Edwards, "Fueling Asia's Recovery."

21. Christian Constantin, *China's Conception of Energy Security: Sources and International Impacts* (University of British Columbia, 2005).

22. Erica S. Downs, *China's Quest for Energy Security* (Santa Monica, Calif.: RAND, 2000).

23. Ibid.

24. Constantin, *China's Conception of Energy Security*.

25. Downs, *China's Quest for Energy Security*.

26. F. K. Chang, "Chinese Energy and Asian Security," *Orbis* 45, no. 233 (2001): 2.

27. Constantin, *China's Conception of Energy Security*.

28. Philip Andrews-Speed, Roland Dannreather, and Xuanii Liao, *Strategic Implications of China's Energy Needs* (Oxford: International Institute of Energy Studies, 2002).

29. "China's Oil Strategy in the 21st Century," *People's Daily*, November 14, 2002.

30. Flynt Leverett and Jeffrey Badar, "Managing China-U.S. Competition in the Middle East," *Washington Quarterly* 29, no. 1 (2005): 187–201.

31. Downs, *China's Quest for Energy Security.*

32. Planning Commission, *First Five-Year Plan* (New Delhi: Government of India, 1948).

33. D. S. Visvanath, *A Hundred Years of Oil: Oil India Limited* (New Delhi: Vikas Publishing House, 1997).

34. R. Bhatia, *Planning for Petroleum and Fertilizer Industries: Programming Model for India* (Oxford University Press, 1983).

35. Planning Commission, *Third Five-Year Plan* (New Delhi: Government of India, 1960).

36. Planning Commission, *Sixth Five-Year Plan* (New Delhi: Government of India, 1979).

37. C. D. Patra, *Oil Industry in India* (New Delhi: Mittal Publishers, 2004).

38. Government of India, *Hydrocarbon Vision 2025* (New Delhi, 2000).

39. Planning Commission, *Integrated Energy Policy* (New Delhi: Government of India, 2006).

40. Personal correspondence with the Energy Security Division of the Ministry of External Affairs, October 2011.

41. See, for example, Lydia Powell, "Oil in United States' Energy Policy: Searching for Clues of Influence" (New Delhi: Samskriti Publications, 2008), and Gabe Collins, Andrew S. Erikson, Yufan Hao, Mikkal E. Herberg, Llewelyn Hughes, Weihua Liu, and Jane Nakano, *Asia's Energy and Resource Nationalism: Implications for the United States, China, and the Asia Pacific Region* (Seattle, Wash.: National Bureau of Asian Research, 2011).

42. China's NOCs were created out of the former Ministry of Petroleum Industry and Ministry of Chemical Industry. Sinopec is the largest Chinese company in terms of revenue, but CNOOC is the most profitable of the NOCs partly because of its focus on crude oil and lack of exposure to the highly controlled domestic market for refined products. Chinese NOCs are operating in thirty-one countries and have equity production in twenty of these. See Julie Jiang and Jonathan Sinton, "Overseas Investments by Chinese National Oil Companies: Assessing Drivers and Impact," Information Paper (Paris: IEA, 2011). The objective of the NOCs is to introduce competition, promote economic efficiency, create a wider share of ownership, and reduce government outlays. See Steven W. Lewis, "China's Energy Study 2000: The Effects of Decentralisation and Privatisation on Energy Infrastructure Development" (unpublished manuscript, 2000), and Barry Naughton, *Growing Out of the Plan: Chinese Economic Reform 1978–1993* (Cambridge University Press, 1996).

43. OVL is a wholly owned subsidiary of the Oil and Natural Gas Corporation (ONGC), India's largest state-owned upstream oil exploration and production company. OVL was formed in 1965 as Hydrocarbon India Private Limited and renamed ONGC Videsh in 1989. Its producing assets include the Greater Nile Oil Project and Block 5A in Sudan, Block 6.1 in Vietnam, Al Furat in Syria, Sakhalin-I, and IEC in Russia, PIVSA (IJV) in Venezuela, and Mansarovar in Colombia. OVL bought U.K.-based Imperial Energy Plc in 2010 and is targeting 60 million tons of overseas oil and gas production by 2025. Information from a presentation made by OVL on "Overseas Investment in

Upstream Oil and Gas: Rationale, Policy, Current Situation, and Assessment of Strategy" at the Observer Research Foundation, New Delhi, on May 23, 2012.

44. Lee, "China's Geostrategic Search for Oil."

45. Elizabeth Mills, "Keep Friends Close but Enemies Closer," *Harvard International Review* (Summer 1989), posted on Web Perspectives on July 10, 2009.

46. Jiang and Sinton, "Overseas Investments by Chinese National Oil Companies."

47. Mills, "Keep Friends Close but Enemies Closer."

48. Ibid.

49. "Sinopec Beats ONGC, Gets Angola Block," *Financial Express,* July 15, 2006.

50. Frederik Balfour, "A Global Shopping Spree for the Chinese," *Business Week,* November 18, 2002, p. 24.

51. Wood Mckenzie Corporate Service, *Chinese NOCs Step up International Expansion* (London, 2010).

52. The Indian minister for petroleum and natural gas during the Petro-Kazakhstan deal commented that Goldman Sachs drove up the price of the asset. Following the deal there was open disagreement between the Indian minister of petroleum, who saw a huge role for diplomacy in energy security, and the head of ONGC, who argued that his primary responsibility was toward his shareholders. Mills, "Keep Friends Close but Enemies Closer."

53. Jiang and Sinton, "Overseas Investments by Chinese National Oil Companies." Among other deals that OVL lost are Omimex de Colombia, a Colombian asset bought by Sinopec in 2006, the Apko oil field off Nigeria that CNOOC took over in January 2006, and Petro-Kazakhstan that CNPC took over in 2005. Out of these, the loss of Petro-Kazakhstan was controversial, as the initial bid by India's OVL was higher than that of CNPC. This may be attributed to the skills of Chinese diplomats, who reportedly played an important role in CNPC's successful bids for oil projects in Venezuela, Sudan, and Kazakhstan. Xiaojie Xu, "China's Oil Strategy toward the Middle East," Baker Institute Working Paper 12 (Rice University, Baker Institute, 2002).

54. OVL, "Overseas Investment in Upstream Oil and Gas." The Chinese spent US$47.57 billion in just two years from January 2009 to December 2010. Jiang and Sinton, "Overseas Investments by Chinese National Oil Companies."

55. OVL's reserves are distributed as follows: 58 percent are in Russia (Shakhalin I), 15 percent in Venezuela, 10 percent in Sudan (undivided), and 9 percent in Myanmar. OVL, "Overseas Investment in Upstream Oil and Gas."

56. IEA, *World Energy Outlook 2012.* BP, "BP Statistical Review of World Energy 2011" (www.bp.com/assets/bp_internet/globalbp/globalbp_uk_english/reports_and_publications/statistical_energy_review_2011/STAGING/local_assets/pdf/statistical_review_of_world_energy_full_report_2011.pdf). Sixty-seven percent of China's oil equity is located in four countries: Kazakhstan, Sudan, Venezuela, and Angola. Jiang and Sinton, "Overseas Investments by Chinese National Oil Companies."

57. OVL, "Overseas Investment in Upstream Oil and Gas."

58. The Cabinet Committee on Economic Affairs set up by the government of India needs to approve of investments by OVL and GAIL. "CCEA Approves OVL's $1 Billion Azerbaijan Acquisition," *First Post Business,* January 13, 2013.

59. OVL, "Overseas Investment in Upstream Oil and Gas."

60. Jiang and Sinton, "Overseas Investments by Chinese National Oil Companies."

61. Xia Yishan, "Analysis of China's Strategy for Energy Security," English translation of the speech (text version) delivered in Chinese at the conference "India's Energy Security: Major Challenges," Observer Research Foundation, New Delhi, February 14, 2006.

62. Ibid.

63. Michael Kavanagh, "Dragon Consortium Wins Iraq Fields Bid," *Financial Times*, June 4, 2012.

64. M. E. Herberg, *Asia's National Oil Companies and the Competitive Landscape of the International Oil Industry* (Seattle, Wash.: National Bureau of Asian Research, 2011).

65. Erica Downs, *Inside China Inc: China Development Bank's Cross-Border Energy Deals* (Brookings Institution, 2011).

66. Ibid.

67. Xiaojie Xu, "Chinese NOCs Overseas Strategy: Background, Comparison, and Remarks" (Rice University, Baker Institute, 2007).

68. Ibid.

69. Jiang and Sinton, "Overseas Investments by Chinese National Oil Companies."

70. Downs, *Inside China Inc.*

71. IEA, "Oil Market Report" (Paris, April 13, 2010).

72. Minxin Pei, *China's Trapped Transition* (Harvard University Press, 2006).

73. Jiang and Sinton, "Overseas Investments by Chinese National Oil Companies."

74. Lleweyn Hughes, *Resource Nationalism in the Asia Pacific: Why Does It Matter?* (Seattle, Wash.: National Bureau of Energy Research, 2011).

75. Erica Downs, "The Chinese Energy Security Debate," *China Quarterly* 177 (March 2007): 21–41, quoting Asia Research Center, "China: Energy Policy and Natural Gas Use," Murdoch University, Western Australia, September 2001, p. 12.

76. Ibid., quoting Lewis, "China's Energy Study 2000: The Effects of Decentralisation and Privatisation on Energy Infrastructure Development."

77. Based on personal communication with sources (confidential).

78. Andrews-Speed, "China's Energy Role in the Middle East and Prospects for the Future."

79. Ibid.

80. Arguments in this section have been expressed in the Observer Research Foundation's weekly energy news monitor and also in short articles.

81. Raghuram Rajan, "The Resource Security Trap," *Mint*, August 9, 2008.

82. Energy poverty is a structural problem that concerns extending energy access to the poor with little or no purchasing power. Energy shortage is a supply-induced problem that represents inability to meet market demand backed by purchasing power. Other qualitative dimensions of energy security include energy price distortions, poor governance of the energy sector, lack of investment in energy production and distribution, local environmental impact of energy projects, and, more recently, scarcity of land and water required for energy generation.

83. All figures are from the World Bank energy database. Government of India figures for per capita energy consumption are different, but World Bank figures have been used for fair comparison of countries.

84. For example, low per capita energy consumption figures could be due to the climatic and lifestyle differences.

85. Firewood (twigs and logs collected informally from fields and forests) and dried animal dung.

86. BP, "BP Statistical Review of World Energy 2011."

87. The use of traditional biomass sources such as firewood and dried animal dung is more expensive because more than 75 percent of the heat generated when these fuels are burnt in rudimentary stoves is wasted and dissipated into the atmosphere. This means that in order to obtain one unit of heat energy, they need to collect biomass with more than three to four times the energy content. In addition, the opportunity cost of human labor used to collect biomass is added to the cost of fuel. In comparison, more affluent households that use modern cooking fuels such as liquefied petroleum gas, natural gas, or electricity do not have to expend human energy and pay less for a unit of useful energy.

88. For example, electricity, natural gas, or petroleum products such as gasoline and diesel fuel.

89. Officially 285 million people do not have access to electricity, which means that they are not connected to the grid. Technically, the government declares a village as "electrified" on the basis of whether or not infrastructure is present to transmit some form of electricity (including electricity obtained through decentralized renewable energy) and not on the basis of whether or not electricity actually flows through the infrastructure. Roughly half of the households connected to the grid receive electricity for only a few hours a day. Even in urban areas, power outages are the norm and not an exception.

90. Figures are from Government of India Census 2011, Sources of Lighting 2001–2011 and Households at a Glance (www.censusindia.gov.in/2011census/population_enumeration.aspx), and the National Sample Survey Organization, Consumer Expenditure NSS Sixty-Eighth Round (http://mospi.nic.in/Mospi_New/site/Home.aspx). As per the IEA, 400 million people in China continue to use biomass as fuel for cooking.

91. Technologies (green or brown) and economic techniques are often mistaken as apolitical solutions to the problems of energy access. Technologies and techniques are deeply political and are unlikely to solve the problem of inequality and energy access simultaneously. Green energy does not reach and sustain lives of the poor for the same economic and social reasons that brown energy does not reach them. The decentralized nature of green energy alone does not guarantee decentralized access to energy.

92. The government's rural electrification programs have extended grid infrastructure to almost 80 percent of the population. However, the government has not been able to ensure that electricity actually flows through these wires. Decentralized schemes based on solar, biomass, and small hydropower have had some isolated successes but have not made a significant difference at the aggregate level. Most of these schemes have proved to be economically unsustainable.

93. India's per capita carbon emissions are as low as 1.7 tons, one third of global average and less than one tenth of the largest emitter, primarily because more than half the

population draws its "energy" only from carbohydrates that they consume as food and the carbon they collect in the form of twigs to burn. This "subsidizes" hydrocarbon and fossil fuel–based energy consumption by the rest of the population. If the population remains energy poor, India's per capita emission levels will remain unaltered, but if they start consuming energy at higher rates, India's emissions profile will change dramatically. This will have a significant impact on global efforts to contain carbon emissions.

94. Central Electricity Authority of India.

95. IEA, *World Energy Outlook 2012*. Until very recently, India's coal imports consisted largely of high-quality coking coal used by the steel sector, as India's coal reserves are relatively poor in quality. In the last few years imports of thermal coal used for power generation have increased because structural, economic, and managerial shortcomings have effectively destroyed India's ability to respond to demand.

96. Ashish Gupta, "India's Coal Supply Security: Pushing Imports at the Expense of Domestic Reforms?" (New Delhi: Observer Research Foundation, 2012).

97. IEA, *World Energy Outlook 2012*.

98. Ibid.

99. Gupta, "India's Coal Supply Security."

100. Reserve Bank of India, *Handbook of Statistics on the Indian Economy 2011–12* (New Delhi, September 14, 2012).

101. Indian Navy, *Indian Maritime Doctrine*. Joachim Betz and Melanie Hanif, *The Formation of Preferences in Two Level Games: An Analysis of India's Domestic and Foreign Policy* (Zurich: German Institute of Global and Area Studies, 2010).

102. Ibid.

103. James Lamount and Geoff Dyer, "India Offers to Protect China's Oil Shipments," *Financial Times,* February 17, 2010.

104. Wang Donghai, "China's Oil Resources Security Strategy," *Journal of Beijing Institute of Technology,* vol. 5 (2003), quoted in the English translation of the speech (text version) delivered in Chinese at the conference "India's Energy Security: Major Challenges," Observer Research Foundation, New Delhi, February 14, 2006.

105. Downs, *China's Quest for Energy Security.*

106. Ibid.

107. The analogy is Anthony R. Turton, "Hydropolitical Dynamic of Cooperation in South Africa: A Strategic Perspective on Institutional Development in International River Basins," in *Transboundary Rivers, Sovereignty, and Development: Hydropolitical Drivers in the Okavango River Basin,* edited by Anthony R. Turton, Peter Ashton, and Eugene Cloete (Pretoria: African Water Issues Research Unit; Geneva: Green Cross International, 2003).

108. IEA, *World Energy Outlook 2012.*

109. Ibid.

110. Ibid.

111. Ibid.

112. Ibid.

113. Ibid.

114. On India, see Indian Navy, *Indian Maritime Doctrine.* On China, see Donghai, "China's Oil Resources Security Strategy."

115. On India, see Planning Commission, *Integrated Energy Policy.* On China, see International Crisis Group, *China's Thirst for Oil,* Asia Report 153 (Zurich, 2008).

116. J. V. Mitchell, "Energy and Security," lecture delivered at the Royal Swedish Academy of War Sciences, Sweden, March 16, 2000.

117. Constantin, *China's Conception of Energy Security.*

118. Planning Commission, *Integrated Energy Policy.*

119. "Inflation Fears Heat up in Chilly China," *Wall Street Journal,* January 19, 2013. "India Hikes Rates by Quarter Point on Oil Fears," *Wall Street Journal,* March 17, 2011.

120. India's exposure to high oil prices is the highest among large oil importers such as China, the United States, and the European Union.

121. IEA, *World Energy Outlook 2012.*

8

Resource Security in Saudi Arabia: Domestic Challenges and Global Implications

KRISTIAN COATES ULRICHSEN

Saudi Arabia is facing a major shift in its local and global energy landscape. Domestic fiscal and energy consumption pressures challenge the redistributive political economy that for decades has underpinned sociopolitical stability in the Saudi Kingdom. Saudi policy responses to the regional upheaval that has rocked the Middle East and North Africa since early 2011 have exacerbated the challenge of sustaining resource security. Moreover, emerging trends in oil and gas production and extraction threaten to reshape the international energy system and move its center of gravity away from the Gulf. The dilemma facing Saudi policymakers is one of balancing domestic sociopolitical stability against the need to reform and diversify economic structures. The critical question is whether the processes of change that will occur are orderly and managed, or disruptive and contested.

This chapter investigates the causes and multiple trajectories of change in Saudi Arabia's socioeconomic model. It begins by examining how dependence on oil revenues has been intertwined with state building and economic development since the 1950s. This leads into a second section that argues that the redistributive system faces interlinked threats to its existence. These are the soaring levels of domestic energy consumption that incrementally eat into overall Saudi production and export figures, as well as a combination of declining field productivity, intensifying international competition from conventional and unconventional sources alike, and potentially weaker global demand for hydrocarbons in a financially and climate-stressed world. The following (third) section addresses the likely challenges that will result from any decline in absolute or relative levels of oil revenue and their implications for domestic sociopolitical stability. These issues will occur against the backdrop of a leadership transition to a newer generation of governing elites in the Kingdom. Finally, the concluding section offers observations on the looming intersection of the multilevel transformations as described in the paper, and explores the geopolitical risks and opportunities that may arise.

From the beginning of Saudi Arabia's emergence as a modern state (in 1932), the accrual and redistribution of oil rents have played the pivotal role in the processes of state formation and subsequent consolidation. As late as the 1940s the political economy of the young state was still rooted in rudimentary and subsistence-based techniques and traditional modes of production located within the boundaries of the village or tribe. A minimal state operated within strict financial constraints and considerable resource poverty, with little distinction between royal and state resources because initially the state appeared little more than an extension of the ruling family. The major sources of economic livelihood remained pastoral agriculture and trade, alongside small-scale artisanal and commercial activities in the towns.[1]

Starting in 1948, a haphazard process of institution building commenced in order to provide an administrative framework to oversee the extraction of oil. This was necessary to demarcate national boundaries and determine property rights for oil-concession holders, channel the incoming revenues into material development by way of seeking support from tribal, merchant, and Bedouin allies, and link the economy into world markets through oil exports. Substantive progress on all these fronts gathered pace following the death of King Abdul Aziz Al-Saud in 1953, whereupon there was no state apparatus capable of administering the country's principal resource. Hence the processes of modern state formation were intricately connected to the receipt and redistribution of revenues generated by the export of oil.[2]

Saudi Arabia, therefore, is a hydrocarbons-based economy. The petroleum sector currently represents 45 percent of GDP and provides roughly 80 percent of the Kingdom's budget revenues, and 90 percent of its export earnings.[3] Oil rents transformed the political economy of Saudi Arabia, reshaped state-society relations during the twentieth century, and influenced the economic development of the redistributive, rent-based ("rentier") state that emerged.[4] The 2012 *BP Statistical Review of World Energy* projects the Kingdom's reserves-to-production ratio to last a further 65.2 years, although this is significantly lower than the estimate given by the same publication just two years earlier, in 2010, which posited a reserves-to-production ratio of 74.6 years.[5] As will be analyzed in full in the following sections, this drop reflects some of the uncertainties over the medium- and longer-term prospects of Saudi energy policy.

Exports of oil started shortly after the end of the Second World War and subsequently tied Saudi Arabia firmly into the international economic system. Strong mutual interdependencies developed between the Kingdom and Western economies, creating powerful linkages between oil-producing and -consuming states in the post-1945 era of industrial reconstruction. Saudi Arabia thus was integrated into the global economy long before the acceleration of global- izing flows and processes of economic globalization in the 1980s and 1990s.[6] However, the structure of the oil sector created the distinctive nature of rentier economies marked by enclave-based development largely isolated from the non- oil economic sector. Moreover, its capital intensity meant that hydrocarbons provided few opportunities for integration with labor markets, accounting for only 1.2 percent of the total workforce in 2004, while the accrual of oil rents to Saudi nationals (via state redistributive and welfare policies) created disincentives toward economic productivity. Dual labor markets emerged as the public sector absorbed Saudi nationals (constituting 86 percent of total public sector employ- ees), while the private sector largely became the preserve of the burgeoning expa- triate workforce (60 percent of the private sector total in 2008).[7]

Saudi Arabia nevertheless differs significantly from the comparable economies of its smaller Arab Gulf neighbors (particularly Kuwait, Qatar, and the United Arab Emirates). It has a much larger population (26.5 million in 2012) and rapid demographic growth that complicates the continued transfer of wealth through the redistribution of oil revenues.[8] Together, these trends have caused disparities in income, wealth, and intrasocietal inequalities spread across several internal fault lines. Regional and sectarian differences reflect the diverse nature of Saudi society and the fact that the Kingdom was created through campaigns of conquest by Abdul-Aziz Al-Saud between 1902 and 1932, leaving subnational fault lines that exist to this day. Heavy dependence on oil revenues generates additional volatilities, because reliance on the fluctuating international price of oil injects a degree of uncertainty into economic performance. Thus, while Saudi Arabia has enjoyed years of successive budget surpluses since oil prices began to rise in 2002, it should not be forgotten that the Kingdom recorded seven- teen consecutive years of budget deficits during the prolonged price slump in the 1980s and 1990s. In 1991 the deficit was equivalent wholly to 19 percent of gross domestic product (GDP), while the lengthy slump caused a protracted economic downturn and placed great strain on the maintenance of the social contract that underpinned the redistribution of wealth and provision of jobs to Saudi nationals.[9]

During the downturn, income per capita more than halved between 1980 and 2000, from US$16,650 to US$7,239, consistent with a general fall in the value of oil exports per capita throughout the Gulf Cooperation Council (GCC,) from US$15,000 to US$6,000 over the same period.[10] A high birth rate of 29 per 1,000 of total population (double that of the United States at 14 per 1,000) and a median age of just 21.6 years further exacerbates the decline and places added pressure on the economy to generate the jobs that will be required to accommodate the resulting youth bulge. In 2000 the scale of the challenge became evident in estimates that 3,474,000 new jobs would be created by 2020, compared to a projected increase in the Saudi labor force of 5,091,000.[11]

Programs of labor nationalization ("Saudization") and economic diversification therefore formed the cornerstone of successive five-year development plans. These began in 1970 as part of an attempt to reduce the direct and indirect reliance on hydrocarbons revenue and to increase the value added and non-oil sectors of the Saudi economy. While initial plans during the 1970s oil boom were characterized by lavish expenditure on prestige projects (often of questionable enduring value) in the context of state-led development, more recent ones have demonstrated a considerable maturation of economic policy objectives. In particular, the seventh (2000–04) and eighth (2005–09) plans shifted the focus of policymaking to embrace the private sector as the engine of economic diversification and growth, embedded within sustainable development policies through investment in human resources and science, technology, and IT.[12]

Economic diversification programs in Saudi Arabia followed a two-pronged approach. One dimension focused on establishing economic cities as hubs of agglomeration and encouraging the creation and diffusion of knowledge, while the other emphasized developing a sophisticated downstream petrochemicals industry, in addition to investing in other energy-intensive industries (such as aluminum) and capital-intensive technological sectors. By 2009 the Kingdom was the fastest growing market in the Middle East for the petrochemical, printing, plastics, and packaging industries and accounted for 70 percent of petrochemical production in the GCC.[13] Interwoven into both the job creation and economic diversification programs was the emergence in the 2000s of an incipient private sector bourgeoisie. This comprised individuals and businessmen involved in the production of value added goods and services, who would be less dependent on the state for the receipt and redistribution of oil rents.[14] Luciani went as far as to label the appearance of an autonomous national bourgeoisie as a "silent transformation," indicative of a shift toward a post-rentier framework of governance.[15]

Against this more positive trajectory of autonomous economic development, several factors continue to constrain the breadth and depth of Saudi diversification, such as the resilience of opaque networks of familial political-economic alliances. These complicate the transition to a market economy with high standards of corporate governance and introduce a measure of conceptual uncertainty into the notion of a "private" sector genuinely operating beyond the realm of the state.[16] Saudi Arabia's relatively opaque business culture became evident in May 2009 when two of the most prominent family conglomerates in Saudi Arabia (the Saad Group and Ahmad Hamad Algosaibi and Brothers) unexpectedly announced a debt restructuring.[17] This affected more than 80 domestic, regional, and international banks, including Citigroup and BNP Paribas. A general lack of transparency and inadequate disclosure of information to investors demonstrated the difficulty in overcoming older ways of conducting business on the basis of informal and familial connections.[18]

Nevertheless, four decades of development plans and substantial investment in industrial projects have failed significantly to lessen the centrality of hydrocarbons in Saudi Arabia's political economy. On the contrary, the processes of industrialization are energy intensive, and most business entities either are hydrocarbon derivatives (such as petrochemicals and plastics) or dependent on cheap feedstock (such as aluminum or cement) for their comparative advantage.[19] Moreover, economic responses to the regional upheaval across the Arab world in 2011 underscored the continuing importance of oil revenues in cushioning potential dissent and conditioning policy choices in the Kingdom. These primarily took the form of two emergency welfare packages collectively worth US$130 billion. This enormous figure exceeded the size of every annual government budget prior to 2007 and included a provision to employ 60,000 additional Saudis in the Ministry of Interior alone. The welfare proposals also contained stipulations for increasing the minimum wage of public sector employees, offering a one-time bonus of a month's pay to all public officials and constructing 500,000 new homes to combat a shortage of social housing.[20]

Saudi Arabia's redistributive economic model faces four major challenges in the years ahead—two internal and two external. The domestic factors are the increasingly unsustainable pattern of domestic energy consumption as well as uncertainty regarding oil reserves, while the international dimensions are, short term, the possibility of a protracted global economic downturn and, medium and longer term, the rebalancing energy landscape across the world. Linking these issues is the common thread of reduced room for maneuver caused by the substantive rises in public expenditure and the political sensitivity of reformulating the networks of subsidy that have underpinned sociopolitical stability for decades. Together, these trends will inject profound new uncertainties into the regional security landscape as existing pillars of domestic and regional stability become increasingly untenable in the longer term.

Saudi oil use nearly has doubled in just eight years, from 1.6 million barrels per day in 2003 to 2.8 million in 2011, while government spending also escalated during the same period. Between 2003 and 2009, the government wage bill rose by 76 percent while the number of employees in the public sector increased by 24 percent, despite the avowed policy of Saudization of the work force.[21] Such rapid rises in domestic consumption represent a problem that will become more challenging the longer it is unresolved. The scale became clear in an official report compiled by the Saudi Electricity Company in the spring of 2011. The report pointed out that nearly one-third of current Saudi oil production (8.5 million barrels per day in 2011) is used to meet local demand, primarily for power generation, and that the revenues from the export of the remaining oil provide nearly 80 percent of government revenue. However, it also warned that if present rates of local consumption continue, current production levels would be unable to meet local demand by 2030. Already, domestic oil consumption increased by 11 percent, in the year between May 2010 and May 2011, and high population growth will translate into increasing future demand for energy. Moreover, a diplomatic communication released by WikiLeaks in 2010 predicted that domestic energy demand would grow 10 percent each year and suggested that the Kingdom's ability to export oil would decline as these domestic requirements escalated.[22]

The diversion of crude oil to meet domestic energy demand therefore imposes a growing constraint on Saudi Arabia's and other GCC states' export capabilities. Aside from Qatar, the increasing shortage of natural gas to fire power plants and generate electricity means that ever-larger amounts of oil are being burned to generate sufficient power to meet the demands of energy-intensive industrialization and high population growth. Between 25 and 30 percent of Saudi Arabian crude currently is being diverted to local use, amounting to some 2.8 million barrels each day. Two reports, both published in 2011, highlighted the dangers hidden within these approaches. The first was a paper published by the British think tank Chatham House, which warned that continuing growth in domestic demand for energy would cause economic and social pressures long before the ending of oil exports. Alarmingly, the authors added that these pressures could come about as early as 2020.[23] Meanwhile, over the summer of 2011 the Riyadh-based consultancy Jadwa Investments drew up a worst-case scenario covering the oil and fiscal challenges in the Kingdom. Their report warned the Saudi government that it faced an especially difficult future if spending and oil trends did not change. Indeed, it raised the prospect of substantial budget deficits by the 2020s and, sensationally, predicted that domestic oil consumption would reach 6.5 million barrels per day by 2030. By this time, it warned, Saudi Arabia could be facing a reduction in foreign assets to minimal levels, rapidly rising debt, and a break-even price of more than US$320 per barrel.[24]

Unsustainable patterns of domestic energy consumption reflect the market-distorting pricing policies that deliver energy at greatly subsidized prices as well as the energy-intensive nature of GCC states' industrialization (and urbanization) projects reliant on cheap feedstock of gas. Both trends support a culture of almost unrestrained energy consumption and are underpinned by the provision of crude oil to local markets at around US$8–10 a barrel, far below the global rate upwards of US$80–90. This imposes a double cost on governments, which must continue to subsidize artificially low domestic prices of oil while incurring a significant opportunity cost because they cannot export and sell at international market prices. As perhaps the most extreme example, Kuwait has not raised electricity prices for individual consumers since 1962, but also in Qatar, domestic consumption of oil has trebled since 2000. Within Saudi Arabia, figures from the Hong Kong and Shanghai Banking Corporation (HSBC) estimate that fuel subsidies cost the Kingdom some US$70 billion each year in lost export revenues alone.[25]

In a political context in which low fuel and electricity prices are a significant mechanism of wealth redistribution, the difficulties of reducing or rolling back subsidized utilities are manifold. In November 2012 the rapid escalation of demonstrations and protesters' demands for regime change in neighboring Jordan, following the announcement of a 53 percent rise in prices of gasoline, cooking gas, diesel fuel, and kerosene to tackle a US$5 billion budget deficit, demonstrated just how volatile the issue could become.[26] Yet, the longer that the Gulf States put off the politically sensitive issues of reformulating the subsidy regimes and the social contract in its current guise, the harder it will become to wean citizens off such mechanisms that increasingly are taken for granted. Resource shortages may therefore develop into intractable threats to security if they call into question the state's capacity to deliver essential goods to its citizen population.

Against this backdrop of demand pressures, there is additional uncertainty over the extent of Saudi Arabia's resource endowment. Another leaked diplomatic cable from WikiLeaks revealed that a senior official at Saudi Aramco had warned the U.S. consul general in Riyadh in 2007 that the Kingdom's oil reserves may have been overstated by as much as 40 percent. The cable noted that "it is possible that Saudi reserves are not as bountiful as sometimes described, and the timeline for production not as unrestrained as Aramco and energy optimists would like to portray."[27] While it is difficult, if not impossible, to verify such claims, it is worth pointing out that Saudi Arabia and several other countries in the Gulf, including Kuwait, the United Arab Emirates (UAE), and Iran, all registered a series of sudden and massive jumps in reserves in the 1980s in a bid to secure larger shares in the OPEC quota system then being introduced. Indeed, Saudi Arabia recorded the largest absolute rise as officials added 85.4 billion barrels to proven reserves in 1988, while the UAE recorded the highest proportionate increase in proven reserves, which jumped by a startling 195 percent in 1986, from 33 billion to 97.2 billion barrels of oil.[28] Further lack of consensus exists regarding the operational state and productivity of the Saudi oil fields. The late Matthew Simmons painted a gloomy picture of aging fields seemingly in a long-term decline that could neither be offset by substantive new discoveries nor reversed by technological improvements in oil field management and enhanced oil recovery.[29] By contrast, Dubai-based energy consultant Robin Mills provides a far more robust and optimistic account of Saudi oil prospects, countering each of Simmons's points in turn and emphasizing the Kingdom's untapped reserves, further exploration potential in gas as well as oil, and much lower production costs.[30] Moving beyond these differing interpretations and potential scenarios, it is nevertheless the case that the greater diversion of crude oil from international markets to domestic use will draw down Saudi Arabia's export potential far sooner than the eventual depletion of its total reserves.

Domestic trends within Saudi Arabia therefore offer some cause for concern. The same can be said of international economic and energy trajectories, which currently do not favor Gulf oil-exporting states. Although the world economy began to rebound in 2009–10 following the global financial crisis of 2007–08, the onset of a double-dip recession and the eurozone crisis hit Western economies hard. In addition, a slowdown of growth in China and other key Asian markets also contributed to a downturn in economic activity in 2011–12. This may become significant as the large spending rises announced in 2011 need oil prices to remain high if they are to be financed properly. In October 2012 the International Monetary Fund (IMF), drawing attention to Saudi Arabia's vulnerability in relying on uncertain revenue flows, warned that the Kingdom could slide into a 0.6 percent budget deficit by 2017 as a result of falling oil prices and increasing state spending.[31] The organization laid out a scenario whereby oil prices fell by US$30 per barrel and remained at that level into the medium term. If this happened, the IMF forecast that the GCC states would begin to go into deficit by 2014, with Bahrain and Oman running deficits of up to 16 percent by 2017 and Saudi Arabia also facing a double-digit deficit by that time.[32]

The fourth vulnerability also is external in the sense that it lies beyond the control of policymakers within Saudi Arabia. This is the looming transformation of the geopolitics of energy arising from the unlocking of massive unconventional reserves such as tight oil and shale gas. A report released in November 2012 by the International Energy Agency predicted that the United States would overtake Russia and Saudi Arabia to become the largest producer of oil (to go alongside surging gas production) by 2017.[33] While the United States has not in actual fact been dependent on Saudi oil (its two largest suppliers are Canada and Mexico), the westward shift of the energy gravity center still is momentous. Significantly, the volume of unconventional oil in the Americas far exceeds Middle Eastern conventional reserves, with an estimated 2.4 trillion barrels in Canada, 2 trillion in the United States and in South America as compared with 1.2 trillion barrels in the Middle East.[34] With technological developments making possible the commercial recovery of ever-larger unconventional resources, the relative absence of equivalent large-scale reserves in the Middle East may become more pronounced. Even within the Gulf, Saudi Arabia could also be squeezed by increasing production in Iraq, if industry estimates of a doubling in Iraqi production from 3 million barrels a day in August 2012 to more than 6 million by 2020 prove correct.[35]

The internal and external trends described above will have a significant impact on national and regional security structures in the Persian Gulf. The shifting of the center of gravity in the global energy landscape away from the Middle East may intersect with the rising geopolitical and geo-economic importance of South and East Asia; in this sense, the Obama administration's much-heralded "pivot to Asia" may be a harbinger of things to come. The dilemma for Saudi policymakers is that domestic production has been at or near full capacity since the late 1990s, while the entry of major new producers may dilute Saudi Arabia's position as the pivotal swing producer capable of regulating global oil prices. To the extent that oil has provided the linchpin both of Saudi domestic stability and of its regional and international power, any loosening of Saudi influence could have multilevel ramifications. These consequences already have become apparent and likely will only become more salient over time. Notably, the uneven depletion of oil reserves across the GCC has diverted Saudi Arabia's own resources of oil and financial assistance to support neighboring states, as occurred in Bahrain in 2011 and with financial packages for Bahrain, Oman, and Jordan unveiled in 2012. This was followed in 2013 by the immediate provision of large-scale financial support to the interim Egyptian government that replaced toppled president Mohamed Morsi in July.[36]

Both as individual members and as a collective organization, the GCC has turned inward in response to the regional pressures generated by the Arab Spring. In December 2012 the annual GCC Summit in Bahrain prioritized closer defense and security cooperation under a vague (and publicly undisclosed) security agreement. The enhanced collection and sharing of data across national boundaries undoubtedly will boost efforts to protect critical national infrastructure and energy installations from attack either by local terror networks or by Iran (in the event of any confrontation between Tehran and the international community). However, a spate of cross-border arrests of opposition activists early in 2013 indicated that the closer security collaboration was targeting internal dissent as well as external aggressors, as the six Gulf monarchies attempted to limit the spread of unrest.[37]

As domestic and regional resource constraints become more pressing, recent experience suggests that the Gulf States will continue their inward turn toward rule by coercion rather than consent. Managing the processes of change will become progressively more difficult if domestic pressures build up without an outlet for consensual reform. Given the high-visibility role of the Gulf States, led by Saudi Arabia, in structures of international governance and the regional security architecture of the Middle East, the danger is that security and stability will become increasingly fragile and transient over time if the patterns of unsustainable energy consumption are inadequately resolved. This raises the prospect that sensitive internal reforms to the sociopolitical and economic structures of rent redistribution may occur against the backdrop of regional upheaval and inject major new uncertainties into the regional security landscape.

The previous section documented how increasing domestic energy consumption posed a challenge to the continuation of the status quo model of wealth redistribution in the Kingdom. This section begins with the second major threat to Saudi Arabia's political economy, namely the rapidly rising break-even price of oil needed to balance the budget and ensure a surplus. Together, these two longer-term challenges constitute an Achilles' heel that, if left unchecked or inadequately tackled, will pose a growing threat to the political survival of the status quo. Moreover, they call into question the viability of the welfare strategies for coopting support and spreading resources that developed in the 1960s and 1970s in times of comparatively smaller populations and seemingly endless resources.[38] The section then continues with an analysis of the unfolding leadership transition in Saudi Arabia as a new generation of officials prepares to take the helm of Saudi policymaking.

The breakeven oil price concerns the price level that will be necessary to sustainably maintain the increases in social and welfare expenditure outlined in the previous section. During the long years of the oil price boom that began in 2003 and has continued, with a major dip in 2008–09, through 2014, Saudi Arabia and the other Gulf States ran significant budget surpluses. As mentioned earlier, this sustained period of capital accumulation sharply contrasted with the prolonged period of low oil prices in the 1980s and 1990s. As oil prices rocketed in the 2000s, collectively, the GCC states acquired US$912 billion of foreign assets in the five years to June 2008.[39] In Saudi Arabia, Jean-François Seznec estimates that oil income rose from US$42 billion in 1999 to US$181 billion in 2006, before soaring to US$211 billion in 2007 and US$307 billion in 2008.[40]

Since 2008, however, Saudi and other Gulf economies were hit first by the rapid slump in oil prices in late 2008 and into 2009, and later, as economies returned to surplus in 2010 and 2011, by the impact of the spending increases.

The volatility of world oil prices highlighted the Gulf States' vulnerability to external factors that directly affect government revenues and that largely are beyond their control. It is within this context that the rises in the breakeven price of oil need to be assessed. This has risen inexorably over the past decade and now is well over US$100 per barrel for resource-poor Bahrain and Oman. The increase in Saudi Arabia has been from US$20 to nearly US$90 per barrel during that time, with the Institute for International Finance forecasting a breakeven price of US$110 by 2015.[41]

The steady rise both in public spending and in the breakeven level leaves the Saudi government (alongside the other Gulf States) dependent on oil prices remaining high. Any significant drop would leave them exposed, and although their massive capital accumulations and budget surpluses in recent years provide a buffer of sorts, they do leave them a hostage to fortune should prices fall and then remain low. It is, after all, only five years since prices temporarily plunged to US$33 a barrel in 2008–09. Furthermore, Saudi Arabia engineered the pledges of US$10 billion of GCC aid each to Bahrain and Oman and US$5 billion to Jordan in 2011, although very little of the money appears yet to have materialized. Yet, with the Arab upheaval coursing through the region, Saudi officials did provide assistance to limit the spread of the unrest, with one estimate of US$25 billion in 2012 alone.[42]

Political leaders and officials both in Riyadh and in the GCC states thus fear the potential unrest that could ensue from the scaling back of the oil-funded redistributive state, particularly if it occurs during times of comparative hardship. The street riots in Yemen in 2005 that followed government efforts to abolish subsidies on diesel provide a case in point.[43] So, too, did the surge in commodity prices in 2007–08, which left states in the GCC, as elsewhere in the Middle East, vulnerable to social unrest and simmering discontent at the rising cost of living.[44] The drawdown of subsidy regimes and the search for resource security is consequently fraught with difficulty. For this reason, stability of access to resources is intertwined with the maintenance of social order, especially in the theoretically depoliticized polities of the Gulf. If well managed, resources can become valuable assets of development, as evidenced most successfully in Norway in the decades following the discovery of North Sea oil and gas.[45] Hence, while resource security has been, and will continue to be, a pillar of internal security in the short to medium term, the way that officials address it will determine the nature of the longer-term economic transformation.

In parallel with these economic and resource security challenges is the imminent political transition to a new generation of Saudi leaders. The death first of Crown Prince Sultan bin Abdul Aziz Al-Saud (October 2011) and then of his successor, Nayef bin Abdul Aziz Al-Saud (June 2012), thrust the issue of succession to the forefront of the domestic agenda. With King Abdullah bin Abdul Aziz Al-Saud nearing ninety years of age and his designated successor, Crown Prince Salman bin Abdul Aziz Al-Saud, in his late seventies, it is likely that the shift toward the "third generation" of grandsons of Saudi Arabia's founding father will occur sooner rather than later. The appointment of a number of younger princes to key positions within the Saudi government and provincial governorships indicates that this process of generational renewal has already begun.[46]

Despite comprising nearly 5,000 members, the Al-Saud family has consistently demonstrated an ability to control the broad pace of domestic change. However, the ruling family is far from a monolithic entity with one official view. Subgroups of brothers and half-brothers historically have formed powerful alliances exercising influence over the direction and formation of policy.[47] Now, the looming transition to the third generation of princes introduces new dynamics into this intrafamilial balancing. The creation of an Allegiance Council (al-Hayaat al-Bayaa) in October 2006, consisting of thirty-five senior sons and grandsons, aimed to formalize the process of future successions and ensure that the Al-Saud reach a quiet consensus around a suitable candidate in a manner similar to the Al-Sabah family council in Kuwait. However, its relevance was called into question in 2009 when the announcement of Prince Nayef as second deputy prime minister (effectively the third-in-line after the king and Crown Prince Salman) appeared to bypass the council and come directly from King Abdullah himself.[48] Yet, during a period of domestic economic challenges, Saudi leadership needs to be focused not only on securing the line of succession but also on formulating longer-term plans for the process of transition toward a post-oil economy.

The reformulation of Saudi Arabia's redistributive political economy is consequently fraught with challenges. Continuing access to resources is intertwined with the maintenance of social order, especially in a theoretically depoliticized system of governance. Energy security operates at interconnected levels in the Arabian Peninsula states. Internally, privileged access to resources through policies of widespread wealth redistribution constitutes powerful centripetal mechanisms and pillars of regime legitimation. Externally, governments' ability to provide these resources to their citizenry is intimately bound up with (and vulnerable to disruption to) the constant and unimpeded flow of revenues from hydrocarbon exports. This, in turn, feeds into a third dimension, which is the energy security requirements of the oil-consuming nations that purchase their oil and gas from the Gulf region. The internal and external dimensions are interlinked as any disruption to one heightens the vulnerability of the other, as the two are contingent on the smooth functioning of each. This was evidenced in al Qaeda in the Arabian Peninsula's specific targeting of the core of regime legitimacy in Saudi Arabia through its attack on the Kingdom's oil-processing facilities at Abqaiq in February 2006.[49]

One dilemma facing officials is that the concept of resource security is nuanced and multidimensional, meaning that individual aspects cannot easily be addressed in isolation. A prime example is the record of Saudi attempts to attain food security by promoting agricultural productivity that paradoxically made the problem of resource insecurity worse. Three decades of state-sponsored agricultural development programs commenced in the 1970s and aimed to increase the Kingdom's self-sufficiency in selected food items. They raised wheat production from 3,000 tons in 1970 to a peak of 3.4 million in 1991, before falling away to 2.5 million tons by 2008.[50] Yet, these policies neither were successful in increasing food self-sufficiency and reducing reliance on imported foodstuffs, nor were they sustainable through careful managing of scarce water resources. Agriculture accounted for a mere 6.5 percent of GDP in Saudi Arabia and a total of 1.6 percent throughout the GCC, but nearly 60 percent of total water consumption usage in 2000.[51] This far outstripped industrial and domestic usage and represented an unsustainable use of resources in what was already one of the most arid regions in the world. In Saudi Arabia the Al-Safi Dairy Farm represented a prominent example of the disjuncture between agricultural use and water scarcity. It is the largest in the world and more than double the size of the biggest dairy farm in the United States, with 37,000 cows producing more than 58 million gallons of milk each year, at an average water cost of nearly 2,300 gallons of water per gallon of milk.[52]

Belated recognition of the intertwined problems of water and food security led to the February 2008 announcement that Saudi Arabia would cease producing grain by 2016. Officials attributed this abrupt reversal in food policy to the impact of climate change, drought, and the depletion of fossil water. All of Saudi Arabia's wheat depended on central pivot irrigation that drew its water from fossil reserves. The drawdown of these reserves clashed with Saudi industrialization plans and rapid population growth, both of which significantly increased the demand for scarce water supplies. It also was proving unsustainable to Saudi Arabia's long-term water security by depleting the nonrenewable sources from the deep aquifers stretching underneath the Eastern Province.[53] Moreover, their interconnected nature meant that shared aquifers could become potential flashpoints of transboundary conflict in the future. An extensive regional aquifer system known as the Eastern Arabian Aquifer extends from central Saudi Arabia to Bahrain and Qatar, while the Kuwait Group Aquifer is hydraulically connected with the Dammam Foundation of the Hasa Group in eastern Saudi Arabia.[54]

Saudi overexploitation of its aquifers for agricultural use began to reduce the water availability and agricultural potential in Bahrain and Qatar.[55] These trends contain the seeds of future political tension over transboundary water resources, particularly as cooperation between GCC member states on utilizing and managing joint aquifers has so far been negligible.[56]

A similar example of the challenge posed by interconnected dimensions of policymaking lies in the recent Nitaqat initiative. This scheme, launched in 2011, classified all private sector companies into three color-coded bands to indicate their level of success in nationalizing their workforces and, in turn, their eligibility for future sponsorship of non-Saudi workers. The proportion of nationals deemed desirable in each sector varied from 6 percent in the construction sector to 19 percent in media and 49 percent in banking.[57] However, the scheme ran into difficulties, with warnings that the increased cost of hiring Saudi nationals could drive as many as one-third of small and medium-sized enterprises out of business. However, a proposal by the Ministry of Labor to introduce fines for private companies hiring too many foreign workers was subsequently criticized by members of the Shura (Consultative) Council, who attacked the plan as being bad for business.[58]

The two cases described above highlight the need for comprehensive measures that tackle issues in their entirety and protect policies from vested interests. The marginalization of the Saudi Arabian General Investment Authority (SAGIA) demonstrates how even ostensibly flagship reform initiatives can become vulnerable to such assault. Launched in 2000 with the strong support of then Crown Prince (now King) Abdullah, SAGIA built alliances with high-level figures within the Saudi bureaucracy and achieved some early success in economic liberalization ahead of Saudi Arabia's accession to the World Trade Organization in 2005. Even at this early stage, though, the academic Steffen Hertog noted that progress was "based on individual, personalized, case-by-case brokerage" and that "the deeper fiefdoms of the Saudi state have proven harder to penetrate."[59] This pessimistic analysis largely has proven true. SAGIA remains in a state of limbo following a series of corruption allegations, changes of leadership, and confusion regarding lack of clarity about the country's foreign investment regime.[60]

A potentially rocky road thus lies ahead for Saudi Arabia, both domestically, in terms of sustainably managing trends in the production and extraction of resources, and internationally, in terms of adapting to the shifting geopolitical balance of resources. Policymakers must be able to operate between and across the two levels in order to address the interrelated issues in an integrated way. The coming transition in global energy resources and within the political economy of Saudi Arabia represents a moment both of challenge but also of opportunity. While moving away from a status quo that has underpinned domestic stability for decades inherently raises a host of sensitive issues, the recent oil boom has provided officials with a strong base from which to make a start. The challenge for officials is one of maintaining control over the pace and extent of reform processes that otherwise may easily develop a momentum and direction of their own.

The concept of resource (and, within that, energy) security therefore is undergoing momentous change across the geopolitical spectrum and within individual regions and economies. It is neither a given that Saudi Arabia will maintain its position as the largest and most important swing producer over the next decade, nor guaranteed that the Kingdom will be able to reduce or address the patterns of unsustainable fiscal and energy policy outlined in this chapter. Moreover, the international politics of climate change likely will become harder for high-income hydrocarbon-producing countries to navigate. The political economy of rent redistribution and patterns of energy-intensive industrialization mean that Saudi Arabia—and the GCC as a whole—must strike a balance between shaping global response mechanisms and decisionmaking processes while simultaneously minimizing the disruptive threat to domestic interests from pressure exerted by international policy responses to the climate change issue.[61] However, Saudi Arabia developed a reputation for obstructionist tactics at successive rounds of negotiations during the 2000s by focusing on the (perceived) negative economic implications of a climate-changed world rather than on the environmental impacts of climate change itself.[62] Thus, in March 2009 during the run-up to the pivotal Copenhagen conference in December, Mohammad al-Sabban, the head of the Saudi delegation to the United Nations Framework Convention on Climate Change (UNFCCC) warned that strict global proposals to mitigate climate change by cutting carbon emissions and reducing dependence on oil represented a "very serious [threat] for oil producing countries and in particular Gulf producing countries," which "stand to lose out to such policies that are biased against oil producers."[63] This obstructionist stance continued through the 2012 climate change conference in neighboring Qatar, as Saudi negotiators joined with counterparts from China, India, and Iran to demand that developed countries reduce their aggregate emissions by an unrealistic 40 to 50 percent below 1990 levels by 2020.[64]

Saudi responses to climate change therefore are consistent with the ruling elites' pursuit of strategies of regime survival by adapting to changes in the international political economy around them. Enormous investments that have been announced in renewable and nuclear energy in Saudi Arabia are designed both to attempt to diversify away from over-reliance on oil and to counter international pressure. If implemented in a careful manner, these mega-projects hold out the possibility of significant job creation and inward investment that can strengthen private sector development. Set against this optimistic scenario is the continuing reliance on the politics of patronage as a tried-and-tested mechanism for ensuring social and political order and the resulting vulnerability to any volatility in international oil price fluctuations as the global energy market itself enters a period of transformative change.

It also is likely that the coming years and decades will see a rising tension between the need to decisively shift into a post-oil era while seeking to maintain the sociopolitical models that have underpinned regime stability thus far. Yet the inability to properly diversify away from dependence on oil revenues will be magnified if and when Saudi Arabia loses its comparative advantage in cheap energy when shale and other unconventional sources come fully on-stream. In addition, Saudi officials must balance between groups that wish to move ahead quickly and others that do not; the far-reaching changes inherent in any move toward post-oil governance threatens the rule by consensus that Saudi monarchs have always sought. Against all these domestic uncertainties, the intersection of local and regional trends across the Arab world with global shifts has the capacity to produce volatile, even game-changing results. With this in mind, the only certainty is that the status quo that has survived the first phase of the Arab Spring upheaval cannot be sustained for much longer, and will, eventually, be transformed. The major questions are in which direction and on whose terms this process will take place.

Notes

1. Tim Niblock, with Monica Malik, *The Political Economy of Saudi Arabia* (London: Routledge, 2007), p. 35.

2. Simon Bromley, *Rethinking Middle East Politics: State Formation and Development* (Cambridge, U.K.: Polity Press, 1994), pp. 144–45.

3. Central Intelligence Agency (CIA), "Saudi Arabia: Economy Overview," *World Factbook* (Washington, November 13, 2012).

4. Fred Halliday, *The Middle East in International Relations: Power, Politics, and Ideology* (Cambridge University Press, 2005), p. 271.

5. British Petroleum (BP), "Statistical Review of World Energy" (June 2012), p. 6; BP, "Statistical Review of World Energy" (June 2010), p. 6. Yearly publications are available in print and online at www.bp.com/en/global/corporate/about-bp/energy-economics/statistical-review-of-world-energy-2013.html.

6. Anoushivaran Ehteshami, *Globalization and Geopolitics in the Middle East: Old Games, New Rules* (London: Routledge, 2007), p. 110.

7. Gary Donn and Yahya Al-Manthri, *Globalisation and Higher Education in the Arab Gulf States* (Oxford: Symposium Books, 2010), p. 37.

8. CIA, "Saudi Arabia: People Overview," *World Factbook* (Washington, November 13, 2012).

9. Darryl Champion, "Saudi Arabia: Elements of Instability within Stability," in Barry Rubin, ed., *Crises in the Contemporary Persian Gulf* (London: Frank Cass, 2002), pp. 130–31.

10. Paul Dresch, "Societies, Identities, and Global Issues," in Paul Dresch and James Piscatori, eds., *Monarchies and Nations: Globalisation and Identity in the Arab States of the Gulf* (London: I. B. Tauris, 2005), p. 16.

11. Donn and Al-Manthri. *Globalisation and Higher Education,* p. 37.

12. Niblock with Malik, *Political Economy of Saudi Arabia,* pp.181–85.

13. Kristian Coates Ulrichsen, *Insecure Gulf: The End of Certainty and the Transition to the Post-Oil Era* (London: Hurst, 2011), p. 102.

14. Giacomo Luciani, "From Private Sector to National Bourgeoisie: Saudi Arabian Business," in Paul Aarts and Gerd Nonneman, eds., *Saudi Arabia in the Balance: Political Economy, Society, Foreign Affairs* (London: Hurst, 2005), p. 144.

15. Ibid., pp.180–81.

16. Chatham House, *The Gulf as a Global Financial Centre: Growing Opportunities and International Influence,* Chatham House Report (London, 2008), p. 48.

17. *The Peninsula* newspaper (Qatar), June 23, 2009.

18. Kristian Coates Ulrichsen, "Repositioning the GCC States in the Changing Global Order," *Journal of Arabian Studies* 1, no. 2 (2011): 237.

19. Steffen Hertog and Giacomo Luciani, "Energy and Sustainability Policies in the Gulf States," in David Held and Kristian Coates Ulrichsen, eds., *The Transformation of the Gulf: Politics, Economics, and the Global Order* (London: Routledge, 2011), p. 239.

20. Steffen Hertog, "The Costs of Counter-Revolution in the GCC," *Foreign Policy* (May 31, 2011).

21. Peter Salisbury, "Spending Increases Oil Shock Risks," *Middle East Economic Digest* 55, no. 27 (July 7, 2011): 30.

22. Christopher Davidson, *After the Sheikhs: The Coming Collapse of the Gulf Monarchies* (London: Hurst, 2012), p. 113.

23. Glada Lahn and Paul Stevens, "Burning Oil to Keep Cool: The Hidden Energy Crisis in Saudi Arabia," Chatham House Report (London: Chatham House, December 2011), pp. 2–3.

24. "Jadwa Forecasts Long-Term Fiscal Problems," *Gulf States Newsletter* 35, no. 906 (August 5, 2011): 12.

25. Kevin Baxter, "Riyadh's Rising Fuel Subsidy Bill," *Middle East Economic Digest* 55, no. 37 (September 16, 2011): 22–23.

26. "Jordan Engulfed in Protests over Fuel Price Hike," *Russia Today,* November 24, 2012.

27. "WikiLeaks Cables: Saudi Arabia Cannot Pump Enough Oil to Keep a Lid on Prices," *Guardian,* February 8, 2011.

28. Robin Mills, *The Myth of the Oil Crisis: Overcoming the Challenges of Depletion, Geopolitics, and Global Warming* (Westport, Conn.: Praeger, 2008), pp. 54–55.

29. See Matthew R. Simmons, *Twilight in the Desert: The Coming Saudi Oil Shock and the World Economy* (Hoboken, N.J.: John Wiley and Sons, 2005).

30. Mills, *Myth of the Oil Crisis,* pp. 108–18.

31. "Riyadh Looking for Bigger Say in IMF," *Gulf States Newsletter* 36, no. 933 (October 11, 2012): 13.

32. "Gulf Arab States Should Cut State Spending Growth: IMF," Reuters, October 29, 2012.

33. "US to Overtake Saudi as Top Oil Producer: IEA," Reuters, November 12, 2012.

34. Amy Myers Jaffe, "The Americas, Not the Middle East, Will Be the World Capital of Energy," *Foreign Policy* (September/October 2011).

35. "Iraq Oil Output to Double by 2020: IEA," *CNN Money,* October 9, 2012.

36. Aaron David Miller, "Why Obama Won't Give (or Get) Much in Saudi Arabia," *American Interest,* March 23, 2014.

37. Kristian Coates Ulrichsen, "Security Comes First," *Majalla,* January 2, 2013.

38. F. Gregory Gause, "The Persistence of Monarchy in the Arabian Peninsula: A Comparative Analysis," in Joseph Kostiner, ed., *Middle East Monarchies: The Challenge of Modernity* (London: Lynne Rienner, 2000), p. 186.

39. "Tracking GCC Foreign Investments: How the Strategies Are Changing with Markets in Turmoil" (Riyadh: SAMBA Financial Group, December 2008).

40. Jean-François Seznec, "The Gulf Sovereign Wealth Funds: Myth and Reality," *Middle East Policy* 15, no. 2 (2008): 99.

41. Hertog, "Costs of Counter-Revolution."

42. 'Saudi Arabia and the United States: Awkward Relations," *Economist,* March 29, 2014.

43. Ginny Hill, "Yemen: Fear of Failure," Briefing Paper (London: Chatham House, January 2010), p. 9.

44. Marie Lillo, "Ensuring Food Security: For the GCC, the Solution Lies in Africa," Gulf Research Centre Report (Dubai: Gulf Research Centre, July 1, 2008).

45. Halvor Mehlum, Kalle Moene, and Ragnar Torvik, "Social Policies and the Phasing in of Oil in the Norwegian Economy" Gulf Research Unit Working Paper (University of Oslo, March 2, 2010).

46. "Attrition among Aging Senior Leadership Will Force Third-Generation Princes up Al-Saud Hierarchy," *Gulf States Newsletter* 36, no. 925 (June 7, 2012): 1.

47. Madawi Al-Rasheed, "Circles of Power: Royals and Society in Saudi Arabia," in Aarts and Nonneman, eds., *Saudi Arabia in the Balance,* pp. 199–208.

48. Eleanor Gillespie, ed., "Politics, Succession, and Risk in Saudi Arabia," *Gulf States Newsletter Special Report* (January 2010): 27.

49. Paul Rogers, "Abqaiq's Warning," *Open Democracy,* March 2, 2006.

50. Andrew England and Javier Blas, "Water Concerns Prompt Saudis to Cease Grain Production," *Financial Times,* February 27, 2008.

51. Mohamed Raouf, "Water Issues in the Gulf: Time for Action," Policy Brief 22 (Washington: Middle East Institute, January 2009), p. 22.

52. "Dairy Kingdom," *Center for Strategic and International Studies Middle East Program Newsletter* (April 2010): 1.

53. Toby Craig Jones, *Saudi Alchemy: Water into Oil, Oil into Water,* Middle East Report 254 (Washington: Middle East Research and Information Project, Spring 2010), p. 29.

54. Raouf, "Water Issues in the Gulf," p. 3.

55. Ilan Berman and Paul Michael Wihbey, "The New Water Politics of the Middle East," *Strategic Review* (1999) (www.iasps.org/strategic/water.htm).

56. Raouf, "Water Issues in the Gulf," p .3.

57. Kasim Randeree, "Workforce Nationalization in the Gulf Cooperation Council States," Center for International and Regional Studies Occasional Paper 11 (Georgetown School of Foreign Service in Qatar, 2012), p. 12.

58. "Saudi Shoura Council Slams Expat Fee Plan," ArabianBusiness, November 20, 2012.

59. Steffen Hertog, *Princes, Brokers, and Bureaucrats: Oil and the State in Saudi Arabia* (Cornell University Press, 2010), pp. 174–76.

60. "Saudi Arabia Reviewing Whole Process of Foreign Investment," *International Financial Law Review* (July 11, 2012).

61. Kristian Coates Ulrichsen, "Rebalancing Global Governance: Gulf States' Perspectives on the Governance of Globalisation," *Global Policy* 2, no. 1 (2011): 71.

62. Joanna Depledge, "Striving for No: Saudi Arabia in the Climate Change Regime," *Global Environmental Politics* 8, no. 4 (2008): 20.

63. "Climate Action Plan to Harm Gulf Economies: Saudi Official," *Saudi Gazette,* March 20, 2009.

64. Andrew Light and others, "Doha Climate Summit Ends with the Long March to 2015" (Washington: Center for American Progress, December 11, 2012).

9

Governance for a Resilient Food System

ALEX EVANS

> *"Starvation is the characteristic of some people not having enough to eat. It is not the characteristic of there not being enough to eat."*
> —Amartya Sen[1]

At the beginning of the twenty-first century, humanity has achieved an astonishing feat. Even as the world's population has grown exponentially—to the brink of the 7 billion mark—it has managed to ensure that food production has kept pace. Yet amid this extraordinary success, there remains an equally arresting failure: the fact that enough food is produced to feed all of the world's inhabitants has not led to all people having enough to eat.

On the contrary, the latest available data from the Food and Agriculture Organization (FAO) suggest that in the period of 2010–12, 852 million people in developing countries were chronically undernourished, with progress on reducing hunger stalled since the onset of the global food price spike in 2008.[2] In the background, there is growing concern about how increasing volatility in the global food system—from food price spikes to the impact of extreme weather events and from shocks to the international trade system to debates over the influence of commodity speculation on food prices—could affect the food security outlook in the future, especially given underlying long-term trends like climate change, population growth, and increasing resource scarcity.

Against this backdrop, this chapter—an edited and updated version of a paper first commissioned by Oxfam and published in June 2011 to coincide with the launch of its Grow campaign on food security—discusses the role of international institutions in contributing to a more resilient food system.

At its core is the argument that access to food matters as much as how much food is produced. As policymakers sought to address food security issues during the 2008 food price spike, they tended to focus on the need to produce more food, overlooking the fact that this is different from ensuring food security for all of the world's people.

As the chapter discusses, poor people and poor countries are particularly vulnerable to different kinds of shocks as well as to slower-onset stresses such as gradual price inflation, declining water availability, or increasing average temperatures that can reduce crop yields. All too often, this vulnerability is most apparent in poor people's food insecurity. This should come as no surprise, given that poor households typically spend 50–80 percent of their income on food.[3]

The need to tackle poor people's particular vulnerability to shocks and stresses leads naturally to the question of how to replace vulnerability with resilience. The technical definition of resilience refers to the capacity of a system (anything from a community to an institution or indeed an ecosystem) to "absorb disturbance and reorganize while undergoing change so as still to retain essentially the same function, structure, identity, and feedbacks."[4] In the context of international development, it can be interpreted more broadly to refer to the ability of poor people to cope with shocks and stresses within a broader context of progress on human development goals.

Tackling this need implies a vision of development that starts from a clear recognition of the threats to poor people and to recent progress in poverty reduction posed by emerging risks like climate change and global economic instability. But it also implies a development agenda that looks beyond the need to defend existing progress against such risks and toward ways of making more progress in spite of disruption and turbulence.

The chapter begins by outlining some critical areas of action for international organizations as they seek to build a more resilient food system. It focuses primarily on actions needed at the supranational level, but also discusses both resilience at the country level and key elements of a longer-term agenda to address core supply and demand fundamentals affecting global food security. It concludes with a brief assessment of how the multilateral system has performed on food security in the six years since the 2008 food price spike.

The Challenge of Building a More Resilient Food System

The period since the onset of the global financial crisis has seen globalization entering an unstable and unpredictable phase, with food prices one of the areas where volatility has been most pronounced. Following a long global slump in prices for most commodities, food prices began to rise sharply in 2006, increasing by 9 percent in that year, 24 percent in 2007, and 51 percent over the twelve-month period to July 2008.[5]

Prices then fell sharply amid the global economic crisis, but soon recovered again, with the FAO Food Price Index surpassing its 2008 peak in 2011. In February 2014, the index stood at 208, compared to 100 in 2002–04 and 227 in 2011.[6]

Why have prices been so volatile? Part of the reason is simply that the supply and demand fundamentals for food have become progressively tighter in recent years. Demand is rising because the world's population is growing and because a larger and more affluent global middle class is switching to more resource-intensive "Western" diets. On the supply side, production has struggled to keep pace. The productivity gains of the "green revolution" have been running out of steam—from around 2 percent a year in the 1970s and 1980s to 1.1 percent a year in the 1990s and the first half of the last decade, with the rate projected to keep falling.[7] Competition for land and water is also limiting the growth of supply, pushing food prices upward in the process.

The convergence of the world's food and energy economies has also emerged as a key factor in food price inflation and volatility. The dependence of modern agriculture on fossil fuels means that high oil prices exert upward pressure on food prices too, as costs increase for on-farm energy use, inputs like fertilizers and pesticides, processing, and transportation. At the same time, high energy costs increase the attractiveness of biofuels as a substitute for fossil fuels, in the process diverting crops to engines instead of plates and creating another source of competition for land.

And while higher average temperatures could lead to higher global crop yields for the next few decades, a warmer world is projected to reduce yields immediately for low latitudes (that is, most developing countries).[8] Moreover, extreme weather events are already affecting yields in many countries (including, for instance, recent droughts in Russia, China, and the United States and floods in Australia and South Africa) and will do so much more in the future.

But food price inflation is not simply the result of supply and demand. Also important is the fact that, as food supply chains have become more globalized and efficient, they have also become more brittle and less resilient. "Just-in-time" logistics can reduce the margin of error and create risks of supply interruptions in extreme circumstances. One of the drivers of the 2008 food price spike was that countries' food stocks had fallen to historically low levels: from more than 110 days' worth before 2000 to just over sixty days' worth in 2004.[9]

Above all, a more globalized food system equals a more interdependent one too—which makes the system vulnerable to zero-sum games when governments or other key players succumb to panic or herd behaviors.

If, for example, key food exporters suddenly reduce or suspend their exports because of domestic unrest over food prices—as more than thirty countries did at the height of the 2008 spike—then import-dependent countries that rely on their exports are left hanging in the wind. By the same token, if import-dependent countries embark on bouts of panic buying on international grain markets to try to build up stockpiles and head off unrest over food prices—as various Middle Eastern and North African governments did in early 2011 as both the Arab Spring and a second food price spike gathered pace—then this too has the effect of worsening the problem for everyone else, as prices are forced still higher.

So what does the multilateral system need to do to reduce food price volatility and improve food security and resilience in developing countries? Four key areas for action stand out.

—*Make markets work better.* Measures are needed to improve markets in periods of tight supply and demand, including food reserves, more effective regulation of commodity futures, and improved market transparency.

—*Reduce the risk of global zero-sum games with food.* Ways are needed to reduce the risk of zero-sum games such as panic buying and export bans, protectionism in agricultural trade, and the need to balance countries' right to decide their own policies with their international responsibilities to their trade partners.

—*Build resilience on the ground and improve access to food.* More work is needed in developing countries, in particular, to improve access to food by scaling up social protection systems and food safety nets.

—*Address long-term supply and demand fundamentals.* More investment is needed in a "twenty-first-century green revolution" that improves output, while reducing resource intensity and using land and crops more efficiently and with less waste.

Making Markets Work Better

The first set of actions centers on recognizing the vulnerability of food markets to supply and demand shocks. As Homi Kharas has put it, "What makes food markets distinctive is that both supply and demand curves are highly inelastic, meaning neither responds much to price changes in the short run. The most basic economics dictates that small shocks in either supply or demand will therefore lead to large price changes."[10] The International Food Policy Research Institute, meanwhile, observes that, while higher food prices should benefit producers even if they cut into the budgets of consumers, "volatile food prices . . . harm both consumers and producers by increasing uncertainty and making it difficult for households to budget for food consumption and to plan for production."[11]

Food Reserves

One set of actions that can be taken to build greater resilience to volatile price changes is to invest in food reserves. Food reserves come in a variety of forms, including community reserves that reduce post-harvest waste and give small farmers more control over when to sell their crops, strategic reserves at the national level that are used to stabilize prices, and international reserves that are available for emergency use (either physical stockpiles or "virtual" reserves based on promises to provide food if it is needed).

However, food reserves do come with costs and trade-offs. Running large inventories is expensive, and no one wants to pay for them unless they have to: private sector companies have no incentive to hold stocks beyond their own needs, while governments tend to want cheap, simple solutions. Food reserves are often complicated to run and can distort prices when reserves are released, in effect reducing farmers' ability to profit from periods of high prices.

In spite of these issues, food reserves have an important role to play in ensuring food security. For example, they can create preparedness for food emergencies, ranging from humanitarian relief operations after disasters to ensuring that a country can still access grain, even if tight international markets have fallen prey to spasms of exports. "Buffer reserves," which are used to stabilize prices rather than react only in emergency conditions, can potentially be used to guard against excessive price volatility, an important factor given the inelasticity of supply and demand for food. Reserves can also provide support to smallholder farmers when the grain used for reserves is sourced from them. (This is the principle of the World Food Program's Purchase for Progress initiative, which purchases food for emergency operations from small farmers in developing countries, rather than from producers in developed countries—thus helping small producers as well as the recipients of food assistance.)

Between the 1960s and 1980s, food reserves were widely used. After that, however, they began to decline, as international financial institution–mandated structural adjustment programs in developing countries insisted on phasing them out, as the private sector moved toward just-in-time supply chains, and as structural oversupply of food, coupled with the high cost of holding reserves, began to make them seem unnecessary. More recently, increased trade liberalization has increased the liquidity of global markets for many foods (although not all: rice markets remain relatively illiquid, for example), further reducing the apparent need for countries to maintain their own stocks.

However, the food price volatility of recent years has brought many of these assumptions into question, and the issue of food reserves is back on the agenda. But there are still important questions about what kind of approach makes most sense in which circumstances. In broad terms, the following are the main options available:

—*Community reserves.* Community reserves buy food from farmers when prices are low and keep it until prices are high enough to cover purchase and management expenses. They can be used as reserves during the seasonal "hunger gap" or as collateral for pre- or post-harvest credit. They also play a social function, by providing food to the poorest families in the community.

—*National-level reserves.* Following the 2008 food price spike, many governments, including Burkina Faso, the Democratic Republic of Congo, Malawi, Nicaragua, Pakistan, and Zambia, decided to scale up their food reserves for emergency use. Using national reserves to stabilize prices is much more contentious, due to risks of corruption, the discouraging effect that buffer stocks have on private stockholdings, the expense involved, and other factors. Major exporter governments can also use stocks to manipulate prices.

—*Regional reserves.* Regional reserves can ensure that food is in the right place when it is needed, while reducing some of the risks associated with national reserves. A range of governments are considering or moving forward with pooled regional arrangements, including the Economic Community of West African States and the ASEAN Plus Three Emergency Rice Reserve (APTERR), which came into force in July 2012.

—*Global reserves.* The World Food Program has proposed creating a global emergency food reserve, which was subsequently included in the G-20's plan of action following summits of both agriculture ministers and heads of government in 2011.

As yet, there is little consensus on which of these options (or a blend of them) makes most sense. However, it is important that countries have the space to try out different approaches and that the results of these experiments are shared, so as to allow improvements to be made over time. What is clear, though, is that the low stock levels that preceded the 2008 food price spike did increase overall vulnerability to food price volatility and that a move toward higher stocks would strengthen global resilience.

Financial Markets and Speculation

A second key issue in the area of making markets work better is the role that financial markets have played in amplifying food price volatility.

There is considerable disagreement about the role that speculation has played in driving food price inflation and volatility. While it is clear that traded volumes of agricultural commodity futures have increased markedly in recent years, this is not the same as saying that speculative activity has been responsible for rising food prices. In some ways, speculation can be seen as a "canary in the coal mine" in that food prices are rising and becoming more volatile for reasons that are very much rooted in the real-world economy.

A further challenge arises from the difficulty of distinguishing in practice between the use of financial futures to hedge against price volatility—something many farmers, food companies, and others engage in—and the use of such instruments purely to make bets on future commodity prices. In reality, these apparently very different activities are two sides of the same coin, and distinguishing between one and the other is not always possible.

These kinds of methodological issues mean that discussions of the role of commodity speculation tend to be studies in carefully worded ambiguity. The International Food Policy Research Institute, for example, undertook a detailed review of the data and concluded, "The results show that speculative activities might have been influential, but the evidence is far from conclusive."[12]

Moreover, badly designed policy intended to tackle the perceived excesses of speculation can itself have negative consequences. While, in the aftermath of the global financial crisis, politicians, campaigners, and the media find it easy to malign commodity traders, new investment in agriculture is urgently needed, including from the private sector, given that part of the backdrop to the 2008 food price spike was a long period of underinvestment in agriculture.

However, while discussion of the role of investors has often fallen prey to exaggeration and stereotypes, private sector involvement in agriculture can cause real problems if it happens in the wrong way.

First, speculation may not be the main cause of food price inflation, but it can still amplify volatility at the margin, particularly given the volumes now being traded. Most investors seeking exposure to commodities have no intention of taking physical delivery of the commodity in question, which means that futures markets cannot altogether lose touch with real-world supply and demand fundamentals. But during periods of high volatility (such as at the height of the 2008 food price spike), futures markets can add "froth" to prices and accentuate the peak of the spike.

Second, large and influential commodity trading firms may have conflicts of interest. For example, Glencore—a major global commodities trading house—published a briefing note in summer 2010 setting out reasons for Russia to impose an export ban on wheat, but failed to disclose until a year later that it had placed a major speculative bet that wheat prices would rise.[13] The Russian government did indeed impose an export ban shortly after Glencore's note was published, sending wheat prices skyrocketing and driving the food price spike that peaked in 2011.

Third, private sector investors in farmland can have strongly negative impacts on poor people if deals are not sufficiently attuned to their needs. While governments and sovereign wealth funds account for the bulk of the trends toward large land deals (discussed more fully in the next section), private sector firms can contribute to the problems of poor environmental impact assessment, displacement of people who may have farmed the land in question for decades despite lacking formal title to it, minimal job creation, and scant benefits to the host country.

As governments assess the need for additional regulation of financial activity in agriculture, given the sector's unique sensitivity, they could start by taking an incremental "no-regrets" approach that opts for modest initial wins while gathering more data about what is happening.

A first step along these lines could be for governments to mandate additional transparency requirements in food commodity futures. At present, many commodity futures contracts are traded over the counter (OTC)—that is, they are negotiated and traded privately between two parties without going through an exchange. Such deals are subject to minimal information disclosure requirements, yet account for enormous sums of money: overall, outstanding OTC commodity derivatives accounted for a notional total of US$2.9 trillion in June 2010.[14] If these OTC contracts instead had to be cleared formally through an exchange (such as the Chicago Board of Trade), this would introduce important new reporting requirements without impeding the capacity of food producers and purchasers to hedge against possible price variations.

At the same time, much greater transparency is needed in the area of food stocks and reserves, where opacity increases the uncertainty faced by markets and, with it, the risk of volatility. Governments, including China and India, have in the past regarded information about agricultural commodity markets, in particular their stock levels, as highly confidential, while detailed knowledge of stocks and harvests has long been a source of competitive advantage for large private sector companies such as Archer Daniels Midland, Bunge, and Cargill. The 2011 G-20 in France secured a significant success in agreeing to set up a new Agricultural Market Information System, with full Chinese and Indian participation. However, the G-20's 2011 action plan went no further than to "urge" large grain traders to participate in it.[15]

Reducing the Risk of Global Zero-Sum Games

A second key area for international action to tackle food price volatility consists of measures to reduce the risk of global zero-sum games in international trade.

As noted, the global food outlook will be heavily shaped by a tighter balance between supply and demand. In such conditions, there are real risks when government actions are motivated by narrow, short-term interests—or outright panic—without regard for the knock-on consequences of their actions.

The 2008 food price spike provided a vivid warning of the need for governments to think holistically about how their actions can affect prices and each other. As prices increased, many import-dependent governments frantically tried to rebuild their depleted food stockpiles by buying up grains and other foodstuffs on international markets—in the process, of course, pushing prices up still higher. The same dynamic was evident again in 2011, when Middle Eastern and North African governments engaged in panic buying of wheat and other commodities to try to contain political unrest (which was itself catalyzed at least in part by food price inflation).

The concerns of import-dependent countries to ensure their food security are also evident in the recent—and enormous—global trend toward large-scale land acquisition or lease deals, mirroring the intensifying global scramble for oil and mineral resources. While precise data on the extent of the phenomenon are hard to find, one compilation of estimates suggests that 79.9 million hectares of land were acquired or leased in land deals between 2001 and 2011, with more than half the total in Africa.[16]

While the dominant players in this trend have been local rather than foreign investors, some Persian Gulf states and Asian countries such as China, India, Japan, and South Korea have been heavily engaged as well. In many cases, land deals have been undertaken with minimal transparency or environmental impact assessment, little employment creation, a majority of crops exported, and minimal consultation or involvement of local people, thousands of whom have found themselves displaced from land that they may have relied on for decades, despite not having had formal title or ownership.[17]

Import-dependent governments are not alone in their susceptibility to zero-sum games. The 2008 food price spike saw more than thirty food exporters imposing export restrictions or outright bans as a means to reduce food prices at home and ease urban unrest over price inflation.[18] This trend was instrumental in bringing the food price spike to its peak, particularly in rice prices, where relatively illiquid international markets for the grain contributed to a sudden outburst of acute price volatility.

In all of these cases, a common theme is that while such actions may make sense for individual governments, the aggregate effect is to increase perceptions of scarcity and the risk of more "resource nationalism." Panic buying and export bans also push prices up still further, worsening the problem they were intended to address in the first place. The potential for positive feedback loops (whereby the effects of a change further amplify that change) is clear, as is the risk of global zero-sum games hallmarked by competition rather than cooperation.

These kinds of dynamics represent a big change for agricultural trade. Until food prices began to rise after 2000, commodity prices, including those for grains and other foodstuffs, had been in a slump for years. Commodities were a buyer's, not a seller's market; the sorts of issues that led to trade disputes and World Trade Organization (WTO) cases tended to be about issues of market access. But with the emergence of food inflation and volatility, a shift toward a seller's market has become evident, in which trade disputes are as likely to be about security of supply as about market access.

These kinds of disputes are not well covered by existing international trade rules, however. Although the General Agreement on Tariffs and Trade (GATT) and the WTO Agreement on Agriculture (AoA) do include rules against export restrictions, important caveats apply, which seriously weaken these rules' effectiveness. One is that while most export restrictions are prohibited under GATT, Article XI of the agreement stipulates that temporary restrictions are allowed "to prevent or relieve critical shortages of foodstuffs or other products essential to the exporting contracting party."[19] And while countries suspending exports are supposed to take account of the effect on importers, notify the WTO that restrictions have been implemented, and provide justification if asked, these requirements do not prevent countries from imposing export bans. Finally, even these modest requirements apply only to developed countries, thus missing key exporters such as Argentina or Thailand.

In the long run, policymakers should aim to agree to new, tougher trade rules designed to prevent a repeat of the kind of volatility seen during the last food price spike. Respect for developing countries' policy space should continue to be an important principle in international trade, as should emphasis on "special and differential treatment" for developing countries. But at the same time, the extent of interdependence in twenty-first-century trade, coupled with the challenging global food outlook, means that sovereign rights need to be coupled with responsibility and with binding rules if countries refuse to display it.

This is unlikely to happen any time soon. The Doha Trade Round, which offers one forum in which the problem could potentially be addressed, remains on life support after more than ten years of negotiations; although the WTO did manage to secure an agreement on agriculture at its 2013 ministerial meeting in Bali, the terms of the deal were modest and included nothing on preventing export bans, which will not be included in the post-Bali work program.[20] Although the French-chaired G-20 in 2011 tried to address the issue of export bans, it too made minimal progress: emerging economies proved bluntly unwilling to relinquish one of the few tools they have to respond to unrest during periods of high food prices, and the G-20 settled instead for a much more modest undertaking to ensure that humanitarian assistance does not get caught up in food export bans.[21]

In the meantime, then, policymakers should focus on more achievable measures that would still have a tangible impact. High on their list should be some form of global emergency management mechanism that provides communication and coordination between countries in conditions of high volatility. This could potentially help to ease some of the risks of panic buying by import-dependent countries, which pushes prices still higher.

Policymakers should also be clear that moving forward with the Doha Trade Round is essential for global food security, however difficult progress has been—in particular, making faster progress on reform of Organization for Economic Cooperation and Development (OECD) farm support policies, which are even more problematic in conditions of high and volatile global food prices.

While having some domestic food production capacity can be an important source of resilience for poor countries during periods of volatility on global food price markets, the capacity to maintain this domestic capacity can be undermined by unfair competition from imports that have been heavily subsidized by rich exporters. While the Doha Trade Round was supposed to eliminate many OECD subsidies (especially export subsidies), numerous loopholes remain in place, allowing the United States and European Union to continue subsidizing their farm sectors.[22]

The recent volatility of food prices makes it more important than ever that developing countries can retain a degree of policy flexibility so as to be able to respond to conditions of volatility. For example, governments need to be able not only to lower tariffs during periods of high prices, but also to raise them if prices subsequently fall. While total food self-sufficiency will rarely, if ever, make sense as a policy objective for developing countries, retaining at least some domestic food production capacity can be an important source of resilience for developing countries, which therefore need to be able to shield domestic producers from extreme price volatility or from sudden surges of imports. This issue remains highly contentious: while the WTO's 2013 ministerial meeting reached consensus on an Indian-led proposal for a "peace clause" on developing countries' right to implement food stockholding policies, this is only an interim solution until a permanent approach is agreed.

Building Resilience at the Country Level

A third key area for action by the international system centers on the need to build resilience and security of access to food within poor countries.

More or less by definition, poor people are the most exposed to high food prices, just as they are to resource scarcity, to climate change, and to shocks and stresses of other kinds. The US$1.25 a day benchmark for defining and quantifying absolute poverty is itself based on an average of national poverty lines that are in turn based largely on a food poverty line that is established by pricing a food bundle that provides a minimum caloric intake.[23]

In part, this vulnerability derives from the fact that poor households spend such a high proportion of their income on basic goods such as food and energy. It is also the result of poor people's high dependence on natural assets, like land, water, fisheries, and forestry: three quarters of the world's poor live in rural areas. And while most of the rural poor are involved in smallholder farming, they have tended to lose as a result of high food prices rather than benefit from them, because low yields per hectare mean that most of them are still net food buyers.

This dependence on natural assets increases poor people's exposure to environmental shocks like droughts or floods. These kinds of shocks often lead to vicious cycles and chronic poverty traps—as, for instance, when droughts force poor families to sell productive assets like livestock or to take children out of school, making eventual recovery more difficult. These kinds of cycles are often a key part of the reason why people become poor in the first place and why it can be so difficult to escape from poverty.[24]

These kinds of shocks and stresses are likely to intensify in the future. Climate change impacts are becoming more evident, more frequent, and more intense. Competition for land and water is intensifying. There is a high risk that inflation and price volatility will continue to affect food and other basic goods.

As ever in development, there is no one-size-fits-all approach. Instead, a whole range of approaches is available to reduce the risks faced by poor people in a volatile world hallmarked by increasing resource scarcity, including some of the most exciting and innovative areas in international development. The following are some of the key elements of this emerging agenda:

—*Strong focus on employment and livelihoods.* While social protection systems (see below) are rightly commanding high levels of attention among donors and civil society organizations, the best form of social protection is a decent job or livelihood. However, the global financial and economic crisis of the last few years has had a strongly negative impact on employment, and past crises have often seen a major lag in employment recovery. An estimated 45 million to 50 million new jobs will be needed every year for the next decade just to keep up with new entrants joining the workforce.[25]

—*Approach to agricultural development centered on small-scale food producers.* As noted, three quarters of the world's poor people live in rural areas, and, of the 3 billion rural people in developing countries, 1.5 billion are in small-scale producer households.[26] At present, the fact that most small farmers are net food buyers means that high food prices have often been a curse rather than a blessing, and small farmers also tend to be most exposed to climate change and weather variability. But when governments get the right conditions in place for small farmers to manage risks such as weather variability and input price fluctuations—as, for instance, in Vietnam, which has gone from being a food-deficit country to a major food exporter, thanks largely to improvements on small farms—agriculture can have an especially powerful role in reducing poverty and building resilience.[27]

—*Strong emphasis on disaster risk reduction (DRR).* This has been the focus of a sharp increase in interest and commitment in recent years. The case of Japan illustrates the value of effective disaster risk reduction. While the tsunami of 2011 was devastating in its impact, the earthquake that triggered it caused minimal direct damage, thanks to Japan's leadership and experience in DRR, from its building codes to high preparedness throughout society. The 2005 Hyogo Declaration on DRR saw 168 governments commit to a ten-year program of integrating DRR into their national development strategies and the work of international agencies.

—*Resilient governance and emphasis on peacebuilding and other approaches to preventing and resolving conflicts.* This is particularly important in the area of natural resource governance, as competition for land and water intensifies and poor people find themselves at risk of having reduced access to natural assets, whether through conflict with others over those assets or through being displaced—both risks that are thrown into especially sharp relief by the emerging trend toward "land grabs." More broadly, the role of the state itself is crucial, including both the state's accountability and legitimacy in the eyes of its citizens and its capacity for managing shocks and enabling other sources of resilience.

—*Social networks.* Poor people generate substantial resilience themselves through friends, families, and local institutions such as religious bodies and community groups. Research undertaken by Oxfam on how the global economic crisis has affected developing countries emphasizes how poor people all over the world have weathered the storm of recent years by "turning to one another to share food, money, and information to recover from lost jobs or reduced remittances."[28]

There are extensive, significant linkages and overlaps across all of these areas, with similar themes cropping up again and again. Five themes consistently emerge as important in building up poor people's and poor countries' adaptive capacity:[29]

—Importance of assets, from land to livestock and from tools for livelihoods to education

—Centrality of institutions and entitlements, in particular, as ways of guaranteeing rights and access to key resources

—Key role of knowledge and information, such as seasonal weather forecasts or agricultural extension services in the farming context

—Value of innovation, which relates to whether systems (governance systems, communities, ecosystems, and so on) are able to adapt and change themselves

—Significance of flexibility and foresight, which is often challenging when governments or individuals are struggling to cope with the present, but nevertheless a crucial component of what makes actors resilient to shocks and stresses.

So building resilience—whether in response to a specific threat or more generally—is emphatically not a separate, stand-alone area of activity. Rather, it is about taking an approach to development itself that is aware of risks and vulnerabilities and that seeks to manage and reduce them at the same time as making progress on development.

This means that investing in resilience can have ripple effects, driving progress on multiple agendas at the same time. Nicholas Stern has argued that social protection is a key part of climate adaptation—for example, the United Kingdom's Overseas Development Institute has undertaken research into the links and overlaps between social protection, climate adaptation, disaster risk reduction, and livelihoods approaches.[30] The peacebuilding nongovernmental organization International Alert, meanwhile, has argued, "Peacebuilding and [climate] adaptation are effectively the same kind of activity, involving the same kinds of methods of dialogue and social engagement, requiring from governments the same values of inclusivity and transparency."[31]

The Special Role of Social Protection Systems

Investing in social protection systems is one of the most crucial areas where progress can be made in improving poor people's resilience, particularly with regard to access to food. Defined as "public actions carried out by the state or privately that can enable people to deal more effectively with risk, vulnerability to crises, or change and that help to tackle extreme and chronic poverty," social protection takes a huge range of forms.[32] The following are among those most relevant to food security:

—Cash and in-kind transfers, like Ethiopia's Productive Safety Net Program, which transfers both cash and food during periods of seasonal food insecurity by providing people with employment on public works projects, or Brazil's Bolsa Familia (family grant) system

—Employment guarantee schemes, like India's National Rural Employment Guarantee Act, which guarantees 100 days of employment a year to poor people in 200 of India's poorest rural districts, often on projects that contribute to sustainable agriculture and climate adaptation, like planting trees or strengthening flood defenses

—Mother-and-child health and nutrition systems or school feeding programs, which are becoming increasingly important in many countries and which form a key plank of Brazil's Fome Zero (Zero Hunger) Program.

Social protection systems like these have crucial advantages as a way of protecting poor people during periods of high or volatile food prices. Because they are targeted at the poorest and most vulnerable people, they are much more affordable for developing countries than economywide subsidies, which often contribute to further inflation. Where food price controls have the potentially disastrous effect of reducing the incentives for farmers to increase food production, social protection systems create no such problems. And where food export restrictions can create catastrophic ripple effects for food-import-dependent countries, social protection systems avoid knock-on effects elsewhere in the world.

So far, though, only some of the people who need access to social protection actually have it. The International Labor Organization, for instance, estimates that only 20 percent of the world's people have access to adequate social protection of any kind.[33] Moreover, a substantial proportion of this total is accounted for by social insurance systems like social pensions or health insurance, where social security is financed by contributions based on the insurance principle of pooling resources with others. These tend to be concentrated in middle-income countries. If the focus is narrowed to social assistance systems—in which public actions are targeted to the neediest people, without depending on contributions—the total is significantly lower, with only around 750 million people enjoying access to some form of social assistance.[34]

But although a major task lies ahead in ensuring access to social protection for everyone who needs it, recent progress has been extremely encouraging, particularly on access to social assistance. Some of the most impressive progress has been in emerging economies like China, India, Mexico, and Brazil, where governments have invested heavily in building up their social protection programs, with striking results, including, in some places, marked reductions in overall levels of inequality.

Where most remains to be done, by contrast, is in low-income countries, especially in sub-Saharan Africa. Here too, progress is being made, but too often the trend is toward small-scale pilot programs that are heavily driven and micromanaged by donors. Where social protection programs in Africa have broken out of this mold and moved toward wider levels of coverage—as, for example, in Ethiopia or South Africa—this has been because an assertive government has taken control of the process. While donors' enthusiasm for social protection is welcome and significant, future progress will depend on their remembering—and being reminded of—two important lessons.[35]

First, in social protection, as in so many other areas of development assistance, there is no one-size-fits-all approach. Social protection takes many forms: what works in one country may be inappropriate, or politically infeasible, somewhere else. Some donors, including the World Bank, have at times been too quick to assume that cash transfers will always be the right approach for all countries.

Second, for social protection to work, it has to be rooted in national politics, not imposed from above. While financing and government capacity are often issues that have to be addressed in scaling up social protection, the biggest barrier to building up social protection in poor countries is often a tough political context (when, for example, policymakers and public debates focus on fears that social protection will encourage dependency, a concern not supported by the evidence, which shows that poor people instead tend to use social transfers as investments).[36]

Addressing Long-Term Supply and Demand Fundamentals

So far, this chapter has focused on measures to increase the resilience of the food system—both internationally, through measures to make markets work better and reduce the risk of zero-sum games in developing countries.

However, measures to increase resilience will be of only limited usefulness if the supply and demand fundamentals for food continue to worsen—in much the same way as effective climate adaptation is no substitute for tackling the underlying causes of climate change through reducing emissions.

As the issue of global food security started appearing on the policy agendas of heads of government from 2007 onward, many of them rushed to the conclusion that their most important task was simply to increase production of food in line with projected demand, such as the World Bank's forecast that 50 percent more food would be needed by 2030 or the FAO's projection that 70 percent more food would be needed by 2050.[37] (This emphasis on production was politically expedient for many OECD countries, as it enabled them to argue for the continuation of farm support regimes.)

Increasing production is certainly *part* of the solution to global food security for all, although making sure that there is enough food for everyone is no guarantee that everyone will get fed. But the challenge goes much further than just increasing yields per hectare or bringing new land into production. Just as important, for example, is the need to achieve dramatic improvements in resource efficiency, in particular, to reduce the demand for water in agriculture (which currently accounts for 70 percent of global freshwater use).

To some extent, aid donors have responded to the need for increased investment in agriculture, in the process beginning to make up for a long period of neglect of the sector. The 2009 L'Aquila G-8 Summit in Italy saw the G-8 and five other donors commit to provide US$22 billion for agriculture and food security, for example, while the 2012 G-8 saw the launch of a "New Alliance for Food Security and Nutrition." However, only US$6 billion of the L'Aquila pledges was new money, and a 2012 monitoring report found that only 22 percent of donors' pledges had been disbursed; the United States had only disbursed 2 percent of its pledge.[38]

In addition, despite the prospect of renewed investment in agriculture, there are hard questions about whether the current tight supply-demand balance for food can be resolved on the supply side alone. The crop yield gains of the twentieth-century green revolution have been running out of steam in recent years. Competition for land is intensifying. Even if the efficiency of agricultural water use improves dramatically, it will still find itself racing against the reduced availability of water as a result of climate change. Other climate impacts, particularly extreme weather events, are likely to reduce crop yields too. Higher energy prices will increase the cost of many inputs that are essential for food production under current agricultural models, including fertilizer and fuel for on-farm energy use, processing, and distribution.

For all of these reasons, it is possible that supply will fail to keep pace with growth in demand, even assuming an immediate and large-scale reversal of the underinvestment in research and development, and in agriculture generally, of recent decades. If demand can be lowered—for food, for nonfood crops, for land, for water, and so on—then this will help to make the overall global food security challenge easier. In particular, four key areas for potential action stand out.

First, a rethink is needed of policies that support the most inefficient biofuels, above all corn-based ethanol. While biofuels still contribute a very small proportion of global liquid fuel needs, they account for a much higher proportion of the net increase in liquid fuels from outside the Organization for Petroleum Exporting Countries. However, they are also having major impacts on food prices: the International Monetary Fund (IMF) has observed that biofuels accounted for almost half the increase in the consumption of major food crops in 2006–07, primarily because of corn-based ethanol in the United States.[39] In 2012 more than 40 percent of U.S. corn production went to ethanol rather than the food chain.

However, despite strong consensus among international agencies including the World Bank, IMF, OECD, and FAO that governments should "remove provisions of current national policies that subsidize (or mandate) biofuels production or consumption,"[40] the United States was until recently unwilling to countenance reform of its Renewable Fuel Standard, both refusing a temporary waiver of it following the severe drought in 2012 and allying with Brazil and others to block action on biofuels in the 2011 G-20.[41] More recently, the U.S. Environmental Protection Agency has proposed reducing ethanol-blending requirements for the first time, although it remains to be seen whether the measure will be implemented in the face of stiff opposition from the agricultural lobby.[42]

Second, new measures should be introduced to reduce the proportion of food that goes to waste, both on the supply side in developing countries, by reducing post-harvest losses and production inefficiencies, and on the demand side in developed countries, by reducing the amount of food that is wasted by food companies, retailers, and consumers. Regulation and incentives are needed to reduce this waste, while individual consumers also need to take responsibility for dramatically reducing the amount of food they throw away.

Third, there is a clear need to encourage the "global middle class" to adopt more resource-efficient diets, above all in developed countries. As the "global middle class" expands and grows more affluent, hundreds of millions more people are moving toward "Western diets" rich in meat, dairy products, and processed foods, all of which are far more resource intensive in terms of grain use, energy use, water use, and, critically, greenhouse gas emissions. However, if the global middle class (and above all its most affluent members in the West) moved to more resource-efficient diets, and in particular ate less meat, this would significantly reduce the demand for grains as feed for livestock and land for grazing; ease a wide range of environmental impacts, particularly in the climate change arena; and greatly improve public health outcomes with regard to obesity and many noncommunicable diseases. However, achieving this result will be difficult, given the very limited progress made on influencing consumers' food choices in most OECD countries.

Finally, policies are needed to stabilize the world's population at low- rather than high-end estimate levels, for example through investing more in areas like girls' education, women's empowerment, and access to reproductive health services. The issue of global population levels is one of the most controversial in the global food security agenda, with much of the controversy stemming from "population bomb" alarmism of the 1970s. In fact, the global picture on population today is far from the Malthusian nightmare of popular imagination: global population growth rates peaked in 1963, at 2.19 percent a year, and have now almost halved, to 1.15 percent a year. If, as projected, growth rates continue to decline, then the world's population will be on course to stabilize within the next century or two.

However, the issue of population still matters for development. Remaining population growth will be heavily concentrated in developing countries, many of them net food importers with poor resource endowments, where resource scarcity is likely to have a powerful impact, including worsening state fragility in many cases. Given higher population growth rates, these countries will have to either improve crop yield productivity or import more food. More broadly, Jeffrey Sachs has argued that population growth matters for development because:

—Families cannot surmount extreme poverty without a decline in the fertility rate.

—A country with rapid population growth faces intense fiscal challenges just to keep up with the population, not to mention achieve economic progress.

—The ecological and (closely related) income consequences of rapid population growth are devastating.

—High rates of population growth threaten the rest of the world by raising pressures for mass migration and local conflict.[43]

A compelling development case can be made for supporting programs to bring down high rates of population growth. Crucially, though, such programs must ensure that women have the power to make their own family planning choices— a task that involves not only the availability of contraception and capacity of the health system, but also a broader agenda of women's empowerment and (especially) girls' education.

Conclusion: Multilateral Effectiveness Six Years after the Food Price Spike

This chapter has outlined an agenda for action on increasing access to food and improving the resilience of the global food system. But a critical question remains: how well is the multilateral system currently placed to deliver this agenda, and how has it performed over the six years since the 2008 food price spike?

Any discussion of this area has to start with the problem of "G-Zero" dynamics in many multilateral contexts, in which, as Ian Bremmer and Nouriel Roubini have put it, "No single country or bloc of countries has the political and economic leverage—or the will—to drive a truly international agenda."[44] This problem has been especially pronounced in a range of multilateral forums that are important for food security.

Following the disappointing outcome of the 2009 Copenhagen Summit, the United Nations Framework Convention on Climate Change process appears to be at risk of sliding into a similar "holding pattern" as that following the Doha Trade Round. The 2012 Rio Conference on Sustainable Development also experienced severe political headwinds and managed to agree on few concrete outcomes of real significance.

Perhaps most disappointing of all, the 2011 G-20 made little progress despite both strong commitment from the French chairs to taking action on food security and a powerful joint analysis paper submitted to the G-20 by nearly a dozen international organizations that was notable for pulling no punches on tough issues like biofuels and export bans. While the G-20 did make progress on agreeing to actions to improve market transparency, it took minimal action on biofuels, export bans, climate change, or financial regulation, despite a strong push by France, the host government, in all of these areas.[45]

If lack of leadership and political space for collective action on food security and wider sustainability is one problem, another is that current multilateral institutions are badly configured to support and facilitate collective action. The multilateral system is particularly weak in the area of crisis management, where it is often unclear which decisionmaking body is supposed to lead. This was a major issue when collective action was needed in 2008 to halt the spate of food export bans, for example.

More broadly, decisionmaking bodies that focus on only one issue struggle to take account of the big picture, often because they only engage one kind of policymaker (that is, environment ministers in environment summits, trade ministers in trade summits, agriculture ministers in agricultural summits, and so on). As a result, a recent trend has been to hand over many "difficult issues" to the level of finance ministers and heads of government, especially through the G-8 and more recently the G-20.

The underlying long-term need is for much more shared awareness and interoperability between governments and international organizations—something that will not be achieved overnight. Much of the progress that is needed will have to come initially through national governments making their own policymaking more coherent, given that the multilateral system generally reflects what happens in national capitals.

For now, governments and international organizations could usefully focus on two actions that they could undertake immediately: upgrading the United Nations Committee on Food Security and improving data collection and analysis.

First, they should work hard to make the United Nations Committee on World Food Security an effective decisionmaking body on food and agriculture issues. While some are skeptical about whether the body will be effective—pointing to its large and unwieldy membership—it has recently been reformed and could potentially emerge as an engine for action. The next step should be for the committee to broker action on a small number of specific, concrete areas and then to follow up with smaller action teams of governments, international agencies, and other actors.

Second, they should focus on improving the collection and analysis of data on food security and related issues. The weakness of data on hunger was thrown into sharp relief by the 2008 food price spike: initially, the FAO estimated that the number of the world's undernourished had surged from 850 million to more than 1 billion, but it then had to suspend publication of its data altogether as a result of methodological problems.[46] The FAO now estimates that 852 million people were chronically undernourished in 2010–12, suggesting that while progress on reducing hunger had stalled as a result of the food price spike, it had not exploded as initially thought; even these new estimates "do not fully reflect the effects on hunger of the 2007–08 price spikes or the economic slowdown experienced by some countries since 2009, let alone the recent price increases."[47]

As well as improving global hunger estimates, the multilateral system should focus on improving the integration of data across issues—an undertaking that would not only give a more accurate overall picture, but also do more to improve system coherence than any number of attempts to "redraw the organogram" in one way or another.

One way of doing this would be to move from the current situation of having a *State of Food Insecurity* report, a *World Development Report,* a *World Energy Outlook,* a *Human Development Report,* and so on and toward requiring all agencies to work together on a single analysis that devotes proper resources to assessing the default trajectory on ending poverty, what could "bend the curve" toward faster progress toward identifying what resources and partnerships are needed to drive the change, what are the key risks to poverty eradication goals and how they can be managed, what are the key environmental risk thresholds that the world faces, and how close will projected global growth trajectories take us to them. The *Global Sustainable Development Report* mandated in the Rio conference's outcome document would be a way of taking this idea forward.

These two proposals are both modest in scope and are made with the often dispiriting current political context in mind. At the same time, though, the key point about sustainability challenges, after all, is that they are unsustainable and will drive their own changes if sufficient action is not taken. Policymakers, researchers, and campaigners need to stay focused on what is necessary as well as what is possible—whether on export bans, biofuels, climate change, multilateral system reform, or other areas.

Recent years have seen numerous global shocks, from 9/11 to two food price spikes and from a financial crisis to ever more frequent and severe extreme weather events. Each of these has opened political space for more radical action, at least for a time. It seems likely that more such shocks will happen in the future. Much will depend on whether advocates for global food security are ready to make full use of them.

Notes

1. Amartya Sen, *Poverty and Famines: An Essay on Entitlement and Deprivation* (Oxford: Clarendon Press, 1981).

2. Food and Agriculture Organization (FAO), *State of Food Insecurity in the World 2012* (Rome, 2012).

3. Alex Evans, *The Feeding of the Nine Billion: Global Food Security in the 21st Century* (London: Chatham House, 2009).

4. Brian Walker, C. S. Holling, Stephen R. Carpenter, and Ann Kinzig, "Resilience, Adaptability, and Transformability in Social-Ecological Systems," *Ecology and Society* 9, no. 2 (2004): art. 5.

5. FAO Food Price Index (www.fao.org/worldfoodsituation/wfs-home/foodprices index/en/).

6. Ibid.

7. Ronald Trostle, *Global Agricultural Supply and Demand: Factors Contributing to the Recent Increase in Food Commodity Prices* (Washington: U.S. Department of Agriculture, Economic Research Service, 2008).

8. Martin Parry, "Humanitarian Implications of Rising Food Prices," Presentation to the Inter-Agency Standing Committee Principals, 2008.

9. Trostle, *Global Agricultural Supply and Demand.*

10. Homi Kharas, "Making Sense of Food Price Volatility" (Brookings, March 3, 2011).

11. International Food Policy Research Institute, *2011 Global Food Policy Report* (Washington, 2012).

12. Miguel Robles, Maximo Torero, and Joachim von Braun, "When Speculation Matters," Issue Brief 57 (Washington: International Food Policy Research Institute, 2009).

13. Javier Blas and Jack Farchy, "Glencore Reveals Bet on Grain Price Rise," *Financial Times,* April 24, 2011.

14. Data from Bank for International Settlements (www.bis.org/statistics/otcder/dt1920a.pdf).

15. John Thompson, "A Missed Opportunity: The G-20 Action Plan on Food Price Volatility and Agriculture," Future Agricultures blog, June 28, 2011.

16. "When Others Are Grabbing Their Land," *Economist,* May 5, 2011.

17. See Klaus Deininger and Derek Byerlee with Jonathan Lindsay, Andrew Norton, Harris Selod, and Mercedes Stickler, *Rising Global Interest in Farmland: Can It Yield Sustainable and Equitable Benefits?* (Washington: World Bank, 2011).

18. See Evans, *Feeding of the Nine Billion.*

19. Jonathan Lynn, "Can Export Bans Be Challenged at the WTO?" *Reuters Global News Journal,* August 12, 2010.

20. See www.fao.org/docrep/019/i3658e/i3658e.pdf.

21. Thompson, *A Missed Opportunity.*

22. Oxfam, "The Time Is Now: How World Leaders Should Respond to the World Food Price Crisis," Briefing Note (Oxford, June 3, 2008).

23. World Bank, *2008 World Development Indicators: Poverty Data—A Supplement to World Development Indicators 2008* (Washington, 2008).

24. Rasmus Heltberg, Steen Jorgensen, and Paul B. Siegel, "Climate Change: Challenges for Social Protection in Africa," paper prepared for conference on social protection for the poorest in Africa, World Bank, Washington, 2008.

25. International Labor Organization, "Concept Note on the Post-2015 Development Agenda" (Geneva, 2012).

26. World Bank, *World Development Report 2008: Agriculture for Development* (New York: Oxford University Press, 2007).

27. Ibid.

28. Duncan Green, Richard King, and May Miller-Dawkins, "The Global Economic Crisis and Developing Countries," Draft research report (Oxford: Oxfam, 2010).

29. Adapted from Africa Climate Change Resilience Alliance, "Consultation Document: The ACCRA Adaptive Capacity Framework" (Kampala: Oxfam International, October 2010).

30. Nicholas Stern, *Key Elements of a Global Deal on Climate Change* (London School of Economics, 2008); Lindsey Jones, Susanne Jaspars, Sara Pavanello, Eva Ludi, Rachel Slater, Alex Arnall, Natasha Grist, and Sobona Mtisi, "Responding to a Changing Climate: Exploring How Disaster Risk Reduction, Social Protection, and Livelihoods Approaches Promote Features of Adaptive Capacity" (London: Overseas Development Institute, 2010).

31. Dan Smith and Janani Vivekananda, "A Climate of Conflict: The Links between Climate Change, Peace, and War" (London: International Alert, 2007).

32. Department for International Development, "Social Protection in Poor Countries," Social Protection Briefing Note 1 (London, 2006).

33. International Labor Organization (www.ilo.org/global/about-the-ilo/decent-work-agenda/social-protection/lang--en/index.htm).

34. Armando Barrientos, Miguel Niño-Zarazúa, and Mathilde Maitro, "Social Assistance in Developing Countries Database Version 5.0," Working Paper (Manchester: Brooks World Poverty Institute; London: Chronic Poverty Center, July 2010).

35. See, for example, Institute of Development Studies, Overseas Development Institute, University of East Anglia, and Regional Hunger and Vulnerability Program, "Social Protection in Africa: A Way Forward" (London: ODI, 2010) (www.odi.org.uk/resources/download/5010.pdf).

36. Chronic Poverty Research Center, *The Chronic Poverty Report 2008–09: Escaping Poverty Traps* (Northampton: Belmont Press, 2008).

37. World Bank, *World Development Report 2008;* FAO, "How to Feed the World in 2050" (www.fao.org/fileadmin/templates/wsfs/docs/expert_paper/How_to_Feed_the_World_in_2050.pdf). Both figures are before additional demands for crops to use as biofuels are taken into account.

38. Ibid. One Campaign, *Agriculture Accountability: Holding Donors to Their L'Aquila Promises* (London, 2012).

39. International Monetary Fund, *World Economic Outlook* (Washington, 2008).

40. "Price Volatility in Food and Agricultural Markets: Policy Responses," Policy report commissioned for the 2011 G-20, June 2, 2011.

41. Gregory Meyer, "US Will Not Ease Corn Ethanol Mandate," *Financial Times,* November 16, 2012; Thompson, *A Missed Opportunity.*

42. See www.ft.com/cms/s/0/fde54b44-4e36-11e3-8fa5-00144feabdc0.html?siteediti on=intl#axzz2x4p8PK00.

43. Jeffrey Sachs, *Common Wealth: Economics for a Crowded Planet* (London: Penguin, 2008).

44. Ian Bremmer and Nouriel Roubini, "A G-Zero World: The New Economic Club Will Produce Conflict, Not Cooperation," *Foreign Affairs* 90, no. 2 (March-April 2011) (www.foreignaffairs.com/articles/67339/ian-bremmer-and-nouriel-roubini/a-g-zero-world).

45. Thompson, *A Missed Opportunity.*

46. David Steven, "How Many People Are Hungry?" Global Dashboard, November 4, 2011 (www.globaldashboard.org/2011/11/04/how-many-people-are-hungry/).

47. FAO, *State of Food Insecurity in the World 2012.*

10

Water Security:
Global Implications and Responses

DANIEL KIM CHAI YEO

"Water, water everywhere, nor any drop to drink," laments the ancient mariner in Samuel Coleridge's poem, the "Rime of the Ancient Mariner." Water is indeed everywhere. It is essential for life, livelihoods, economies, and industries, but it is this ubiquity that makes its coherent management such a challenge. "Water" has different meanings in different contexts, resulting in approaches that are disconnected and at times contradictory.

While the need for water is universal, essential in every region around the world, it is also deeply specific to national and local context. The nature of water supply, the climate, and the uses of water are defined largely by geographic, societal, and economic contexts. The responses to water challenges in a temperate climate with high population density but low population growth, like the United Kingdom, are very different from those in a highly variable climate with rapid population growth and a large rural population, like Ethiopia. Water also reaches across sectors, acting as a critical input and enabler in the extraction and use of other resources, such as food or energy—making its management a truly cross-cutting resource challenge.

Water use is a transnational challenge—but one that differs from others with subtly different characteristics and therefore responses. Climate change, terrorism,

The views expressed in this piece are the author's and are not necessarily representative of the Global Green Growth Institute or the government of Ethiopia. All errors and omissions are the author's responsibility.

and financial stability all require coordinated global responses, but water use is a global challenge where the solutions are at national and subnational levels. At the same time, national policies (or their absence) can have implications beyond national borders, so multilateral action on water is needed to facilitate and coordinate responses rather than homogenize or consolidate them.

In that regard, is water security really a *global* issue? What are the real water security issues at a national level? What are the global implications of a country's water insecurity or its response to water insecurity? What shape should multilateral action take, and how does it relate to national responses?

Currently, the complexity of water and the range of issues involved are not adequately reflected in the political or popular discourse, which tends to condense water into an issue of global scarcity requiring a global response. This chapter therefore starts by focusing on where water plays a critical role in global strategic resource challenges. It is divided into three sections. The first frames water security as a crosscutting challenge in the context of global resource scarcity; the second highlights how this plays out at a national level by exploring the impacts of and responses to water insecurity in Ethiopia; the third steps back up to the global level to reflect on the role of the international institutional architecture in addressing national water security challenges.

A Complex and Crosscutting Resource

Water is a universal resource—one that every country and person needs. It is directly relevant in all of our lives. However, it is a complex resource cutting across multiple dimensions of security, geography, and scale. It is one of the most basic human needs, essential for drinking, cooking, washing, and cleaning. But it is also an economic resource, vital for growing crops, keeping livestock, producing goods, and providing services. This distinction between economic and social value has been a core tension in historic attempts to fashion multilateral responses to water. The highly contested Principle 4 of the 1992 Dublin Principles[1] emphasized water as a source of economic value over water as a human right, only to be superseded in 2010 by a United Nations (UN) Human Rights Council resolution recognizing water (and sanitation) as a human right derived from other rights in the Universal Declaration of Human Rights.[2] The challenge of resolving conflicting demands and values remains at the heart of effective water management.

Water also affects other resources, particularly the production of food and generation of energy. This interdependency between resource issues can act as a multiplier, amplifying local issues into systemic impacts. If water problems affect the food or energy system, they can become national security and stability issues; they can also become regional stressors if they negatively affect the shared use of water between states.

Water challenges affect every scale of society, from the community to the nation and beyond. But responding to water challenges at one level comes with its own consequences, often unintended, at other scales. For example, domestic water policies can have transboundary impacts, affecting other national contexts, while national responses can have local distributional impacts. This multiscalar, multisectoral relevance means that different actors are responsible for dealing with different dimensions of water, further complicating efforts at a collective and strategic response.

In the context of global resource scarcity, water is a very different beast from other resources. Water itself does not have much direct commercial value. Instead, water's economic value is derived from its essential role in the extraction or production of other, more commercially valuable resources. However, this use is often misinterpreted and misunderstood. It is commonly noted that only 1 percent of the world's water is freshwater or that agriculture accounts for the vast proportion of water use (around 70 percent).[3] What is often overlooked is that only 9 percent (3,800 cubic kilometers) of globally available freshwater is extracted for human use, meaning that, globally, water is not as scarce as one might think (although there are parts of the world where scarcity is a major issue). In any case, water use figures only provide one perspective. To understand the links with other resource issues, it is more useful to look at the role that water plays in various sectors of the economy rather than at which sector is the biggest user of water.

For example, while agricultural irrigation may account for major water withdrawals, irrigation is, in fact, only a modest part of global agricultural water consumption: less than 20 percent of the world's cultivated land is under irrigation (around 300 million hectares), with rain-fed agriculture practiced on the remainder. However, the land under irrigation accounts for more than 40 percent of the world's food production,[4] highlighting two critical dimensions of water for food security.

First, the 40 percent of the world's food production that is dependent on irrigation largely coincides with physical water scarcity—locations where more than 75 percent of river flows are withdrawn for agriculture.[5] As food demand rises, water availability will increasingly be a limiting factor in production. Without further improvements in water productivity or major shifts in production patterns, the amount of water consumed by evapotranspiration in agriculture will increase by 70–90 percent by 2050.[6] This increase in water stress also will increase the vulnerability of food production to weather shocks such as drought, which can be compounded by spillover effects. For example, in 2010 major droughts severely affected wheat producers around the world. In Russia, grain was lost in one quarter of the sown area, equal to around 2.3 percent of global production.[7] This loss alone was not enough to trigger a price spike (the stocks-to-use ratio was well above that of previous price spikes); however, in the context of a relatively recent previous price spike, it provoked a Russian export ban, which did trigger a dramatic increase in prices and extended the food price crisis with a second peak.

Second, at a human scale, the majority of farmers still depend on rainfall for their livelihoods, so when the rains fail, their incomes suffer. This, in turn, affects their ability to access food and undermines their food security—at this scale, access (generally through affordability) is a more significant determinant of food security than availability. Effective water management can help to "insulate" farmers from climatic variability—either by shifting to irrigation or by improving rain-fed systems (for example, by conserving soil moisture).

So irrigation demand is a critical stressor of water availability in some contexts, increasing vulnerability, while in other contexts, increasing irrigation or improving rain-fed systems can play a key role in reducing vulnerability to existing and future climatic variability. In this way, water for agriculture is both a stressor of and a solution to food security.

Irrigation is a predominantly consumptive process—most water used is "consumed" by the crops grown and effectively lost to the immediate environment. Water use in the energy sector is very different—of the 580 cubic kilometers of freshwater withdrawn for energy production each year, only 66 cubic kilometers are actually consumed.[8] The rest is returned, so energy is not a major user of water in terms of volume.

However, water is a critical component of energy production. Hydropower is the most obvious connection, but, by necessity, hydropower tends to be located where there is an abundant, reliable supply, so ironically, the role of water is less significant in hydropower production than in thermal energy generation. Thermal power requires water to generate steam, which needs high-quality water to minimize fouling and calcination of turbines and boilers. Therefore, insufficient, unreliable, or poor-quality water can act as a limiting factor for energy production. Given that thermal power still represents almost 80 percent of global power generation,[9] the quality and availability of water for thermal energy production are more critical, but overlooked, issues for global energy markets. The International Energy Agency's *World Energy Outlook 2012* highlighted the widespread nature of this vulnerability:

> The vulnerability of the energy sector to water constraints is widely spread geographically, affecting, among others, shale gas development and power generation in parts of China and the United States, the operation of India's highly water-intensive fleet of power plants, Canadian oil sands production, and the maintenance of oil-field pressures in Iraq.

What is particularly noteworthy is just how far and wide the implications reach—from conventional to nonconventional, from development to generation, across geographies and climates, and at all levels of development and capacity. Water for energy is vital for security of production in almost all contexts.

In industry, water lives up to its physical attributes—it is clear and invisible. Most goods and products depend on water: some are literally made up of it, such as beer, while others need water for their manufacture, such as clothing and textiles. Water is therefore deeply embedded in many goods and products. This concept is increasingly used to provide a "water footprint" for products—typically to illustrate how thirsty a product is (that is, how much water is needed to produce it; also referred to as virtual water). However, the absolute water footprint of a product needs to be coupled with the context. Water is not the same around the world: a liter of water in the Brazilian rain forests has a very different significance than a liter of water in the Kalahari desert. Instead, it is more useful to see that trading this "virtual water" allows water-poor states to resolve their water insecurity by importing goods and products with high water content rather than producing them from their own water resources. Similarly, water-rich states can export their water resources in the form of products far more easily than directly transporting their water. This interdependency is a fundamental yet invisible aspect of global trade.

The International Institute for Hydraulic and Environmental Engineering estimated global virtual water trade between nations to be 1,040 cubic kilometers a year, of which 67 percent relates to international trade of crops, 23 percent to trade of livestock and livestock products, and 10 percent to trade of industrial products.[10] To put that into perspective, this is equal to around one quarter of global water withdrawals (approximately 3,829 cubic kilometers a year), meaning that virtual water is already a significant part of the global water system and can help to mitigate physical scarcity where water demand exceeds natural supply.

Ethiopia: Opportunities and Challenges of Water Security

Although there are specific areas where competing uses of water clash with physical or temporal scarcity, outside of these hotspots, it is the role of water in other resources that raises the biggest global challenges. Given its crucial role in the extraction and use of other resources, water has the potential to act as a limiting factor and therefore as one of the first "pinch points" for wider resource scarcity. This resource challenge merits more global attention than it currently receives. But it is as complex and multifaceted as it is crosscutting. The exact nature of water challenges is highly location specific, so the global picture needs to be complemented by an understanding of differing national contexts and the links between them.

Given the importance of context, it is not possible to explore the issues of water management fully without examining national cases. This section highlights some of these national dimensions through a case study of Ethiopia, a country that encapsulates many of the biggest water challenges and illustrates some water issues that have been insufficiently addressed. Ethiopia has a very difficult climate, with diverse water security concerns at subnational, national, and regional scales. Perhaps most important, the government has demonstrated the political will and leadership to address these, but has limited resources and capacity to do so. Identifying these limitations will facilitate a more pragmatic consideration of multilateral responses addressed at the end of this chapter.

The Federal Democratic Republic of Ethiopia has one of the lowest levels of gross domestic product (GDP) per capita in Africa, but under the firm leadership of the late Meles Zenawi, the country experienced consistently strong growth (averaging 10 percent a year over the last three years). Ethiopia's Growth and Transformation Plan (GTP) aims to continue this with an ambitious goal of quadrupling GDP per capita and becoming a middle-income country by 2025 through "agricultural development–led industrialization."[11] This plan is complemented by the country's bold and unique Climate-Resilient Green Economy Initiative, which aims to achieve this growth with no net increase in greenhouse gas emissions and with a reduction in climate vulnerability.[12] This commitment to an alternative high-growth pathway is notable, not least because it comes from a low-income country, but also because it is distinct from both developed and emerging economy models of growth. The ambition to follow a different growth paradigm makes Ethiopia a particularly interesting country to study within the water context.

Ethiopia's target growth sectors include floriculture, sugar, leather, cement, and gold mining, all of which depend on water as a critical input or a process enabler. With 47 percent of the economy stemming largely from rain-fed agriculture, the Ethiopian economy is already closely linked to rainfall, and water will continue to play a key part in its future growth. Water is also critical to the country's goals of reducing poverty. Only 68.4 percent of the population has access to water,[13] creating a significant health burden and consuming valuable productive time, limiting the potential of households to generate income and grow out of poverty. The World Bank has estimated that hydrological variability in Ethiopia slows the country's growth rate 38 percent and increases poverty 25 percent.[14] Given these links, water clearly is central to Ethiopia's ambitious economic and social plans.

The Ministry of Water, Irrigation, and Energy (formerly the Ministry of Water Resources) leads the water sector component of the GTP, focusing on three areas: hydropower, irrigation, and access.[15]

On hydropower, the objective is to tap the country's underused potential, increasing available hydropower capacity elevenfold to reach 24,092 megawatts and generate around 106,000 gigawatt hours of electricity a year. This involves the development of several cascades of dams in the main rivers of the Nile, Baro-Akobo, and Omo-Gibe basins. These plans have implications for regional relations—both negatively through the potential disruption of watercourses and positively through the potential to export power and build stronger economic ties with neighboring countries. Within Ethiopia, the construction of dams in sensitive areas has entailed the relocation of ethnic minorities and the repurposing of lands, which, despite a clear resettlement policy and resettlement action plans, has still provoked anger and accusations of human rights abuses.

Ethiopia has plans to scale up irrigation massively to improve agricultural productivity. The GTP identified 5 million hectares of land as suitable for medium- to large-scale irrigation, which would represent a fiftyfold increase in land under irrigation. Although deemed suitable for irrigation, only a small proportion of these sites have been fully evaluated for their water resources (3 million hectares might be a more likely estimate, but would still represent a substantial increase).

The third plank of Ethiopia's water policy is to deliver universal access to drinking water, jumping from 68.4 to 98.5 percent of the population with access to a water supply by 2015 and to reduce the proportion of nonfunctioning facilities to 10 percent.[16] This ambitious goal involves reaching the hardest-to-reach communities in remote or geographically challenging locations. Furthermore, achieving this coverage requires a commensurate ambition to achieve physical and financial sustainability and ensure that it is permanent.

These very ambitious plans will require significant monies and capacity to deliver. Although Ethiopia is willing to commit its own funds to achieve its ambitions,[17] it currently lacks the domestic financial resources to finance them fully and so will require considerable additional resources. But this support has not been forthcoming, as international opinion and concerns over environmental and social impacts have deterred development partners and private investors from investing in dams and large-scale irrigation. Instead, they prefer to focus on the less politically contentious issue of access to water, sanitation, and hygiene (WASH), which reflects the approach of development partners to water globally. Even then, the WASH sector is not fully funded: the recently launched US$2.5 billion One WASH National Program has a 32 percent funding shortfall, despite widespread support.

In addition to and as a contributor to underinvestment, the practical delivery of Ethiopia's bold political ambitions risks being undermined by weak implementation capacity at the regional and subnational levels.[18] This weak capacity varies between locations, but typically includes lack of human resources, insufficient financial management (staff and processes), poorly implemented procurement processes, and lack of funding for basic operational items such as fuel.[19] These limitations can undermine the confidence of development partners, leading to increased bureaucracy and fiduciary requirements, which further exacerbate delivery capacity—completing the vicious circle.

The implications of Ethiopia's water use extend beyond its borders: it shares most of its water resources with the ten riparian countries of the Nile basin. The Nile is divided into two main subbasins, the White Nile and the Blue Nile (Abbay)—the latter of which lies mainly in Ethiopia and is responsible for 85 percent of the river flow in the Nile. The Nile basin is peculiar from a hydropolitical perspective in that the downstream riparian nation (Egypt) has historically exerted the most control over the river[20]—principally through the 1929 agreement between Egypt and the United Kingdom and the 1959 agreement between Egypt and Sudan, which allocate 55.5 billion cubic meters (bcm) of water to Egypt each year.

Over the last decade, through the Nile Basin Initiative (an informal dialogue process), the countries of the Nile basin have been working to find more mutually beneficial arrangements so that all riparian nations can share the benefits of the Nile. Analysis shows that, while the resources of the Nile are limited, there is enough water to meet the planned objectives of all riparians (including preserving Egypt's 55.5 bcm).

Ten years of dialogue through the Nile Basin Initiative have led to the development of the more formal Cooperative Framework Agreement (CFA), setting out the rules of the game for the Nile. Intense negotiations were concluded around thirty-eight out of thirty-nine articles—with the remaining stumbling block being the status of historic water agreements (Article 14b). Despite this, in May 2010, five upstream riparians (Ethiopia, Kenya, Rwanda, Tanzania, and Uganda) decided to forge ahead, with Burundi and the Democratic Republic of Congo declining to sign after coming under heavy pressure from Egypt. The CFA required the ratification of six of the (then) nine riparian countries in order to establish the Nile Basin Commission—a permanent river basin organization that would unlock previously identified cooperative investment projects. Cooperation in the Nile had reached an impasse until the unforeseen fall of Mubarak's regime in Egypt. In 2011, Burundi agreed to sign, and the CFA reached its six-country requirement.[21]

While the disjointed evolution of the CFA appears to reflect a breakdown in regional cooperation and an uncertain institutional future for Nile cooperation, the CFA has neither dampened collaboration nor exacerbated conflict.[22] Despite major headlines and rhetoric to the contrary, Egypt, Ethiopia, and Sudan have continued to work together on the Grand Ethiopian Renaissance dam (GERD), with a joint panel of experts acting as a consultation mechanism. This has not resolved every issue, but it has allowed a more pragmatic approach: because the new dam will have minimal impact on flows once complete, the focus is on agreeing to a regime for filling it. So far it appears that regional cooperation has trumped national identities and tension. After a brief suspension of the tripartite committee in December 2013, and following the recent election, Egyptian Prime Minister Abdel-Fattah Al-Sisi and Ethiopian Prime Minister Hailemariam Desalegn announced in July 2014 that the committee will resume work and agreed on seven principles relating to water use:

1. Respecting the principles of dialogue and cooperation as a foundation for mutual interests

2. Giving priority to establishing regional projects to develop financial resources to meet the growing demand on water and face water shortages

3. Respecting international law principles

4. Resuming immediately the activities of the tripartite committee

5. The Ethiopian government commits to avoiding any possible harm the dam could inflict on Egypt's water usage

6. The Egyptian government commits to constructive dialogue with Ethiopia that takes into consideration the latter's development needs

7. Committing to act in good faith under the framework of the tripartite committee.

While there are still some outstanding issues to resolve, it is clear that the leaders of Egypt, Ethiopia, and Sudan see more value in collaboration than conflict.

On top of the institutional and political challenges, weather and climate play a defining role in managing water. Much has been written about Ethiopia's climate and the potential impacts of climate change. However, limited historical data and a highly complex intersection of climate systems mean that even the most sophisticated climate models do not agree. As a result, there is much uncertainty about some aspects of climate change projections in Ethiopia—specifically rainfall.

Rainfall and temperature remain the two most significant climate variables for Ethiopia. Historically, Ethiopia has seen a consistent upward trend in temperature, with limited variability between months and between years. Climate models agree that the upward trend in temperature is likely to continue, accompanied by a likely decrease in temperature variability.

The picture on rainfall is more complicated. Ethiopia has three distinct rainfall regimes:

—*West:* One long rainy season, *kiremt* (June–September)

—*Central and Eastern: Kiremt* (June–September) is the main rainy season, preceded by smaller *belg* rains (March–May). There is a short hot, dry period known as *bega* (October–January)

—*South and Southeastern:* February–May is the main rainy season (*gu*) and is separated from a secondary rainy season in October–November (*deyr*) by two pronounced dry seasons.

Models suggest that the pattern of rainfall across a given year is not likely to change significantly, but there is no clarity across climate models about whether overall trends are increasing or decreasing. Instead, year-to-year rainfall variability remains the key driver of climate vulnerability and is likely to increase in the future—leading to an increase in extreme events. This is not to discount the significant uncertainty around overall rainfall trends, which should be a key marker, particularly in the arid south where there is already some evidence of drying.[23] There is also a risk that key periods of seasonal rainfall in some areas may change (namely, the *belg* and the *gu* rains).

Although more research, improved data, and model development are needed to understand the likely direction and impacts of climate change in Ethiopia, tackling current rainfall variability clearly will benefit the country regardless of climate change. This means that the international emphasis on future climate change as opposed to existing variability runs the risk of distracting from the real issues that will benefit the country. However, this dynamic also creates a window of political opportunity where, with the right framing, more attention and energy can be brought to bear on this core issue of vulnerability in Ethiopia.

Ethiopia is coming to grips with its water security issues, with a clear set of bold plans, backed by political vision. However, implementation has been stalled by a combination of underfunding and critical capacity gaps at the local level. The country has an opportunity to stimulate the implementation of these plans by aligning with international interests—principally climate change (through accessing global climate finance). However, difficult choices will persist with regard to the role of water in modernizing the country: allegations of human rights abuses closely related to hydropower and irrigation remain a significant barrier to international support. But even with sufficient funding, major problems with delivery endure, and the government of Ethiopia has recognized the need to continue focusing its attention and that of development partners on the core issues of public policy and the translation of political ambition into practical reality.

Ethiopia, as with many countries, will require more support internationally. Given that Ethiopia's water security can have global implications, there is a clear need to take a coordinated and focused multilateral approach to supporting the country in responding to the complex and crosscutting challenges of water. The exact nature of this response is the subject of the final section of this chapter.

The Role of Multilateralism in Water Security

The case of Ethiopia highlights some practical issues at a national level. In particular, international support is a key element of domestic ambitions. Ethiopia is not unique in this; water-insecure countries need support, but the national water context will vary across continents, cultures, and climates. Given this, how far can the global architecture address a local issue?

The evidence to date suggests that there is a long way to go. In institutional terms, the global architecture for water lacks strategic coherence. Different perspectives on water and perceptions of "the water crisis" create balkanized institutional structures, where, for example, water for people is considered separate from water for agriculture. As referenced above, the issue of water as a human right or as an economic good continues to be contested, despite the UN Human Rights Council's resolution stating that water and sanitation are a human right.

UN Water is the international mechanism intended to support states in their water-related efforts. It consists of twenty-six UN organizations and seventeen non-UN partners. Needless to say, it is an unwieldy institution. In parallel to this formal structure is the UN Secretary General's Advisory Board on Water and Sanitation, which aims to catalyze cooperation but instead has further complicated an already messy landscape.

Outside the UN, there are several stakeholders including the World Water Council, Stockholm World Water Week, the Asia Pacific Water Forum, the Global Water Partnership, and the Sanitation and Water for All Partnership—each working to achieve coherence and coordination.

Recognizing the shared risks that it faces from ineffective water management and limited international coordination, the private sector has also established several water initiatives including the World Economic Forum's Global Agenda Council on Water Security, the Water Futures Partnership, and the 2030 Water Resources Group. Finally, civil society networks and campaigns such as the Freshwater Action Network and End Water Poverty are working to bring local perspectives to global issues. They often perceive private sector engagement as threatening the human right to water (a legacy of the historical conflict over the Dublin Principles).

The UN agenda for post-2015 provides an example of how this fragmentation of institutions and actors plays out. The agenda aims to establish a set of global goals for reducing poverty and achieving sustainable development. In the discussions to date, water has been identified as a critical issue that has been split into three streams: drinking water and sanitation, water resource management, and wastewater management. This very compartmentalization stems from the lobbying of diverse actors in pursuit of their own agendas and worldviews. Furthermore, the discussions on water tend toward technical, technocratic issues rather than the wider policy challenges. At present, the post-2015 approach to water lacks coherence, failing to frame the strategic or policy implications and challenges or to draw the links and contradictions between policy issues.

Global Water Priorities and National Contexts

Currently, the complexity of water and the range of issues involved are not adequately reflected in political or popular discourse. Instead, global narratives of scarcity, conflict, and drought-induced disaster dominate, pointing to economizing and efficiency as the solutions, often with a strong technological bent. In some cases, there is just cause for alarm: Sana'a could well be one of the first cities to run out of water, India is systematically allocating too much of its limited groundwater, and China's planned coal-fired power stations will stress the limit of water supplies in several regions and beyond.[24]

However, this is not true everywhere, least of all in Africa, where many countries use less than 5 percent of their available water resources and the dominant challenge lies in increasing the productive use of water, not reducing use.[25] Here the key issues are ineffective governance, underinvestment, and mismanagement, which result in the absence of infrastructure to provide water access, to translate water use into economic growth, or even simply to mediate and determine water usage. It is these more complex social, political, and state capacity issues, rather than physical availability, that hold back progress. As highlighted above, the solutions to these problems are very different from a supply-and-demand challenge, and there is real danger in applying a uniform solution to very distinct contexts.

Toward a Global Agenda on Water Security?

Are there global implications of a country's water insecurity? As Professor Aaron T. Wolf, a renowned water mediator and facilitator at Oregon State University, concludes, "Violence over water does not seem strategically rational, hydrographically effective, or economically viable."[26] Despite the appeal of a narrative of impending "water wars," there is more evidence of countries collaborating over water than fighting over it. Although the role of water as a driver of conflict or collaboration is still unclear, water more often acts as a vector of existing conflict than as a cause in its own right. The spillover risks of a nation failing to manage water properly are much more indirect than open conflict. Water problems can hinder the ability of a country to produce food and generate energy, which poses risks to the food system and the global economy. Similarly, inequitable access to water or extreme scarcity can amplify other risks that undermine the perceived legitimacy of a state, risking instability and state failure.[27] Given the highly political nature of water, domestic policies and actions on water can have impacts on interstate relations and become framed as "hard security" issues—regardless of the facts or evidence. Therefore, both the failure of a country to manage its own water-related risk and the efforts of a country to address these risks can have global implications.

Responding to this complexity requires a multilateral architecture that seeks to enable and facilitate national change rather than prescribe solutions. Water has been prominent in global discourses for some time and is increasingly so, but a coherent framework and a clear actionable agenda are still lacking. Such an agenda needs to be able to frame a common set of issues that encompass the full range of water dimensions, yet be sufficiently flexible to support national contexts. Three core challenges encapsulate the diversity and complexity of water risks facing nations, and each will have a different degree of relevance depending on context:

—*Challenge 1: Providing universal access.* It is remarkable that in a modern world nearly a billion people still are without reliable access to safe drinking water.[28] Much progress has been made,[29] but governments urgently need to accelerate the infrastructure and associated maintenance systems to deliver safe water to everyone, both now and in the face of future demographic changes.

—*Challenge 2: Staying within natural constraints.* It is easy to make the mistake of treating water as a resource with limited reserves, such as a fossil fuel. But water is infinitely recycled throughout the planet: the water we have is the same water we have always had, so it is, in a sense, infinite. However, that does not mean that there are no limits. A more appropriate characterization of water constraints is as a flow problem, not a stock problem, where there is not enough water at a particular point in time and space. This includes better management of water-related risks such as droughts or floods, building in resilience and buffers to uncertainty, shocks, and stresses.

—*Challenge 3: Sharing benefits.* Water is used to generate economic and societal benefits. It is both an economic resource and a public good. How are decisions made about the uses of water and who shares in the benefits generated? This is at once a technocratic issue about allocation regimes as well as a deeply political issue about how a society chooses to use its resources. To use a coined word, this may well be a "satisficing" agenda, where countries need to manage their water "well enough" to maintain legitimacy.

How could multilateralism help to support and enable these outcomes at a national level?

—*Agree on a common agenda.* Agreeing on a clear and common agenda would help to focus existing energy and activity. A starting point would be to frame the debate around support for national responses as well as mediation around the international implications of these responses. International norms can also buttress national responses. For example, the UN Guiding Principles on Business and Human Rights require governments to protect the human right to water through transparent regulation and businesses to respect the human right to water and provide transparent access to remedy (both judicial and nonjudicial measures to redress negative impacts where people are harmed by business activity).

—*Develop evidence-based decisionmaking.* The absence of high-quality and practicable data is a major limiting factor in developing decent policy. A reliable and regular monitoring system is needed to help countries to assess where they are and to track progress across a range of agreed water security indicators. This can build on existing tools such as UN Water's Key Water Indicator Portal Project and the Wealth Accounting and Valuation of Ecosystem Services Initiative. It also involves understanding what sorts of interventions are effective in delivering real-world change. There is limited understanding of successful approaches to water resource management at a strategic and policy level.

—*Broker collaboration and implementation.* Partnerships are the flavor of the month, but there is a need to focus on high-quality partnerships between governments and across sectors. Institutions like the embryonic UN Partnership Facility could catalyze the development and coordination of trusted, quality partnerships, supported by the UN Global Compact, to gather and share learning from existing partnerships and initiatives.

—*Resolve conflict and build trust between actors.* Regional initiatives such as the Nile Basin Initiative or the South Asia Water Initiative can serve as mediation mechanisms to build trust between riparian states through joint analysis and improved understanding of the available water resources in a basin. Sharing the problem can help to identify mutually beneficial solutions and establish a platform for resolving conflict.

—*Share technical assistance and knowledge.* Technical assistance from multilateral and bilateral donors should be better coordinated and made available to decisionmakers to provide a neutral base of evidence to support decisionmaking and analysis. Development partners should align their activities to support and facilitate national systems and processes, based on the domestic context of water-insecure countries.

Water is a key global issue, acting as a "pinch point" for other global resource challenges and a stressor for wider global issues. It represents a particular type of transnational problem where the challenges and solutions are national, but where domestic water insecurity and responses to it can have global implications. Countries need international support to improve progress on the management of water-related risks, and multilateral support and coordination are vital to manage the transnational implications. The current responses are too fragmented and do not reflect the complexity of these issues. A more coherent global agenda on water must be in place to corral energy, expertise, and resources so that states facing domestic water challenges can confront those difficulties and act to mediate transnational risks.

Notes

1. The Dublin Statement on Water and Sustainable Development, also known as the Dublin Principles, was agreed on January 31, 1992, at the International Conference on Water and the Environment in the run-up to the Earth Summit.

2. Resolution A/HRC/15/L.14 (http://ap.ohchr.org/documents/dpage_e.aspx?si=A/HRC/15/L.14) also clarified an earlier General Assembly resolution (64/292 of July 28, 2010), which "recognized the right to safe and clean drinking water and sanitation as a human right that is essential for the full enjoyment of life and all human rights."

3. World Water Assessment Program, "Water in a Changing World," World Water Development Report 3 (Paris: UNESCO, 2009), p. 99 (www.unesco.org/new/en/natural-sciences/environment/water/wwap/wwdr/wwdr3-2009/).

4. Food and Agriculture Organization (FAO), *The State of Food Insecurity in the World 2012: The Multiple Dimensions of Food Insecurity* (Rome, 2013). FAO, International Fund for Agricultural Development, and World Food Program, "State of Food Insecurity in the World 2012: Economic Growth Is Necessary but Not Sufficient to Accelerate Reduction of Hunger and Malnutrition" (Rome: FAO, 2012).

5. Comprehensive Assessment of Water Management in Agriculture, *Water for Food, Water for Life: A Comprehensive Assessment of Water Management in Agriculture* (London: Earthscan; Colombo: International Water Management Institute, 2007), p. 14.

6. Ibid.

7. U.S. Department of Agriculture, Foreign Agricultural Service, "Global Crop Production Analysis," Commodity Intelligence Report (Washington, August 2010).

8. International Energy Agency, *World Energy Outlook 2012* (Paris, 2012).

9. International Energy Agency, *Key World Energy Statistics* (Paris, 2013).

10. A. K. Chapagain and Arjen Y. Hoekstra, "Virtual Water Flows between Nations in Relation to Trade in Livestock and Livestock Products," Research Report 13 (Delft, The Netherlands: UNESCO, Institute for Water Education, 2003).

11. The plan is available at www.mofed.gov.et/English/Resources/Documents/GTP%20English2.pdf.

12. See www.epa.gov.et/Download/Climate/Ethiopai's%20Vision%20for%20a%20Climate%20Resilient%20Green%20Economy.pdf.

13. Ministry of Water, "Irrigation and Energy Six-Month Review," February 2014.

14. Claudia Sadoff, *"Managing Water Resources to Maximize Sustainable Growth: A World Bank Water Resources Assistance Strategy for Ethiopia,"* Water P-Notes 13 (Washington, D.C.: World Bank, 2008).

15. This is set out in the GTP's "Water Sector Development Plan 2002–2016" (www.mowr.gov.et/attachmentfiles/Downloads/Water%20Sector%20Development%20Program%20Vol.1.doc).

16. Ministry of Health and Ministry of Water and Energy, "Universal Access Plan" (Addis Ababa: MOH/MOWE, December 2011) (www.cmpethiopia.org/content/download/361/2226/file/UAP%20Executive%20Summary.pdf).

17. For example, construction of the Grand Ethiopian Renaissance dam has begun based on national finance and a national bond scheme.

18. Ethiopia is subdivided administratively into regions, zones, woreda, and kebele.

19. For full details, see the One WASH National Program Fiduciary Risk Assessment (www.cmpethiopia.org/content/download/934/4384/file/FRA%20Mitigation%20plan%20March%2025,%202014%20.pdf).

20. Given that water flows downhill, upstream riparians generally are able to dictate the amount of water in a basin.

21. Although the creation of the Republic of South Sudan is yet another complicating factor.

22. In fact, the Nile Basin Initiative itself has not restricted unilateral or multilateral investments.

23. Chris Funk, Jim Rowland, Gary Eilerts, Emebet Kebebe, Nigist Biru, Libby White, and Gideon Galu, "A Climate Trend Analysis of Ethiopia," U.S. Geological Survey Fact Sheet 2012–3053 (Sioux Falls, S.D.: Earth Resources Observation and Science Center, 2012).

24. Greenpeace China, "Thirsty Coal: A Water Crisis Exacerbated by China's New Mega Coal Power Bases" (Beijing: Greenpeace China/Chinese National Academy of Sciences, 2012).

25. Mike Muller, "Rocks, Hard Places, and Road Blocks: Challenges on the Paths to Water Security in Africa," presentation at the Water Security, Risk, and Society Conference, Oxford University, April 16–18, 2012 (www.water.ox.ac.uk/120416conference/3-muller.pdf).

26. Aaron T. Wolf, "Conflict and Co-Operation over Transboundary Water," Human Development Report Office Occasional Paper (New York: United Nations Development Program, 2006) (http://hdr.undp.org/en/reports/global/hdr2006/papers/Wolf_Aaron.pdf).

27. U.S. Office of the Director of National Intelligence, "Global Water Security: Intelligence Community Assessment," ICA 2012-08 (Washington, 2012).

28. In 2012 the World Health Organization/UNICEF Joint Monitoring Program noted that 768 million persons were without such access.

29. The Millennium Development Goal of halving the global number of persons without access to water was met in 2012, but largely through progress in China.

11

Oil, Domestic Politics, and International Conflict

JEFF D. COLGAN

The global oil industry profoundly shapes the politics and economic development of producer countries, and those that interact with them. Recent research and interest provides a superb opportunity to reflect upon the progress social scientists have made in understanding the politics of oil, and the many questions left unanswered.[1] In this chapter, I focus primarily on the security dimensions of energy and, more specifically, on oil. The sheer importance of oil to the modern global economy makes it the logical starting point of any inquiry into the role of energy in international security. It also has specific characteristics that are not necessarily shared by other energy sources, such as the ease of centralization of revenues and a fungible world commodity market based on ocean-going shipping.

Oil is special. Oil-exporting states, called petrostates, engage in about 50 percent more international conflict than non-petrostates, on average.[2] They are at higher risk of civil wars and domestic strife. Their economic growth is weaker than it ought to be given the vast potential of their natural resources, and more volatile than in non-petrostates.[3] They are more likely to be corrupt, but under the right conditions oil income can be channeled to provide a rich variety of valuable public goods and feed sustainable institutions.[4]

This chapter originally appeared in *Energy Research & Social Science*, vol. 1, 2014, pp.198–205 (© 2014 Elsevier).

The net impact of oil on a country, both domestically and in its foreign policy, depends critically on its domestic politics, especially the preferences of its leaders. For instance, the tendency of petrostates to get into international conflicts cannot be explained without disaggregating the group and appreciating the role of revolutionary petrostates. This subset of states—those with revolutionary leaders—represents a special threat to international peace and security, initiating roughly three and a half times more interstate conflicts than a typical state. There are some recurring tendencies, however, across almost all oil-producing states. These tendencies are driven by common incentives generated from oil income, and these common incentives are identifiable in both domestic and foreign policy. Yet for virtually all of the things that we most want to know about a country—the rate at which it develops economically, the likelihood that it gets into international wars, the degree to which peace and order are kept at home— the effect of oil depends upon a complex interaction with the country's domestic institutions, politics, and historical legacy.

Oil is a sweeping force in politics around the contemporary world, especially in producer countries. The next part describes the distinctive characteristics of petrostates, both domestically and in terms of their foreign policy. I then describe and explain the systematic variation among petrostates' international aggression. Finally, I consider policy implications with a summary and conclusions.

The Petrostate Syndrome

I use the term *petrostate* to mean any country that has annual net oil export revenue of at least 10 percent of its gross domestic product (GDP). Such petrostates have a number of characteristics in common, which I describe here as the "petrostate syndrome." Examples include Saudi Arabia, Iraq, Iran, Russia, Norway, Venezuela, Ecuador, Nigeria, Angola, Algeria, Libya, and Sudan. Petrostates are thus a very diverse group geographically, culturally, and economically, making the similarities that we observe among them all the more striking. Naturally, there are exceptions: Norway, for instance, is quite distinct from the rest of the petrostates, and enjoys a high level of political and economic development that is consistent with the other countries of Scandinavia. Thus Norway seems largely unaffected by the negative side effects of the oil industry experienced in many petrostates, while still reaping many of the benefits. Nonetheless, the patterns and similarities among the group of petrostates as a whole are striking.

Other oil producers, even if not meeting the definition of petrostate just stated, might also experience some petrostate characteristics, albeit to a lesser degree. Examples include Mexico, Malaysia, Egypt, Colombia, and Argentina. Even Canada and the United States might experience some aspects of the petrostate syndrome, especially in oil-producing regions like Alberta or Louisiana, though the effects are typically heavily mitigated by the diversity of the national economy and the strength of political institutions.[5]

The Resource Curse

One of the best-known traits of petrostates is that they suffer from the "resource curse." The resource curse is not one characteristic, but rather a collection of negative economic and political phenomena, each of which is more likely to be observed in a petrostate than in other kinds of countries. Economically, the resource curse typically means: [6]

—increased corruption

—high income inequality

—currency volatility and appreciation (Dutch Disease)

—uneven regional economic development

—high unemployment

—low rates of female labor-force participation

—increased state ownership of business

Each of these phenomena, along with the exact causal mechanisms linking oil to these effects, is debated by scholars. Dutch Disease, by which changes in the value of the petrostate's currency affect the viability of other economic sectors such as manufacturing, is often thought to be responsible for some but not all of the economic problems. Enduring questions of energy poverty and energy justice are additional economic issues that are not limited to the resource curse or even to petrostates.[7]

Originally, the resource curse was also thought to mean weak or negative GDP growth, but the evidence on that question is actually quite mixed.[8] Sovacool, for instance, investigates the extent to which oil and gas has hindered economic development in Southeast Asian producers, and concludes that a hydrocarbons industry is neither a blessing nor a curse.[9] His research focuses primarily on socioeconomic indicators, however, and does not include an analysis of how oil income affects democratization or civil conflicts.

Politically, the resource curse typically means:[10]

—durable authoritarianism

—low levels of political accountability

—more frequent civil violence, possibly including civil war

—weak governance institutions

—increased gender inequity

—grievances stemming from environmental degradation or forcible migration in oil-producing regions, or both

As with the economic effects, the exact symptoms and causal mechanisms linking oil to politics are debated by scholars. For instance, many studies have considered the effect of oil on democratization and regime type. Most scholars agree that rentier politics are at least partially responsible, whereby resource-rich governments use low tax rates, high public spending, and patronage to maintain their authority, resulting in lower levels of democratic accountability.[11] The low rate of tax collection is often viewed as critical, because taxation is an important step in state formation, as it helps to cement a social contract between a state and its citizens. Taxation is also viewed as a key element of governance capability, so its absence (or reduced role) in petrostates is often viewed as hindering institutions and democracy.[12] Other causal mechanisms suggested by scholars include: corruption,[13] capital immobility (elites in petrostates impede democratization because they fear that it will lead to expropriation of their assets),[14] or geopolitics (powerful oil-importing states supporting friendly autocratic regimes in petrostates).[15] This area of research remains unsettled and open for future research.

Proclivity to Provide Energy Subsidies

Although not typically included in the concept of the resource curse, one of the other common characteristics in the domestic political economy of petrostates is the use of energy subsidies. Subsidies for energy cost governments billions of dollars globally.[16] In 2012 the total cost of fuel subsidies was $525 billion, a 30 percent increase over the previous year.[17] Energy subsidies can appear in multiple forms, including subsidies for residential heating and industrial uses, but the most common form is for transportation fuels: gasoline and diesel. Fuel subsidies are politically popular, but they can be fiscally unsustainable, especially when combined with rapid demographic growth and rising energy prices.[18]

Many countries, both petrostates and non-petrostates, subsidize energy. What sets petrostates apart is the increased likelihood that the government will subsidize energy and the larger magnitude of those subsidies, as compared to non-petrostates.[19] The difference is attributable to the fact that the domestic population typically feels some sense of national ownership over the oil reserves, and fuel subsidies are an administratively easy way to redistribute some of the wealth generated by a petrostate's geological endowment.

The consequences of withdrawing energy subsidies, however, are no different in petrostates than in non-petrostates. Once established, fuel subsidies are remarkably difficult to reduce or eliminate, as price increases linked to reductions in subsidies often set off political demonstrations and riots.[20] National leaders are often concerned that such demonstrations, sparked by fuel subsidies, could spread to other political and economic grievances, thereby generating a significant challenge to the stability of the regime. Fuel subsidies affect a wide cross-section of the population, are highly visible, and are typically seen as a direct measure of the extent to which a government is providing for its people. Consequently, efforts to reduce energy subsidies frequently meet with strong social resistance.[21] In Nigeria, such efforts have repeatedly caused protests and riots, forcing the government to back down. In Jordan, the government has unsuccessfully tried to reform subsidies on multiple occasions, leading to large-scale demonstrations which on one occasion brought down the prime minister. In Bolivia, the government raised gasoline and diesel prices in January 2011, leading protesters to ransack government offices, block a main highway, and lead a transportation strike, before subsidies were reinstated five days later. Increases in fuel prices sparked anti-governments riots in Kyrgyzstan in 2010, in which at least four protesters were killed. Similarly, changes in energy prices or subsidies have caused major protests in Ecuador, Indonesia, Bulgaria, and elsewhere.[22]

Successful energy subsidy reform is relatively rare.[23] Governments often cannot credibly commit to use the savings generated by a cut in fuel subsidies on public goods and services. The rare cases of successful reform typically occur in states that (i) face significant fiscal pressures and (ii) have already established a history of significant repression (for example, Iran, Syria). Thus fuel subsidies are persistent and widespread around the world. Future research could fruitfully explore the causes of such subsidies, effective methods for reforming them, and their connection to social and political instability.

Common Foreign Policy Behaviors

It is not only in domestic politics that petrostates share commonalities. There are some typical behaviors of petrostates in foreign policy, too. They include:
   —elevated military spending
   —large foreign aid donations to other developing countries
   —funding of foreign insurgencies or terrorists, or both
   —checkbook diplomacy (use of foreign aid and commercial relationships to accomplish foreign policy objectives).[24]

All of these tendencies derive from the ease with which oil revenues can be centralized and controlled by the state's leadership, and thus spent on foreign policy. Naturally, not every petrostate will exhibit all of these behaviors, as the state's particular circumstance and other idiosyncratic factors can override them. Nonetheless, the tendencies form a discernible pattern. Each of these behaviors is especially likely in periods of high oil prices. For instance, President Chávez of Venezuela engaged in a significant military spending spree as prices rose in the period 1998–2008.[25]

Perhaps the most provocative of these tendencies is the funding for foreign insurgencies that petrostates provide. Many non-petrostates also provide such funding, but among petrostates the behavior appears especially common. For instance, the Saudi regime provided billions of dollars for the Afghani mujahedeen during the Soviet occupation in the 1980s. The Libyan government under

Qadhafi provided material support for at least thirty foreign insurgencies around the world and was implicated in several major acts of international terrorism. The Chávez government in Venezuela was accused of providing support for the FARC and other rebel groups in neighboring Colombia. Iraq and Iran have each funded insurgencies on the other's territories, as well as groups in other neighboring states, especially in or near Israel. Iran has been especially supportive of Hezbollah and Hamas, and a branch of the Iranian Revolutionary Guard, the Quds force, is widely suspected of conducting joint operations on foreign soil with Hezbollah.[26] The relationship between oil income and funding for foreign insurgences is ripe for future research.

Beyond the petrostates themselves, recent research has identified eight different causal mechanisms—most of which are understudied—linking the global oil industry to international conflict:

—resource wars, in which states try to acquire oil reserves by force;

—petro-aggression, whereby oil facilitates domestic political control of aggressive leaders like Saddam or Khomeini;

—externalization of civil wars in petrostates;

—financing for insurgencies, such as Iranian oil money to Hezbollah;

—conflicts over potential oil-market domination, such as the United States' conflict with Iraq over Kuwait in 1991;

—control over transit routes, such as shipping lanes and pipelines;

—oil-related grievances, whereby the presence of foreign workers in petrostates helps extremist groups like al Qaeda recruit locals;

—and as an obstacle to multilateral cooperation, such as when an importer curries favor with a petrostate to prevent multilateral cooperation on security issues.[27]

The most widely discussed mechanism is a resource war over possession of oil reserves, but the threat of such wars is often exaggerated.[28] The other mechanisms are less well appreciated, and collectively they make oil a leading cause of war. Understanding these mechanisms can help policymakers design grand strategy and allocate military resources.

Petro-Aggression: The Difference That Revolutionary Governments Make

While petrostates share many similarities and common behaviors, they differ systematically in at least one important respect: the degree to which they engage in aggressive foreign policy.[29] The difference in aggression among petrostates is caused principally by the preferences and beliefs of a country's political leadership, which in turn is shaped in important ways by whether the government came to power through a domestic revolution. International war or conflict is

Figure 11-1. *Interstate Conflict Rate, by Government Type*

Conflicts instigated per year

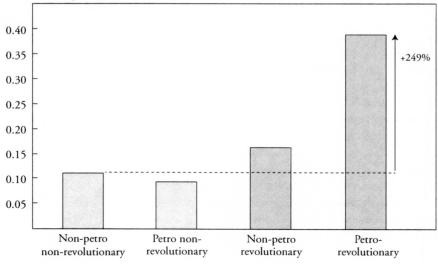

Source: J. D. Colgan, *Petro-Aggression: When Oil Causes War* (Cambridge University Press, 2013).

more probable following a domestic revolution, regardless of whether the country has oil.[30] Yet, as figure 11-1 shows, the combination of oil and revolutionary government creates an especially high propensity to instigate international conflict. Petro-revolutionary states are roughly three and a half times as likely to instigate a militarized interstate dispute (MID) than are non-revolutionary, non-petrostates.

Figure 11-1 was generated from a statistical regression model in which the dependent variable (the measured outcome) is the count of MIDs instigated by a given country per year. The full model is presented elsewhere,[31] but it is helpful to recap some of the details about the variables here. MIDs are a class of international events in which a state threatens, displays, or uses force against another state or states.[32] The MIDs data come from the Correlates of War (COW) project. The figure only includes MIDs in which the country was coded as the attacker (using the COW "revisionist" variable); it does not include any MIDs in which it was the target of some other country's aggression. The statistical model that generated the graph controls for other variables that could affect a country's propensity to instigate conflict, such as the state's population and military capabilities.[33] Much of the data is drawn from the World Bank but other sources are used.[34] The quantity measured on the y-axis is thus the predicted annual rate of conflict for a "typical state" (that is, a state in which all control variables are set to their mean values) in each of the four categories: petrostate/revolutionary, petrostate/non-revolutionary, and so on. Note that the difference between petro-revolutionary states and all the other types of states in figure 11-1 is highly statistically significant.[35] It is also worth noting that the pattern in the raw data looks much the same as the one in this figure. The pattern is not generated by the statistical modeling, only clarified by it.

The evidence reflects the important distinction between revolutionary and non-revolutionary governments and leaders. A revolutionary government is one that "transforms the existing social, political, and economic relationships of the state by overthrowing or rejecting the principal existing institutions of society."[36] Revolutions are a subset of the broader category of regime changes, which includes coups, assassinations, revolts, and foreign occupations or installations. Some of these events can be a part of a revolution (for example, a coup), but they are not necessarily revolutionary on their own. For a government to be coded as revolutionary in figure 11-1, it must satisfy two criteria: the leader must have come to power through use of armed force, widespread popular demonstrations, or similar uprising; and once in power, the government must have implemented radical domestic changes for the purpose of transforming the organization of society, including its social, economic, and political institutions and practices.[37] The data set codes seventy-seven revolutions worldwide in the period 1945–2004. A revolutionary leader is an individual who takes power in a country through a revolution that he helped to lead. According to the data set coding rules, "It is possible for more than one person to have 'led' a revolution (e.g., Lenin and Stalin in Russia, Naguib and Nasser in Egypt, and al-Bakr and Hussein in Iraq), but the leadership is restricted to its senior leaders."

Why Oil and Revolution Produce Aggression

Profits from the oil industry affect a petrostate's foreign policy in multiple ways. One of the most important but subtle incentives is that oil facilitates risk taking by petrostate leaders. Oil income can be easily seized by the head of state, thereby giving the leader financial resources that can be redistributed in exchange for political support (and creating the resource curse discussed above). Consequently, a petrostate leader often faces very little domestic political accountability, which reduces the leader's risk of domestic punishment for risky decisions (like starting wars) and engaging in foreign policy adventurism. In non-petrostates, the risk of being punished for losing an international war (such as being removed from office, nonviolently or otherwise) is a significant deterrent to leaders who are deciding whether to initiate a war.

Oil also creates other incentives, some of which alleviate aggressive behavior. For instance, oil rents create financial incentives to avoid international conflicts that might interrupt the country's oil export sales. Oil exports are the financial lifeblood of many petrostates, by their very nature, and any significant interruption of those exports can compromise the economy and cause significant fiscal strain for the government. For example, despite his fiery rhetoric against the United States, Venezuela's President Chávez did not follow through on his threats to cut off oil exports to the United States, most likely because he realized how valuable those exports were to his government. Another potential cost of conflict is the loss of assets invested overseas that are frozen or seized after the outbreak of conflict, such as when the United States froze Iranian assets in 1980 during the embassy hostage crisis. Given the nature of petrostates' economies, they are likely to hold sizable overseas assets (recently in the form of sovereign wealth funds). There are also long-term costs to conflict for petrostates: oil-consuming states respond to price volatility with energy diversification (for example, nuclear, coal) and investment in alternative fuels.[38] For these reasons, petrostates face significant incentives to maintain international peace and stability and to prevent the interruption of oil exports.[39] The net impact of oil's multiple effects on foreign policy depends critically on a petrostate's internal politics, and especially on the leader's preferences. Revolutionary governments are more likely to have aggressive preferences for two reasons.[40] First, revolutionary politics tend to select leaders who are, typically, more risk tolerant and ambitious to revise the status quo than non-revolutionary leaders. If a leader does not have such characteristics, he (or she) is unlikely to ever successfully lead a revolution. While all leaders take some risks, revolutionary leaders take more (often risking injury, imprisonment, exile, or death to come to power). Likewise, all leaders need ambition to take office, but not all leaders seek to fundamentally alter the societal status quo once in office. Second, the domestic political constraints that normally serve to restrain an aggressive leader from taking a country into international conflict get overturned and temporarily jettisoned during and immediately after a revolution. In short, revolutionary states are more likely to instigate conflicts than non-revolutionary states, all else equal, and that tendency is independent of the presence of oil.

These two factors—oil income and revolutionary government—interact in a complex way. For states in which a revolutionary government has taken power, oil increases the state's propensity to instigate international conflicts. The combination of a risk-tolerant revolutionary leader, financial resources for military activities, and a high degree of political autonomy generated by oil income facilitates state aggression, which in turn frequently leads to conflict. The disincentives to conflict generated by oil (such as the potential disruption of oil export sales) are typically overpowered when the petrostate's government is revolutionary. Not only does this make the petrostate more likely to engage in military conflict, it is also more likely to be targeted by the international community for economic sanctions.[41] Oil wealth in the absence of a revolutionary government, however, tends to have little or no net impact on a state's degree of aggression, due to countervailing incentives such as the possible cost of lost oil exports. In other words, the opportunity costs of disrupted oil exports do not change much if the petrostate's government is revolutionary compared to if it is non-revolutionary, but the domestic political risks and benefits do change. Thus in a non-revolutionary context, the incentives stemming from oil appear to be roughly offsetting, meaning that non-revolutionary petrostates have about the same propensity for instigating conflict as non-revolutionary non-petrostates.

Several countries have exhibited petro-aggression. (Detailed case studies are available elsewhere.)[42] Libya under Qadhafi, for instance, participated in four wars with its neighbor Chad, and a variety of conflicts with other states such as Sudan, Tanzania, and the United States. It also supported insurgencies, opposition movements, and terrorists in more than thirty countries worldwide. Under Saddam Hussein's leadership, Iraq invaded first Iran and then Kuwait. Saddam fit the mold of a petro-revolutionary leader: he seized power by force, revolutionized his country's domestic politics, and then used oil income to centralize power. And in Iran, the revolutionary government led by Ayatollah Ruhollah Khomeini did not initiate the Iran-Iraq war, but it did decide to continue the war for many years after Hussein repeatedly sued for peace. In other displays of aggression, Iranian leaders expressed a desire to see Israel wiped off the map; its people chanted "Death to America" in the streets; and the country instigated various low-level military conflicts with its neighbors. All of these behaviors, along with its pursuit of nuclear weapons, can be attributed in part to its petro-revolutionary regime.

One might wonder whether petro-aggression is really due to the fact that most petrostates are in the Middle East, a conflict-prone region. Research to date has focused primarily on the Middle East, so it is appropriate to be cautious about extrapolating outside of the region. However, three reasons lead to confidence in the findings. First, there are statistical controls in the analysis that ought to isolate a "Middle East effect" for international conflict, to the extent that this exists. The evidence observed in figure 11-1 already accounts for regional differences in the rate of conflict. Second, a big part of why the Middle East is so conflict prone is precisely because of the oil.[43] Not all states in the Middle East tend to conflict, but those that are petro-revolutionary are exceptionally so. Petro-aggression helps to explain the variation. And third, the political dynamics described in this chapter appear to apply to revolutionary governments outside

the Middle East, such as in Venezuela and Sudan. For instance, while fortunately the so-called Bolivarian Revolution led by Hugo Chávez did not lead
to any wars, his panoply of aggressive foreign policy activities, such as military
mobilization and threats against Colombia in 2008, were consistent with the
theme of petro-aggression.

Consequently, the combination of oil and revolutionary government leads to
aggressive foreign policy, whereas oil income on its own (without revolutionary
government) tends to have no such effect. One might also wonder whether oil
plays a causal role in the onset of revolutions, but the evidence does not appear
to support that possibility. While oil does create some grievances and financing
possibilities for rebels, it also often creates durable autocratic regimes supported
by oil-financed patronage. Empirically, petrostates were led by revolutionary governments for almost exactly the same number of years in the data set (15.8 percent), on average, than non-petrostates were (15.6 percent).[44] Subsequent statistical analysis and qualitative study also suggests no reason to believe that oil
systematically helps cause revolutions, though it might have played that role in
individual cases (for example, the Iranian revolution).[45]

Policy Considerations

I have thus far described some of the established and cutting-edge scholarly
research on the impact of oil income on state behavior. The work of applying
that research to specific policy problems remains to be done. Research can contribute to policy in three ways. First, it informs intelligence estimates: the elevated conflict propensity of petro-revolutionary states should be taken seriously,
perhaps more seriously than it has in the past. Second, it reinforces an existing set
of reasons why it is desirable to reduce global oil dependence. And third, it provides further incentive to support institutions that avoid or mitigate the resource
curse in oil-producing states.

Better Intelligence Estimates: Iraq, July 1990

Petro-revolutionary states are high-risk candidates for initiating international
conflict. This insight ought to inform policymakers' decisions. For instance, in
the period preceding the Iraqi invasion of Kuwait in August 1990, U.S. policymakers observed conflicting signals of Iraq's intentions and debated their
meaning. Some members of the intelligence community argued that there was
a high probability of an attack on Kuwait, but the Department of State was not
convinced and argued that the crisis would likely pass.[46] This meant that President George H. W. Bush received mixed messages. The confusion was certainly
understandable: there was a jumble of mixed signals, and wars are inherently

difficult to predict. And of course, the research on petro-aggression did not exist in 1990, and thus the mechanisms linking oil revenues to greater risk taking and foreign policy aggression were not well understood. With the power of hindsight, certain clues stand out more clearly: Hussein had come to power in a domestic revolution, with all of the risk tolerance and ambition typical of a revolutionary leader, and Iraq's government was clearly supported by oil money. Still, given the research advances in understanding petro-aggression since that time, current and future policymakers ought to shift their prior beliefs about revolutionary and petro-revolutionary leaders and consider them as high-risk candidates for initiating international conflict. Had the research on petro-aggression existed in 1990, the State Department's analysts might have had a deeper sense of foreboding when confronted with warnings of Iraqi troop movements near the border of Kuwait.

Knowing that a state is a high-risk candidate for aggression could have real consequences in resolving crisis situations. If it had been clear to U.S. policymakers in 1990 that the Iraqi invasion was coming, they would have had more time to consider the appropriate response to such an invasion before it occurred. With more time and better information, they might have concluded that the United States was indeed willing to go to war in defense of Kuwait. Armed with that resolve, Washington might have been able to convey to Hussein in clear and unambiguous terms the consequences of his planned invasion, before he invaded. History might have taken a different course.

Ending the Oil Addiction

The second major implication of this chapter is to add to the growing list of reasons why policymakers should do more to reduce dependence on oil. Oil income funds petro-revolutionary states, which fuels their aggression and creates international conflict. The United States and its allies have substantial military deployments that are directly or indirectly connected to the global oil industry.[47] When added to the other negative consequences of the global oil industry—which include environmental degradation, economic volatility, political corruption, and more frequent civil wars in oil-producing countries[48]—the case for ending the world's continued dependence on petroleum as a primary source of energy grows stronger. Policies and technologies that create incentives for alternatives to oil, especially those that are based on renewable sources, have potentially very positive consequences for global affairs.

Continued dependence on oil is a problem regardless of where the oil comes from.[49] The global oil market is highly integrated and fungible, meaning that if one country stops importing from petrostates, the latter will typically be able to switch customers, selling the same quantity to other countries. Thus, reducing oil imports without reducing consumption will not lower the global oil price, nor decrease petrostates' revenues, nor prevent petro-aggression.

Energy independence, properly conceived, is desirable and feasible for the United States in the medium to long term. Energy independence does not require energy autarky—that is, self-sufficiency in energy. Instead, we should think of energy independence as minimizing the harmful externalities associated with energy production and consumption, and reducing the risk of supply disruptions to a managerial rather than strategic problem. In practical terms, it requires an end to the stranglehold that petroleum has on the transportation sector. Energy independence probably requires commercially viable alternatives to petroleum as a fuel for transportation. There are some technologies already, and more being developed, that could help with this goal. Plotting a strategy toward genuine energy independence lies far beyond the scope of this chapter, however.[50] Still, the payoff from such a strategy should not be lightly dismissed.

Mitigating the Resource Curse

Even so, oil is going to be a vital part of the global economy for at least a few more decades, and probably longer.[51] As a consequence, we need a set of policies to address the harmful geopolitical consequences of the oil sector during that period of transition. Specifically, we need to increase our efforts to better manage the resource curse in oil-producing countries.

Efforts by developed countries to alleviate the resource curse typically are viewed in terms of altruistic, humanitarian goals. Yet developed countries should recognize that these efforts serve their own selfish interests. The same mechanisms that underlie the resource curse have serious consequences for international security in the form of petro-aggression when a revolutionary government comes to power. The nearly inevitable consequence is that developed countries feel compelled to manage the resulting conflicts and wars. The United States spends billions of dollars annually on its military presence in the Middle East and North Africa, and that presence is intimately tied up in its efforts to secure stability in the global oil market.[52] Civilian efforts to manage the resource curse, by putting in place institutions, norms, and practices to better manage the inflow of oil income and enhance domestic political accountability, are in everyone's interest. Initiatives such as Publish What You Pay or the Extractive Industries Transparency Initiative are probably necessary (though insufficient) steps toward that goal.[53]

Policies designed to mitigate the resource curse remain contentious and encounter significant resistance. For instance, a decision in August 2012 by the U.S. Securities and Exchange Commission established a short-lived set of rules for financial reporting on oil-production activities in foreign countries, following passage of the Dodd-Frank Act in Congress.[54] The decision was only narrowly passed, by a vote of two to one, with two abstentions. Then in July 2013, the law was struck down by a federal court after a legal challenge from the American Petroleum Institute. The research described in this chapter should encourage policymakers to counter the reluctance in the oil industry to take steps to increase transparency and actively manage the effects of the resource curse.

Conclusion

Oil politics is a major force in global and domestic politics, especially in developing countries. One might ask whether we should expect other forms of energy, such as natural gas or renewable energy sources, to pose similar political dynamics. That question is very much an open one and should be investigated by researchers. Still, I conjecture that oil is actually distinct from other energy sources in some important ways. As mentioned earlier, it has some specific characteristics that are not necessarily shared by other energy sources. For instance, the world oil market is characterized by a single, relatively uniform price (accounting for transportation costs and differences in crude oil quality), which is not true of natural gas. Oil profits are also easily seized by governments, which might not be true of profits in the renewable energy sector. For those reasons and others, this chapter has focused on oil as a distinct topic worthy of study in its own right.

Oil-producing states are characterized by some similarities. They are vulnerable, for instance, to the resource curse, which leads to pervasive corruption, wasted public spending, volatile economic growth, and more frequent civil wars and domestic conflict. Yet while common tendencies are observable among the group of petrostates, there are also important and systematic differences. States that are petro-revolutionary—having both oil income and a revolutionary leader—tend to instigate conflicts at a rate three and a half times that of a comparable "typical" state (one without oil or a revolutionary leader). Indeed, the tendency of petrostates to get into international conflicts cannot be explained without disaggregating the group. The research described in this chapter thus emphasizes the point that oil does not have a single, monolithic effect, but rather it interacts with domestic politics in a complex way.

Nonetheless, that complexity should not obscure the difficult questions raised by the research presented here. Ample evidence shows that money consumers in developed countries spend on gasoline is contributing to the resource curse and petro-aggression experienced in the developing world. The list of negative consequences of dependence on oil is growing longer, and the case for reducing oil dependence is growing stronger.

Notes

1. Also see B. K. Sovacool, "What Are We Talking About? Analyzing Fifteen Years of Energy Scholarship and Proposing a Social Science Research Agenda," *Energy Research and Social Science* 1, no. 1 (2014); and K. Hancock and V. Vivoda, "International Political Economy: A Field Born of the OPEC Crisis Returns to Its Energy Roots," *Energy Research and Social Science* 1, no.1 (2014).

2. Counting all conflicts, regardless of whether they are instigators or targets. See J. D. Colgan, "Oil and Revolutionary Governments: Fuel for International Conflict," *International Organization* 64 (2010): 661–94; J. D. Colgan, *Petro-Aggression: When Oil Causes War* (Cambridge University Press, 2013); and J. D. Colgan, "Oil and Resource-Backed Aggression," *Energy Policy* 39 (2011):1669–76.

3. R. M. Auty, *Resource-Based Industrialization: Sowing the Oil in Eight Developing Countries* (Oxford University Press, 1990); J. D. Sachs and A. M. Warner, *Natural Resource Abundance and Economic Growth* (Cambridge, Mass.: National Bureau of Economic Research, 1995); and X. Sala-i-Martin and A. Subramanian, *Addressing the Natural Resource Curse: An Illustration from Nigeria* (Cambridge, Mass.: National Bureau of Economic Research, 2003).

4. M. L. Ross, *The Oil Curse: How Petroleum Wealth Shapes the Development of Nations* (Princeton University Press, 2012); P. J. Luong and E. Weinthal, *Oil Is Not a Curse: Ownership Structure and Institutions in Soviet Successor States* (Cambridge University Press, 2010).

5. E. Goldberg, E. Wibbels, and E. Mvukiyehe, "Lessons from Strange Cases: Democracy, Development, and the Resource Curse in the U.S. States," *Comparative Political Studies* 41 (2008): 477–514.

6. The literature on these effects is vast, but some of the most important work includes R. M. Auty, *Resource-Based Industrialization: Sowing the Oil in Eight Developing Countries* (Oxford University Press, 1990); J. D. Sachs and A. M. Warner, *Natural Resource Abundance and Economic Growth* (Cambridge, Mass.: National Bureau of Economic Research, 1995); Sala-i-Martin and Subramanian, *Addressing the Natural Resource Curse: An Illustration from Nigeria;* Ross, *The Oil Curse;* J. A. Robinson, R. Torvik, and T. Verdier, "Political Foundations of the Resource Curse," *Journal of Development Economics* 79 (2006): 447–68; M. Humphreys, J. Sachs, and J. E. Stiglitz, *Escaping the Resource Curse* (Columbia University Press, 2007).

7. B. K. Sovacool, *Energy & Ethics Justice and the Global Energy Challenge* (Houndmills, Basingstoke, Hampshire: Palgrave Macmillan, 2013); B. K. Sovacool, "Deploying Off-Grid Technology to Eradicate Energy Poverty," *Science* 338 (October 5, 2012): 47–48.

8. Ross, *The Oil Curse;* Luong and Weinthal, *Oil Is Not a Curse: Ownership Structure and Institutions in Soviet Successor States.*

9. B. K. Sovacool, "The Political Economy of Oil and Gas in Southeast Asia: Heading towards the Natural Resource Curse?" *Pacific Review* 23, no. 2 (May 2010): 225–59.

10. Arguably the best single-volume discussion of these effects is Ross, *The Oil Curse.* There are also some skeptics of the political resource curse, notably S. Haber and V.

Menaldo, "Do Natural Resources Fuel Authoritarianism? A Reappraisal of the Resource Curse," *American Political Science Review* 105 (2011):1–26; M. Herb, *All in the Family: Absolutism, Revolution, and Democracy in the Middle Eastern Monarchies* (State University of New York Press, 1999); and D. Acemoglu, S. Johnson, J. A. Robinson, and P. Yared, "Income and Democracy," *American Economic Review* 98 (2008): 808–42.

11. Ross, *The Oil Curse;* E. Goldberg, E. Wibbels, and E. Mvukiyehe, "Lessons from Strange Cases: Democracy, Development, and the Resource Curse in the U.S. States," *Comparative Political Studies* 41 (2008): 477–514; H. Mahdavy, "The Patterns and Problems of Economic Development in Rentier States: The Case of Iran," *Studies in Economic History of the Middle East: From the Rise of Islam to the Present Day* (Oxford University Press, 1970); T. L. Karl, *The Paradox of Plenty* (University of California Press), 1997; M. L. Ross, "Does Oil Hinder Democracy?" *World Politics* 53 (2001): 325–61; E. Bellin, "The Robustness of Authoritarianism in the Middle East," *Comparative Politics* 36 (2004): 139–57.

12. Karl, *The Paradox of Plenty.*

13. M. S. Fish, *Democracy Derailed in Russia: The Failure of Open Politics* (Cambridge University Press, 2005).

14. C. Boix, *Democracy and Redistribution* (Cambridge University Press, 2003); T. Dunning, *Crude Democracy: Natural Resource Wealth and Political Regimes* (Cambridge University Press, 2008).

15. E. Bellin, "The Robustness of Authoritarianism in the Middle East," *Comparative Politics* 36 (2004): 139–57.

16. D. G. Victor, *The Politics of Fossil-Fuel Subsidies* (Geneva: International Institute of Sustainable Development, 2009). See www.iisd.org/gsi/sites/default/files/politics_ffs.pdf.

17. V. Walt, "Why Global Fuel Prices Will Spark the Next Revolutions," *Time,* Nov. 28, 2012.)

18. Victor, *The Politics of Fossil-Fuel Subsidies.*

19. A. Cheon and J. Urpelainen, "Oil Prices and Energy Technology Innovation: An Empirical Analysis," *Global Environmental Change* 22 (2012): 407–17.

20. Victor, *The Politics of Fossil-Fuel Subsidies.*

21. See Victor, *The Politics of Fossil-Fuel Subsidies;* H. A. Bienen and M. Gersovitz, "Consumer Subsidy Cuts, Violence, and Political Stability," *Comparative Politics* 19 (1986): 25–44. Bienen and Gersovitz emphasize that subsidy cuts alone are not fundamental causes of instability, but rather act in combination with other factors.

22. S. Gupta, M. Verhoeven, R. Gillingham, C. Schiller, A. Mansoor, J. P. Cordoba, "Equity and Efficiency in the Reform of Price Subsidies: A Guide for Policymakers," IMF Staff Report (Washington: International Monetary Fund, 2000).

23. For some examples of relatively successful subsidy reform efforts, see M. B. J. Clements, D. Coady, M. S. Fabrizio, M. S. Gupta, M. T. S. C. Alleyne, and M. C. A. Sdralevich, *Energy Subsidy Reform: Lessons and Implications* (Washington: International Monetary Fund, 2013).

24. Colgan, *Petro-Aggression: When Oil Causes War;* Ross, "Does Oil Hinder Democracy?"

25. J. D. Colgan, "Venezuela and Military Expenditure Data," *Journal of Peace Research* 48 (2011): 547–56.

26. Colgan, *Petro-Aggression: When Oil Causes War.*

27. J. D. Colgan, "Fueling the Fire: Pathways from Oil to War," *International Security* 38 (2013): 147–80.

28. M. T. Klare, *Resource Wars: The New Landscape of Global Conflict* (New York: Holt Paperbacks, 2002).

29. For a richer and more detailed treatment of petro-aggression, see Colgan, *Petro-Aggression: When Oil Causes War.*

30. J. D. Colgan, "Domestic Revolutionary Leaders and International Conflict," *World Politics* 65 (2013): 656–90.

31. Colgan, "Oil and Revolutionary Governments"; Colgan, *Petro-Aggression: When Oil Causes War.*

32. While there is heterogeneity in these events, from full-fledged wars to relatively minor disputes, they provide considerable information about a state's interstate conflicts.

33. The statistical model is described in Colgan, "Oil and Revolutionary Governments," and Colgan, *Petro-Aggression: When Oil Causes War.* The model includes the following variables: GDP per capita (logged), population, Polity IV score, number of other countries with which the state shares a border, the percentage of the population that is Muslim, and dummy variables indicating the cold war time period, whether the state was a major power, and the state's geographic region. Some models also include country-fixed effects and the results are consistent.

34. World Bank data are used for GDP per capita, population, and the state's geographic region, while COW data provide the number of other countries with which the state shares a border and whether the state was a major power; see Colgan, "Oil and Revolutionary Governments," and Colgan, *Petro-Aggression: When Oil Causes War.*

35. Specifically, the petrostate and petro-revolutionary dummy variables are positive and statistically significant at $p < 0.05$ levels. The petrostate variable itself is negative and statistically significant in some but not all models. The only other consistently statistically significant variable is the number of other countries with which the state shares a border (which is positively correlated with conflicts), though population size is also significant whenever country-fixed effects are not used. Note that the difference between non-revolutionary petrostates and non-revolutionary non-petrostates is small and not statistically significant.

36. See J. D. Colgan, "Measuring Revolution," *Conflict Management and Peace Science* 29 (2012): 444–67. Walt and Huntington use similar definitions. See S. M. Walt, *Revolution and War* (Cornell University Press, 1996), p. 12, and S. P. Huntington, *Political Order in Changing Societies* (Yale University Press, 1968), p. 264.

37. For more detail on the coding rules, see Colgan, "Measuring Revolution." Note that leaders of entirely new countries are not coded as revolutionary, even if they led a war of independence, nor are leaders who are installed by foreign occupations.

38. Oil must compete with other energy alternatives in the long run, and international conflict drives up the cost of oil relative to its competitors. This was evident in the

change in the energy consumption profile of the United States and other Western states in the 1970s, when questions about the cost and reliability of the oil supply were being raised: oil lost market share to other energy sources and was essentially eliminated from use for electricity generation. At least for large exporters of oil, interruptions of supply caused by international conflict raise the risk that consuming nations will permanently alter their consumption patterns away from oil. See Cheon and Urpelainen, "Oil Prices and Energy Technology Innovation."

39. The expectation that oil exports create incentives for petrostates to avoid international conflict touches on the larger issue of the general relationship between trade and conflict. The argument here is consistent with those scholars (Keohane and Nye; Russett and O'Neal) who argue that trade has a pacifying effect, though this effect is disputed by some (Barbieri). See R. O. Keohane and J. S. Nye, *Power and Independence* (Boston: Little Brown, 1977); B. Russett and J. R. O'Neal, *Triangulating Peace: Democracy, Interdependence, and International Organizations* (New York: W.W. Norton, 2001); and K. Barbieri, *The Liberal Illusion: Does Trade Promote Peace?* (University of Michigan Press, 2005).

40. Colgan, "Domestic Revolutionary Leaders and International Conflict."

41. J. D. Colgan, "Oil and Resource-Backed Aggression," *Energy Policy* 39 (2011): 1669–76.

42. Colgan, *Petro-Aggression: When Oil Causes War*.

43. Ibid.

44. Colgan, "Oil and Revolutionary Governments."

45. Colgan, *Petro-Aggression: When Oil Causes War*.

46. C. Alfonsi, *Circle in the Sand: Why We Went Back to Iraq* (New York: Doubleday, 2006).

47. J. Duffield, *Over a Barrel: The Costs of U.S. Foreign Oil Dependence* (Stanford, Calif.: Stanford Law and Politics, 2007).

48. Ross, *The Oil Curse*.

49. Cutting imported oil does have some benefits, such as reducing a country's vulnerability to an oil embargo, but this is less important than it might appear. Embargoes are rare and short lived; the 1973 oil crisis had more to do with other factors like nationalization of oil sectors and U.S. price controls than the embargo itself; and since 1973, the United States and other major oil consumers have put in place significant emergency management systems and petroleum reserves. See E. Gholz and D. G. Press, "Protecting 'The Prize': Oil and the U.S. National Interest," *Security Studies* 19 (2010): 453–85, and J. D. Colgan, "The International Energy Agency," GPPI Policy Paper Series no. 6 (Berlin: Global Public Policy Institute, 2009).

50. Others are working on this problem. See, for example, D. Sandalow, *Freedom from Oil: How the Next President Can End the United States' Oil Addiction* (New York: McGraw-Hill, 2007).

51. K. Crane, A. Goldthau, and M. Toman, *Imported Oil and U.S. National Security* (Santa Monica, Calif.: RAND, 2009); J. M. Deutch and J. R. Schlesinger, *National Security Consequences of U.S. Oil Dependency* (New York: Council on Foreign Relations Press, 2006).

52. Crane, Goldthau, and Toman, *Imported Oil and U.S. National Security*.

53. The Natural Resources Charter is a promising step toward a more comprehensive approach. See http://eiti.org/, www.publishwhatyoupay.org/, and http://naturalresourcecharter.org/.

54. J. D. Colgan, "Regulating the Resource Curse," *Foreign Policy*, August 27, 2012

12

Russia Gambles on Resource Scarcity: Energy Intrigues in a Time of Political Crisis

PAVEL K. BAEV

Russia is so richly endowed with many and varied natural resources—from land and water to oil and gold—and has inherited from the Soviet industrialization such a strong industrial and technological capacity to extract and process these resources that its potential as a global supplier of primary commodities might appear supreme. Yet many of the extraction industries suffer from underinvestment in their production assets, and Russia's economic development resolutely slowed to a 2–3 percent crawl in 2012–13 after the five quarters long and 12 percent deep contraction in 2008–09. This diminishing output from Russia's uniquely deep resource base cannot be explained by the impact of the global financial-economic crisis or sanctions. The demand for mineral resources remained strong as China and other emerging economies kept growing even as the United States and the European Union (EU) contracted and is on track as of early 2014. At the same time, the emergency monetary policies (such as the quantitative easing) have generated speculative pressure on the primary commodities markets, so oil prices, which are a common point of reference for commodities, have remained high.

The prime reason for the apparent stagnation in the Russian extraction industries is the intrusive state policy, which sets ambitious goals and seeks to turn export strength into political influence but also exhibits predatory practices shaped by massive corruption. This dominance of political agenda over economic rationale makes Russia both similar to other resource-exporting states and special in the distorting power of its politics. The fundamental principle of expanding strong state control over the development of prime natural resources, first of all oil and gas, fits perfectly into the well-researched trend of resource nationalism.[1] This state empowerment, however, is emasculated by low capacity for central planning and government's inability to control the "state" companies, effectively privatized by political clans, which pursue their parochial agendas by awarding the most lucrative pieces in the value-generating systems to quasi-private companies. The oil and gas sector produces up to 50 percent of revenues for the federal budget, and state policy is focused accordingly. Within this incoherently controlled sector, the natural gas industry—dominated heavily by Gazprom—is the most politicized and faces the gravest challenges.

This chapter examines the pre-sanctions turmoil in Russia's policy for development of its natural resources and evaluates possible changes in the context of transformation of the quasi-democratic (and deeply corrupt) authoritarian regime. The main focus is on the oil and gas industries, which are of crucial importance for Russia's progress—or lack of thereof. Other parts of the energy sector (including the nuclear industry) are addressed briefly, as are related environmental problems (such as global warming). At the same time, many significant extraction industries (for instance, the production of gold) and the whole agricultural sector (which shapes the politicized debates on food security) are left out of the analysis. The first section evaluates the impact on energy policymaking of the crisis in Putin's regime. The second examines changes in the key guidelines for Russia's energy policy. The following three sections look into the growing problems for Russia in the European energy market, the limited opportunities for expanding into the Asia-Pacific markets, and the prospects for developing Russia's mineral resource base.

Distortion of the Energy Policy by the Crisis of Putin's Regime

The eruption of mass street protests in Moscow in December 2011 illuminated the maturing of a complex crisis of Putin's populist authoritarian regime, and the ebb in protest activity since autumn 2012 signifies a transformation rather than a de-escalation of this crisis of governance.[2] The fears and disorganization that this crisis has generated in the Kremlin manifest themselves in political zigzags in every direction, from the Arctic to Syria to Crimea, and in the execution of key tasks in economic and foreign policies. The centrality of energy in Putin's management of state affairs has been somewhat diminished by the commitment to prioritize other urgent challenges, including the massive and patently infeasible (at a total cost of US$750 billion to 2020) rearmament program and the heavily indebted pension system.[3] Decisionmaking on energy policy is more than ever shaped by conflicting demands and crisis-driven changes of direction, so that short-term imperatives prevail over strategic priorities. The bargaining over take-overs and tax cuts has become more tumultuous but somewhat less opaque than it used to be because the interests of key players have come into sharper conflict, while Putin's control and arbitration have become less de rigueur.

The production of doctrines of various kinds—from the Military Doctrine to the Information Security Doctrine and the Food Security Doctrine—is a typi-cal feature of hyper-centralized economic management, which has little capac-ity for the intrusive Soviet-style central planning. The energy sector has its own set of strategic guidelines that generally have even less connection with reality than most other wishful prescriptions.[4] Thus the emphasis on reducing state control in the Energy Strategy 2020 (approved in 2003) was undermined by the de facto expropriation of the largest oil company, Yukos, and the forecast of steady growth of production in the Energy Strategy 2030 (approved in 2009) was proven wrong by the deep decline and sluggish recovery in the course of the ongoing economic turmoil.[5] In the series of goal-setting articles that Vladimir Putin published on the electoral trail in early 2012, remarkably little attention was given to the energy sector, while in his address to the parliament in Decem-ber 2012, he asserted, "The capacities of the raw materials–based economy model are exhausted."[6] The newly developed Energy Security Doctrine is supposed to be a coherent set of updated guidelines, but it does not resolve the contradic-tion between long-term and immediate priorities. The goal of securing growth in production of energy resources requires an increase in investments, first of all domestic, but the need to increase budget revenues dictates higher taxation of the energy sector, which curtails the base for these investments.[7]

This contradiction is not addressed in the current decisionmaking, which is heavily tilted toward immediate issues. The progressive confiscation of profits in the energy sector is causing much dismay among stakeholders, who engage in fierce lobbying for tax breaks, arguing that their profit margins are shrinking due to steady growth of operational costs.[8] The government is indeed taxing the vol-ume of production and revenues from export and cannot shift to taxing profits due to the lack of reliable data on corporate production and operational costs, so even in the rare situation of relatively stable prices (as in 2012–13), compa-nies have had to cut investment budgets. Cost cutting is not an option because various forms of corruption, particularly in "social responsibility" projects, take a heavy toll. The inevitable consequence of shrinking profits is the escalation of intra-elite squabbles, and while in 2013 attention in Moscow was focused on the clan feuds in the defense-industrial complex, culminating in the ignominy of former defense minister Anatoly Serdyukov, the intensity of intrigues in the oil and gas elites is not much lower. The key figure in these intrigues is former

deputy prime minister Igor Sechin, who combines the positions of chief executive officer in the state-owned company Rosneft and secretary of the presidential
Commission for Strategic Development of the Fuel and Energy Sector.[9] Exploiting his close ties with Putin, Sechin has defied the efforts of Dmitri Medvedev's
government to assert authority in setting the rules for the energy business and
at the same time has moved aggressively against other "oil oligarchs," including
even Gazprom's chief executive, Aleksei Miller.[10]

These cutthroat intrigues camouflage an important swing in Putin's engagement with the energy sector as his attention span narrows. The gas business
attracted his prime attention in the second half of the 2000s, but he now appears
to be more interested in oil. The mammoth deal on takeover of TNK-BP by
Rosneft—by striking separate bargains with British Petroleum and the Russian
Alfa Access Renova consortium amounting to US$56 billion—is evidence of this
change of heart.[11] It can perhaps be explained by the significantly deeper financial flows in the oil sector and by the accumulating problems in the gas sector,
where, as we shall see, Gazprom needs a lot of support in the struggle for export
markets, thus becoming a political liability rather than an asset. An important
consequence of this reorientation of "supreme" attention is a smaller geopolitical
profile of the Russian energy complex. Political interference cannot alter the fact
that the oil business operates in an environment shaped by global market forces
and that softer Kremlin management of the gas business helps to consolidate the
trend of liberalization, in which market rules prevail over political ambitions.

Overall, the fast-moving crisis of Putin's regime increases the uncertainty and
aggravates the distortions in the energy sector because political control is tightening but losing coherence. Policymakers are intimately aware of the anxiety
of stakeholders but have to prioritize extraction of dividends at the expense of
investment in modernization.

The Vision Wandering: From Energy Superpower
to Modernization to Reindustrialization

Russia's spectacular richness in natural resources is confidently perceived by the
elites and society at large as a major source of strength and indeed as an element
of national identity. Yet this perception is mixed with reservations about the infe-
rior status of being an exporter of oil, minerals, and timber to more developed
states, as captured by the oft-used label of "raw material appendage."[12] The pride
in possessing a treasure chest is blended with greed that cries against granting
hungry outsiders access to it on the cheap, and both translate into widespread
worries about unfair distribution of the rents. At the same time, the dissatisfac-
tion with the high dependency on the export of primary commodities evolves

into concerns about vulnerability to sharp price volatility. These mixed feelings are stirred by the widespread expectations of a new wave of global economic crisis and underpinned by unease about the astounding rise of China, which emerges as the major source of highly politicized demand for every kind of primary commodity and energy source.

When the proposition of becoming an energy superpower was initially advanced by Putin in the early 2000s, it was far less controversial and reflected perfectly the high expectations in Russia of a "great leap forward" in prosperity and rehabilitation of its compromised international status.[13] In fact, the assumption of perpetually climbing commodities prices, dubious as it might seem today, was in tune with the "peak oil" school of thought that was gaining ground in the international debates.[14] These assumptions materialized in the remarkable fact that Russia, with 7–8 percent of proven oil reserves (about the same volume as Kuwait and the United Arab Emirates), competed with Saudi Arabia, with one of the lowest ratios of resources to production, for the position of the world's top producer of oil.[15] Putin also placed strong emphasis on development of the nuclear industry, presuming that the Chernobyl syndrome had dissipated and that Russia could turn its technological base into a major foreign policy asset. What shattered that energy-centric thinking was the economic crisis of 2008–09, which hit Russia harder than any of the G-20 economies and placed oil prices on a gradually sloping plateau. That shock paved the way for a swing in official discourse accomplished by President Medvedev, who unfurled the slogan of "modernization" and placed priority on developing high-tech industries; the export of natural resources was merely a means to that end.[16] Few of his projects came close to implementation, but the heavy emphasis in official rhetoric on reducing petro-dependency and setting Russia on a track of technological revolution made a difference in public perceptions of the value of natural resources.

Reclaiming the supreme power through the heavily manipulated elections in 2012, Putin has not tried to switch back to an energy-centric discourse; instead, he has discarded most of the "modernization" talk as subversive advocacy of political liberalization that plays into the hands of the opposition, which suddenly has gained worrisome street power. His trademark slogan of "stabilization" has little, if any, convincing force in the environment of fast-moving and uncontrollable changes, so he has put forward the idea of "reindustrialization," which appears promising in the context of the disarray in the postindustrial economies of the European Union. The problem with this course is that reviving old Soviet industries, especially the production of armaments, by means of massive state investments and guaranteed acquisition of their production, amounts to attempting to replicate a failed economic model. Mikhail Khodorkovsky, who has emerged as one of the most influential political thinkers despite his long imprisonment, criticizes this Putin-style state capitalism as the road to a "primitive economy where business cannot develop outside several narrow sectors supported by [the] state," leading to slow growth and backwardness resembling a "cross between Argentina in the 1970s and Venezuela today."[17]

This course has important implications for the energy sector because the giant manufacturing enterprises require a lot of cheap energy and consume great volumes of raw materials, while their production typically amounts to "value detraction."[18] Labor costs are set to increase because Putin needs to mobilize support among the working class, which generates demands from the factory bosses for lower energy tariffs and lower commodity prices, which are poorly compatible with Russia's long-negotiated accession to the World Trade Organization (WTO).[19] Lobbying for subsidies and state orders tends to be far more efficient in the "market" of bureaucratic control than investment in energy efficiency or environmental protection, while the political priority of the climate change issue, which has never been high, has all but disappeared.[20] Russia thus finds itself disengaged from the spectacular innovations in the global energy market, downplaying (as denial has become impossible) the "shale gas revolution" championed by the United States and dismissing the EU efforts to tap into renewable energy sources as "green protectionism."

Being the largest energy producer in the world, Russia lacks a coherent vision for turning its riches into a driver of economic development in the mainstream of global innovations rather than merely a means of securing regime survival. It is stuck in the old-fashioned pattern of extracting oil and gas, which is unsustainable as access to modern technologies is denied, while production costs rise to overtake the falling benefits.

Energy Troubles in the European Market and the Reform of Gazprom

It was in energy exports to the European market, first of all to Germany, that the Soviet Union accomplished a memorable breakthrough in the 1970s. In the assessments of Russian energy strategists, this market had remained pivotal in the volume of profits and political dividends to be harvested—up until 2014.[21] Experts and politicians staffing the European Commission arrived in the mid-2000s at the opposite conclusion—that the EU dependency on Russian hydrocarbons constitutes a security challenge—and now insist with new vigor on their prescriptions for reducing imports from this erratic supplier. What is remarkable about this clash of policy prescriptions for and against energy partnership is that both sides have got it wrong.

There is a natural complementarity between Russia's abundance in energy resources, which are available for transportation westward through well-developed infrastructure, and Western (as well as Eastern and Central) Europe's deficiency in them, which is aggravated by falling production. This seemingly perfect fit is, however, distorted by deepening disagreements between multiple energy policies in this supposedly carefully regulated interface. From the early 2000s, Russia saw the main problem for expanding its position on the European energy market as being transit, which was perceived not only as a cost issue but also as a political vulnerability. In oil politics, Moscow has successfully resolved this problem by building terminals in Primorsk (eliminating transit through Estonia and Latvia) and Novorossiysk (eliminating transit through Ukraine), while at the same time controlling the main channel for oil exports from Kazakhstan and accepting with surprising indifference the opening of a Caucasian corridor along the Baku-Tbilisi-Ceyhan pipeline.[22]

The situation in the gas business was far more complicated, and the Russian-Ukrainian gas skirmish in the first days of 2006 raised alarm in EU quarters about the heavy politicization of this business on the Russian side. These worries blended with the strong activist demands for emissions reductions, leading to an attempt to shape a common energy policy aimed at significantly reducing total energy consumption, including gas imports from Russia, by 2020.[23] Policymakers in Moscow interpreted this set of guidelines as an exercise in wishful "green" thinking far detached from economic realities and took the fiasco of the United Nations Copenhagen Climate Summit in December 2009 as proof of ever-expanding demand. Protracted economic crisis in Europe has revised these assessments downward, but what is more striking is the stubborn refusal of the European Commission to modify the energy policy according to the demands of financial austerity, so the emphasis on stimulating the use of renewable sources by generous subsidies remains strong.[24]

The year 2012 marked a turning point in gas relations between Russia and the EU, one clear indication of which was the shrinking volume of exports by as much as 10 percent. Russian energy champion Gazprom managed to restore its market share in 2013 by granting price cuts to its most privileged customers, but was caught flat-footed with the launch of the European Commission probe into its alleged abuse of market monopolization in East and Central Europe.[25] Disappointment in Gazprom's inefficiency and disgust with its symbiotic relations with the Kremlin were growing even among its traditional partners, such as the German giant E.ON, and a new high in this distancing was marked by the collapse of the long-dragging Shtokman project in mid-2012.[26] Putin keeps trying to shelter Gazprom from the EU investigation and blasts the so-called "Third Energy Package" as a "harmful document," but he is gradually realizing that the gas business is no longer a useful political instrument and that the scope of problems in its rehabilitation has grown beyond his capacity for "manual management."[27]

The execution of the ill-conceived policy of opening new export channels to the saturated European market has brought endless complications in Russia's relations with two of its key gas partners—Ukraine and Turkey. In Ukraine, the government of Victor Yanukovich was eager to leave behind the angst of the "gas war" of January 2009 but still wanted to deny Gazprom the rights to control the complex system of gas pipelines and storage facilities. Putin tried to prop up the government by granting it a huge loan and a cut in the gas price, but that generosity failed to prevent the collapse of the Yanukovich administration in February 2014. Russia's annexation of Crimea has brought not only a sharp crisis in relations with tumultuous Ukraine, but also a deep confrontation with the EU, in which gas matters will inevitably come into play. The plan to circumvent the Ukrainian transit by constructing the South Stream pipeline across the Black Sea is not only hugely cost-inefficient but also requires consent from Turkey, which is conditional on expanding the flow of hydrocarbons into that prospective "hub."[28] Russia is not comfortable with the idea of making Turkey a major player in the European gas market, but its plans for capturing a dominant position in the southeastern corner of this market are undermined by the EU objections and serious decline in the purchasing power of local consumers.

Diversification Russian Style: Challenges in the Asia-Pacific Energy Markets

Most of Russia's undeveloped and underexplored energy reserves are found to the east of River Yenisei, and it makes perfect economic sense to connect the exploitation of these greenfields with the fast-growing demand in Asia-Pacific. Ideas about and orders for expanding the flow of oil and gas in the eastern direction have been presented and issued so many times that it is astounding that the share of Russian exports in the petro-export market is still in the single digits. Many European politicians have concluded that the talk about reorienting energy trade is merely a bargaining tool for Moscow in its strategy to defeat the EU directive for diversification.[29] Indeed, only one group of projects has been successfully developed in the vast area of the Far East—on Sakhalin Island. All credit belongs to Western majors that executed these projects on the basis of production-sharing agreements made in the mid-1990s, while the slowdown in expanding these developments is the result of Gazprom's hostile takeover of the Sakhalin-II project in 2006.[30] Every oil and gas field in East Siberia poses a particular upstream challenge, but the endless procrastination with bringing the new reserves online cannot be explained away merely by geologic peculiarities and lack of infrastructure. It is primarily the result of policy faults.

What underpins Moscow's slowness in exploring and exploiting the energy base in the Far East is the profound unease in its relations with China, which are formally cordial but shaped by worries about the insatiable appetite for every kind of mineral resource, on the one hand, and disdain about corrupt inefficiency, on the other.[31] The key project in these energy relations is the oil pipeline grandly called East Siberia–Pacific Ocean (ESPO or VSTO), and while China was ready to buy all available oil and more on long-term contracts, Russia undertook a major effort to extend the pipeline to the Kozmino terminal facing the Sea of Japan. The prospect of heavy dependency on exports to China was thus avoided (costs notwithstanding), but finding oil for filling the strategic pipeline remains an open question.[32] Moscow is adamantly opposed to letting Chinese companies take shares, not to mention ownership, in energy projects in East Siberia, but Russian companies developing these greenfields demand tax cuts and subsidies, which the stressed federal budget can ill afford.[33] It makes little sense to divert oil from West Siberia eastward because the costs of transportation are higher, while prices are subject to the same fluctuations.

The prospects for exporting gas to the Asia-Pacific markets are even more uncertain, despite International Energy Agency (IEA) estimates that in 2020 as much as 55 billion cubic meters (bcm) would go to China and 20 bcm would go to other regional consumers; regional consumers presently receive 12 bcm, and China receives nothing.[34] In the aftermath of the September 2012 Asia-Pacific Economic Cooperation Summit in Vladivostok, Putin directed energy companies to concentrate their efforts on conquering the respective markets, but negotiations with China remained deadlocked over the disagreement on prices.[35] The Ukrainian crisis brought a breakthrough, enabling Putin to sign a deal with China during a visit to Shanghai on May 20, 2014. To deliver such volumes—exporting 38 bcm of gas annually over 30 years, worth US$400 billion—Gazprom would need to develop two major greenfields in Eastern Siberia (Kovykta and Chayanda) and construct a pipeline, which would require investing at least US$55 billion, while China provided a pre-payment of some US$25 billion.[36] The deal is far more important for Russia than for China, which already has seen increases in gas imports from Turkmenistan—currently amounting to 35 bcm and could reach 70 bcm by 2020. Putin managed to secure more favorable terms than he had any right to expect based on the desperate situation he found himself in, but the economic fundamentals of the mega-project are still quite weak—and it is export to the European market that will keep Gazprom in business in the years ahead.

Export-oriented development of mineral resources could have been a strong driver for growth in Russia's economically depressed Far East. Instead, it is impeded by state policy that advances cost-inefficient mega-projects (like the ESPO) and places harsh restrictions on foreign investments, driven by the fear of losing control over the imagined riches.

The Prospects for Developing Russia's Mineral Resource Base in the Global Environment of Scarcity and Saturation

One advantage of asserting firm state control over the extraction and export of natural resources should have logically been improved capacity for strategic planning. In fact, however, it has turned the industries into hostages of political squabbles with a pitifully short time horizon. For that matter, even the mighty Gazprom has never been able to approve its annual investment plans until the last quarter of the respective year, and the deviation from the original estimate in most cases has exceeded 25 percent.[37] There are few reasons to expect that Rosneft, which has become the largest oil company in the world, first by grabbing the assets of the forcefully bankrupted Yukos and then by acquiring the conflict-ridden TNK-BP, would do any better in this department.[38] The long-term investments in production assets suffer most from this political mismanagement of the energy business, while the mega-projects on laying "strategic" pipelines have advanced with remarkable enthusiasm, primarily because of plentiful opportunities for misappropriation and embezzlement.

Russian leadership makes high promises regarding improvement of the investment climate, and Putin declared a particular goal of moving Russia up 100 positions from a ranking of 118 in the *Doing Business* rating compiled by the World Bank.[39] Similar promises were made on multiple occasions during Medvedev's presidency, but the course on providing direct support and protection to national champions like Gazprom and Rosneft, while also granting privileges to quasi-independent and well-connected companies like Novatek, deterred Western investors, who must also account for the risks related to the flourishing culture of administrative corruption. The deep crisis in Russia's relation with the West as a result of the annexation of Crimea in March 2014 has caused a massive exodus of investment capital and is certain to affect profoundly the implementation of many oil and gas projects. In 2012 Gazprom finally opened for exploitation the giant Bovanenkovskoe gas field on the Yamal Peninsula, and in late 2013, the controversial Prirazlomnaya platform in the Pechora Sea produced the first oil, but many other projects, including Shtokman in the Barents Sea, are postponed indefinitely as Western majors suspend their engagement. Instead of the envisaged progress from strength to strength, many experts now predict a decline in Russian oil production and an even bleaker future for the gas sector, even if the sanctions are lifted in the near future.[40]

It makes much more economic sense for the "champions" and the "favorites" to exploit their monopolistic positions and political connections than to run with the fast-moving energy market and invest in dubious innovations. As a result, Russian mainstream analysis of global energy developments tends to be not only rigidly conservative but also self-serving, so that only the trends that fit the interests of the stakeholders are recognized as real. The fundamental proposition in the corporate and political thinking about the future of Russia's reliance on the export of primary commodities is that of their assuredly increasing value determined by the aggravating scarcity. This mind-set finds abundant corroboration in Western neo-Malthusian forecasts of escalating competition for depleting resources.[41]

In particular, Russian energy-political strategizing has been centered on the advent of the golden age of gas, but the real features of this transition to the most energy-efficient and environment-friendly source, as outlined by the IEA, have turned out to be very different from Putin's and Sechin's expectations.[42] Instead of "eternal delight" (in William Blake's words) for suppliers, who would be able to dictate prices, a buyers' market is fast taking shape, with competing sources and spot prices detached from price fluctuations in the oil market. The main driver of this spectacular change is the American shale gas revolution, which Gazprom tried to deny up until the moment when the United States overtook Russia as the top gas producer.[43] This corporate dinosaur cannot rationally relate to the new environment, and the symbiotic relationship with the Kremlin will be able to shelter it from the long-overdue reform and unbundling only so far.

The situation in the oil sector is slightly different, and the problem for Russia is not that it will soon step down from its position as the top producer in the world as Saudi Arabia and the United States increase their output, and Mesopotamia becomes the major oil province, but that the expansion of global supply might reduce prices from historic highs to a more reasonable plateau.[44] Cost-efficiency of many upstream projects, particularly in East Siberia, is presently secured only by time-limited tax cuts, but sliding prices could force the companies to freeze unprofitable fields, while the contraction of revenues might force the government to close tax loopholes, leading to a vicious cycle of self-propelling production cuts.[45] Execution of the much-trumpeted projects in the Arctic seas retreats into the indefinite midterm future (as exemplified by the Shtokman joint venture), while far less spectacular projects to produce "tight" or "shale" oil in the old "brown" fields in the Volga area, where infrastructure is available, could have granted the best chance for the Russian oil business to escape from the taxes-versus-investment trap if the participation of the Western partners were not interrupted by sanctions.

The situation in the nuclear industry is rather similar, as rigid state control keeps it on the conservative more-of-the-same track. The disaster at Japan's Fukushima power station made remarkably little impression on the Russian public's attitude to the "peaceful atom," and Rosatom's ambitious plans to build a string of new reactors are impeded only by the plain fact that the costs to produce electricity on the ten operational plants are significantly higher than the state-controlled tariffs, so the industry depends heavily on subsidies, and each new reactor (twenty-eight are constructed or planned) adds to the volume of deficit subsidized by the federal budget.[46] The only way to compensate for these losses is to expand the export of nuclear technologies, and Rosatom is quite successful in the Asia-Pacific markets, despite the negative resonance from the Bushehr project in Iran.[47] Most of the projects in this expanding portfolio are, however, political in nature, and their profitability is highly problematic.

One massive factor of insecurity for the Russian energy sector is political turbulence in the wider Middle East, which could affect producers of global significance. For that matter, the civil war in Libya in 2011 helped Gazprom to expand its exports to the European market by as much as 15 percent, but the relative de-escalation of conflicts in North Africa in 2012 wiped away those gains, only to be interrupted by the terrorist attack on the Amenas gas complex in Algeria in January 2013, which set off a new wave of violent conflicts, allowing Gazprom to expand its export yet again. Very probable steady progress in developing huge oil and gas resources in Iraq could transform the paradigm of the global market from scarcity—envisioned many times and coming close to happening on several occasions—to abundance. Russia is politically unprepared for this shift.

Conclusions

Russia has great advantages in the global market as a major exporter of energy resources, raw materials like timber or diamonds, and primary commodities such as steel and aluminum, but reliance on the revenues from these exports has grown so much in the course of the 2000s that a rich fusion of political and economic ills producing a uniquely Russian case of "resource curse" has become the main challenge for its future. The common paradox in Medvedev's appeal for modernization and Putin's pursuit of reindustrialization is that the discourse of overcoming the unacceptable dependency on petro-profits and the inappropriate specialization on the lowest links in the supply chain blossom in parallel with the deepening of this dependency and narrowing of this specialization. The politics of harvesting the dividend from the simplest exploitation of natural riches triumphs over the ambitions for upholding Russia's great-power status and worries about price volatility.

Russia could have become a key part of the solution to the global problem of the exhaustion of traditional sources of energy. Instead, it has transformed itself into a major factor of uncertainty in this problem. The global energy industry is undergoing a spectacular transformation based on the introduction of modern technologies, and Russia could have used the strength of its natural sciences to generate innovations for a high-tech oil and gas sector. It is, however, so worried about a possible breakthrough from scarcity to plenty that modernization of the energy industry has stalled. Instead of strategic planning and long-term investment in developing the resource base, the prevalent policy is driven by profit maximization and bureaucratic predation, and these unhealthy short-term priorities are accentuated by the fast-developing crisis of Putin's corrupt rent distribution regime. Russian politicians are keen to fan the popular perceptions of greedy multinational corporations and aggressive state actors that are plotting to gain access to Russian oil and minerals, but there is hardly any recognition of responsibility for delivering on the obligations determined by Russia's special place as a high-capacity supplier in the global division of labor. The globalized world is typically seen as more brutally competitive than it really is, but this vision is not translated into readiness to invest in strengthening Russia's competitiveness. Natural resources can be a major source of strength if developed responsibly, but they can also sustain bad policies—and Russia has turned itself into a test case for this sustainability.

Notes

1. For a noteworthy examination of this trend, see Ian Bremmer and Robert Johnson, "The Rise and Fall of Resource Nationalism," *Survival* 51, no. 2 (2009): 149–58.

2. On the character of protests, see Vladimir Gelman, "The Regime, the Opposition, and Challenges to Electoral Authoritarianism in Russia," *Russian Analytical Digest* 118, no. 2 (October 2012): 8–10. On the "hybrid" character of Putin's regime in comparison with China, see Bobo Lo and Lilia Shevtsova, "A 21st Century Myth: Authoritarian Modernization in Russia and China" (Moscow: Carnegie Endowment for International Peace, Moscow Center, July 2012).

3. On the costs of rearmament, see Jim Nichol, "Russian Military Reform and Defense Policy," CRS Report 7-5700 (Washington: Congressional Research Service, August 2011) (www.fas.org/sgp/crs/row/R42006.pdf). On the deadlock in reforming the pension system, see Aleksei Kudrin, "No Winners in the Proposed Reform," *Vedomosti,* September 6, 2012 (in Russian).

4. On the doctrine obsession, see Julian Cooper, "Reviewing Russian Strategic Planning: The Emergence of Strategy 2020," NDC Research Review (Rome: NATO Defense College, June 2012) (www.ndc.nato.int/research/series.php?icode=9).

5. The orchestrated bankruptcy of Yukos and imprisonment of its owner, Mikhail Khodorkovsky, derailed the promising U.S.-Russian energy partnership. On the impact of that enforcement of political will, see Martin Sixsmith, *Putin's Oil: The Yukos Affair and the Struggle for Russia* (New York: Continuum, 2010).

6. The key tasks in advancing toward a "new economy" are defined by Vladimir Putin, "On Our Economic Tasks," *Vedomosti,* January 30, 2012 (in Russian). The official translation is at http://eng.kremlin.ru/news/4739.

7. The final draft of this doctrine was discussed at the meeting of the presidential Commission for Strategic Development of the Fuel and Energy Sector in order to make it ready by November 2012. However, it was not adopted as of February 2013. The official translation of Putin's remarks is at http://eng.kremlin.ru/news/4553.

8. Oil companies take a cue from Gazprom's determined resistance to even modest tax hikes. See Yekaterina Strukova, "New Russian Exempts: Gazprom's Battle against Taxes," *RBC,* October 22, 2012 (in Russian) (http://top.rbc.ru/economics/22/10/2012/675419.shtml).

9. On Sechin's breakthrough with the creation of this commission, see Catherine Belton, "Putin Steps up Battle with PM over Energy," *Financial Times,* June 15, 2012.

10. On the disorganization of government energy policy, see Anastasia Bashkatova, "The Energy Ministry between Sechin and Dvorkovich," *Nezavisimaya Gazeta,* October 11, 2012 (in Russian).

11. For a skeptical assessment of this deal, see Vladimir Milov, "Zastoi Is Back: What Comes from the Takeover of TNK-BP by Rosneft," Forbes.ru, October 23, 2012 (in Russian) (www.forbes.ru/sobytiya-column/177892-zastoi-vozvrashchaetsya-chto-budet-posle-togo-kak-rosneft-kupit-tnk-bp).

12. The official use of this self-derogatory term can be traced from Putin's speeches at the start of his era in early 2000 (http://archive.kremlin.ru/eng/text/news/2000/01/122336.shtml) to Medvedev's exhortations at the end of his disappointing presidency (http://kremlin.ru/news/13065).

13. For an examination of this proposition, see Pavel K. Baev, *Russian Energy Policy and Military Power: Putin's Quest for Russia's Greatness* (London: Routledge, 2008).

14. For a sound revisiting of those debates, see Daniel Yergin, *The Quest: Energy, Security, and the Remaking of the Modern World,* ch. 11 (New York: Penguin Press, 2011).

15. See International Energy Agency (IEA), *World Energy Outlook 2012* (Paris: OECD, 2012), p. 98.

16. For a balanced assessment of prospects for Medvedev's "modernization," see Clifford G. Gaddy and Barry W. Ikes, "The Russian Economy through 2020: The Challenge of Managing Rent Addiction," in *Russia in 2020: Scenarios for the Future,* edited by Maria Lipman and Nikolay Petrov, pp. 165–86 (Moscow: Carnegie Endowment for International Peace, Moscow Center, 2011).

17. See the interview of Mikhail Khodorkovsy in "Money Doesn't Smell, Isn't It So, Mr. Dudley?" Forbes.ru, November 21, 2012 (in Russian) (www.forbes.ru/sobytiya/lyudi/215553-mihail-hodorkovskii-o-prodazhe-tnk-vr-dengi-ne-pahnut-ne-pravda-li-mister-dadl).

18. On the phenomenon of value detraction, see Anders Åslund, *Building Capitalism: The Transformation of the Former Soviet Bloc* (Cambridge University Press, 2002), particularly pp. 125–26. For his more recent assessment, see Anders Åslund, "How Putin Is Turning Russia into One Big Enron," *Moscow Times,* November 21, 2012.

19. Putin found it difficult to square his new industrial priorities with the old plan for joining the WTO. See Anna Koroleva, "Defense against the WTO," *Expert,* November 22, 2012 (in Russian). For a solid analysis, see Dominic Fean, "Decoding Russia's WTO Accession," Russie.Nei.Visions 64 (Paris: Institut Français des Relations Internationales, February 2012).

20. See Adnan Vatansever and Anna Korppoo, "A Climate Vision for Russia: From Rhetoric to Action," Policy Outlook (Moscow: Carnegie Endowment for International Peace, Moscow Center, August 2012).

21. A valuable source on the ambitions and shortfalls of the Soviet energy policy is Thane Gustafson, *Crisis amid Plenty: The Politics of Soviet Energy under Brezhnev and Gorbachev* (Princeton University Press, 1989).

22. For an inflated evaluation of the importance of this corridor, see S. Frederick Starr and Svante Cornell, eds., *The Baku-Tbilisi-Ceyhan Pipeline: Oil Window to the West*

(Johns Hopkins University, School of Advanced International Studies, Central Asia-Caucasus Institute, 2005).

23. See European Commission, "A European Strategy for Sustainable, Competitive, and Secure Energy," Green Paper COM(2006)105 (Brussels, 2006) (http://ec.europa.eu/energy/strategies/2006/2006_03_green_paper_energy_en.htm).

24. For my evaluation of these diverging guidelines, see Pavel Baev, "Russian Energy as a Challenge and a Bonus for European Security," *Studia Diplomatica* 64, no. 1 (March 2012): 91–100.

25. On the weakness of Gazprom's position, see Aleksei Khaitun, "Gazprom on Clay Feet," *Nezavisimaya Gazeta,* October 9, 2012 (in Russian). Nadezhda Petrova, "Gazprom and Thunder," *Kommersant-Dengi,* September 10, 2012 (in Russian).

26. For an acerbic comment, see Anders Åslund, "Why Everyone Is Avoiding Gazprom," *Moscow Times,* August 22, 2012.

27. Putin criticized the EU energy policy at the joint press conference with German Chancellor Angela Merkel on November 16, 2012. The official translation is at http://eng.kremlin.ru/transcripts/4645.

28. For a more elaborate evaluation of these intrigues, see Pavel Baev and Indra Øverland, "The South Stream versus Nabucco Pipeline Race," *International Affairs* 68, no. 5 (September-October 2010): 1075–90.

29. For a discussion of this bargaining, see Pavel Baev, "Asia-Pacific and LNG: The Lure of New Markets," in *Pipeline, Politics, and Power: The Future of EU–Russia Energy Relations,* edited by Katinka Barysch (London: Centre for European Reform, 2008).

30. See Michael Bradshaw, "A New Energy Age in Pacific Russia: Lessons from the Sakhalin Oil and Gas Projects," *Eurasian Geography and Economics* 51, no. 3 (September 2010): 330–59.

31. For a sharp comment on the limits of these relations, see Bobo Lo, "A Partnership of Convenience," *International Herald Tribune,* June 7, 2012. For a sober view from Moscow on China's rise, see Fedor Lukyanov, "Hegemonic It Is Not," *Gazeta.ru,* June 7, 2012 (in Russian) (www.gazeta.ru/column/lukyanov/4616101.shtml).

32. The issue of pricing was resolved after some bickering, but Chinese requests for additional deliveries are usually turned down. See Isabel Gorst, "Hello ESPO: Russian Oil Looks East," *Financial Times,* February 29, 2012. "Russia Refused China Request for Extra Oil," Reuters, Match 5, 2012 (www.reuters.com/article/2012/03/05/petrochina-russia-oil-idUSL4E8E510I20120305).

33. See Kirill Melnikov, "More Preferences to the Oil Companies," *Kommersant,* November 23, 2012 (in Russian).

34. See IEA, *World Energy Outlook 2012,* p. 149.

35. For an Asia-skeptic assessment, see Sergei Kulikov, "The World Doesn't Need Russian Gas That Much," *Nezavisimaya Gazeta,* September 4, 2012 (in Russian).

36. On Gazprom's unenthusiastic response to Putin's orders, see Mikhail Serov, "Gazprom Is Instructed to Turn Eastward," *Kommersant,* October 30, 2012 (in Russian). Igor Naumov, "Gas Is Given the Eastward Order," *Nezavisimaya Gazeta,* November 21, 2012 (in Russian).

37. Thus the investment program for 2012 was corrected downward by 20 percent, and the plan for 2013 aims to keep it on this low level. See "Gazprom Invests the Old Way," *Kommersant*, November 21, 2012 (in Russian).

38. On the market view of TNK-BP, see Catherine Belton and Guy Chazan, "Sechin's Hard Sell at Western Investors," *Financial Times*, October 9, 2012.

39. In the 2012 rating, Russia advanced to the 112th place. See Mikhail Sergeev, "Investment Growth Has Effectively Stopped," *Nezavisimaya Gazeta*, November 23, 2012 (in Russian).

40. See, for instance, Kenneth Rapoza, "Is Russia Ready for Life after Oil?" *Forbes*, October 3, 2012 (www.forbes.com/sites/kenrapoza/2012/10/03/is-russia-ready-for-life-after-oil/).

41. For a balanced report, see Philip Andrews-Speed, Raimund Bieschwitz, Tim Boersma, Corey Johnson, Geoffrey Kemp, and Stacy D. VanDeveer, *The Global Resource Nexus: The Struggle for Land, Energy, Food, Water, and Minerals* (Washington: Transatlantic Academy, May 2012).

42. See the section "Are We Entering a Golden Age of Gas?" in IEA, *World Energy Outlook 2011* (Paris, 2011), pp. 170–73.

43. On the reckoning with the reality of the shale gas revolution, see Ivan Rubanov, "Shale as Cleansing Flame," *Expert*, November 5, 2012 (in Russian). Svetlana Melnikova, "Europe's Hydrocarbon Future," *Nezavisimaya Gazeta—Energiya*, October 9, 2012 (in Russian).

44. For a sharp examination of production facts and figures, see Mark Adomanis, "Is Russia the World's Largest Oil Producer?" *Forbes*, November 20, 2012 (www.forbes.com/sites/markadomanis/2012/11/20/is-russia-the-worlds-largest-oil-producer-it-all-depends-on-whom-you-ask/).

45. For a sober view, see Chris Weafer, "What the U.S. Oil Revolution Means for Russia," *Moscow Times*, November 21, 2012.

46. On the shaky economic foundation for these plans, see Anastasiya Baskatova, "Risky Priorities of Russian Modernization," *Nezavisimaya Gazeta*, November 21, 2012 (in Russian).

47. On the current portfolio of nuclear orders, see Vadim Ponimarev, "Expansion Abroad," *Expert*, October 22, 2012 (in Russian).

PART III

The Critical Actor

13

Challenges to Sustainable Growth after the Great Recession: How America Can Lead

JOSHUA MELTZER, DAVID STEVEN, AND CLAIRE LANGLEY

In January 2000 President Bill Clinton argued that the United States had entered the new century from a position of unparalleled strength. "Never before has our nation enjoyed, at once, so much prosperity and social progress with so little internal crisis and so few external threats," he said in his final State of the Union address. "We will make America the safest big country on Earth. We will pay off our national debt for the first time since 1835. We will bring prosperity to every American community. We will reverse the course of climate change and leave a safer, cleaner planet. America will lead the world toward shared peace and prosperity, and the far frontiers of science and technology."[1]

Despite this optimistic prognostication, the millennial decade was one of profound crisis, with serious consequences for the United States' security and prosperity and for the sustainability of the American dream. The dot-com market crashed in March 2000, the latest in a chain of asset price bubbles that burst in Japan in 1991 and East Asia in 1997.[2] The attacks of 9/11 drew the United States into expensive and inconclusive wars that caused significant damage to its international reputation.[3] In 2007 the property market collapsed, triggering near-meltdown in the financial sector, and then a brutal recession saw the median American family lose 40 percent of its wealth.[4]

At the end of what he described as "a difficult decade," President Barack Obama's State of the Union address was very different in tone from that given by President Clinton ten years earlier.[5] He painted a picture of the economic "devastation" that had hit ordinary people and their resulting loss of faith in America's government, business, and media. It was time, he argued, to start anew and rebuild the American dream, drawing on the country's history of "stubborn resilience in the face of adversity" and the core ideals and values that had made it strong.

Despite the result of the 2012 election, however, Americans remain deeply divided over the country's future direction. According to a survey of political values across the past quarter century, partisan division was fairly stable until 2002, after which it increased rapidly.[6] The public is especially split on the scope and performance of government, the role of the state in helping the poor, and the need for regulation to protect the environment.[7] These divisions have shaped the U.S. response to the financial crisis. In September 2008, the initial phases of the banking bailout became enmeshed in the American election, and in the summer of 2011, fundamental disagreements about government debt brought the country close to a deliberate default.[8] In recent years, fiscal battles have brought the country's politics close to gridlock, and in 2013 the Republican refusal to pass a budget led to a federal government shutdown for sixteen days.[9]

America is not alone in its lack of direction, of course. The European Union remains incapable of solving the euro crisis, leading to expectations that a supposedly "irrevocable" currency union will shrink or could even disintegrate.[10] China and India face significant headwinds over the coming years, as China is confronted by its own asset bubble and demographic decline and India, by a combination of political gridlock and economic slowdown.[11] Their recent success has also brought new challenges, as their middle classes become increasingly demanding and assertive. At a global level, globalization's "long crisis" has exposed the fragility of the international system.[12] The G-20 has failed to emerge as a steering committee for the global economy, while Rio+20 has once again demonstrated how little the set-piece summit has to offer.[13]

As governments devote an increasing proportion of their energy to fighting short-term crises, longer-term challenges have been left largely unaddressed. In 2008 an energy and food price shock coincided with and contributed to the acute phase of the financial crisis.[14] Commodity markets then crashed before rebounding sharply and now remain in a volatile state that is challenging for both producers and consumers of natural resources. High energy prices have been an obstacle to recovery in America and Europe, with an increase in the oil price of US$10 per barrel thought to cut growth in the countries belonging to the Organization for Economic Cooperation and Development (OECD) by 0.2 percent.[15] Conversely, many energy exporters are vulnerable to falling prices, with their "fiscal breakeven point" having increased dramatically as they use subsidies and other transfers to try to dampen political unrest. In 2012, due to adverse weather resulting in drought conditions in the United States, another food crisis was intensifying, with 60 percent of American farms experiencing drought in August 2012 and "major impacts on the production of many field crops this year, particularly corn, soybeans, sorghum, and hay."[16]

Climate change impacts are already being felt in the United States. The most recent decade was the nation's hottest on record, and temperatures will continue to rise, with the next few decades projected to see another 3.6°C to 7.2°C of warming in most areas.[17] Certain types of weather events have become more frequent or intense, including heat waves, heavy downpours, and, in some regions, floods and droughts. Sea levels are rising, oceans are becoming more acidic, and glaciers and Arctic sea ice are melting. These changes and others yet to come will affect human health, water supply, agriculture, transportation, energy, and other aspects of society.[18]

Climate change may have slipped down the international agenda, but global greenhouse gas emissions have rebounded much more sharply than expected after the financial crisis.[19] They have now reached the level at which they would need to peak if the world is to have a 50 percent chance of limiting warming to below 2°C.[20] Although many countries now have voluntary commitments to reduce their greenhouse gas emissions, implementation of a binding agreement to reduce emissions has been delayed until at least 2020. And recent analysis from the United Nations Environment Program (UNEP) showed that, even if nations meet their current climate pledges, greenhouse gas emissions in 2020 are likely to be 8 to 12 gigatons of CO_2-equivalent (GtCO_2e) above the level needed to have a good chance of remaining below 2°C by 2020 on the lowest-cost pathway.[21]

Other "planetary boundaries" are also being threatened, with some scientists warning that global ecosystems are on the verge of a "state change that will be extremely disruptive to civilization."[22] A substantial shift is needed in patterns of global growth if the world is to avoid irreversible environmental damage, as its urban population is slated to grow by another billion in just fifteen years and, if economies are robust, a further 4 billion people will join the global middle class.[23] The world remains far from any consensus on how to achieve this shift, despite attempts to focus attention on "green growth" at the Rio+20 Summit.

Although Americans on both sides of the political divide believe their country should continue to play an active role in responding to global problems, the nature and direction of American leadership remain controversial. About two thirds of Americans believe the country benefits from globalization, but this is below the average for twenty-five countries.[24] The American public is also relatively skeptical about international financial regulation, with a slight majority fearing that a new regulatory body would make the American economy less productive (compared with an average of a third in other countries). Although there is widespread concern about high commodity prices (especially as they feed through to the gas pump), improving energy independence, principally by exploiting shale gas, has persuaded some policymakers that the United States can now insulate itself from turbulence in the Persian Gulf and other energy-producing hot spots.

Support for robust action at a global level to tackle climate change and other environmental problems is weak, with only a minority of Republicans believing there is solid evidence that the Earth is getting warmer.[25] In the run-up to the 2012 presidential election, tropical storm Sandy is estimated to have caused US$20 billion in damage to New York, New Jersey, and surrounding areas,[26] with scientists arguing that climate change has already increased the likely frequency and ferocity of extreme weather events of this sort.[27] Although this has increased pressure on American politicians—a fact acknowledged by President Obama as he won reelection—it is far from certain that this will translate into increased international engagement by the United States.[28]

The current impasse may be temporary, however. Both domestically and internationally, the process of political change is probably only beginning to gather momentum. President Obama's reelection is an anomaly in a period when incumbent governments have had a miserable time at the polls and populist movements and fringe parties have thrived.[29] In the United States, the Tea Party has attacked the political establishment from the right, and the Occupy movement has had a similar, if less far-reaching, impact from the left. The Arab Spring, itself a reaction to economic stagnation, will continue to reshape multiple countries, with highly unpredictable results. Across the world, many countries will experience further political disruptions, with the next ten years likely to be a fertile period for policy innovation. Elites find themselves broadly discredited, and outsiders will continue to have unusual opportunities to bring new ideas—both good and bad—into the mainstream, if they can make effective and entrepreneurial use of popular frustration with the status quo.[30]

This chapter represents an initial attempt to understand the directions this change is likely to take. It is written with three assumptions:

—First, although the U.S. economic model has many strengths, its resilience has been weakened. Acute economic, social, and environmental challenges will need to be addressed in either the short or the long term. It is currently unclear whether this will lead to only minor changes in the American economic model or to a more significant transformation.

—Second, the U.S. response to this era of crisis will be an important factor affecting how other countries react, given the size and influence of the U.S. economy, its position as a "necessary but not sufficient" actor on most global issues, and its potential for technological and social innovation.

—*Third, there is little point in expecting the United States to adopt or advocate policies that run counter to its interests and values.* It is therefore necessary to understand the drivers of and obstacles to change in the United States and use them to draw conclusions about the types of solutions that are most likely to emerge, after an era of crisis.

The chapter is divided into three sections. In the first, we review the evolution of the U.S. economy in recent decades and the positive and negative effects of the growth it has provided, with a focus on economic, social, and environmental outcomes.

In the second section, we analyze the shifting interests of different groups in American society and the structural, institutional, and cultural factors that will inform the process of change. This allows us to identify four broad scenarios for the evolution of the U.S. economy, each of which represents a plausible pathway from the current crisis toward a new growth model and political settlement.

In the third and final section, we set out policy recommendations that cover the areas of employment, investment in the future, energy, fiscal rebalancing, and American opportunities for global leadership during President Obama's second term.

The U.S. Economy: How It Works and What It Delivers

The following analyzes how the U.S. model works, focusing on what it has achieved in terms of economic, social, and environmental outcomes.

Economic Outcomes

The United States is the world's foremost economic power. Since the end of World War II, its economy has achieved relatively steady growth, low unemployment and inflation, and rapid advances in technology. This prosperity underpins American global leadership, supporting a military that dwarfs its rivals, maintaining America's place at the heart of the international system, and influencing other countries through trade, investment, the diffusion of technologies, and the spread of scientific, economic, and legal models.[31]

In the postwar period, gross domestic product (GDP) has grown in real terms by an average of 2.9 percent a year, or 1.7 percent on a per capita basis, with the economy more than six times larger in 2012 than it was in 1945.[32] Over the long term, the economy has been highly successful in creating employment, with an average of 1.3 million new jobs created each year and an unemployment rate below 6 percent.[33] The average worker is also much better paid, with mean annual earnings for males having doubled in the postwar period.[34]

During this time, the United States has placed a premium on the role of the private sector as the main driver of innovation and productivity and constrained the role of the government in the economy. The American economy consistently ranks highly when compared with its competitors and is currently fifth in the World Economic Forum's Global Competitiveness Index.[35] Its other key strengths are the size of its domestic market, the flexibility of its labor market, its commitment to innovation, and the sophistication of its business sector.

Labor productivity, which has grown at an average annual rate of 2.4 percent since World War II, has been underpinned by high levels of research and development (R&D). The United States spends about 3 percent of GDP on R&D, about average for the OECD.[36] However, it is home to the world's best universities and research institutions, with eight American universities ranked among the top ten in 2013 and with the United States accounting for more than a third of citations in the world's science and engineering journals and registering more than half the world's patents.[37] The public sector, meanwhile, has invested in breakthrough R&D, such as through the Defense Advanced Research Projects Agency, which created the Internet.[38] This has allowed the country to remain at the forefront of sectors with high growth potential, such as information technology, biotechnology, pharmaceuticals, personal services, and renewable energy.[39]

The economy is highly entrepreneurial, with Americans more likely to set up new businesses than the citizens of comparable countries and workers prepared to relocate to seek work.[40] Given their depth and sophistication, the U.S. financial markets, including the capital venture sector, provide funding for start-ups with high growth potential: firms less than five years old accounted for almost two-thirds of net jobs created in 2007.[41] Established American companies tend to be more decentralized than their competitors and more open to innovation.[42] American consumers also appear to be unusually willing to try new products and services.[43]

The Great Recession, however, has heightened concerns that the U.S. economic model is failing to deliver to its full potential. The recession, which began in December 2007, was the longest and deepest of the eleven experienced since the war.[44] Recovery has been anemic, with the economy only returning to its prerecession size in the third quarter of 2011.[45] Moreover, the economy faces many longer-term threats:

—*Competitiveness is being eroded.* Since 2005, the United States has experienced the largest drop in its score on the World Economic Forum's Global Competitiveness Index of any country.[46] Business leaders have low levels of trust in the ability of politicians, government, and other institutions to support growth, believe that regulation places too great a burden on the private sector, and are concerned about a lack of macroeconomic stability.[47] A majority expect American competitiveness to continue its decline.[48]

—*The economy is struggling to generate sufficient new jobs.* Before 1990, the United States returned to prerecession levels of employment within an average of just six months after the recovery was complete. Since then, however, it has experienced two "jobless recoveries" (1990 and 2001), and it is now in the midst of a third, in which employment is expected to take up to five years to recover.[49] As a result, long-term unemployment has been an increasing problem. Only 4 percent of the unemployed had been out of work for more than a year in 1980. This number rose to about 10 percent of total unemployed before the financial crisis and reached nearly 30 percent of the total by 2010.[50]

—*Many workers are not seeing an increase in their earnings.* Until 1970, male workers saw their wages increase by about 25 percent per decade.[51] Since then, however, they have done much less well, with real median earnings now lower than they were forty years ago, a period when the proportion of men in full-time work shrank significantly. Poorly educated men have performed especially badly, with men who failed to complete high school seeing their earnings eroded by 66 percent. Women are more likely to work and have seen their earnings grow, but this has not been sufficient to compensate families for the loss of male earning power. As a result, most households have become poorer.

—*Investment in infrastructure and human capital is not world class.* The United States is ranked nineteenth in the world on the World Economic Forum's Index of Quality of Overall Infrastructure Investment.[52] The country needs US$2.2 trillion worth of investment in infrastructure over the next five years, US$1.18 trillion of which has not been budgeted.[53] School-level education is at or below the average standards for the OECD, despite relatively high levels of expenditures per student.[54] Publicly funded higher education is under pressure, with cuts from both federal and state budgets. Student debt is a growing problem, with US$956 billion in loans now outstanding.[55]

—*Growth has been fueled by high levels of indebtedness.* Total public and private debt grew to almost three times the level of U.S. GDP in 2008, with a third of this debt outstanding to households and about half of the rise in consumer spending during the boom years accounted for by increased household debt.[56] Since the financial crisis, households and businesses have begun to pay down their debt, and they are moving toward sustainable debt levels.[57] The deleveraging process, however, is delaying recovery, with the most indebted households seeing the fastest decline in consumption during the Great Recession. Business investment remains low as a percentage of GDP.[58]

—*The United States faces growing fiscal pressures.* The national debt fell throughout the postwar period, before rising dramatically in two waves (1981–95 and 2001–12), reaching 122 percent of GDP in 2013.[59] Tax cuts and spending increases fueled the debt after 2001, whereas during the recession, this long-term trend was exacerbated by a loss of tax revenue, an increase in entitlement spending, and the stimulus package and bailout, with the debt held by the public reaching 73 percent of GDP in 2013 from 40 percent of GDP in 2007.[60] The January 1, 2013, fiscal agreement raised income taxes on individuals earning over US$400,000 and made the rest of the Bush-era tax cuts permanent. A decision on sequestration—the mandated cuts in defense and nondefense spending of US$1.2 trillion over ten years—was pushed back from January 1 to March 1, 2013. The ultimate reductions in spending authority amounted to approximately US$85.4 billion during fiscal year 2013 and a further US$109.3 billion a year from 2014 to 2021. These cuts contributed to short-term effects such as increased unemployment levels of approximately 7 percent in the fourth quarter of 2013, but long-term forecasts estimate that economic growth will pick up in 2014, strengthening the labor market and shrinking the unemployment rate to 5.5 percent by 2018.[61]

—*The U.S. economy is affected by broader global imbalances.* The current account deficit rose steadily from 1991, peaking at 6 percent of GDP in 2006, but has now fallen to slightly less than 3 percent of GDP. With Americans saving less than the country's investment needs, the counterpoint is trade surpluses run by countries such as Germany and China, where consumption levels are low and the economy is highly reliant on exports to debtor countries. Ben Bernanke, former chairman of the Federal Reserve, has argued that a "global savings glut" is an important source of global financial instability and that, in the medium term, it can be effectively addressed if countries with "unsustainable trade surpluses" export less and consume more, whereas countries such as the United States with "large, persistent trade deficits must find ways to increase national saving, including putting fiscal policies on a more sustainable trajectory."[62] The sustainability of the trade deficit will depend on ongoing foreign appetite for American assets.

Social Outcomes

Since World War II, economic growth has delivered substantial benefits for the American people, who are richer, healthier, and better educated than they were sixty years ago. The average American born today can expect to live ten years longer than one born in 1950.[63] Literacy levels have reached 99 percent, and 70 percent of Americans who completed high school in 2009 went on to enroll in higher education.[64] American average income is now nearly 8.5 times higher than postwar levels.[65] Moreover, basic needs account for a decreasing share of the consumption basket: food nearly has halved its share of disposable income, while money spent on recreation has more than quadrupled.[66] In comparative terms, the United States ranks at the top of the OECD for income and for the quality and affordability of its housing provision. Americans also rate their quality of life more highly than the average for the OECD.[67]

Not all trends have been positive, however, especially in recent decades. Median family income shrank for most Americans between 2001 and 2007 and then fell significantly between 2007 and 2010.[68] Poorer American families (below the fortieth income percentile) saw their net worth fall consistently throughout the decade, while all but the richest 10 percent saw precrisis gains wiped out by the fall in house prices, leaving them poorer than at the beginning of the decade.[69] For more than half of American families, in other words, economic growth is no longer translating into higher living standards.

Inequality has risen steeply and is now one of the highest in the OECD, second only to Mexico. After taking into account the redistributive impact of government taxes and transfer payments, the Gini coefficient for American disposable income rose from 0.37 in 1979 to 0.49 in 2007.[70] Although poor and middle-class Americans have seen their living standards stagnate in recent years, the top 1 percent earned 20 percent of income in 2010, and the top 10 percent earned almost half of all income.[71] Household income is increasingly derived from capital, rather than from labor (although there were significant capital losses during the recession), and capital income has become steadily more concentrated among the richest households.

At the same time, economic mobility has been declining, with fewer people able to move through income brackets due to ability and hard work.[72] By some measures, the United States is now less mobile than many countries in Europe. Parental socioeconomic status, for example, is moderately correlated with children's educational attainment and income in the United States.[73] Although 84 percent of Americans earn more than their parents did, Germany and Canada both perform better on this indicator.[74] Intergenerational mobility, which increased until the 1970s, also fell significantly in the 1980s and has remained unchanged since then.[75]

The drivers of inequality and a lack of mobility are complex.[76] Increased competition from trade has created incentives for businesses to increase their efficiency and use technology that reduces the need for low-skilled labor. However, this effect is tempered by the fact that approximately 70 percent of American imports come from developed countries with similar wage costs.[77] Foreign direct investment and the offshoring of jobs might also have contributed to inequality, with the OECD finding that outward foreign direct investment has had some impact, although mainly on the upper half of the distribution.[78] Technology has also replaced low-skilled work and increased the demand for high-skilled work, driving wage differentials, while immigration may also have depressed wage costs.

Although these global drivers have an impact on the U.S. economy's ability to deliver broad-based social outcomes, other factors are under national control:

—*Poor education outcomes* at primary and secondary school levels, especially in the worst schools, have contributed to the decline in mobility, as have the increasing costs of the university system and of elite universities in particular. Students from wealthier families are much more likely to attend a four-year college program than their less-wealthy counterparts, whereas fewer than 10 percent of students at Harvard, Yale, and Princeton receive Pell Grants, a federal scholarship for low-income students. Education has become less of a government priority, accounting for 13 percent of government expenditures in 2009, compared with 23 percent in 1970.[79]

—*Tax and transfer payments* have had less of a redistributive impact over time.[80] The United States is below the OECD average for the progressivity of its tax system, and its transfers are relatively modest and not well targeted.[81] Although effective federal tax rates have fallen for all income groups, richer Americans now pay a small proportion of a much larger income in tax.[82]

—*Deregulation of the labor market* has also had a negative impact on the distribution of income, with the rise in inequality since the 1980s occurring in tandem with a near halving of the rate of union membership.[83] Deregulation, however, has had a broader impact on the market, increasing competition, expanding economic activity, and creating employment, which has partially offset the downward pressure on wages from less-regulated labor markets.[84]

—The rising cost of *housing* (34 percent of average household expenditures), especially during the property bubble, the need to spend more on *personal insurance and pensions* (11 percent), and more expensive *health care* have all placed pressure on living standards.[85] Health care is an especially pressing problem, with the United States already spending more than any other OECD country on health—18 percent of GDP in 2011, compared with below 12 percent in Australia, Canada, Germany, and the United Kingdom.[86] Notwithstanding the recent health care reforms, health costs as a percentage of GDP are expected to increase to 34 percent by 2040.[87]

There are signs of popular discontent with the American economic system, with only a third now believing that it delivers fair outcomes for middle- and working-class citizens.[88] Although 68 percent of Americans say that they have achieved or will achieve the American dream, the proportion that believes they are richer than their parents were at a similar age has fallen 13 percentage points over the past thirty years.[89] Fewer than half of parents now expect their children to enjoy a better standard of living than they did.

Environmental Outcomes

Over the past half century, the United States has made important progress in its domestic environmental quality and has led on international environmental challenges such as depletion of the ozone layer. In the 1960s and 1970s, American progress on the environment was underpinned by the rise of environmental movements, which increased awareness about the effects of economic growth on the environment. Many of the key American environmental advocacy groups were created then, such as the World Wildlife Fund (1961), the Environmental Defense Fund (1967), and Friends of the Earth (1969). The president created the White House Council for Environmental Quality in 1969 and the Environmental Protection Agency in 1970.[90] Congress passed the Clean Air Act and the Clean Water Act in 1970 and 1972, respectively.[91]

Broadly speaking, American environmental laws and regulations are guided by the twin goals of protecting the environment for future generations while interfering as little as possible with the efficiency and growth of the economy. All U.S. environmental regulation is subject to rigorous cost-benefit analysis, where environmental and human health benefits are quantified and considered alongside the costs to industry and the broader economy. The United States pioneered market-based approaches to delivering environmental improvements, through a series of experiments that date back to the 1960s.[92] A full cap-and-trade system for regulating sulfur dioxide was launched in 1990 and has delivered significant reductions in emissions at a lower cost than a regulatory option and at a quarter of the original government cost estimates.[93]

Over recent decades,

—Air quality has improved significantly, with reductions in levels of six common pollutants ranging from 7 percent for eight-hour ozone to 75 percent for annual sulfur dioxide from 1990 to 2010.[94]

—The Clean Water Act has led to significant improvements in the quality of the water received by households and triggered a rapid recovery of heavily polluted urban waterways.[95]

—The efficiency with which the economy uses resources has also improved steadily. The amount of energy needed to produce a dollar of GDP (after adjustment for inflation) has almost halved since 1980, although the United States still ranks only sixty-one in the world on this measure.[96]

Internationally, the United States has played an important role in agreeing to international environmental treaties such as the 1973 Convention on International Trade in Endangered Species, the 1987 Montreal Protocol on Substances That Deplete the Ozone Layer, and the 1989 Basel Convention on the Control of Transboundary Movements of Hazardous Wastes and Their Disposal. The basis for American engagement on these issues reflected several drivers, including concentrated advocacy by American environmental organizations and a calculation that the economic costs of addressing these environmental challenges would be minimal for the United States and overshadowed by the environmental benefits. The benefits of the Montreal Protocol, for example, were expected to exceed the costs by a factor of sixty-five, even if the United States implemented it unilaterally.[97] Implementation by other countries made an already attractive proposition even more compelling.

Over time, however, the environment has become an increasingly contentious political issue. In 1992 environmental issues were a relatively minor source of partisan division, with large majorities of both Republicans and Democrats agreeing that stricter laws and regulations were needed to protect the environment.[98] Today, the environment is more divisive than any issue apart from the social security net, with Democrats now twice as likely to favor environmental controls as Republicans.[99]

Similar divisions have opened up between the United States and other countries on global environmental issues, especially over climate change. In the negotiation of the United Nations Framework Convention on Climate Change, which was agreed to in 1992 and entered into force in 1994, the United States stressed scientific uncertainty and was an early advocate of taking action on the basis of cost-benefit analysis.[100] In 1997 President Bill Clinton signed the Kyoto Protocol but resolved not to submit it for ratification "until key developing countries [also] commit to binding targets."[101] President George W. Bush definitively ruled out ratification in 2001, promising instead to "develop technologies, market incentives, and other creative ways to address global climate change."[102]

These divisions complicated American efforts to respond to future environmental challenges, which include the following:

—*Securing access to resources.* The United States consumes about a quarter of the world's energy and, until recently, had experienced a steady erosion of its energy security.[103] All but one of the postwar recessions in the United States has been preceded by a pronounced increase in the price of crude oil, and all but one oil market disruption has been followed by a recession.[104] The Great Recession is no exception, with food and energy prices peaking in the summer of 2008 after a long period of decline.[105] Recovery has also been hampered by the resurgence of prices after 2010 and by uncertainty about future oil prices.[106] Rapid growth in demand from emerging markets has been the primary driver of higher and more volatile commodity prices, indicating the potential for increased competition for resources in both the short and long terms.[107]

—*Tackling climate change.* During the past twenty years, the United States has experienced intense international pressure to reduce its carbon emissions, which in 2011 were more than double those of the European Union on a per capita basis and almost three times those of China.[108] U.S. emissions rose strongly before the recession but have since fallen, due to a combination of higher prices, lower growth, increased use of natural gas, and tighter regulations reducing the competitiveness of coal. Emissions in 2011 were 8.5 percent lower than in 2005, putting the United States on a trajectory that would allow it to meet its voluntary commitment under the Copenhagen Accord (a 17 percent reduction in emissions by 2020, from the same baseline).[109] However, even if all countries meet their Copenhagen commitments, the world will still be on track for warming at levels well above 2°C, ensuring ongoing international pressure on the United States to move toward, or beyond, its long-term target (an 83 percent reduction by 2050).[110]

—*Responding to extreme weather events.* The United States has proven relatively vulnerable to extreme weather events, although China and India face greater risks (ranking nineteen and twenty-two places, respectively, above the United States on an index based on fatalities and economic impacts from 1990 to 2009).[111] Hurricane Katrina was America's costliest natural disaster, and tropical storm Sandy again showed the vulnerability of coastal cities. The economic loss from a storm of the same intensity is estimated to double every ten years. If the 1926 Great Miami hurricane were to hit again in the 2020s, it could be expected to cause US\$500 billion worth of damage (more than six times the cost of Hurricane Katrina), or about 3 percent of GDP.[112] Drought is also a significant threat, as seen during the 2012 heat wave, which has had a global impact on food security.[113] Even before Sandy, more than two thirds of the American public believed that global warming was already affecting weather patterns in the country.[114] This anxiety is now likely to have intensified.

—*Coping with water stress.* The United States is ranked as "high risk" on the Water Stress Index, although, again, the threats facing China and India are greater.[115] The U.S. Southwest, Southeast, and West all experience chronic water scarcity, due to unsustainable patterns of building and economic growth, and more than 1,100 counties (one third of all counties in the lower forty-eight U.S. states) will experience a high risk of water shortages by mid-century, with more than 400 of these facing an extremely high risk of water shortages.[116] Temperatures for 2012 through June were the warmest since records began in 1895, and the drought was the worst in more than fifty years.[117] It seems certain to have a significant impact on world food markets, with the U.S. corn crop forecast to be the lowest in fourteen years and the U.S. Department of Agriculture predicting cascading price rises for soybeans, animal feed, meat, and dairy products.[118]

The American Growth Model under Threat

As this review has demonstrated, in the postwar period the United States has had an impressive track record in delivering economic growth, boosting the living standards of its citizens, and improving environmental standards. America now appears to have reached an inflection point, however, with a significant majority of its residents believing that the country is heading in the wrong direction.[119]

The reasons for their concern are clear. The resilience of the economy has been challenged by a series of financial shocks, some starting in the United States (the dot-com crash and the housing crisis) and some originating internationally (the East Asian financial crisis and the euro crisis), but with an impact on growth in the United States. Although the U.S. economy has a good track record in bouncing back from shocks, deleveraging in the wake of the Great Recession has hindered its most recent recovery.

The failure to deliver rising living standards to the majority of Americans is not a recent phenomenon, but until recently it was masked by rising debt and asset prices (both mostly tied to residential property). Americans are currently experiencing an uncharacteristic loss of optimism about their country's ability to provide opportunities and social mobility for the middle and working classes, and this has led to anxiety about the sustainability of the American dream.

Environmental threats, finally, pose a serious threat to the United States. The country has a dominant share of global resource markets, but it will face growing competition from emerging markets and possibly also from the next wave of developing countries. Climate change remains the greatest environmental challenge, with the United States certain to face continued pressure to accelerate the rate at which it lowers its extremely high per capita level of greenhouse gas emissions.

There is, moreover, a lack of consensus about how to address these problems, with intense partisan divisions over how to respond to the financial crisis, whether and how to tackle economic stagnation among the middle and working classes, and what role government should play in tackling environmental problems. This uncertainty makes the future highly unpredictable. In the next section, we explore the interests, norms, and values that will inform the future evolution of American society and the balance it needs to strike between economic growth, social values, and environmental constraints.

Where Next for the United States after the Great Recession?

"We have involved ourselves in a colossal muddle, having blundered in the control of a delicate machine, the working of which we don't understand," wrote John Maynard Keynes in 1930 as the Great Depression deepened.[120] Despite the crisis, however, the human race had not lost its ingenuity, he believed, nor the capacity for its members to work together to provide themselves with higher living standards. The turmoil of the present would soon pass, Keynes argued, but only if policymakers avoided mistakes that would drive them deeper into trouble.

Keynes would find much to recognize in the modern predicament. The Great Recession has been described as the greatest economic challenge the world has faced since the 1930s.[121] More than five years since the leaders of the G-20 countries met in London and promised to "restore confidence, growth, and jobs," the global economy remains extremely fragile, with the International Monetary Fund warning that recovery in the United States remains vulnerable to "fiscal uncertainty, weakness in the housing market, and potential spillovers from Europe."[122] The American economy continues to add jobs, but only at roughly the same rate as the increase in its labor force, leaving unemployment rates stubbornly high.[123]

A crisis often creates a window in which change is possible. There are, however contrasting visions for the direction the United States should take.[124] Republicans and Democrats remain divided on the role of government, the speed of fiscal retrenchment, the distributional impact of taxation and transfers, and policies on energy and the environment. What, then, can be said about the course the United States will set over the next twenty years? What impact will it have on patterns of growth and quality of life of the American people? And how will decisions made by the world's largest economy affect people from other countries and the global environment? This section sets out some of the drivers that will determine the United States' options, based on the norms, interests, and values that ensure that its choices are likely to be distinctive from those made by other countries.

America's Dynamic Demography

A country's demography offers a window to its future. In coming decades, the United States faces a surprisingly positive demographic picture, one that will set it apart from other developed countries, while posing fresh challenges to global sustainability.

The most striking factor is the speed of American population growth. There are projected to be more than 400 million Americans by mid-century, about 90 million above the current level.[125] Only India, Nigeria, Pakistan, and Tanzania will gain more people by 2050. In contrast, other major powers (China, Russia, Japan, and the European Union) will see their populations decline. As a result, the United States will age much less rapidly than many expect. America's median age is increasing only slowly and is expected to be at about forty years for much of the century. In contrast, Japan's median age will exceed fifty years in 2025, as will Germany's in 2040. Extraordinarily, on this measure China will be an older country than the United States before the end of *this* decade.

The United States will not be immune to the challenges of an aging society, of course, especially as its disproportionately large baby boom generation (born 1946–64) enters retirement.[126] According to the Congressional Budget Office, health and security spending is on a trajectory that will see it grow from 10 percent of GDP to 16 percent over twenty-five years.[127] At the same time, the workforce is shrinking as a proportion of the total population, albeit more slowly than in most other developed countries.[128] Fewer workers will need to be more productively employed if they are to provide baby boomers with a comfortable retirement. This difficult transition will be relatively short-lived, however.

By 2040, old-age dependency will have stabilized, with little further aging until deep into the twenty-first century.[129]

America's population growth will be confined to its towns and cities as rural areas continue to lose population. By 2050, the U.S. urban population will have grown by more than 100 million (roughly the same size as the entire American population at the beginning of World War I).[130] This growth will be driven mainly by first- and second-generation immigrants, as the United States continues to have significantly higher rates of net migration than any other G-20 country. As a result, the country's cultural makeup will continue to change rapidly, with non-Hispanic whites expected to be a minority of the population before 2050.

These demographic changes have the following implications:

—*Cities will be critical to rates and patterns of economic growth.* Urban centers that have high concentrations of educated workers, especially those with scientific and technological skills, will account for a growing share of American GDP.[131] Cities that create jobs will thrive and see their population grow, while the poorest-performing ones will see their population shrink. This evolutionary dynamic will enhance the ability of the United States to adapt to new economic forces and to make a smoother exit from legacy industrial sectors.

—*A growing population will consume more.* Developed countries with stable populations can expect demand for resources to fall, possibly significantly, if efficiency gains also accelerate. The United States, however, is emphatically not in this group. The U.S. government will be under significant pressure to provide tens of millions more people with high standards of living. Such a large number of additional American consumers will inevitably have a significant impact on the global economy and environment.

—*Consumption patterns may shift.* Changes in the configuration of American cities and in the preferences of city dwellers could have a pronounced impact on consumption patterns. Will American cities become more densely populated over time and therefore efficient in their use of resources?[132] Will the United States' long love affair with the automobile begin to dwindle as young Americans drive less than previous generations did at the same age?[133] And will there be an ongoing dematerialization of the economy as consumers switch from physical goods to virtual services?

Demographic trends will also fuel broader social and cultural changes. At present, younger generations are likely to be significantly more progressive than other voters, although how this translates into political preferences will shift as they age.[134] As intergenerational transfers grow, political friction may increase between the young and the old, especially as high participation rates continue to give older voters disproportionate electoral power.[135] Climate change could also emerge as a source of political division, especially as cities continue to be hit by extreme weather events or if a growing proportion of the young become convinced that they will see dangerous levels of climate change within their lifetime.

A changing ethnic balance will also lead to a political realignment. Nonwhite ethnic groups are much poorer than whites, with more than a quarter of Hispanics and African Americans living in poverty.[136] Both groups are highly aspirational. Although they are much less likely than whites to believe that they have already achieved the American dream, they are more likely to think that they will achieve it in the future.[137] They will therefore continue to value growth, but only if it delivers broad income gains. At the same time, however, nonwhites are significantly less conservative than whites and more likely to support direct government action to tackle poverty.[138] They will also become an increasingly powerful lobby for change if their aspirations continue to be frustrated.

Deepening Political Distrust

Although demography will drive change in American society, the country's political system is likely to continue to frustrate those who wish to see decisive government action. Polarization in the United States has been increasing since the 1970s as political extremes increase their representation in Congress, parties become more ideologically homogeneous, and the differences between them become more stark.[139] In a parliamentary system, this might translate into decisive implementation of policy platforms, but the separation of powers and the dramatically increased use of the filibuster in the Senate make it much harder for any party to impose its will.[140]

Polarization may prove especially problematic during turbulent times, limiting the United States' ability to respond to unfamiliar challenges. An international review of the political response to past financial crises shows that they are more likely to lead to "greater ideological polarization in society, greater fractionalization of the legislative body, and a decrease in the size of the working majority of the ruling coalition."[141] Coalitions become smaller, governments weaker, and the opposition stronger. This pattern seems to be repeating itself in the wake of the Great Recession, not just in the United States but also across the Western world.

At the same time, a broader loss of trust in elites is making it harder to build the consensus needed to tackle complex challenges. In the run-up to and in the aftermath of the Great Recession, policymakers, regulators, and financial institutions have been widely perceived as having failed to protect the public good. Alan Greenspan, chairman of the Federal Reserve under four presidents, was lauded as "the maestro" for his control of the U.S. economy.[142] After the financial crisis, however, he admitted to being reduced to a "shocked state of disbelief" by the failure of the market adequately to manage risk. The Financial Inquiry Commission, meanwhile, catalogued a series of "dramatic failures" in government regulation and corporate governance.[143] It found that government agencies were "always behind the curve," both before and during the crisis. They had allowed the financial system "to race ahead of our ability to protect it."

The discrediting of elites is more than a short-term trend. Confidence has been falling in most major institutions, often over many decades. The military is the only institution that a majority of Americans trust, commanding greater respect than in the 1970s. Even organized religion is now trusted by fewer than half of Americans. Confidence in business is low and has fallen significantly since the turn of the century, while faith in banks has collapsed in the wake of the financial crisis. Unions are as distrusted as big business. The presidency is the most trusted of the major political institutions (but with a rating of only 37 percent), along with the Supreme Court (also 37 percent). Congress has always been especially unpopular, but has seen a further collapse in its approval ratings since 2004.

In part, these ratings reflect a broader trust deficit across society, with only 44 percent of Americans agreeing that "most people can be trusted."[144] Trust has declined steadily since the mid-1960s and is currently lower among young people than older people, among nonwhites than whites, and among the less educated than those with a college degree.[145] Inequality appears to fuel distrust, as vulnerable groups react to their own insecurity by being less willing to take the risk of placing their faith in others.[146] If the gulf between ethnic groups, the rich and poor, and the haves and have-nots remains wide, then levels of mistrust are likely to remain high in American society.

Although the combination of polarization, loss of trust in elites, and gridlock suggests that the U.S. government will continue to lack direction, this may create space for other actors to challenge the status quo. This challenge could take many forms, including protest movements such as Occupy or the Tea Party, innovation by for-profit or social entrepreneurs, or leadership from states or cities that emerge as laboratories for new approaches. The drivers of political and social change, in other words, may be more likely to come from the margins than from the center.

A New Era of Global Leadership

Although the United States is certain to face headwinds in the coming decades, this does not mean that its stance will be a pessimistic one. Although fears of America's decline will continue to surface, a more confident narrative is likely to predominate at most times.

Even during the crisis, a slim majority of Americans remained optimistic about the country's future over the next fifty years.[147] At the ballot box, meanwhile, they consistently reward optimistic politicians over negative ones.[148]

A blind analysis of the speeches of presidential candidates between 1900 and 1984[149] showed that the candidate who sounded the least pessimistic was elected on 80 percent of occasions, creating strong incentives for politicians to emphasize the potential for renewed American leadership.

At the same time, the United States will be able to draw on enduring *absolute* geopolitical strengths, even if its relative power continues to diminish due to the economic success of rising powers. It will continue to benefit from its

—Position as a *dominant security actor*, which it seems certain to maintain for at least another generation, and its privileged position in most *global institutions*[150]

—*Internal security*, which is more robust than that of countries such as India (currently tackling a Naxalite insurgency in 125 of its 640 districts) or China (reported to be spending as much on domestic security as on defense)[151]

—*Growth potential*, especially when compared with the European Union, but more generally if it manages to use its leadership in key export sectors to exploit the purchasing power of a growing global middle class[152] or if one or more of the emerging economies suffers an interruption to its growth.

Energy is set to become an additional source of American leadership. High prices send powerful market signals, as last seen during the energy crisis of the 1970s, which led to both rapid increases in energy efficiency and a substantial growth in supply.[153] On the demand side, a similar shift in American demand is under way today in response to the price shocks of the past five years and to government-mandated improvements in vehicle fuel efficiency standards that are expected to reduce U.S. carbon dioxide emissions by 4.7 billion metric tons by 2025.[154] As a result, despite population growth, the U.S. Energy Information Administration expects growth in energy use to slow to 0.3 percent a year between 2010 and 2035 and per capita consumption to fall to 0.6 percent in that period.[155]

The supply response has been even stronger. As prices have risen, global investment in development has grown sharply. According to Barclays Capital, oil and gas companies will spend nearly US$723 billion on exploration and production in 2014, a 6 percent increase on 2013, with investment increasingly directed toward unconventional and deepwater oil and gas.[156] This investment is expected to bring significant new production on stream, with the United States one of five countries that account for slightly under two thirds of new development. American unconventional oil is now estimated to be profitable when the West Texas Intermediate benchmark for oil is at US$55 to US$65 per barrel (it has been above this level for most of the past five years).[157]

The prospects for natural gas have been fundamentally transformed, in what one analyst has described as the "the greatest revolution in the United States energy landscape since the Second World War."[158] Until recently, the United

States was expecting to become increasingly dependent on imported gas, with Alan Greenspan warning the House of Representatives' Committee on Energy and Commerce that "earlier periods of relative [gas] abundance and low prices" were probably over and that the United States should increase liquefied natural gas (LNG) imports in order to reduce domestic price volatility.[159] As late as 2006, the International Energy Agency predicted that growth in production in the gas sector would be driven by the Middle East and Africa.[160] However, U.S. reserves have grown by about 70 percent during the past decade.[161] Production increased by a factor of six between 2007 and 2011, with a gas glut leading to a substantial reduction in prices and a growing gap between the cost of gas in North America and the price paid in Europe or Asia.[162]

Although energy will provide a geopolitical boost for the United States, the environmental consequences of these rapid changes to the energy sector remain hard to predict. Global demand for energy is still expected to grow rapidly, despite gains in energy efficiency, whereas the diffusion of new techniques for extracting unconventional oil and gas will see a growth in estimates of remaining reserves of fossil fuels. The trajectory of emissions will depend on the quantity of "new carbon" that is successfully extracted, its price, and whether the energy source it replaces has higher (coal) or lower (nuclear, renewables) emissions. Pressure on U.S. emissions is likely to be downward, especially if combined with regulation (limiting coal, supporting renewables) and a carbon price.[163] At a global level, however, this could be offset by increased exports of American coal and by lower-than-expected energy prices. The International Energy Agency has modeled a "golden age of gas" and finds a marginal impact on emissions, leaving the world on a trajectory toward a 3.5°C increase in temperatures, even before additional supplies of unconventional oil are factored into the mix.

Overall, it seems highly likely that the United States will continue to play an assertive global role, supported by a public that overwhelmingly believes that it is best for the United States to be active in global affairs.[164] This, however, is equally *unlikely* to translate into a willingness to see American sovereignty constrained by international agreements, especially in contentious areas such as the environment. Formal treaties, meanwhile, will prove almost impossible to ratify, as can be seen by the fate of the relatively anodyne United Nations Convention on the Law of the Sea, which remains far from Senate ratification even after twenty years, and the recent failure in the Senate of a United Nations treaty banning discrimination against people with disabilities.[165] In a partisan age where appeals to sovereignty still have political salience, gaining the support of two thirds of the Senate to pass a treaty poses an almost insurmountable obstacle. If the United States is to contribute to international action on global challenges, it will seldom be via this formal route.

Moreover, the United States is likely to use its leadership to enhance its growth prospects, given the speed with which its population continues to grow. This is likely to bring it into conflict with those who believe that it needs to shift to a much less resource-intensive economic trajectory. Given the choice between fast growth and green growth, the United States is likely to favor the former over the latter.

Scenarios for the Future

In the run-up to Rio+20, the High-Level Panel on Global Sustainability set out a plan of "global action . . . to enable people, markets, and governments to make sustainable choices."[166] The priorities for the future, the panel argued, were "to eradicate poverty, reduce inequality, and make growth inclusive, and production and consumption more sustainable, while combating climate change and respecting a range of other planetary boundaries." It called on all countries to adopt a strategy for sustainable development and to measure the implementation of this strategy through a set of goals that would reflect equally "the economic, social, and environmental dimensions of sustainable development and the interconnections between them."

A vision of this kind has no chance of adoption in the United States. In this chapter, we have argued that there are powerful reasons for the United States to address threats to its current growth model, given the vulnerability of the current model to shocks, the failure of the American dream to deliver for a growing proportion of citizens, and the seriousness of climate change and other environmental challenges. However, we have also demonstrated that change will not be easy to achieve and will almost certainly not follow the pathway suggested by those who wish to see a substantial shift from growth to equity and environmental protection. American leaders are elected by a growing population that places a high value on prosperity. They are unlikely to be returned to office if they fail to deliver economic success, nor will they be rewarded at the ballot box if they are seen as being insufficiently assertive in advancing American interests on the international stage.

Change to the American system may be needed, but the approach recommended by the United Nations and endorsed at Rio+20 has little appeal to either the American public or its elite. Many Americans remain strongly resistant to any role for the international system in regulating or restraining American growth. If anything, this hostility is growing. Agenda 21, a voluntary action plan agreed to at the first Rio Summit in 1992, was denounced at the Republican National Committee in 2012 in a resolution condemning "extreme environmentalism, social engineering, and global political control" that was inherently hostile to the American way of life.[167]

American policymakers therefore face a paradox. On the one hand, the need for—and perhaps also the demand for—a new growth model is strong. On the other hand, the obstacles to its creation are daunting. Although predicting the future is an invidious task, especially when levels of global uncertainty are so high and American politics is so finely divided, we see four broad scenarios that could result from the interplay of these contrasting forces.

SCENARIO 1: MUDDLE THROUGH. This scenario sees a continuation of business-as-usual, with a slight rebalancing of growth from the richest Americans to the middle classes, as a result of a combination of recovery, growth in high-value exports, and an increase in income taxes for higher earners. A period of high energy prices stimulates significant gains in energy efficiency, but also sees the United States emerge as a major producer of unconventional oil as well as unconventional gas. This increases American energy security, but carbon emissions are only reduced slowly, as cheaper energy prices stimulate demand and reduce the competitiveness of renewables. Pressure is placed on China and India to discover and develop their own unconventional carbon reserves, with an inevitable impact on climate trajectories. Policymakers increasingly focus on adaptation to climate impacts and on geo-engineering as a potential route to reducing atmospheric concentrations of greenhouse gases.[168] Internationally, levels of trust and cooperation between major powers are low, while a growing number of countries face powerful protest movements from both ends of the political spectrum.

SCENARIO 2: GOING FOR GROWTH. This scenario builds on scenario 1 but assumes a singular focus on growing the economy. Unconventional oil and shale gas are rapidly exploited and often exported, with lower energy prices boosting the economy. Domestic demand for coal continues to fall, but low-cost coal is sold aggressively to emerging markets. Consumption remains a key driver of economic growth, which is rapid but unevenly distributed, with some metropolitan areas prospering and others experiencing a steep decline in their wealth and population. The labor market performs strongly, but it does not generate the jobs needed to reduce income inequality. Economic mobility also remains low, but, on the whole, urban voters continue to support "growth first" politics. American greenhouse gas emissions fall, but only slowly, while its coal exports boost emissions in other countries. Declining federal government support for renewable energy means that gas does not become a bridging fuel to zero-carbon energy sources. American resilience to risk is strengthened by an improved fiscal position, but increased resources—diplomatic, military, and economic—are used to react to, rather than manage, crises, both overseas and at home. America leads still, but in a highly competitive and often fractious world.

SCENARIO 3: INTELLIGENT DESIGN. This scenario is also consistent with strong levels of economic growth but includes a more deliberate attempt to reinforce positive trends, restrain negative ones, and increase American resilience to a range of risks. Successive presidents focus on employment through renewed public investment in education and training, additional support for sectors with high export potential, and innovative approaches to regulation, especially in the financial sector. The Federal Reserve places greater emphasis on its mandate to maximize employment, alongside its current focus on interest rates and price stability.[169] In the energy sector, the government takes a strategic approach to augmenting the country's new opportunities, with policies to maximize the potential of gas to reduce emissions (for example, use in transportation) and some contribution from the energy sector to fiscal consolidation (through lower fossil fuel subsidies and increased use of taxation or market instruments).[170] None of these measures is especially dramatic, but taken together they have a definite impact on sustainability and allow the United States to provide somewhat higher levels of leadership internationally. As a result, geopolitical outcomes are more cooperative, with some innovations in global governance, even though important stresses remain unaddressed.[171]

SCENARIO 4: EMERGENCY RESPONSE. Policy is driven in unpredictable directions by a series of shocks, such as a further breakdown in global financial systems, serious conflict or state failure, or a series of extreme weather events or clear evidence of disruptive climate change. In response to one or more of these shocks, the United States becomes a highly directive actor as it mobilizes what it perceives to be an urgent threat to its security. At a global level, net economic impact is negative, possibly strongly so, as growth slows in some countries. The impact on sustainability is hard to predict. It is most likely to be positive if an environmental shock triggers the crisis, although even then outcomes will be highly dependent on the timing of the event and the extent to which appropriate technologies are primed for rapid diffusion. The impact on geopolitics will also be mixed, especially if the world divides into victims and villains (with the United States on either side) and if coercive measures (for example, trade sanctions) are used to deliver change. This scenario becomes an increasingly likely successor to the previous scenarios, assuming that patterns of growth take the world further outside the "safe operating space for humanity."[172]

Determining the Future

These scenarios have very different probabilities of being realized. In the short term, *muddle through* is the most plausible course of action for the United States at the national level at least. Pockets of innovation will be found at the state and metropolitan levels and in the private sector, of course, but they are unlikely to have a decisive impact, given opposing trends in other states and business sectors. Fiscal tightening is likely to reduce space for the adoption of new policies, while any restriction on growth in existing industries will be strongly resisted while unemployment levels remain high. In his second term, President Obama may find that the rewards for U.S. leadership are likely to be low, a product of an unsettled and often chaotic international environment. Increased strategic competition between the United States and China would be highly likely under this scenario.[173]

The prospects for a resurgent American economy should not be discounted, however. Growth is currently quite strong,[174] and new housing construction has increased substantially.[175] Assuming some stabilization in the euro zone and no significant weakening in the emerging economies, the United States could now see a rapid recovery after some false starts. *Going for growth* is a plausible scenario in this case, especially if more metropolitan areas aggressively pursue growth strategies. Internationally, under this scenario, the United States will sit somewhere in between the rest of the West and the rising powers, with the wealth and established institutions of the former, but the population growth, rapid urbanization, and appetite for resources of the latter.

Shocks have the potential to make it impossible for the United States to continue to follow the *muddle through* scenario. In the short term, a returning financial crisis is the greatest risk, either in the euro zone or in one or more emerging markets. Conflict—in Iran, for example—cannot be ruled out, and political disturbance in a major oil producer (Iran, Saudi Arabia, Russia, or Venezuela) would have a dramatic impact on energy markets. Environmental shocks are inherently unpredictable, but they are expected to become more frequent as climate change intensifies. In the *emergency response* scenario, much will depend on the resilience of American society (defined as the capacity to *absorb disturbance and reorganize while undergoing change*) and on policies that reinforce that resilience.[176] As was seen during the early phase of the Great Recession, the window in which reforms can be implemented is small. It is therefore critical that potential responses have already been developed and are ready for rapid deployment.

Intelligent design is the preferred scenario for those who are convinced of the importance of sustainable development. This scenario does not require a sudden and unrealistic change of political and economic direction. Instead, a set of disparate policies will have the cumulative effect of pushing the United States onto a growth trajectory that is somewhat more sustainable than the current one. Over time, a new economic model emerges as political and economic incentives shift and the new direction becomes self-reinforcing. This scenario is far from being an easy option, however. On the one hand, even in the best case, environmental sustainability would still be some way off. Climate stabilization, in particular, is likely to remain a distant goal, with the chance of global warming remaining below 2°C now remote. On the other hand, most of the policies that might underpin this scenario face daunting obstacles. Significant political skill will be needed to shift American society onto this path.

So what reforms or policy innovations are both consistent with the *intelligent design* scenario and likely to gain traction within contemporary America, given the country's history, current preferences, and future opportunities and risks? First, a future direction *cannot rely too heavily on the federal government*. Until the 1970s, the postwar U.S. economic policy was underpinned by a form of Keynesian economics that relied on the market but also the government for distributional issues and used fiscal policy to smooth economic cycles and achieve key social and environmental goals. Keynesian policies came under sustained pressure, however, as economic growth began to slow, the oil crisis fueled inflation, and a combination of the Vietnam War and the cost of social programs increased budgetary pressure.[177] The result was a shift to a monetarist economic underpinning for economic policy, based on a view that government intervention in the market was a source of instability and on policy prescriptions that increased the role of the private sector through deregulation and the privatization of government-owned assets.

Today, the role of government appears to have hit another inflection point, but its future direction is hotly contested. There is strong support for a substantial further reduction in the size of government. The Path to Prosperity, a Republican budget proposal for 2012, envisaged reducing the size of government to 20 percent of GDP, while placing renewed emphasis on "the timeless principles of the American idea: free enterprise and economic liberty; limited government and spending restraint; traditional family and community values; and a strong national defense."[178] The proposed budget argued for a reversal of a "shortsighted financial regulatory overhaul [that] failed to fix what was broken on Wall Street" and attacked the "environmental activism" of the federal government.

An alternative vision is more supportive of a return to a mixed model that delivers new approaches to service delivery and regulation, while imposing more modest spending cuts. During its first term, the Obama administration created fewer regulations than its predecessors, but it has been more prepared to impose regulations in "economically significant" areas, where costs are above US$100 million.[179] It has also established a new Consumer Financial Protection Bureau that is expected to take an aggressive approach to its mission, making "markets for consumer financial products and services work for Americans."[180] But even if these trends continue, the role of government will remain constrained, given traditionally low levels of government expenditures, the need to tackle the deficit, and low levels of public confidence in the government's ability to deliver change.

Second, a new growth model is only likely to prosper if it *generates wealth for all segments of society*. U.S. citizens have a relatively high tolerance for inequality. Only a slim majority believes that it is the government's responsibility to take care of people who cannot take care of themselves, with support for a social safety net declining over the past twenty years.[181] It is highly unlikely that any political party will win support if it sets the reduction of inequality as a primary policy goal. However, it is equally unlikely that patterns of growth that fail to deliver benefits to the middle classes can be sustained indefinitely. The politically salient yardstick, therefore, is an absolute one (most Americans are seeing improvements in their living standards), not a relative one (the gap between rich and poor is closing), although the latter may follow from or be required to deliver the former.

Governments are therefore likely to place considerable emphasis on the ability to generate more and better employment, with 21 million new jobs needed by 2020 for unemployment to sink below 5 percent.[182] In addition, productivity gains must also support higher wages if household incomes are once again to continue to rise. In part, this is likely to depend on the United States' ability to exploit emerging international export opportunities in societies with growing numbers of consumers. President Obama has set a target of doubling American export growth by 2015, with his National Export Initiative claiming that an additional 1.2 million jobs were supported by exports between 2009 and 2011 and that U.S. exports hit an all-time record of US$2.2 trillion in 2012, supporting an additional 9.8 million jobs.[183]

Finally, policies will need to fulfill at least *a narrow vision of environmental sustainability,* based on two key areas:

—*Greater resilience in the face of crisis.* Federal, state, and city governments will see their credibility undermined if they fail to manage risks effectively. The economic crisis is far from over, with the euro remaining under serious threat. The world also faces significant geopolitical risks, including the aftermath of the Arab Spring and potential conflict with Iran, either of which could have a dramatic impact on energy markets. This suggests that the United States is highly unlikely to be able to avoid future shocks but will prosper to the extent that it is adaptable in the face of them.

—*Protection from immediate environmental impacts.* American public opinion on climate change is influenced by short-term weather trends, with abnormal shifts in local temperature associated with a stronger belief in global warming.[184] Natural and environmental disasters—such as Sandy and Katrina—also increase concern about climate change, with more than 80 percent of Americans saying that they experience an extreme weather event or natural disaster each year.[185] Action that explicitly aims to address these threats, either directly or indirectly, is therefore more likely to be supported than more general appeals to protect the planet, especially as weather extremes continue to increase.[186]

On the basis of these criteria, we have developed a series of policy recommendations that are most likely to push the United States toward the more proactive approach outlined in the *intelligent design* scenario. Many of these policies would also push the United States toward the *going for growth* scenario, but without the social and environmental benefits of the preferred scenario.

We do not expect all of these policies to be implemented in the short term, but implementing even a handful of them would nudge the United States toward a more sustainable trajectory. This would, in turn, provide a foundation for a new era of leadership from the United States on issues that will have a decisive impact on global prosperity and security in the twenty-first century.

America's Future Direction

We have argued that the United States faces economic, social, and environmental challenges that cannot be effectively managed given existing policies. However, significant social and political factors block many options for a future direction. In this section, we set out policies that, though challenging to implement, are within the realm of the politically possible. Our expectation is that demand for new policies will grow as globalization continues to be gripped by its long crisis and that the United States remains relatively well placed to pioneer new approaches, given its geopolitical position, wealth, and appetite for innovation. We therefore expect opportunities to break the gridlock, although the windows for reform will often be fleeting.

We group recommendations into four areas:

—*Employment,* which is the most urgent priority to accelerate American recovery from the Great Recession, while addressing underlying structural issues that have led to a decade of poor economic outcomes for most citizens

—*Investment in the future,* which is the key marker of whether the United States is prepared to make farsighted decisions or whether its resources and political attention are increasingly absorbed by current consumption and immediate crises

—*Energy,* where new opportunities exist to make strategic use of a larger energy endowment, while reinforcing the trend toward lower demand for resources, with a significant impact on the sustainability of the U.S. growth model

—*Fiscal rebalancing,* where the United States must insulate economic recovery from the process of fiscal reform while also reducing and stabilizing the debt.

Finally, we explore the implications of these policies for renewed American leadership internationally, arguing that President Obama and his successors after

2016 have the opportunity to reenergize the country's foreign policy if they build on a platform of domestic actions that enhance the sustainability of America's society and economy.

Tackling the Jobs Crisis

Nearly 9 million jobs were lost in the Great Recession and its immediate aftermath.[187] During the recovery, policy has had a modest impact on increasing employment, with the Congressional Budget Office estimating that the Recovery and Reinvestment Act has led to between 0.2 million and 1.2 million additional people in current employment, with a peak impact on employment at the end of 2010.[188] At the state level, labor markets were strongest in those states that increased government expenditures fastest between 2007 and 2010.[189] But the federal stimulus spending created jobs at an estimated cost of US$125,000 per job.[190]

As noted by Ben Bernanke, former chairman of the Federal Reserve, "The rate of improvement in the labor market has been painfully slow."[191] At the rate of job creation in the 2000s, it would take until 2020 to fill the current jobs gap, with Bernanke blaming the troubled housing sector, fiscal contraction at the federal and state levels, and financial stresses in the euro zone. The Federal Reserve, tired of waiting for Congress to act, launched a new round of quantitative easing based on its expectation that economic growth would not otherwise "be strong enough to generate sustained improvement in labor market conditions.[192] This new commitment does not have a fixed end date but is tied to clear evidence that the labor market is improving. This marks increased commitment from the Federal Reserve to "forward guidance," signaling that it is prepared to boost aggregate demand (and, as a result, tolerate higher inflation), until the economy has fully recovered.[193]

Prospects for U.S. growth have improved, but are still highly vulnerable to shocks. The housing market appears to have stabilized, deleveraging is advanced, and companies are sitting on large reserves of cash. The immediate priority, therefore, is to maintain quantitative easing and strengthen the signal sent to the market by underlining the importance of the dual mandate (in contrast to current legislative attempts to remove the Fed's goal of maximizing employment), while maintaining the current consensus on the Federal Open Market Committee behind a "highly accommodative stance of monetary policy" until employment has increased substantially.[194] The key domestic threat to employment growth derives from the prospect of premature fiscal tightening. Internationally, U.S. leadership is needed, especially within the G-20, to manage contagion more aggressively within and from the euro zone and to respond to signs of economic fragility in the emerging powers.

Beyond the immediate economic crisis, the focus needs to shift to structural factors, through efforts to tackle long-term unemployment and geographic and skills mismatches between the labor market and labor force. During the recession, there was a substantial increase in the mismatch between available jobs and the skills of workers available to fill them, with industrial mismatch accounting for about a third of the increase in unemployment (geographic mismatch did not play a significant role).[195] Although this was primarily a cyclical phenomenon with levels of mismatch quickly returning to prerecession levels—mostly as a result of more rapid recovery in sectors such as construction, manufacturing, and retail that were fastest to shed jobs during the downturn—workers with obsolete skills are disproportionately likely to lose their job during a recession.[196] Large numbers of workers have been unemployed for more than six months or have exited the labor force entirely.[197] Most of these potential workers will lose skills and motivation the longer they are out of work, leading to what Ben Bernanke has warned of as "modest increase in the sustainable, long-run rate of unemployment,"[198] with the natural rate of unemployment now estimated to have increased to between 5.2 and 6 percent.[199]

A related problem is the long-term failure to generate sufficient jobs that support a middle-class income. At least in its early stages, the recovery has seen a further shift toward low-wage jobs, with mid-wage jobs accounting for 60 percent of the jobs lost in the downturn, but only 22 percent of those added in its aftermath.[200] Looking forward, the workforce faces significant structural challenges. During the next decade, it will continue to age, increasing the importance of the participation rates of older workers. The skills gap is also likely to increase, with the McKinsey Global Institute projecting that in 2020 there will be about 6 million too few jobs for those who have not completed a high school education and a shortage of workers able to fill jobs that require advanced technical degrees.[201] The major priority is to address the skills gap, while also undertaking the following:

—*Implementing an emergency package for the long-term unemployed to increase their chances of finding work as the recovery proceeds, with the aim of bringing the natural rate of unemployment back down to about 5 percent.*[202] Options include targeted retraining schemes for the long-term unemployed or wage subsidies for employers who provide them with jobs, drawing on the more successful elements of Germany's Hartz Reforms.[203]

—*Supporting the rebound of manufacturing after the recession, with the aim of creating middle-class jobs and supporting robust local economies.*[204] The future for U.S. manufacturing is in high-end industries, which are likely to prosper as manufacturing becomes increasingly reliant on technology, less centered on mass production, and less determined by access to cheap labor.[205] This will require greater support for innovation.

—Capitalizing on the opportunities for growth that can be found in America's cities, especially as they continue to experience rapid population growth. They have the greatest ability to escape partisan gridlock at federal levels, offering what Bruce Katz calls a "historic opportunity to usher in a new era of pragmatic, collaborative federalism that capitalizes on the economic power of metropolitan areas and the policy creativity of state and local leaders."[206] Katz proposes that the federal government fund state and metropolitan development strategies on a competitive basis and with regard to their contribution to national objectives, such as the goal of doubling exports.

Investing for Tomorrow

A willingness to invest in future generations is critical to the long-term success of any society. In recent decades, however, the United States has seen a rise in consumption, an increase in debt, and a failure to invest adequately in education, infrastructure, and the innovation needed to sustain prosperity.

The American education system has important strengths, including its elite higher education sector. Its schools, however, are failing large numbers of students, with American students ranking below average for science and only average for mathematics when compared with other OECD countries.[207] The failure to provide a decent education to black and Latino students is especially consequential, given that they lag two to three years behind their white counterparts.[208] This will have an intensifying economic impact as the workforce becomes increasingly populated by these groups. Creating better and more affordable education opportunities means reducing costs, improving quality, and ensuring that the education system is equipping graduates with the skills needed for the twenty-first century, with a particular focus on poorly performing groups of students. Challenges include the high costs of elite institutions and higher education, limited access to scholarships and grants, mounting student debt, and inequitable payback schemes.

Priorities include the following:

—Making higher education more affordable and accessible for a greater number of students, thus narrowing the educational opportunity gap. This can be done by increasing state-sponsored financial aid and granting programs (that is, making further investments in Pell Grant scholarships), providing payment options for students at different income levels, or freezing or cutting tuition rates.[209] Reform of the student loan payback system is especially important, enabling borrowers to cap their payments at a percentage of income (that is, at 10 percent of what they make every month).[210]

—Improving educational outcomes. This can be done by reviewing curricula and assessment systems to match outcomes relevant to future economic

opportunities and social challenges. All of the world's top-performing and rapidly improving systems have curriculum standards that set clear and high expectations for what students should achieve.[211]

—*Addressing the skills gap among adult workers.* This can be done by creating more partnerships between businesses and educational institutions and focusing on workforce development. Investment could be increased through Skills for America's Future, an industry-led initiative that improves industry partnerships with community colleges and builds a nationwide network to maximize workforce development strategies, job training programs, and job placement.[212] There is also potential to focus federal and state assistance for training on firms and sectors that have the greatest potential to produce high-paid jobs (with randomized trials to measure what works).[213]

Infrastructure is another area where the United States is falling behind, with a pronounced impact on future competitiveness.[214] According to the American Society of Civil Engineers, the United States should spend US$1.7 trillion by 2020 to upgrade infrastructure, and current investments are falling short of what is needed by US$94 billion a year.[215] It currently spends only 2.4 percent of GDP on infrastructure,[216] compared with 5 percent in Europe and 9 percent in China.[217] As well as improving competitiveness, smart investment in infrastructure could put the U.S. economy on a lower-carbon path.

The United States should develop a national infrastructure plan or strategy that strengthens federal support and improves cooperation between all levels of government and the private sector. For example, Obama has proposed a partnership to rebuild America that will leverage private capital to upgrade infrastructure. In order to increase the sustainability of America's infrastructure, specific priorities include the following:

—*Increasing investment in low-carbon mass transportation,* thereby reducing fuel use, air pollution, and greenhouse gas emissions, while improving the quality of urban life.[218] Moreover, by one estimate the economic gains are significant, with every US$1 spent on public transportation increasing GDP by up to US$3.50.[219]

—*Promoting innovative financial mechanisms to support green infrastructure investments,* through entities such as Connecticut's Clean Energy Finance and Investment Authority, which helps to reduce pressure on public budgets, and the State of New York's US$1 billion Green Bank to help to fund clean energy investments.[220]

—*Making infrastructure more resilient to extreme weather events and other natural disasters,* given the heightened vulnerability of many U.S. urban areas to a range of threats.[221]

Finally, policies are needed to increase innovation, especially in areas that will equip the United States to compete in industries with high growth potential.

President Obama in his 2013 State of the Union address said, "Now is the time to reach a level of research and development not seen since the height of the Space Race."[222] Since the 1960s, the U.S federal rate of investment in R&D as a percentage of GDP has declined from nearly 1.3 percent to 0.9 percent, damaging the global competitiveness of U.S. industries.[223] The government should increase federal funding for R&D, especially in clean energy and other low-carbon areas, but also in sectors where the United States holds significant research capacities, including biotechnology, genetics, and nanotechnology. Priorities include the following:

—*Enhancing the United States' attractiveness as a place for investment* by removing barriers in the tax code, creating new financial mechanisms that combine public and private funding streams, and increasing investment in seed capital and technology funding programs, such as the Small Business Innovative Research Program, which provides about US$1 billion a year to small businesses for early-stage R&D projects.[224]

—*Supporting entrepreneurship* through effective immigration policies that attract a highly skilled labor force. H1-B visas are strongly associated with innovation in science, technology, and engineering.[225] The cap on these visas should therefore be raised to address shortages of skilled labor.

—*Supporting innovation in clean energy and low-carbon technologies* through a cohesive set of federal, state, and local low-carbon economic growth strategies that will help to increase America's leadership in these sectors.[226]

Fueling the Future

America's energy prospects have changed radically in recent years, as higher energy prices have combined with modest technological innovation to increase reserves of unconventional gas and, more recently, unconventional oil. This is already having an economic impact, with energy prices lower in the United States than in Europe or Asia. In his 2012 State of the Union address, President Obama claimed that shale gas alone will lead to the creation of 600,000 new jobs by 2020.[227] Gas production is likely to exceed consumption within a decade, though prices are already low (indicating a gas glut).[228] This creates the potential for exports, supporting the development of stronger and more resilient global LNG markets.[229] However, the long-term benefits of gas and, in particular, the impact on climate change are uncertain. Natural gas has been presented by the American Gas Association as a "bridge" to renewable energy technologies since the early 1980s, but it is unclear whether it is a bridge to nowhere.[230] Much will depend on the extent to which coal is displaced, whether investment in renewables is crowded out, how quickly tight oil production increases, and the boost to demand from lower prices.

Policies are therefore needed to direct demand for gas, especially through faster switching from coal to gas for power generation. Coal is still projected to provide 38 percent of U.S. electricity in 2035, compared with 45 percent in 2010.[231] Earlier decommissioning of inefficient coal plants should be encouraged through ongoing tightening of regulations.[232] There is a real danger, however, that the decline in coal production will be limited by an increase in exports, displacing carbon emissions overseas. Exports in 2011 were almost double those of two years earlier and have continued to rise rapidly.[233] New coal terminals are planned, with the Environmental Protection Agency calling for a study of the climate change effects of exporting coal from the United States to Asia.[234] Europe, suffering comparative energy scarcity, is also a growing market for American coal.[235]

There is also potential for displacing oil in transportation, especially in heavy-vehicle fleets (using compressed natural gas) or the greater use of electric cars (assuming that the electricity comes from gas-powered generation). In the medium term, there may be potential for increased use of natural gas light vehicles, which are already made and sold abroad by most major manufacturers, including Ford and General Motors.[236] Again, however, the net effect on emissions will be reduced if energy prices are lower than would otherwise have been expected.

As a zero-carbon base-load source of electricity, there is renewed debate on the role that nuclear energy should play in reducing U.S. greenhouse gas emissions. Nuclear energy is currently the fourth-largest source of energy production and provides more than 20 percent of U.S. electricity. However, since the Three Mile Island nuclear incident, building nuclear power plants has become increasingly costly, and no reactor has been built in the United States since 1977. In addition, the nuclear meltdown at Fukushima Daiichi in 2011 again highlighted the costs of nuclear energy. The Obama administration has offered loan guarantees to support the construction of four new reactors, although it had difficulty finalizing the terms with private sector partners.[237] The Nuclear Regulatory Commission has also received active applications for twenty-eight new reactors, though many are unlikely to be built.[238] President Obama's goal of generating 80 percent of future electricity from clean energy sources by 2035 probably cannot be met without at least some increased role for nuclear energy.

Carbon pricing is a key priority for a more sustainable energy policy. It has the potential to ensure that recent shifts in patterns of energy demand are reinforced, while favoring the supply of low-carbon fuels.[239] A carbon price, by increasing the costs for carbon-intensive industries, would be an incentive for innovation in green technologies that reduce carbon dioxide emissions, complementing other government policies supporting R&D in clean energy.[240] However, a carbon price should be supplemented by the following:

—Better regulation of the shale gas industry, in particular to reduce methane leakage, which is essential if gas is to deliver the expected environmental benefits over coal

—Promotion of investment in gas infrastructure (such as pipelines and refueling infrastructure or standards) and of standards for the use of gas in transportation[241]

—A clean energy standard in the power sector equivalent to a target of 80 percent clean energy by 2035, which would reduce the sector's emissions by 60 percent by 2035[242]

—Policies to promote higher-density urbanization, more energy-efficient buildings, better public transportation links, and less reliance on automobiles[243]

—Continued use of regulation to promote more efficient energy use and ensure rapid improvements in the efficient use of resources by energy-intensive sectors, where the government is able to demonstrate substantial environmental benefits at an acceptable cost.

Fiscal Rebalancing

In the medium term, the United States needs fiscal reform that puts the country on a pathway to sustainable economic growth. However, it must also avoid a sharp near-term fiscal contraction that could endanger the recovery.[244]

The first priority is to manage continued fiscal stalemate in the wake of the compromise deal struck on January 1, 2013, when Congress passed the American Taxpayer Relief Act. This made permanent the Bush-era income tax cuts for those earning under US$400,000 and permanently patched the alternative minimum tax, extended emergency unemployment insurance benefits for a year, averted scheduled cuts to Medicare payments to doctors, and delayed the large automatic cuts in discretionary spending by two months.[245] The measures in this bill will not be enough to resolve the country's long-term budget problem, and US$1.4 trillion in additional savings are required to stabilize the public debt over this decade.[246]

The short-term nature of the deal on the debt ceiling, the need to set a new budget, and the need to deal with spending cuts under the sequester all ensure that fiscal issues will continue to dominate American politics. Despite intense partisan differences on this issue, policymakers need to send a clear signal that expenditures will not be significantly cut until the recovery has become entrenched and the labor market has shown significant signs of recovery. Medium- and long-term fiscal retrenchment should then be used as a "reverse stimulus" when growth is strong, restraining inflation and allowing interest rates to rise more slowly than would otherwise be the case.

A related priority is to address the fiscal crisis at the state and city levels; thirty-one states faced a US$55 billion shortfall in fiscal 2013, and a growing number of municipalities filed for bankruptcy.[247] States have felt the impact of the sequestration, with more than US$5 billion in cuts levied against states in 2013.[248] As the State Budget Crisis Task Force has demonstrated, state budgets have become procyclical, while their deficits are now structural and will not necessarily be closed as the economy recovers.[249] Without action, fiscal pressures are likely to have a serious impact on regional and local labor markets and on education, health, and social sector expenditures. In Alabama, for example, the Jefferson County bankruptcy has seen residents in some of the poorest districts cut off from water mains and sanitation.[250]

Beyond the overall aim of reducing public debt and putting the federal budget on a sustainable trajectory, a fiscal reform package should have three aims:

—*Reform the tax code* in ways that tackle income inequality by restructuring provisions for lower- and middle-income taxpayers. Allowing the Bush tax cuts to expire for incomes above US$400,000 was a first step toward addressing this challenge.

—*Cut inefficient subsidies,* especially those for fossil fuels, in line with the commitment made by leaders at the G-20 in Pittsburgh in 2009. Removing these subsidies may be feasible as part of a broader fiscal package, raising up to US$52 billion in additional revenue at a time when the oil and gas sector is performing strongly and does not need public support.[251]

—*Shift taxation from labor to carbon.* Although a carbon tax is politically difficult, it may win support if it is revenue neutral or is used to prevent income taxes from rising. At US$15 per metric ton of carbon dioxide and rising 4 percent in real terms to 2050, it could raise revenues of US$80 billion initially and US$310 billion by 2050, while also reducing U.S. carbon dioxide emissions by 2.5 metric tons (34 percent) by 2050.[252]

Conclusion: Renewing America's Global Leadership

We live in an era of rapid change and great uncertainty. This crisis of globalization can best be understood as a crisis of unsustainability as the world struggles to provide a decent standard of living to more than 7 billion people at a time when resources are constrained, natural systems are under threat, and international and national institutions are ill equipped to manage contemporary risks.

This is not an easy world in which to lead. Trust is low within and between countries. Levels of uncertainty are high, complicating geopolitical calculations and hampering investment decisions. Governments spend much of their time fighting fires and have little time to shape new policies, approaches, and solutions. The United States' effectiveness in acting alone is diminished, particularly in nondefense-related areas such as economic and environmental challenges, where the rising powers have not yet been prepared to invest in global leadership. The result is a leadership deficit on the defining challenges of our age: building a more resilient economic system, creating productive employment for the world's young people, fostering stable markets for food, energy, and other natural resources, and supporting efforts to stabilize the climate.

Is America equipped to renew its leadership on these issues? It has huge potential for technological and social innovation. Its economy has global reach, and its policies and actions shape markets. Favorable demographics, a strengthening economy, growing energy reserves, and a robust and durable geopolitical position all provide the basis for it to take a more confident and assertive stance.

However, American global leadership needs to be underpinned by a robust economy that delivers outcomes for a wider range of its population and at an acceptable environmental cost. Policies that address the key economic, environmental, and social challenges outlined in this chapter will ultimately be the main drivers and determinants of the scope and effectiveness of the United States' global leadership.

These policies would provide a robust foundation for a new era of American leadership, helping President Obama and his successors to strengthen major alliances and to become a more effective actor in key international forums such as the G-20 and the United Nations. In particular, opportunities for international cooperation exist in the following areas:

—*Building the knowledge base needed to underpin international action.* Many of the world's leading scientists are American, and U.S. research centers have comparative advantage across multiple fields. New approaches to both "big" and "open" data have been pioneered in the United States, offering new opportunities to analyze complex crosscutting global issues. The United States should do more to deploy these resources internationally, establishing analytical resources that build consensus on the scope of problems and the nature of potential solutions.

—*Pivoting to the global jobs crisis.* It is not just America and Europe that lack jobs. The job crisis is global. It is most pressing in regions that have the largest proportion of young people in their populations and have the potential to collect a demographic dividend if they can expand their workforce at sufficient speed, but risk a destabilizing demographic disaster if they fail.[253] For example, in Africa millions of youth are flooding into the workforce each year, while 60 percent of the continent's unemployed are between fifteen and twenty-four years of age.[254] American leadership on global employment and on the education and skills needed to underpin it is essential, especially when the G-20 finally is able to turn its attention from the fallout of the 2008 financial crisis.

—*Strengthening the global trade system.* The United States continues to benefit significantly from global trade, and, as 95 percent of consumers reside outside the United States, access to the markets of large emerging economies such as Brazil, China, and India will be increasingly important sources of growth for U.S. businesses. The United States should reinvigorate the World Trade Organization (WTO) as the key venue for trade liberalization, which first will require finishing enough of the WTO Doha Trade Round to declare the round over, thus creating political space for the WTO to focus on new trade priorities such as green energy, food security, and electronic commerce.

—*Demonstrating leadership on energy, food, and other resources.* Resource markets are likely to remain volatile for some years, complicating relationships between major powers, weakening strategically significant fragile states, and discouraging investors from making long-term commitments. The United States, which is enjoying increasing resource security, has new potential to work with China and India, countries that are increasingly exposed to global resource markets. In particular, by exporting the technological and regulatory know-how that has underpinned its shale gas revolution, it can diversify global energy production while promoting a relatively clean energy source. It should also lead on extractive transparency, helping to ensure that supplier countries are more likely to escape from the resource curse. Domestic action on energy subsidies, meanwhile, will make credible the G-20's commitment to reducing global subsidies, while the Obama administration should deepen its support for efforts to provide universal access to modern energy sources by 2030.[255]

—*Reframing action on climate change.* Concerted international action on climate change has no prospect of success without U.S. leadership. In his second term, President Obama has found his position on climate substantially strengthened by the fact that American emissions are falling and are projected to continue to do so. Countries are committed to once again trying to negotiate a new treaty on climate, this time by 2015. The Obama administration should provide an early signal of its level of ambition for this treaty and what it expects other large economies to contribute in terms of timelines and targets for reducing greenhouse gas emissions. It also has the opportunity to open up new space on issues such as black carbon, the Arctic, and noncarbon greenhouse gases such as methane.

President Obama is likely to spend a growing proportion of his second term on foreign policy, especially after the midterm elections in 2014, when attention will begin to focus on electing his successor. He will find that many of America's partners face sustainability challenges that are often more pressing and far-reaching than those experienced by American citizens, sheltered as they are by prosperity, abundant natural resources, and distance from most of the world's trouble spots. This will provide him with an opportunity to begin to forge a new consensus on tackling the most pressing global risks.

As a second-term president, Barack Obama will benefit from the authority that accrues to leaders the longer they spend on the world stage. In his first speech to the United Nations, he told world leaders that they could be remembered for putting off hard choices and failing to adjust to the challenges of the twenty-first century or they could be remembered for their willingness "to see the shoreline beyond the rough waters ahead." He now has an opportunity to help the world to strike out for that shoreline, but like any American president after an election, his time is already running out.[256]

Notes

1. William J. Clinton, "Address before a Joint Session of the Congress on the State of the Union" (American Presidency Project, 2000) (www.presidency.ucsb.edu/ws/index.php?pid=58708#axzz1xmaikXTb).

2. Charles P. Kindleberger, *Manias, Panics, and Crashes: A History of Financial Crises* (New York: John Wiley and Sons, 2001).

3. Amy Belasco, *The Cost of Iraq, Afghanistan, and Other Global War on Terror Operations since 9/11* (Washington: Congressional Research Service, 2011).

4. Federal Reserve, "Changes in U.S. Family Finances from 2007 to 2010: Evidence from the Survey of Consumer Finances," *Federal Reserve Bulletin* 98, no. 2 (June 2012): 1–80 (www.federalreserve.gov/pubs/bulletin/2012/PDF/scf12.pdf).

5. White House, "Remarks by the President in State of the Union Address" (Washington, January 27, 2010) (www.whitehouse.gov/the-press-office/remarks-president-state-union-address).

6. Pew Research Center, "Partisan Polarization Surges in Bush, Obama Years: Trends in American Values, 1987–2012" (Washington, 2012) (www.people-press.org/2012/06/04/section-1-understanding-the-partisan-divide-over-american-values/).

7. Ibid. Council on Foreign Relations, "U.S. Opinion on the Global Economy," in *Public Opinion on Global Issues: A New Digest of U.S. and International Attitudes* (New York: Program on International Policy Attitudes, 2009) (www.cfr.org/world/us-opinion-global-economy/p20137).

8. Coleen Murray, "Treasury Notes: As U.S. Reaches Debt Limit, Geithner Implements Additional Extraordinary Measures to Allow Continued Funding of Government Obligations" (Washington: U.S. Department of the Treasury, 2011) (www.treasury.gov/connect/blog/Pages/Geithner-Implements-Additional-Extraordinary-Measures-to-Allow-Continued-Funding-of-Government-Obligations.aspx).

9. U.S. Congressional Budget Office, "Economic Effects of Reducing the Fiscal Restraint That Is Scheduled to Occur in 2013" (Washington, 2012) (www.cbo.gov/publication/43262).

10. Martin Wolf, "A Permanent Precedent," *Financial Times*, May 17, 2012.

11. Michael Pettis, "The Contentious Debate over China's Economic Transition," *Policy Outlook* (Washington: Carnegie Endowment for International Peace, March 25, 2011) (www.carnegieendowment.org/files/china_econ_transition.pdf).

12. Alex Evans, Bruce Jones, and David Steven, *Confronting the Long Crisis of Globalization: Risk, Resilience, and International Order* (Washington: Brookings, 2010).

13. Richard Black, "Rio Summit: Little Progress, 20 Years On," BBC, June 22, 2012 (www.bbc.co.uk/news/science-environment-18546583).

14. Derek Headey, Sangeetha Malaiyandi, and Shenggen Fan, "Navigating the Perfect Storm: Reflections on the Food, Energy, and Financial Crises," IFPRI Discussion Paper 00889 (Washington: International Food Policy Research Institute, 2009) (www.ifpri.org/sites/default/files/publications/ifpridp00889.pdf).

15. Organization for Economic Cooperation and Development (OECD), *OECD Economic Outlook 2012* (Paris, 2012), table 1.3 (www.oecd.org/eco/economicoutlookanalysisandforecasts/economicoutlook.htm).

16. U.S. Department of Agriculture, "U.S. Drought 2012: Farm and Food Impacts" (Washington, November 9, 2012) (www.ers.usda.gov/topics/in-the-news/us-drought-2012-farm-and-food-impacts.aspx).

17. U.S. Environmental Protection Agency, "Future Temperature Changes" (Washington, n.d.) (www.epa.gov/climatechange/science/future.html).

18. Federal Advisory Committee, "Draft Climate Assessment Report" (Washington: National Climate Assessment and Development Advisory Committee, U.S. Global Change Research Program, January 2013) (http://ncadac.globalchange.gov/download/NCAJan11-2013-publicreviewdraft-fulldraft.pdf).

19. Carbon Dioxide Information Analysis Center, "Fossil-Fuel CO_2 Emissions" (Washington: Oakridge National Laboratory, 2012) (http://cdiac.ornl.gov/trends/emis/meth_reg.html). Oakridge National Laboratory, "Carbon Dioxide Emissions Rebound Quickly after Global Financial Crisis" (Washington: December 5, 2011) (www.ornl.gov/info/press_releases/get_press_release.cfm?ReleaseNumber=mr20111205-00).

20. International Energy Agency, "Global Carbon-Dioxide Emissions Increase by 1.0 Gt in 2011 to Record High" (Paris, May 24, 2012) (www.iea.org/newsroomandevents/news/2012/may/name,27216,en.html).

21. United Nations Environment Program, "The Emissions Gap Report 2013: A UNEP Synthesis Report" (Nairobi: United Nations Environment Program, 2013).

22. Anthony D. Barnosky, Elizabeth A. Hadly, Jordi Bascompte, Eric L. Berlow, James H. Brown, Mikael Fortelius, Wayne M. Getz, John Harte, Alan Hastings, Pablo A. Marquet, Neo D. Martinez, Arne Mooers, Peter Roopnarine, Geerat Vermeij, John W. Williams, Rosemary Gillespie, Justin Kitzes, Charles Marshall, Nicholas Matzke, David P. Mindell, Eloy Revilla, and Adam B. Smith, "Approaching a State Shift in Earth's Biosphere," *Nature* 486 (June 7, 2012): 52–58.

23. Homi Kharas, "The Emerging Middle Class in Developing Countries," OECD Working Paper 285 (Paris: OECD Development Center, 2010) (www.oecd.org/social/povertyreductionandsocialdevelopment/44457738.pdf).

24. Council on Foreign Relations, "U.S. Opinion on the Global Economy."

25. Chris Borick and Rabe Barry, "Continued Rebound in American Belief in Climate Change: Spring 2012 NSAPOCC Findings" (Washington: Brookings, June 11, 2012) (www.brookings.edu/research/papers/2012/06/~/media/Research/Files/Papers/2012/6/11%20climate%20rabe%20borick/NSAPOCC_Belief_Spring%20Formatted.pdf).

26. "Eqecat Sees Sandy-Insured Losses up to $20 Billion in U.S.," Reuters, November 1, 2012 (www.reuters.com/article/2012/11/01/us-storm-sandy-losses-idUSBRE 8A00V620121101).

27. Mark Fischetti, "Did Climate Change Cause Hurricane Sandy?" *Scientific American,* October 30, 2012 (http://blogs.scientificamerican.com/observations/2012/10/30/ did-climate-change-cause-hurricane-sandy/). See also C. H. Greene, "An Arctic Wildcard in the Weather," *Oceanography* 25, no. 2 (2012): 7–9 (www.tos.org/oceanography/ archive/25-2_greene.html).

28. White House, "Remarks by the President on Election Night" (Washington, November 7, 2012) (www.whitehouse.gov/the-press-office/2012/11/07/remarks-president-election-night).

29. Jordi Vaquer, "Reclaiming Democratic Demands from the Populists," Open Democracy, July 10, 2012 (www.opendemocracy.net/jordi-vaquer/reclaiming-democratic-demands-from-populists).

30. Conor Friedersdorf, "The Cult of Smartness: How Meritocracy Is Failing America," *Atlantic,* June 14, 2012.

31. White House, "National Security Strategy" (Washington, 2010) (www.white house.gov/sites/default/files/rss_viewer/national_security_strategy.pdf).

32. U.S. Bureau of Economic Analysis, "National Economic Accounts: Gross Domestic Product" (Washington, U.S. Department of Commerce, 2012) (www.bea.gov/national/ index.htm). U.S. Census Bureau, "Historical National Population Estimates: July 1, 1900, to July 1, 1999" (Washington: Population Estimates Program, Population Division, June 28, 2000) (www.census.gov/popest/data/national/totals/pre-1980/tables/popclockest.txt).

33. These data are for 1948–2011 and from the U.S. Bureau of Labor Statistics (http://data.bls.gov/cgi-bin/surveymost?bls).

34. Michael Greenstone and Adam Looney, "Trends," *Milken Institute Review* (Third Quarter 2011): 11.

35. World Economic Forum, *The Global Competitiveness Report 2013–2014* (Geneva, 2013).

36. European Commission, Eurostat: R&D expenditure data compiled using OECD figures, 2011 (http://epp.eurostat.ec.europa.eu/statistics_explained/index.php/ R_%26_D_expenditure). OECD, *OECD Economic Outlook 2012.* World Bank, World DataBank: World Development Indicators (Washington, 2012) (http://databank.world bank.org/ddp/home.do).

37. Times Higher Education, "World University Rankings 2013–14" (London, 2013) (www.timeshighereducation.co.uk/world-university-rankings/2013-14/world-ranking). National Science Foundation, "Academic Research and Development," in *Science and Engineering Indicators 2012,* ch. 5 (Washington, 2012) (www.nsf.gov/statistics/seind12/ c5/c5h.htm). U.S. Patent and Trademark Office, "Extended Year Set: Patents by Country, State, and Year—All Patent Types" (Washington, 2011) (www.uspto.gov/web/offices/ac/ ido/oeip/taf/cst_allh.htm).

38. Mitch Waldrop, *DARPA and the Internet Revolution: 50 Years of Bridging the Gap* (Washington: U.S. Department of Defense, Defense Advanced Research Projects Agency, 2008).

39. Lauren Setar and Matthew MacFarland, "Top 10 Fastest-Growing Industries," *IBISWorld,* Special Report (April 2012) (www.ibisworld.com/Common/MediaCenter/Fastest%20Growing%20Industries.pdf).

40. Abdul Ali, Candida Brush, Julio De Castro, Julian Lange, Thomas Lyons, Moriah Meyskens, Joseph Onochie, Ivory Phinisee, Edward Rogoff, Al Suhu, and John Whitman, *National Entrepreneurial Assessment for the United States of America: 2010 United States Report* (Babson Park, Mass.: Global Entrepreneurship Monitor, 2010). Kelly Services, "Talent Mobility: The Evolving Workforce" (KellyOCG, November 2011) (www.kellyocg.com/Knowledge/Kelly_Global_Workforce_Index/Talent_Mobility_-_The_Evolving_Workforce/).

41. Dane Stangler and Robert E. Litan, "Where Will the Jobs Come From?" in *Firm Foundation and Economic Growth,* Kauffman Foundation Research Series (Kansas City: Ewing Marion Kauffman Foundation, 2009).

42. Amar Bhide, *The Venturesome Economy: How Innovation Sustains Prosperity in a More Connected World* (Princeton University Press, 2008).

43. Ibid.

44. National Bureau of Economic Research, "U.S. Business Cycle Expansions and Contractions" (Cambridge, Mass, 2010) (www.nber.org/cycles.html).

45. C. K. Elwell, *Economic Recovery: Sustaining U.S. Economic Growth in a Post-Crisis Economy* (Washington: Congressional Research Service, 2012) (www.fas.org/sgp/crs/misc/R41332.pdf).

46. World Economic Forum, *The Global Competitiveness Report 2012–2013* (Geneva, 2012) (www3.weforum.org/docs/WEF_GlobalCompetitivenessReport_2012-13.pdf).

47. Ibid.

48. Michael E. Porter and Jan W. Rivkin, *Prosperity at Risk: Findings of Harvard Business School's Survey on U.S. Competitiveness* (Harvard Business School, 2012).

49. James Manyika, Susan Lund, Byron Auguste, Lenny Mendonca, Tim Welsh, and Sreenivas Ramaswamy, *An Economy That Works: Job Creation and America's Future* (San Francisco: McKinsey Global Institute, 2011).

50. World Bank, World DataBank.

51. Greenstone and Looney, "Trends."

52. World Economic Forum, *Global Competitiveness Report 2013–2014.*

53. American Society of Civil Engineers, *Report Card for America's Infrastructure* (Reston, Va., 2009), p. 7 (http://infrastructurereportcard.org/sites/default/files/RC2009_full_report.pdf).

54. OECD, *Lessons from PISA for the United States: Strong Performers and Successful Reformers in Education* (Paris, 2011).

55. Federal Reserve Bank of New York, *Quarterly Report on Household Debt and Credit* (New York, November 2012) (www.newyorkfed.org/research/national_economy/householdcredit/DistrictReport_Q32012.pdf).

56. Charles Roxburgh, Susan Lund, Tony Wimmer, Eric Amar, Charles Atkins, Ju-Hon Kwek, Richard Dobbs, and James Manyika, *Debt and Deleveraging: The Global Credit Bubble and Its Economic Consequences: Updated Analysis* (San Francisco: McKinsey Global Institute, 2011).

57. Ibid.

58. Karen Dynan, *Is A Household Debt Overhang Holding Back Consumption?* (Washington: Brookings, 2012); U.S. Department of Commerce, *National Data: GDP and Personal Income* (Washington, 2012) (www.bea.gov/iTable/index_nipa.cfm).

59. "U.S. Total Government Debt," USGovernmentSpending.com, 2013 (www.usgovernmentspending.com/spending_chart_1940_2016USp_13s1li011lcn_H0t_US_Total_Government_Debt).

60. U.S. Congressional Budget Office, "The Budget and Economic Outlook: Fiscal Years 2012 to 2022" (Washington, 2012) (www.cbo.gov/sites/default/files/cbofiles/attachments/01-31-2012_Outlook.pdf).

61. U.S. Congressional Budget Office, "Economic Effects of Policies Contributing to Fiscal Tightening in 2013" (Washington, November 2012).

62. Federal Reserve, "Chairman Ben S. Bernanke at the Banque de France Financial Stability Review Launch Event, Paris" (Washington, February 18, 2011) (www.federalreserve.gov/newsevents/speech/bernanke20110218a.htm).

63. United Nations Department of Economics and Social Affairs (UNDESA), *World Population Prospects, the 2010 Revision* (New York, 2010) (http://esa.un.org/unpd/wpp/index.htm).

64. Ibid. U.S. National Center for Education Statistics, "Digest of Education Statistics: Table 276, College Enrollment of Recent High School Completers" (Washington, 2011) (www.census.gov/compendia/statab/2012/tables/12s0276.xls).

65. U.S. Bureau of Economic Analysis, "National Income and Product Accounts Tables" (Washington, 2012) (www.bea.gov/iTable/iTable.cfm?ReqID=9&step=1). Anthony B. Atkinson, Thomas Piketty, and Emmanual Saez, "Top Incomes in the Long Run of History," *Journal of Economic Literature* 49, no. 1 (2011): 3–71 (http://elsa.berkeley.edu/~saez/atkinson-piketty-saezJEL10.pdf).

66. Atkinson, Thomas, and Saez, "Top Incomes," table 2.3.5.

67. OECD, Better Life Index 2012 (www.oecdbetterlifeindex.org).

68. Federal Reserve Bank of New York, "Quarterly Report on Household Debt and Credit" (New York, May 2012) (www.newyorkfed.org/research/national_economy/householdcredit/DistrictReport_Q12012.pdf).

69. Ibid.

70. OECD, "Income Distribution: Inequality Measure" (http://stats.oecd.org/Index.aspx?DatasetCode=INEQUALITY). Congressional Budget Office data are based on market income, before taxes and government transfers.

71. Uri Dadush, Kemal Dervis, Sarah Puritz Milsom, and Bennett Stancil, *Inequality in America: Facts, Trends, and International Perspectives* (Washington: Brookings, 2012), p. 14.

72. U.S. Department of the Treasury, *Income Mobility in the U.S. from 1996 to 2005* (Washington: U.S. Government Printing Office, 2007) (www.treasury.gov/resource-center/tax-policy/Documents/incomemobilitystudy03-08revise.pdf).

73. OECD, "A Family Affair: Intergenerational Social Mobility across OECD Countries," in *Economic Policy Reforms: Going for Growth 2010,* ch. 5 (Paris, 2010).

74. OECD, "Growing Income Inequality in OECD Countries: What Drives It and How Can Policy Tackle It?" Paper presented at Forum on Tackling Inequality, Paris, May 2, 2011; Pew Research Center, "Partisan Polarization Surges."

75. Linda Levine, *The U.S. Income Distribution and Mobility: Trends and International Comparisons* (Washington: Congressional Research Service, 2012) (www.fas.org/sgp/crs/misc/R42400.pdf).

76. OECD, *Divided We Stand: Why Inequality Keeps Rising* (Paris, 2011).

77. International Monetary Fund, "IMF e-Library Data" (Washington, 2011) (http://elibrary-data.imf.org/). This figure represents imports in goods to the United States from developing countries, excluding Brazil, Russia, India, China, and South Africa (the BRICS). The figure is substantially higher for emerging and developing countries, at 55 percent, which includes the BRICS.

78. Paul Krugman, "Trade and Inequality Revisited," voxEU, June 15, 2007 (www.voxeu.org/index.php?q=node/261); OECD, *Divided We Stand*.

79. World Bank, World DataBank.

80. OECD, *Divided We Stand*.

81. Levine, *U.S. Income Distribution*.

82. Tax Policy Center, "Historical Effective Federal Tax Rates for All Households, April 4, 2011" (www.taxpolicycenter.org/taxfacts/displayafact.cfm?Docid=456).

83. U.S. Bureau of Labor Statistics, "Economic News Release: Union Membership (Annual)" (Washington, 2012) (www.bls.gov/news.release/union2.toc.htm).

84. OECD, *Divided We Stand*.

85. U.S. Bureau of Transportation, Statistics, Research, and Innovative Technology Administration, "4-2 Average Household Expenditures by Major Spending Category: 2010" (Washington, 2012) (www.bts.gov/publications/pocket_guide_to_transportation/2012/html/figure_04_02_table.html).

86. OECD, "OECD Health Data: How Does Germany Compare?" (Paris, 2012) (www.oecd.org/health/healthpoliciesanddata/BriefingNoteGERMANY2012.pdf).

87. Executive Office of the President, Council of Economic Advisers, "The Economic Effects of Health Care Reform on Small Business and Their Employees" (Washington, July 25, 2009) (www.whitehouse.gov/assets/documents/CEA-smallbusiness-july24.pdf).

88. Atlantic/Aspen Institute, "The Atlantic/Aspen Institute American Values Survey" (Washington, 2012) (www.slideshare.net/BMGlobalNews/the-atlanticaspen-institute-american-values-survey).

89. Pew Charitable Trusts, *Economic Mobility and the American Dream: Where Do We Stand in the Wake of the Great Recession?* (Washington, 2011) (www.pewtrusts.org/uploadedFiles/wwwpewtrustsorg/Reports/Economic_Mobility/Economic_Mobility_Post_Recession_Poll.pdf).

90. White House, "About the Council on Environmental Quality" (Washington, 2012) (www.whitehouse.gov/administration/eop/ceq/about). U.S. Environmental Protection Agency, "EPA History" (Washington, 2012) (www.epa.gov/history/).

91. U.S. Environmental Protection Agency, "Clean Air Act" (Washington, 2012) (www.epa.gov/air/caa/); U.S. Environmental Protection Agency, "Clean Water Act" (Washington, 2012) (http://cfpub.epa.gov/npdes/cwa.cfm?program_id=45).

92. Jan-Peter Voss, "Innovation Processes in Governance: The Development of Emissions Trading as a New Policy Instrument," *Science and Public Policy* 5, no. 34 (2007–6): 329–43.

93. Gabriel Chan, Robert Stavins, Robert Stowe, and Richard Sweeney, "The SO_2 Allowance Trading System and the Clean Air Act Amendments of 1990: Reflections on Twenty Years of Policy Innovation" (Harvard Kennedy School, 2012) (www.hks.harvard. edu/m-rcbg/heep/papers/SO2-Brief_digital_final.pdf). Clean Air Market Programs, "Cap and Trade: Acid Rain Program Results" (Washington: U.S. Environmental Protection Agency, n.d.) (www.epa.gov/capandtrade/documents/ctresults.pdf).

94. U.S. Environmental Protection Agency, "Six Common Pollutants," in *Our Nation's Air: Status and Trends through 2010*, Report EPA-454/R-12-001 (Washington, 2012).

95. U.S. Environmental Protection Agency, "Progress in Water Quality: An Evaluation of the National Investment in Municipal Wastewater Treatment" (Washington, 2000) (http://water.epa.gov/polwaste/wastewater/treatment/benefits.cfm).

96. U.S. Energy Information Administration, "Country Analysis Brief: Total Primary Energy (Quadrillion Btu)" (Washington, 2012) (www.eia.gov/countries/country-data.cfm?fips=US&trk=m#tpe).

97. Scott Barrett, *Why Cooperate? The Incentive to Supply Global Public Goods* (Oxford University Press, 2007).

98. Pew Research Center, "Partisan Polarization Surges."

99. Ibid.

100. U.S. Congress, Joint Economic Committee, *The 1990 Economic Report of the President: Hearings before the Joint Economic Committee, Congress of the United States, One Hundred First Congress, Second Session, January 24 and 30, February 2 and 8, and March 15, 1990* (Washington, 1990), p. 212 (http://openlibrary.org/b/OL1986428M/1990_Economic_report_of_the_President). Intergovernmental Negotiating Committee for a Framework Convention on Climate Change, "Preparation of a Framework Convention on Climate Change: Set of Informal Papers Provided by Delegations, Related to the Preparation of a Framework Convention on Climate Change, Note by the Secretariat, Second Session, June 19–28, 1991," ref A/AC.237/Misc.1, 13, 94 (Bonn, 1991) (http://unfccc. int/documentation/documents/advanced_search/items/6911.php?priref=600000014).

101. Ibid, p. 2.

102. White House, "Text of a Letter from the President to Senators Hagel, Helms, Craig, and Roberts, March 13, 2001" (Washington, 2001) (http://georgewbush-white house.archives.gov/news/releases/2001/03/20010314.html).

103. Worldwatch Institute, *The State of Consumption Today* (Washington, 2011) (www.worldwatch.org/node/810).

104. James D. Hamilton, "Oil Prices, Exhaustible Resources, and Economic Growth" (University of California San Diego, October 18, 2011) (http://dss.ucsd.edu/~jhamilto/handbook_climate.pdf).

105. Joachim von Braun, "High and Rising Food Prices: Why Are They Rising, Who Is Affected, How Are They Affected, and What Should Be Done?" Paper presented at U.S. Agency for International Development (USAID) conference on "Addressing the Challenges of a Changing World Food Situation: Preventing Crisis and Leveraging Opportunity," April 11, 2008 (www.ifpri.org/sites/default/files/pubs/presentations/2008 0411jvbfoodprices.pdf). U.S. Energy Information Administration, "Short-Term Energy Outlook" (Washington, July 10, 2012) (www.eia.gov/forecasts/steo/index.cfm).

106. Muriel Boselli, "Oil Price Still Serious Risk to Global Recovery: IEA," Reuters, May 16, 2012. John Elder and A. Serletis, "Oil Price Uncertainty," *Journal of Money, Credit, and Banking* 32 (2010): 400–16 (http://papers.ssrn.com/sol3/papers.cfm?abstract_id=908675).

107. International Monetary Fund (IMF), *World Economic Outlook: Tensions from the Two-Speed Recovery—Unemployment, Commodities, and Capital Flows* (Washington, 2011) (www.imf.org/external/pubs/ft/weo/2011/01/index.htm).

108. U.S. Energy Information Administration, "International Energy Statistics: Per Capita Carbon Dioxide Emissions from the Consumption of Energy (Metric Tons of Carbon Dioxide per Person)" (Washington, 2013) (www.eia.gov/cfapps/ipdbproject/iedindex3.cfm?tid=90&pid=45&aid=8&cid=regions&syid=2006&eyid=2010&unit=MMTCD).

109. U.S. Energy Information Administration, "Total Carbon Dioxide Emissions from the Consumption of Energy (Million Metric Tons), 1980 to 2011" (Washington, 2013) (www.eia.gov/cfapps/ipdbproject/iedindex3.cfm?tid=90&pid=44&aid=8&cid=US,&syid=1980&eyid=2010&unit=MMTCD). U.S. Department of State, Office of the Special Envoy for Climate Change, "Letter to Mr. Yvo de Boer Regarding the Copenhagen Accord" (Washington, January 28, 2010) (http://unfccc.int/files/meetings/cop_15/copenhagen_accord/application/pdf/unitedstatescphaccord_app.1.pdf).

110. United Nations Environment Program, "The Emissions Gap Report 2013."

111. Sven Harmeling, *Global Climate Index 2011: Who Suffers Most from Extreme Weather Events? Weather-Related Loss Events in 2009 and 1990 to 2009* (Bonn: Germanwatch, 2011).

112. Roger A. Pielke Jr., Joel Gratz, Christopher W. Landsea, Douglas Collins, Mark A. Saunders, and Rade Musulin, "Normalized Hurricane Damage in the United States: 1900–2005," *Natural Hazards Review* 9, no. 1 (2008): 29–42. For GDP projections, see U.S. Congressional Budget Office, "Budget and Economic Outlook: Fiscal Years 2011 to 2021" (Washington, 2011) (www.cbo.gov/publication/21999).

113. James Hansen, Makiko Sato, and Reto Ruedy, "Perceptions of Climate Change: The New Climate Dice" (Columbia University, 2012) (www.columbia.edu/~jeh1/mailings/2012/20120105_PerceptionsAndDice.pdf).

114. Yale Project on Climate Change Communication and George Mason University Center for Climate Change Communication, *Extreme Weather, Climate, and Preparedness in the American Mind* (Yale University, 2012).

115. Maplecroft, "Maplecroft Index Identifies Bahrain, Qatar, Kuwait, and Saudi Arabia as World's Most Water-Stressed Countries" (Bath, May 25, 2011) (http://maplecroft.com/about/news/water_stress_index.html).

116. Office of the Director of National Intelligence, "Global Water Security, 2012" (Washington, 2012) (www.dni.gov/files/documents/Newsroom/Press%20Releases/ICA_Global%20Water%20Security.pdf). Natural Resources Defense Council, "Climate Change, Water, and Risk: Current Water Demands Are Not Sustainable," NRDC Factsheet, 2010 (www.nrdc.org/globalWarming/watersustainability/files/WaterRisk.pdf).

117. National Oceanic and Atmospheric Administration, National Climatic Data Center, "State of the Climate: National Overview, June 2012" (Washington, 2012) (www.ncdc.noaa.gov/sotc/national/2012/6).

118. "GRAINS-U.S. Corn Firm, Soybeans Slip on Rain Forecasts," Reuters, August 2, 2012. U.S. Department of Agriculture, Economic Research Service, "U.S. Drought 2012: Farm and Food Impacts" (Washington, 2012) (www.ers.usda.gov/newsroom/us-drought-2012-farm-and-food-impacts.aspx).

119. Answers to this question vary from 53 to 74 percent saying the wrong track; 26 to 43 percent say the right track in various polls conducted this year. See Marist College Institute for Public Opinion, "McClatchy-Marist Poll National Survey, March 26, 2012" (http://s3.documentcloud.org/documents/328329/mcclatchy-marist-poll-politics.pdf); "Right Direction or Wrong Track: 29% say U.S. Heading in Right Direction," Rasmussen Reports, August 1, 2012 (www.rasmussenreports.com/public_content/politics/mood_of_america/right_direction_or_wrong_track/). Naftali Bendavid, "Country Is Headed in Wrong Direction, 74% Say," *Wall Street Journal*, October 13, 2011 (http://online.wsj.com/article/SB10001424052970204774604576627180456112672.html).

120. John Maynard Keynes, *The Great Slump of 1930* (London: Nation and Athenaeum, 1930).

121. Group of Twenty, "London Summit: Leaders' Statement" (London, April 3, 2009) (www.canadainternational.gc.ca/g20/summit-sommet/g20/declaration_010209.aspx?view=d).

122. Ibid. IMF, *World Economic Outlook: Growth Resuming, Dangers Remain* (Washington, 2012).

123. Gary Burtless, "Employment Gains Keep Pace with Population Growth, but Leave Job Deficit Unchanged" (Washington: Brookings, August 3, 2012) (www.brookings.edu/blogs/jobs/posts/2012/08/03-jobs-burtless).

124. White House, "Blueprint for an America Built to Last" (Washington, January 24, 2012) (www.whitehouse.gov/sites/default/files/blueprint_for_an_america_built_to_last.pdf). Mitt Romney, "Mitt Romney Delivers Remarks: Freedom and Opportunity," March 30, 2012 (www.mittromney.com/blogs/mitts-view/2012/03/mitt-romney-delivers-remarks-wisconsin-freedom-and-opportunity).

125. UNDESA, *World Population Prospects*.

126. U.S. Census Bureau, "The Older Population: 2010" (Washington, November 2011) (www.census.gov/prod/cen2010/briefs/c2010br-09.pdf).

127. U.S. Congressional Budget Office, "The 2012 Long-Term Budget Outlook: Federal Debt Held by the Public, 1912 to 2037" (Washington, June 2012) (www.cbo.gov/sites/default/files/cbofiles/attachments/06-05-Long-Term_Budget_Outlook.pdf).

128. UNDESA, *World Population Prospects*.

129. U.S. Congressional Budget Office, "2012 Long-Term Budget Outlook."

130. UNDESA, *World Urbanization Prospects*. Negative Population Growth, "Historical U.S. Population Growth by Year 1900–1998" (Alexandria, Va., 2012) (www.npg.org/facts/us_historical_pops.htm).

131. Michele Hoyman and Christopher Faricy, "It Takes a Village: A Test of the Creative Class, Social Capital, and Human Capital Theories," *Urban Affairs Review* (January 2009) (http://papers.ssrn.com/sol3/papers.cfm?abstract_id=1313563). Stefan Kratke, "'Creative Cities' and the Rise of the Dealer Class: A Critique of Richard Florida's Approach

to Urban Theory," *International Journal of Urban and Regional Research* 34 (2010): 835–53 (http://onlinelibrary.wiley.com/doi/10.1111/j.1468-2427.2010.00939.x/abstract).

132. Edward L. Glaeser and Matthew E. Kahn, "Sprawl and Urban Growth," NBER Working Paper 9733 (Cambridge, Mass.: National Bureau of Economic Research, 2003) (http://people.missouristate.edu/davidmitchell/Urban/Sprawl%20and%20Urban%20Growth.pdf).

133. U.S. Federal Highway Administration, "Highway Statistics 2008: Licensed Drivers, Vehicle Registrations, and Resident Population" (Washington, 2008) (www.fhwa.dot.gov/policyinformation/statistics/2008/dv1c.cfm).

134. David Leonhardt, "Old vs. Young," *New York Times,* June 22, 2012 (www.nytimes.com/2012/06/24/opinion/sunday/the-generation-gap-is-back.html?_r=1).

135. U.S. Census Bureau, "Voting and Registration: Historical Time Series Tables" (Washington, 2012) (www.census.gov/hhes/www/socdemo/voting/publications/historical/index.html).

136. Mark Hugo Lopez and D'Vera Cohn, "Hispanic Poverty Rate Highest in New Supplemental Census Data" (Washington: Pew Hispanic Center, November 8, 2011) (www.pewhispanic.org/2011/11/08/hispanic-poverty-rate-highest-in-new-supplemental-census-measure/).

137. Pew Charitable Trusts, "Economic Mobility and the American Dream: Examining Racial and Ethnic Differences," Fact Sheet, March 2012 (www.pewtrusts.org/uploadedFiles/wwwpewtrustsorg/Reports/Economic_Mobility/Pew-Economic-Mobility-Race.pdf).

138. Frank Newport, Jeffrey M. Jones, and Lydia Saad, "Democrats More Liberal, Less White Than in 2008: Party Generally Looks Demographically Similar to 2008," Gallup Politics, November 7, 2011 (www.gallup.com/poll/150611/democrats-liberal-less-white-2008.aspx). Pew Research Center, "American Values Survey: Question Database—40e: It Is the Responsibility of the Government to Take Care of People Who Can't Take Care of Themselves" (Washington, 2012) (www.people-press.org/values-questions/q40e/government-should-care-for-people-who-cant-care-for-themselves/#race).

139. Nolan McCarty, Keith T. Poole, and Howard Rosenthal, *Polarized America: The Dance of Ideology and Unequal Riches (Walras-Pareto Lectures)* (MIT Press, 2006).

140. "The Negative Impact of the Use of Filibusters and Holds" (Washington: Brookings, June 23, 2010) (www.brookings.edu/research/testimony/2010/06/23-filibuster-mann).

141. Atif Mian, Amir Sufi, and Francesco Trebbi, "Resolving Debt Overhang: Political Constraints in the Aftermath of Financial Crisis," NBER Working Paper 17831 (Cambridge, Mass.: National Bureau of Economic Research, February 2012) (http://faculty.arts.ubc.ca/ftrebbi/research/mst4.pdf).

142. Bob Woodward, *Maestro: Greenspan's Fed and the American Boom* (New York: Simon and Schuster, 2000).

143. Financial Crisis Inquiry Commission, "The Financial Crisis Inquiry Report: Final Report of the National Commission on the Causes of the Financial and Economic Crisis in the United States" (Washington: Government Printing Office, January 2011) (www.gpo.gov/fdsys/pkg/GPO-FCIC).

144. Harvard Kennedy School, "2006 Social Capital Community Survey, National Sample" (Harvard University, 2006) (www.hks.harvard.edu/saguaro/pdfs/2006SCCSbanner.pdf).

145. Ibid. Robert D. Putnam, *Bowling Alone: The Collapse and Revival of American Community* (New York: Simon and Schuster, 2000).

146. Paul Taylor, Cary Funk, and April Clark, *Americans and Social Trust: Who, Where, and Why* (Washington: Pew Research Center, 2006) (http://pewresearch.org/assets/social/pdf/SocialTrust.pdf).

147. Pew Research Center, "Economy Dominates Public's Agenda, Dims Hopes for Future: Less Optimism about America's Long-Term Prospects" (Washington, January 20, 2011) (www.people-press.org/2011/01/20/section-2-views-of-long-term-future-past/).

148. Pew Research Center, "The Generation Gap and the 2012 Election: Angry Silents, Disengaged Millennials" (Washington, November 3, 2011) (http://pewresearch.org/pubs/2122/generation-gap-barack-obama-mitt-romney-republicans-democrats-silent-generation-millenials-genxers-baby-boomers).

149. H. M. Zullow and M. E. P. Seligman, "Pessimistic Rumination Predicts Defeat of Presidential Candidates, 1900–1984," *Psychological Inquiry* 1, no. 1 (1990): 52–61.

150. White House, "National Security Strategy."

151. Shrey Verma, *Far-Reaching Consequences of the Naxalite Problem in India: Understanding the Maoist Problem* (Santa Clara, Calif.: Rakshak Foundation, 2011) (www.rakshakfoundation.org/wp-content/uploads/2011/08/White-Paper-on-Naxalite-Movement-in-India.pdf). "Spending Shows Focus on Internal Threats," *Wall Street Journal,* March 5, 2012 (http://blogs.wsj.com/chinarealtime/2012/03/05/china-spending-shows-focus-on-internal-threats/).

152. Uri Dadush and William Shaw, *Juggernaut: How Emerging Markets Are Reshaping Globalization* (Washington: Carnegie Endowment for International Peace, 2011) (http://carnegieendowment.org/2011/05/31/juggernaut-how-emerging-markets-are-reshaping-globalization/10a2).

153. International Energy Agency, *Worldwide Trends in Energy Use and Efficiency* (Paris, 2008).

154. U.S. Energy Information Administration, "Total Carbon Dioxide Emissions." National Highway Traffic Safety Administration, "Corporate Average Fuel Economy for MY 2017–MY 2025 Passenger Cars and Light Trucks," Final Regulatory Impact Analysis (Washington, August 2012), p. 55.

155. U.S. Energy Information Administration, *Annual Energy Outlook 2012 with Projections to 2035* (Washington: U.S. Government Printing Office, 2012) (www.eia.gov/forecasts/aeo/pdf/0383(2012).pdf).

156. "Global 2014 E&P Spending Outlook: North American Spending to Accelerate," Barclays Capital, December 9, 2013 (www.pennenergy.com/content/dam/Pennenergy/online-articles/2013/December/Global%202014%20EP%20Spending%20Outlook.pdf).

157. Leonardo Maugeri, "Oil: The Next Revolution; The Unprecedented Upsurge of Oil Production Capacity and What It Means for the World," Discussion Paper 2012-10

(Harvard Kennedy School, Belfer Center for Science and International Affairs, 2012) (http://belfercenter.ksg.harvard.edu/publication/22144/oil.html).

158. Florence Gény, "Can Unconventional Gas Be a Game Changer in European Gas Markets?" (Oxford Institute for Energy Studies, December 2010) (www.sbc.slb.com/SBCInstitute/Publications/~/media/Files/Point%20of%20View%20Docs/Can%20Unconventional%20Gas%20be%20a%20Game%20Changer%20in%20European%20Gas%20Markets.ashx).

159. Federal Reserve Board, "Testimony of Chairman Alan Greenspan: Natural Gas Supply—Before the Committee on Energy and Natural Resources, U.S. Senate, July 10, 2003" (www.federalreserve.gov/boarddocs/testimony/2003/20030710/default.htm).

160. International Energy Agency, *World Energy Outlook 2006* (Paris: OECD, 2006).

161. U.S. Energy Information Administration, "U.S. Proved Reserves Increased Sharply in 2010" (Washington, August 2, 2012) (www.eia.gov/todayinenergy/detail.cfm?id=7370).

162. U.S. Energy Information Administration, "Natural Gas–Shale Gas Production (Billion Cubic Feet)" (Washington, 2012) (www.eia.gov/dnav/ng/ng_prod_shalegas_s1_a.htm). U.S. Energy Information Administration, "Global Natural Gas Prices Vary Considerably" (Washington, September 30, 2011) (www.eia.gov/todayinenergy/detail.cfm?id=3310).

163. Henry D Jacoby, Francis O'Sullivan, and Sergey Paltsev, "The Influence of Shale Gas on U.S. Energy and Environmental Policy," Report 207 (MIT Joint Program on the Science and Policy of Global Change, 2011) (http://globalchange.mit.edu/files/document/MITJPSPGC_Rpt207.pdf).

164. Pew Research Center, "Partisan Polarization Surges."

165. Andrew Hart, Bruce Jones, and David Steven, *Chill Out: Why Cooperation Is Balancing Conflict among Major Powers in the New Arctic* (Washington: Brookings, 2012). Jennifer Steinhauer, "Dole Appears, but G.O.P Rejects a Disabilities Treaty," *New York Times,* December 4, 2012 (www.nytimes.com/2012/12/05/us/despite-doles-wish-gop-rejects-disabilities-treaty.html?_r=0).

166. United Nations Secretary General's High-Level Panel on Global Sustainability, "Resilient People, Resilient Planet: A Future Worth Choosing" (New York, 2012) (www.un.org/gsp/sites/default/files/attachments/GSP_Report_web_final.pdf).

167. National Federation of Republican Assemblies, "RNC Adopts Resolution Exposing Agenda 21" (Destin, Fla., January 18, 2012) (www.republicanassemblies.org/rnc-adopts-resolution-exposing-agenda-21/).

168. Jason Blackstock, "Researchers Can't Regulate Climate Engineering Alone," *Nature* 486 (June 14, 2012).

169. Marc Labonte, *Changing the Federal Reserve's Mandate: An Economic Analysis* (Washington: Congressional Research Service, 2012) (www.fas.org/sgp/crs/misc/R41656.pdf).

170. U.S. Senate Committee on Energy and Natural Resources, "Natural Gas for Transportation" (Washington, July 24, 2012) (www.energy.senate.gov/public/index.cfm/democratic-news?ContentRecord_id=123ecf9c-af80-4dbb-b6d4-e328cd0a53ab).

Alternative Fuels Data Center, "Federal Incentives and Laws for Natural Gas" (Washington: U.S. Department of Energy, 2012) (www.afdc.energy.gov/laws/laws/US/tech/3253).

171. Warwick J. McKibbin, Adele Morris, and Peter J. Wilcoxen, "The Potential Role of a Carbon Tax in U.S. Fiscal Reform" (Washington: Brookings, July 24, 2012) (www.brookings.edu/research/papers/2012/07/carbon-tax-mckibbin-morris-wilcoxen).

172. Anthony D. Barnosky, Elizabeth A. Hadly, Jordi Bascompte, Eric L. Berlow, James H. Brown, Mikael Fortelius, Wayne M. Getz, John Harte, Alan Hastings, Pablo A. Marquet, Neo D. Martinez, Arne Mooers, Peter Roopnarine, Geerat Vermeij, John W. Williams, Rosemary Gillespie, Justin Kitzes, Charles Marshall, Nicholas Matzke, David P. Mindell, Eloy Revilla, and Adam B. Smith, "Approaching a State Shift in Earth's Biosphere," *Nature,* vol. 486 (June 7, 2012): 52–58.

173. Kenneth Lieberthal and Wang Jisi, *Addressing U.S.-China Strategic Distrust,* John L. Thornton China Center Monograph 4 (Washington: Brookings, 2012).

174. U.S. Bureau of Economic Analysis, "National Income and Product Accounts GDP: Third Quarter 2012" (Washington, 2012) (www.bea.gov/newsreleases/national/gdp/gdpnewsrelease.htm).

175. Alex Kowalski and Prashant Gopal, "Housing Starts Jump 15% to Four-Year U.S. High," Bloomberg, October 17, 2012 (www.bloomberg.com/news/2012-10-17/housing-starts-in-u-s-surged-in-september-to-four-year-high.html).

176. Evans, Jones, and Steven, *Confronting the Long Crisis.*

177. Labonte, *Changing the Federal Reserve's Mandate.*

178. House Committee on the Budget, "The Path to Prosperity: Restoring America's Promise; Fiscal Year 2012 Budget Resolution" (Washington, 2012) (www.gop.gov/resources/library/documents/budget/path-to-prosperity.pdf).

179. John M. Broder, "Powerful Shaper of U.S. Rules Quits, with Critics in Wake," *New York Times,* August 3, 2012 (www.nytimes.com/2012/08/04/science/earth/cass-sunstein-to-leave-top-regulatory-post.html?_r=1).

180. Consumer Financial Protection Bureau, "Learn about the Bureau" (www.consumerfinance.gov/the-bureau/).

181. Pew Research Center, "Partisan Polarization Surges."

182. Manyika and others, *An Economy That Works.*

183. International Trade Administration, "Jobs Supported by Exports: An Update" (Washington: U.S. Department of Commerce, March 12, 2012) (www.trade.gov/press/press-releases/2012/jobs-supported-by-exports-031212.pdf); International Trade Administration, "National Export Initiative Fact Sheet," (Washington: U.S. Department of Commerce, 2013) (http://trade.gov/nei/).

184. P. G. Egan and M. Mullin, "Turning Personal Experience into Political Attitudes: The Effect of Local Weather on Americans' Perceptions about Global Warming," *Journal of Politics* 74, no. 3 (July 2012): 796–809.

185. Yale Project on Climate Change Communication and George Mason University Center for Climate Change Communication, *Extreme Weather.*

186. Hansen, Sato, and Ruedy, "Perceptions of Climate Change."

187. Center on Budgets and Policy Priorities, "Chart Book: The Legacy of the Great Recession" (Washington, September 11, 2012) (www.cbpp.org/cms/index.cfm?fa=view&id=3252).

188. U.S. Congressional Budget Office, "Estimated Impact of the American Recovery and Reinvestment Act on Employment and Economic Output from April 2012 through June 2012" (Washington, 2012) (http://cbo.gov/sites/default/files/cbofiles/attachments/08-23-2012-RecoveryAct.pdf).

189. Michael Greenstone and Adam Looney, "The Role of Fiscal Stimulus in the Ongoing Recovery" (Washington: Brookings, 2012) (www.brookings.edu/blogs/jobs/posts/2012/07/06-jobs-greenstone-looney).

190. Daniel J. Wilson, "Fiscal Spending Jobs Multipliers: Evidence from the 2009 American Recovery and Reinvestment Act," Working Paper 2010-17 (San Francisco: Federal Reserve Bank of San Francisco, 2011) (www.frbsf.org/publications/economics/papers/2010/wp10-17bk.pdf).

191. U.S. Federal Reserve, "Speech by Chairman Ben S. Bernanke at the Federal Reserve Bank of Kansas City Economic Symposium, Jackson Hole, Wyoming, August 31, 2012" (www.federalreserve.gov/newsevents/speech/bernanke20120831a.htm).

192. Federal Reserve Bank, Press Release, September 13, 2012 (www.federalreserve.gov/newsevents/press/monetary/20120913a.htm).

193. Scott Sumner, "e-Targeting the Fed," *National Affairs* 9 (Fall 2011): n.p. (www.nationalaffairs.com/publications/detail/re-targeting-the-fed).

194. Robin Harding and James Politi, "Fed Risks Political Fallout from QE3," *Financial Times,* September 14, 2012 (www.ft.com/intl/cms/s/0/b7de9070-fe77-11e1-8028-00144feabdc0.html#axzz26TJAxKZu). Federal Reserve Bank, Press Release.

195. Ayşegül Şahin, Joseph Song, Giorgio Topa, and Giovanni L. Violante, "Mismatch Unemployment" (New York: Federal Reserve of New York, 2012) (www.newyorkfed.org/research/economists/sahin/USmismatch.pdf).

196. Nir Jaimovich and Henry E. Siu, "The Trend Is the Cycle: Job Polarization and Jobless Recoveries" (University of California Berkeley, March 31, 2012) (http://faculty.arts.ubc.ca/hsiu/research/polar20120331.pdf).

197. U.S. Bureau of Labor Statistics, "Economics News Release: Table A-15. Alternative Measures of Labor Underutilization" (Washington: U.S. Department of Labor, September 7, 2012) (www.bls.gov/news.release/empsit.t15.htm).

198. Federal Reserve Bank, "Testimony of Chairman Ben S. Bernanke at the Committee on the Budget, U.S. House of Representatives, Washington, D.C.—The Economic Outlook and the Federal Budget Situation" (New York, February 2, 2012) (www.federalreserve.gov/newsevents/testimony/bernanke20120202a.htm). Chairman Bernanke presented identical remarks before the Committee on the Budget, U.S. Senate, on February 7, 2012.

199. Ibid.

200. National Employment Law Project, "The Low-Wage Recovery and Growing Inequality," Data Brief (New York, August 2012) (www.nelp.org/page/-/Job_Creation/LowWageRecovery2012.pdf?nocdn=1).

201. Manyika and others, *An Economy That Works.*

202. Justin Weidner and John C. Williams, "What Is the New Normal Unemployment Rate?" *FRBSF Economic Letter,* February 14, 2011 (www.frbsf.org/publications/economics/letter/2011/el2011-05.html).

203. Lena Jacobi and Jochen Kluve, "Before and After the Hartz Reforms: The Performance of Active Labour Market Policy in Germany," ZAF 1/2007 (Nuremburg: Institute for Employment Research, 2007) (http://doku.iab.de/zaf/2007/2007_1_zaf_jacobi_kluve.pdf).

204. Martin Neil Baily, "U.S. Manufacturing Makes a Comeback" (Washington: Brookings, 2012) (www.brookings.edu/research/opinions/2012/05/18-manufacturing-comeback-katz-baily).

205. "A Third Industrial Revolution," *Economist,* April 21, 2012 (www.economist.com/node/21552901).

206. Bruce Katz, "Will the Next President Remake Federalism?" (Washington, Brookings, March 18, 2012) (www.brookings.edu/research/articles/2012/03/18-federalism-katz).

207. OECD, "Pisa 2009 Results: Executive Summary" (Paris: OECD, 2010), fig. 1 (www.oecd.org/pisa/46643496.pdf).

208. McKinsey and Company, *The Economic Impact of the Achievement Gap in America's Schools* (New York, 2009) (http://mckinseyonsociety.com/downloads/reports/Education/achievement_gap_report.pdf).

209. Meghan Brenneman, Patrick Callan, Peter Ewell, Joni Finney, Dennis Jones, and Stacey Zis, *Good Policy, Good Practice II: Improving Outcomes and Productivity in Higher Education: A Guide for Policymakers,* Joint Report (Washington: National Center for Public Policy and Higher Education and National Center for Higher Education Management Systems, November 2010).

210. Democratic National Committee, "2012 Democratic National Platform: Moving America Forward" (www.democrats.org/democratic-national-platform).

211. McKinsey and Company, *How the World's Best-Performing School Systems Come Out on Top* (New York, 2007) (http://mckinseyonsociety.com/downloads/reports/Education/Worlds_School_Systems_Final.pdf).

212. White House, Office of the Press Secretary, "President Obama to Announce Launch of Skills for America's Future" (Washington, October 2010).

213. Harry J. Holzer, "Raising Job Quality and Skills for American Workers: Creating More-Effective Education and Workforce Development Systems in the States," Discussion Paper 2011-10 (Washington: Hamilton Project, 2011) (www.hamiltonproject.org/files/downloads_and_links/11_workforce_holzer_paper.pdf).

214. World Economic Forum, *Global Competitiveness Report 2011–2012.*

215. American Society of Civil Engineers, *Report Card for America's Infrastructure.*

216. U.S. Congressional Budget Office, *Public Spending on Transportation and Water Infrastructure* (Washington, 2010) (www.cbo.gov/sites/default/files/cbofiles/ftpdocs/119xx/doc11940/11-17-infrastructure.pdf).

217. Pinaki Chakraborty and Yan Zhang, "Economic Reforms and Infrastructure Spending: Evidence from China and India," UNU Research Paper 2009/43 (Tokyo: United Nations University, 2009) (www.wider.unu.edu/publications/working-papers/research-papers/2009/en_GB/rp2009-43/).

218. World Resources Institute, "EMBARQ: The WRI Center for Sustainable Transport" (Washington, 2012) (www.wri.org/project/embarq).

219. Glen Weisbrod and Arlee Reno, *Economic Impacts of Public Transportation Investment,* Report prepared for the American Public Transportation Association, October 2009.

220. Ken Berlin, Reed Hundt, Mark Muro, and Devanshree Saha, *State Clean Energy Finance Banks: New Investment Facilities for Clean Energy Deployment,* Report by the Brookings-Rockefeller Project on State and Metropolitan Innovation (Washington: Brookings, 2012). NYGreenBook, "About My Green Bank" (http://greenbank.ny.gov/About-NY-Green-Bank.aspx).

221. Stephanie Chang, "Infrastructure Resilience to Disasters," *Bridge* 39, no. 4 (Winter 2009): 36–41 (www.nae.edu/File.aspx?id=17673).

222. White House, Office of the Press Secretary, "Remarks by the President in State of the Union Address" (Washington, February 12, 2013) (www.whitehouse.gov/the-press-office/2013/02/12/remarks-president-state-union-address).

223. Ibid.

224. Michael Rambert and Sidney Wigfall, "Leveraging Private Equity with Government Business Incentive Programs," *American Venture Magazine* (July 2002).

225. William Kerr and William Lincoln, "The Supply Side of Innovation: H-1B Visa Reforms and U.S. Ethnic Invention," NBER Working Paper 15768 (Cambridge, Mass.: National Bureau of Economic Research, 2010).

226. Bracken Hendricks, Sean Pool, and Lisbeth Kaufman, "Low-Carbon Innovation: A Uniquely American Strategy for Industrial Renewal," Report for the Center for American Progress and Global Climate Network (Washington, May 2011).

227. White House, "2012 State of the Union Address" (www.whitehouse.gov/photos-and-video/video/2012/01/25/2012-state-union-address-enhanced-version#transcript).

228. U.S. Energy Information Administration, *Annual Energy Outlook 2012.*

229. Michael Levi, "A Strategy for U.S. Natural Gas Exports," Discussion Paper 2012-04 (Washington: Hamilton Project, 2012) (www.brookings.edu/~/media/research/files/papers/2012/6/13%20exports%20levi/06_exports_levi.pdf).

230. Joe Romm, "Natural Gas Is a Bridge to Nowhere—Absent a Serious Price for Global Warming Pollution," Think Progress, January 24, 2012 (thinkprogress.org/climate/2012/01/24/407765/natural-gas-is-a-bridge-to-nowhere-price-for-global-warming-pollution/).

231. U.S. Energy Information Administration, "Projected Retirements of Coal-Fired Power Plants" (Washington, July 31, 2012) (www.eia.gov/todayinenergy/detail.cfm?id=7330).

232. Ibid. U.S. Energy Information Administration, "27 Gigawatts of Coal-Fired Capacity to Retire over Next Five Years" (Washington, July 27, 2012) (www.eia.gov/todayinenergy/detail.cfm?id=7290).

233. U.S. Energy Information Administration, *Quarterly Coal Report* (Washington, October 2012) (www.eia.gov/coal/production/quarterly/).

234. Ben Jervey, "Coal Train to Boardman: EPA Warns of 'Significant' Public Health Threats in Northwest Coal Export Proposal," Desmogblog.com, April 26, 2012 (http://desmogblog.com/coal-train-boardman-epa-warns-significant-public-health-threats-northwest-coal-export-proposal).

235. Ed Crooks and Sylvia Pfeifer, "U.S. Coal Exports to Europe Soar," *Financial Times,* October 3, 2012 (www.ft.com/cms/s/0/fbf0b9fa-0d63-11e2-97a1-00144feabdc0. html#axzz291Mf1lxR).

236. Natural Gas Vehicles for America, "United States Senate Energy and Natural Resources Committee—Opportunities for Current Level of Investment in, and Barriers to, the Expanded Usage of Natural Gas as a Fuel for Transportation" (Washington, July 24, 2012) (www.ngvc.org/pdfs/Statement_of_NGVA_SperawFinal.pdf).

237. White House, "Obama Administration Announces Loan Guarantees to Construct New Nuclear Power Reactors in Georgia" (Washington, February 16, 2010) (www. whitehouse.gov/the-press-office/obama-administration-announces-loan-guarantees-construct-new-nuclear-power-reactors). Jim Snyder and Katarzyna Klimasinska, "Constellation Nuclear Loan Pullout Tests Obama Resolve to Revive Industry," Bloomberg, October 12, 2010 (www.bloomberg.com/news/2010-10-12/constellation-nuclear-loan-guarantee-pullout-tests-obama-s-taste-for-risk.html).

238. U.S. Energy Information Administration, "Energy in Brief" (Washington, 2012) (www.eia.gov/energy_in_brief/nuclear_industry.cfm).

239. Some useful sources are given by Brad Plumer, "The U.S. Is Getting More Oil-Efficient—but Not Quickly Enough," *Washington Post,* February 24, 2012 (www. washingtonpost.com/blogs/ezra-klein/post/americas-getting-more-oil-efficient--but-not-quickly-enough/2012/02/24/gIQAvV6lXR_blog.html).

240. Richard G. Newell, Adam B. Jaffe, and Robert N. Stavins, "The Induced Innovation Hypothesis and Energy-Savings Technological Change," in *Technological Change and the Environment,* edited by Arnulf Grubler, Nebojsa Nakicenovic, and William D. Nordhaus (Washington: Resources for the Future, 2002), p. 97.

241. Christopher R. Knittel, "Leveling the Playing Field for Natural Gas in Transportation," Discussion Paper 2012-03 (Washington: Hamilton Project, 2012) (www.hamilton project.org/files/downloads_and_links/06_transportation_knittel.pdf).

242. Hamilton Project, "Promoting Clean Energy in the American Power Sector," Policy Brief 2011-04 (Washington, 2011) (www.hamiltonproject.org/files/downloads_ and_links/05_clean_energy_aldy_brief.pdf).

243. William E. Rees, "Building More Sustainable Cities," *Scientific American,* March 12, 2009 (www.scientificamerican.com/article.cfm?id=building-more-sustainable-cities).

244. U.S. Federal Reserve, "Speech by Chairman Ben S. Bernanke."

245. Michael Greenstone and Adam Looney, "The Fiscal Cliff and Our Long-Run Budget Challenge" (Washington: Brookings Institution, January 4, 2013) (www.brookings. edu/blogs/jobs/posts/2013/01/04-fiscal-cliff-budget-greenstone-looney).

246. Richard Kogan, "To Stabilize the Debt, Policymakers Should Seek Another $1.4 Trillion in Deficit Savings" (Washington: Center on Budget and Policy Priorities, January 9, 2013).

247. Phil Oliff, Chris Mai, and Vincent Palacios, "States Continue to Feel Recession's Impact" (Washington: Center on Budget and Policy Priorities, 2012) (www.cbpp.org/ files/2-8-08sfp.pdf).

248. State Budget Crisis Task Force, *Report of the State Budget Crisis Task Force, Final Report* (New York, 2014) (www.statebudgetcrisis.org/wpcms/wp-content/images/ SBCTF_FINALREPORT1.pdf).

249. State Budget Crisis Task Force, *Report of the State Budget Crisis Task Force* (New York, 2012) (www.statebudgetcrisis.org/wpcms/report-1).

250. Brian Wheeler, "The Scandal of the Alabama Poor Cut off from Water," BBC News, December 14, 2011 (www.bbc.co.uk/news/magazine-16037798).

251. Oil Change International, "The Price of Oil" (Washington, 2012) (http://price ofoil.org/fossil-fuel-subsidies/).

252. Warwick J. McKibbin, Adele Morris, and Peter J. Wilcoxen, "Potential Role of a Carbon Tax" (Washington: Brookings, July 24, 2012). An additional estimate of possible tax revenues from a carbon tax was presented by the Congressional Research Service in September 2012. See Jonathan Ramseur, Jane Leggett, and Molly Sherlock, *Carbon Tax: Deficit Reduction and Other Considerations,* Congressional Research Service (CRS) Report for Congress (Washington, September 17, 2012). See also the recommendations on international policy in this chapter.

253. David Bloom and David Canning, "The Health and Wealth of Nations," *Science,* February 18, 2000 (www.sciencemag.org/content/287/5456/1207.short).

254. African Development Bank, OECD, United Nations Development Program, and United Nations Economic Commission for Africa, *African Economic Outlook 2012: Promoting Youth Employment* (Abidjan: African Development Bank, 2012) (www.iza.org/conference_files/worldb2012/rielaender_j8363.pdf).

255. Hilary Clinton, "Energy Diplomacy in the 21st Century," Speech at Georgetown University, October 18, 2012 (www.state.gov/secretary/rm/2012/10/199330.htm).

256. "Obama's Speech to the United Nations General Assembly," *New York Times,* September 24, 2009 (www.nytimes.com/2009/09/24/us/politics/24prexy.text.html?pagewanted=all).

14

Governance Challenges and the Role of the United States in the New Energy Landscape

KEVIN MASSY

Much of the discussion on global energy governance has focused on ways in which states competing for finite resources can work together to ensure the stability or sustainability of energy production, trade, or consumption for mutual benefit. In general, energy trade is governed reasonably successfully by the logic of the market, with price signals determining the levels of supply, demand, and investment. Even in a system of self-interested actors who operate in isolation and see energy as a zero-sum calculation (if I get the next barrel of oil, you don't), the simple presence of the next barrel of oil—or cubic foot of gas or ton of coal—lowers the price and increases global welfare irrespective of who gets it.

However, the market works only if certain conditions are met: participants must have access to sufficient information to make informed investment decisions, capital and goods have to be allowed to flow to where they can realize their economic value, competition must be permitted, and transactions have to consider the full costs associated with them. Where such criteria are not present, the market is likely to fail, leading to either overinvestment or underinvestment, with negative consequences for stability, production, and consumption. This chapter identifies five factors that are likely to challenge the functioning of the market in the current energy landscape. It posits that a shifting macroeconomic landscape, the increasing prominence of new state-backed actors, the increasing technical and political complexity around energy production, the globalization of technology itself, and the externalized costs of greenhouse gas emissions should force a reassessment of global energy governance. It poses that the United States finds itself in a unique position to address these challenges and to promote improved market function and overall energy governance.

Governance Challenges in the New Energy Landscape

Five factors are challenging the functioning of the energy market and will require a reassessment of global energy governance.

Changing Consumer-Producer Dynamics

The energy sector is witnessing a structural and permanent shift in global consumption and production patterns. For the past fifty years, the predominant consumer-producer relationships in the energy sector were between the oil-producing regions of the Middle East and the industrial economies of the Organization for Economic Cooperation and Development (OECD). While this axis of energy trade prevailed, energy governance was determined by bilateral contracts—both financial and political—between producers and consumers and by organizations representing producer and consumer nations. The formation of the Organization of Petroleum Exporting Countries (OPEC) in 1960 and the manifestation of the market power of producers in the oil shock of 1973 were countered by the formation of the International Energy Agency (IEA) that same year. Throughout the last quarter of the twentieth century and the first decade of the twenty-first, trade in global energy—the vast majority of which was in crude oil—took place within a framework of OPEC-IEA governance. While one does not need to be an energy analyst to know that oil markets have not functioned flawlessly during that time, this framework provided some price stability to market participants, mainly by offering transparency and certainty around the volume of supply and demand. Through OPEC's production targets and the IEA's thorough demand assessments, consumers and producers have had access to the information necessary to formulate reasonable expectations about the future and therefore to set prices.

Toward the end of the 2010s, economic, demographic, and technological shifts began to erode the traditional axis of energy trade and the relevance of the existing oil market–governance framework. Following two decades of rapid economic growth, China became the world's largest net energy consumer in 2010. In 2013 it overtook the United States to become the largest net importer of oil (the United States regained the top spot in 2014). India has overtaken Russia as the world's third largest energy consumer and is expected to see its energy demand more than double between 2010 and 2035.[1] The Middle East and Latin America are expected to see their energy demand rise 62 and 54 percent, respectively, over the same period.[2] The growth in demand from emerging-market countries—particularly in Asia—is coinciding with a decline in demand among the OECD countries owing to increased efficiency and stable or declining populations. The long-term structural shift to lower growth and even contraction in demand in the OECD countries was accelerated by the sharp economic downtown triggered by the 2008 financial crisis. The result is a picture of future global energy demand that looks very different from that in the past: according to BP, 93 percent of demand growth between 2010 and 2030 is projected to come from countries outside the OECD.[3] Two other factors are changing the demand-supply landscape: the widespread commercialization of technology to produce previously uneconomic "unconventional" oil and gas resources in the United States has transformed the country's energy situation, with the IEA saying that the United States is already the largest producer of hydrocarbon liquids in the world. The resurgence of production in the world's traditional consumption center is also coinciding with a surge in consumption in the world's traditional production center. At around 3 million barrels a day, Saudi Arabia's oil consumption is nearly equal to that of India—a country with more than 1 billion more people. Like its neighbors in the Persian Gulf (the United Arab Emirates and Kuwait are already net gas importers), Saudi Arabia faces a chronic shortfall in natural gas in the near future. For now, Saudi Arabia is able to burn crude oil for power generation at a high economic opportunity cost. Rising populations and rising demand for electricity and water (made through power-intensive desalination processes) are likely to put even more pressure on governments in the region to use more of their own hydrocarbons domestically or to import.

The implications of the changing supply-demand landscape for energy governance are profound. As the industrial world makes up a smaller and smaller proportion of global demand, the IEA in its current form will become a less representative mouthpiece for consuming nations. With China and India not full members of the OECD and therefore not represented in the IEA, the major drivers of demand are not part of the conversation.[4] At the same time, the increasing dysfunction of OPEC, driven by both political and economic divergences among the group's members, is leading to reduced certainty with regard to production. On the supply side of the ledger, the prospects for decreased effectiveness are equally clear. With many OPEC producers, including Saudi Arabia, the cartel's de facto leader, increasingly dependent on high oil prices to sustain domestic political stability through the provision of generous social spending programs, the ability of OPEC to address market volatility through changes in the volume of production is now limited by a significantly higher lower-price bound than in the past. Internal divisions within the cartel along political and sectarian lines have reduced its ability to coordinate production objectives. The reemergence of

Iraq as a major oil producer threatens to limit the effectiveness of OPEC even further. The unwillingness of a Shia-led Iraq, whose political leadership has little incentive to cooperate with Sunni-led Saudi Arabia on any issue, to submit to production quotas has the potential to erode what is left of the quota discipline among OPEC's other members.

Increasing Prominence of National Oil Companies in Global Energy Markets

A direct consequence of the structural changes in the global energy market is a greater prominence of state-owned entities from import-dependent countries, usually in the form of national oil companies (NOCs). For countries that have an increasing need for oil and gas and that see energy as a strategic necessity, access to physical energy resources—rather than reliance on the functioning of the market—is paramount. These emerging economies are more likely to equate energy security with energy equity, leading them to take financial positions in physical resources or production and infrastructure assets via their NOCs. The increasing prominence of emerging market state-owned companies in energy development projects overseas presents several governance-related challenges. The first are the motivations and, perhaps more important, the *perceived* motivations of NOCs. Under the old energy supply-demand paradigm, in which industrial, liberal, market-based economies accounted for the majority of global energy demand, the principal investors in the global energy sector were private companies whose overriding objective was to maximize profits and shareholder value; NOCs in resource-rich countries alternately courted and spurned international oil companies (IOCs) according to technical requirements and political expediency. In the new paradigm, the emergence of NOCs from resource-poor countries looking to acquire energy interests abroad is changing the calculation of both IOCs and NOCs from resource-rich nations. Unlike IOCs, with which they are in direct competition, the motivations of these NOCs are more likely to be perceived to combine commercial interests with geopolitical goals. In many cases, these resource-poor NOCs have access to abundant capital courtesy of their home governments, giving them the ability to accept less attractive terms for energy deals than their shareholder-bound IOC competitors. The implications of this competitive advantage are profound. With the ability to invest in projects that are uneconomic for private sector companies, NOCs can make deals that are backed by political forces, even if not motivated by political ends.

The displacement of IOCs by NOCs also has implications for the stability of host countries. The presence of energy companies in countries with weak institutions and high levels of instability and political risk is not a new phenomenon. However, while IOCs have operated in many of the world's most fragile states for decades, they have done so according to internationally monitored levels of operational and ethical transparency demanded by shareholders and, increasingly, Western governments. The United States, Canada, and Europe now require that listed energy and extraction companies disclose payments they make to foreign governments over a certain threshold—an example of one of the latest manifestations of this phenomenon. While such laws or protocols ensure a minimum standard of ethical business operations for IOCs, many NOCs have no compunctions about following them.

This distinction has implications for energy-related governance regimes with regard to safety, human rights, and corruption. The challenge of governance is particularly acute in new energy-producing states with no history of institutional management of hydrocarbon sectors such as Ghana, Kenya, Mozambique, and Tanzania, all of which have made large discoveries of oil and natural gas in recent years.

The emergence of resource-poor NOCs poses other important governance challenges both for private sector companies and for governments of market-based economies. With the increased complexity, scale, and capital intensity of oil and gas projects, energy investments come with a corresponding increase in the level of financial risk. To mitigate the risks, companies are more and more looking to partner with others in the joint development of projects. There is a long history of partnership between private sector multinational enterprises; however, given the greater role of national oil companies and state-owned enterprises, the new partnerships are increasingly between private multinationals and NOCs. IOC-NOC partnerships on complex, multibillion-dollar projects present new risks. In the event of an accident or a dispute between the partners, private companies may not have recourse to the same liability protocols or dispute resolution mechanisms as they do when dealing with other commercial counterparties. In the event of a NOC refusing to accept liability, abrogating a contract, or otherwise failing to adhere to accepted business practices, it will be harder for their private sector partners to seek redress.

For governments, NOCs present a further challenge with regard to inward investment. As North America experiences a resurgence in hydrocarbons production, many NOCs are vying to invest in assets and projects that come with the benefit of being based in countries with stable political climates, established property rights, and strong rule of law. However, host governments in Washington and Ottawa have shown themselves cautious—if not hostile—toward allowing such investment. The most high-profile example of this phenomenon was the attempted takeover by the Chinese National Offshore Oil Corporation (CNOOC), China's state-controlled oil and gas company, of Unocal, a California-based oil company, in 2005. The bid was aborted in the face of fierce political resistance in the United States. However, the recent discovery of abundant reserves of economic oil and gas in the United States in the wake of the shale gas boom as well as a desire to acquire the technology to replicate the success back home have led to a new wave of multibillion-dollar investments by NOCs in the United States. To date, these investments have mostly taken the form of the acquisition of minority stakes in U.S. or IOC-owned operations. As the United States and Canada continue to see increases in their reserve estimates, their stable political and financial conditions are likely to attract higher levels of investment from NOCs. It is more likely than not that the United States will again face the prospect of a large NOC takeover in the near future. The way in which it handles such prospective transactions will have serious implications on both the economic and diplomatic fronts and for the stability of global energy supplies.

Technical Complexity of Energy Projects and "Frontier" Production

As the world's demand for oil and gas rises and production from traditional hydrocarbon regions declines, countries and companies are having to look to ever more complex and challenging frontiers for production. In addition to venturing into new political frontiers such as sub-Saharan Africa, companies are having to consider more and more complex and costly projects to secure supplies and replace reserves. Development of oil and gas in deepwater offshore fields, the extraction of oil from bitumen (oil, or tar, sands), and the development of "stranded" gas assets through the construction of vast liquefied natural gas infrastructure demonstrate the length to which IOCs—often in partnership with independent private companies or NOCs—are having to go.

This push for new production opportunities comes with new technical risks for which governance structures are absent or only partially in place. The 2010 blowout of the Macondo well in the U.S. Gulf of Mexico, which was exploring for oil more than 50 miles from shore and more than 5,000 feet beneath the surface of the ocean, demonstrated the technological complexity of modern oil production projects. The aftermath of the accident, in which oil spilled into the ocean for eighty-nine days, highlighted the inability of regulators and companies themselves to respond adequately to accidents and, later, the complexity of assessing damages and assigning liability.

In some cases, frontier production can combine both technical and political risk. Perhaps the best example of this is the prospect of energy development in the Arctic. According to the U.S. Geological Survey, the Arctic holds roughly 20 percent of the world's undiscovered oil and gas, most of which is located offshore on the continental shelves of the five Arctic littoral states: the United

States, Canada, Russia, Norway, and Demark (through its control of Greenland). The prospect of energy production in the Arctic is not new: wells have been drilled north of the Arctic Circle for decades. However, with high oil prices, increasing demand for new sources of production, and improved technology, the energy resources of the region are likely to be explored with more interest than ever before. The Arctic presents unique challenges in the realm of global energy governance. There is no overarching set of standards or principles for energy development in the region. While such a regime may be impractical, it is in the interests of all host countries and industry alike to avoid a "race to the bottom" with regard to standards and regulatory oversight in Arctic energy production. The situation presents an opportunity for leadership from the companies with the capital, technology, project management ability, and accountability to take the lead in partnership with host governments to ensure that the risks of frontier production are fully understood and internalized.

Globalization of Energy Technologies

A related, but distinct, trend that is increasing the challenge of energy governance is the diffusion of energy technologies to emerging and developing-market countries. With the latter projected to account for the vast majority of the increase in energy demand in the future, they are designing, acquiring, and implementing technologies that were previously the exclusive preserve of industrial countries. The transmission of complex energy-related technologies to new markets offers significant opportunity as more countries harness advanced exploration, production, and consumption knowledge to meet their requirements. However, this diffusion comes with the risk that countries adopting new technologies will be able to externalize some of the risks and costs of adoption. The most prominent example in this regard is civil nuclear power. In the latter half of the twentieth century, the majority of civil nuclear power deployment was concentrated in countries that had either experience with a military nuclear program, a strong technical and institutional base, or both. The likely newcomer nuclear energy states of the twenty-first century have neither of these characteristics. Having purchased four reactor units from South Korea in 2009, the United Arab Emirates is planning to have its civil nuclear power program operational by 2017—one of the most ambitious timelines for deployment in history. While the country has a high level of sovereign wealth enabling it to attract large amounts of expatriate expertise, its capacity to develop and sustainably operate, maintain, and regulate a civil nuclear program is subject to question.[5] The International Atomic Energy Agency, the nuclear body of the United Nations, states that countries looking to implement nuclear power need to be "intelligent customers" of the technology and that countries using nuclear power should not rely on external parties to oversee nuclear power projects.[6] The necessity for robust regulation of the nuclear power sector was forcefully articulated by the Fukushima accident in Japan in March 2011, which saw the meltdown of three nuclear reactors. While the earthquake and the tsunami that were the proximate causes of the accident could not have been prevented, a subsequent Japanese government inquiry found that the accident was a "profoundly man-made disaster," and the result of a culture of "reflexive obedience" and "insularity" on the part of regulatory authorities.[7] If Japan, a country with decades of civil nuclear power experience and a sophisticated industrial and academic base, can suffer from a lack of regulatory oversight, the risk is at least as great in newcomer countries with no experience in the nuclear sector and brand-new institutional frameworks. The United Arab Emirates is far from alone in its quest for civil nuclear power, and the cause for concern is more pronounced in other countries with serious ambitions: Jordan and Vietnam are both in the advanced stages of negotiating contracts with reactor vendors; Turkey has signed an agreement with Russia for the provision of a new nuclear plant on its Mediterranean coast; and Saudi Arabia has ambitious plans for developing nuclear power to address its rapidly growing demand for electricity. The globalization of nuclear energy technology—and particularly its introduction in the politically volatile Middle East—presents a profound governance challenge for the international community on both safety and nonproliferation grounds. The challenge of regulating regulators in an industry in which an accident, sabotage, or intentional misuse could have wide-ranging international consequences at present is being only partially met by a patchwork of voluntary associations and concepts of best practice. As the number of countries in the nuclear energy sector expands, a greater degree of coordination and governance will be necessary to reduce the risk of serious security and environmental catastrophes. Nuclear power is not the only technology whose international diffusion presents risks and related governance challenges. The genetic modification of organisms for the production of new fuels poses risks in both developed and emerging markets. While genetic modification has the potential to produce replacements for petroleum-based liquid fuels—whether through the modification of algae to produce "drop-in" fuels that substitute for gasoline or through the use of genetically engineered bacteria to break down certain organic matter to produce ethanol—the consequences of such organisms escaping from a controlled lab environment into the wild are unknown but potentially devastating.

This dynamic is also likely to manifest itself in the production of "unconventional" hydrocarbon resources such as shale gas and "tight oil." Such production relies on the practice of hydraulic fracturing (or fracking), which involves the high-pressure injection of large volumes of water and chemicals into subsurface geologic structures. While fracking is at the heart of the U.S. hydrocarbon boom, several European countries have enforced moratoria on the practice out of concern over potential detrimental effects to water and land resources. Even in countries, such as the United States, where the technique is permitted, resistance from environmental groups and local stakeholders has led to greater demands for transparency on the part of producers. Any major accident involving hydraulic fracturing, particularly one in which local water supplies become polluted, would have wide-ranging implications for the practice worldwide. As such, the countries that are expecting to benefit from both the production and consumption of the new volumes of gas being made available by hydraulic fracturing have an interest in creating and enforcing a standards regime that ensures that the practice is carried out at the highest levels of safety and sustainability.

Climate Change and Geo-Engineering

One of the largest market failures related to the energy sector has been the ongoing externalization of the climate-related costs associated with the burning of fossil fuels. The collective-action problem around anthropogenic climate change is a subject that has filled volumes of books and reams of academic journals. However, as the international community continues to search for an effective, feasible solution to the problem, other governance challenges are coming to the fore. Faced with the risk of irreversible climate change resulting from carbon dioxide emissions, the international community has singularly failed to implement a regime that is considered effective and equitable by all members. In the absence of an overarching global mechanism for mitigating greenhouse gases, several innovative measures involving direct intervention in the Earth's biosphere or atmosphere are being considered to address global warming. While such measures—termed "geo-engineering"—have traditionally been considered an insurance policy or a "Plan B" in the global response to climate change, they are now gaining prominence as serious possibilities.

Geo-engineering projects proposed to date can be divided into two major categories: carbon dioxide reduction (CDR) measures, which involve the removal of carbon dioxide from the atmosphere, and solar radiation management (SRM) measures, which involve direct intervention to reduce the effects of solar radiation on the planet.[8] Proposed CDR techniques include carbon capture and sequestration facilities and the addition of millions of tons of minerals into the oceans to absorb carbon and mitigate acidification; possible SMR measures include the emission of large quantities of sulfur dioxide into the atmosphere to block the warming effects of solar radiation and the "seeding" of clouds to increase the amount of sunlight reflected.

While the merits of each of these measures as a means of reducing greenhouse gasses is a matter of debate, the possible side effects or unintended consequences of their deployment throw up a stark set of governance challenges. Geo-engineering measures are designed to be locally deployable and globally effective. It is not inconceivable that an individual state, particularly one that feels itself more at risk from climate change than others, could implement a geo-engineering project that could have wide-ranging global implications. Moreover, nothing is limiting the deployment of geo-engineering measures to state actors. In 2012, Russ George, a U.S. businessman, undertook a small-scale geo-engineering experiment by releasing iron into the ocean off the Pacific coast of Canada in order to trigger the growth of plankton. As plankton absorb carbon dioxide and have the potential to retain it when they die and sink to the bottom of the ocean, George and his company, Planktos Corporation, saw the potential for a CDR project that could reduce atmospheric carbon dioxide levels and—if combined with a mechanism to sell credits for the carbon his company had sequestered—make money. While the results of George's experiment were inconclusive, the experiment demonstrated the challenges of geo-engineering governance. In the event that a well-financed nongovernmental organization, private corporation, or individual wishes to engage in large-scale geo-engineering, it is not clear what legal constraints exist to regulate or prohibit them from doing so.

Geo-engineering has garnered only limited attention from policymakers to date. As noted in a 2013 report by the U.S. Congressional Research Service, while some geo-engineering activities may be covered under the terms of existing treaties or laws, such governance "tend[s] to fall within the provisions of legal instruments designed to regulate the uses of particular environments (e.g., space, atmosphere, ocean, land)."[9] Even in cases where there is the prospect for geo-engineering to be subject to existing governance structures, the jurisdictional applicability of such laws or agreements to new technologies may be subject to challenge. In many cases, governments will have to determine the desirability of putting in place governance structures for geo-engineering. The risks of not engaging with the issue of geo-engineering governance are substantial. The unilateral application of systems or technologies without sufficient safeguards or information could lead to catastrophic consequences. The introduction of alien species or materials to the oceans, for example, could have a detrimental effect on marine habitats, the water cycle, or weather patterns. An effective SRM project would block the symptoms of global warming, but not the cause, leaving the Earth vulnerable to a warming shock in the event that the SRM measures are disrupted or discontinued. However, serious engagement with geo-engineering governance also comes with risk. Governments may be wary of investing effort in formulating a series of rules for geo-engineering governance, because such engagement has the potential to serve as formal recognition of the legitimacy of the technologies being considered. If and when a decision is made to address the issue of governance, policymakers will have to engage with issues of jurisdiction and equity. These issues will be particularly difficult for the United States to address. Among those international agreements that may be seen to have indirect applicability to the governance of geo-engineering, the United States is not a party to at least three: the Kyoto Protocol, the Convention on Biological Diversity (the agreement that George and Planktos Corporation were accused of violating), and the United Nations Convention on the Law of the Sea.

The United States: Cornerstone of Energy and Environmental Governance

Changing economic, technological, and environmental factors are likely to present significant new challenges for energy governance in the coming decade. With shifting patterns of global production and consumption for fossil fuels, incumbent international institutions will struggle to provide the information that traders and investors need to maintain stability in global energy markets. In the absence of new governance structures, both the reduced level of clarity around information on supply and demand as well as the inability of some large producers to respond to price signals due to domestic political constraints may lead to greater uncertainty among investors and therefore greater volatility in global energy markets. The increasing number of actors and jurisdictions in the global oil and gas sector may also increase the challenges of governance. Increased NOC activity in the global energy sector has the potential to improve overall consumer welfare through increased supply of oil, gas, and other energy sources. However, with competition between profit-hungry IOCs and energy-hungry state-backed NOCs, the incentive to subvert or circumvent accepted business norms to win contracts—whether through technically illegal means or not—is high. The displacement of IOCs by NOCs carries the risk of companies with relatively transparent operations and a high level of public accountability being replaced by companies subject to less external scrutiny. While cash-rich NOCs from energy-poor nations may bring large amounts of investment into the energy sector, particularly in developing countries, such investments may come with a cost in terms of environmental performance or good governance. With governments as their major shareholders, NOCs also present a potential challenge to their private sector business partners, as they may be less inclined to submit to the conventional legal mechanisms for resolving commercial disputes and determining liability. Moreover, NOC interest in investment in developed countries poses a governance challenge for national and state governments that need to determine a transparent approach to the evaluation of bids on their relative commercial and political merits.

The new energy landscape will pose technical as well as political governance challenges. The global diffusion of energy technologies raises the prospect of overinvestment by countries and companies in technically complex projects (such as civil nuclear power, hydraulic fracturing, and chemically produced algal biofuels) that may fail to fully internalize risk. The challenge is compounded by the risk of "global feedback" that comes with the use of energy technologies by an increasing number of actors and the need for governance regimes to take account of the use of such technologies wherever they are used. The currently ungoverned arena of geo-engineering presents a challenge that marries technical and transboundary governance challenges with the signal failure of a meaningful collective response to climate change.

Fortunately, for nearly all of the obstacles outlined above one actor has the ability to shape the governance agenda positively for the new energy landscape: the United States.

On the issue of changing consumer-producer dynamics, the United States has, thanks to the boom in shale gas and tight oil production, the prospect of regaining the title of being simultaneously both the world's biggest consumer and biggest producer of oil. In this position, it will hold sway with both consumers and producers. On the consumption side, the United States will remain the single most prominent voice in the IEA and the largest holder of strategic petroleum reserves. It also has the opportunity to serve those non-IEA members nations, such as China and India, that will make up the vast majority of growth in demand in the coming decades. In addition to serving as an increasing source of secure, market-driven supply, the United States has the opportunity to alter the structure and reduce the volatility of the global oil market due to the specific geologic nature of its "unconventional" resources. Owing to its ability and willingness to invest in spare production capacity, Saudi Arabia has been the world's pivotal "swing producer"—and therefore de facto price setter—since the latter half of the twentieth century. Due to the distributed nature of shale gas and tight oil production, which can be likened to a flexible manufacturing process more than traditional "lumpy" production, the United States will have an opportunity to offer its own version of "spare capacity": particularly during periods of low prices, companies in the United States will be able to respond relatively quickly to market signals and cut production to balance the oil market.[10] On the production side, the United States offers a much-needed source of competition, which is likely to lead to a decrease in resource nationalism (as resource-holding governments have to contend with attractive alternatives) and a corresponding increase in the efficiency of production by NOCs.

With regard to the increasing prominence of NOCs in global energy markets, the United States has a unique opportunity to build trust and exert positive influence in the relationships between resource holders and state-backed investors. Like private sector companies, NOCs prioritize three things in their search for new energy sources: abundant resources, low geopolitical risk, and stable investment terms. The United States now provides all three of these conditions. For China, home to some of the world's most ambitious NOCs, the United States is an explicit target in its plans to double its overseas production by 2015; its three largest companies, which have already invested billions of dollars in U.S. shale assets, plan to follow that with tens of billions more in the coming years. NOCs from other countries, including India and Korea, have also invested in U.S. shale-related assets. For the United States, this situation offers an important opportunity in its interaction with NOCs and, by extension, in its ability to shape relationships between NOCs and other host governments. By requiring outside investors to adhere to nondiscriminatory minimum standards as a condition of entry, the United States can bring a higher level of transparency to the operations of NOCs. This can work to the benefit of both consumers—who will gain from the additional supply—and the NOCs themselves. One of the greatest challenges faced by NOCs is the perception that they are tools of a broader foreign policy. By allowing them to enter on comparable commercial terms and to compete on an equal footing with other companies, the United States could go a long way to building trust and reducing the suspicion surrounding NOCs.

The United States also has an opportunity to build trust with NOCs in third countries. Having secured resources in Africa, South America, and elsewhere, several NOCs, particularly those from China, are entering a second phase in their interactions with host governments in which they are experiencing contract disputes, obsolescing bargains, and other complexities associated with foreign direct investment. The United States, which has a long history of addressing these kinds of challenges, can serve as a valuable source of information and advice to these companies as they navigate political risks. Such efforts will encourage NOCs to see themselves as part of the broader international energy community, making them more likely to use established mechanisms for dispute resolution and, over time, more likely to adhere to broader norms and best practices.

On technical complexity and "frontier" production and globalization of energy technologies, the United States is uniquely placed to set the governance agenda. The global oil and gas industry is evolving to one in which technology is becoming as critical a factor in success as access to resources. The United States has both. Texas is home to one of the fastest-growing oil production regions in the world and to the world's most advanced oil and gas technology hub. Other U.S. states also have world-leading educational and research and development facilities. As a result, the engineers and technicians who will be needed to access the world's increasingly hard-to-develop resources will either get their training in the United States or work for U.S.-based firms, or both. The United States also has several of the "frontier" conditions that are found elsewhere. Including ultra-deepwater and "pre-salt" fields in the Gulf of Mexico, offshore Arctic fields in Alaska, and onshore "unconventional" shale gas and oil fields in Texas, North Dakota, and Pennsylvania, the United States is likely to play host to some of the most challenging prospects for oil and gas development. The ability of U.S. companies to establish the industry standards and practices for global offshore and onshore oil and gas development and the ways in which state and federal regulators set the framework for operation in such areas will give it a central role in energy governance for "frontier" production worldwide.

The United States also has a central role to play in the globalization of energy technology. In the wake of the Fukushima tragedy in Japan, the civil nuclear scandal in Korea, and the pullback from nuclear power in Western Europe, the United States has become even more critical as a benchmark for best practice in the civil nuclear sector. As the Japanese nuclear industry has undergone a period of intense—and long overdue—reform, Japanese regulators have looked to the United States as a model for their institutional restructuring. Despite U.S. firms losing out to a Korean consortium in a bid to supply reactors to the United Arab Emirates, Korean firms are now seeking approval from the U.S. Nuclear Regulatory Commission for the winning reactor design. As more details of the level of corruption in the Korean nuclear industry emerge, the United Arab Emirates and other emerging countries are likely to seek both endorsement and additional services from the United States as they proceed with their nuclear programs. While the United States is unlikely to build large numbers of new nuclear power plants itself, it will nevertheless enjoy continued prominence in the civil nuclear industry as a standard setter and supplier of technical services.

The United States has a similar opportunity as a central actor in the design and distribution of unconventional oil and gas production. Thanks to a combination of government support and favorable economic conditions, including private mineral rights, access to capital, and an established supplier base, the United States has served as the cradle of the shale gas and "tight" oil industries. It has therefore captured the first benefits of such unconventional production. Other countries are likely to take longer to develop their own unconventional onshore resources. As they do so, they will have the opportunity to learn from the experience of the United States. For the United States, this creates a double opportunity: it will bring a welcome addition to the export of high-value goods and services, and it will give the United States the chance to set the global standard for hydraulic fracturing and associated services.

The final, and perhaps the most important, governance arena in which the United States holds a critical position is global climate change. With regard to geo-engineering, the United States will have an opportunity to set some of the early policy and regulatory frameworks as entrepreneurs develop and pilot their concepts. However, the United States will struggle to muster the moral authority to regulate the actions of countries that see themselves as facing an existential threat from climate change. Having not ratified the Kyoto Protocol, the signature multilateral initiative for addressing greenhouse gas emissions, the United States will have limited political leverage if it attempts to regulate other approaches to climate change mitigation. In contrast, on the broader climate change issue the United States is the only country that can unilaterally move the world to a mean-ingfully lower-carbon future. At first glance, this proposition appears unlikely. Asia's rapid growth in energy demand will have to be met with fossil fuels under any scenario, meaning that global carbon emissions will continue rising at an unsustainable rate as efforts to get an internationally binding agreement on emis-sions reductions stall and investments in low-carbon technologies falter in the economic downturn. In its most recent annual assessment, the IEA concluded, "Taking all new developments and policies into account, the world is still failing to put the global energy system onto a more sustainable path." The resurgence of U.S. oil and gas production initially appears to add to the challenge: by adding to global reserves of hydrocarbons, the shale gas and tight oil revolution can be seen as extending the carbon-based economy. However, there is a way in which the United States can use its oil and gas bonanza to take a leadership role in climate change mitigation and to put itself back at the forefront of global trade.

Irrespective of actions by OECD countries, China, India, and other emerging nations will burn oil, gas, and coal in ever greater quantities for the foreseeable future. Given its huge reserves of hydrocarbons, the United States could posi-tion itself as perhaps the principal beneficiary of this demand by permitting and supporting the free export of oil and natural gas, both of which are currently inhibited to varying degrees. Such a policy should involve the expedited permit-ting of oil and gas production and ancillary pipeline infrastructure projects and the enabling of crude oil and gas exports, which are currently subject to policy restrictions or prohibitions. The policy would strengthen both the country's fiscal position through export revenues and job creation and enhance the stability of global markets through increased supply and the deepening of partnerships with key consumers such as China and India.

Such a policy of hydrocarbon development can be consistent with leadership on climate change if, as a condition of the development and export of its oil and gas, the United States puts a domestic price on carbon. This would achieve three powerful objectives. First, it would provide a market-based incentive to reduce emissions in a transparent, cost-effective way. Second, it would demonstrate to the international community that the United States takes climate change seriously and is willing to introduce measures to address it. Such an overture would increase Washington's credibility in discussions of emissions reductions and encourage other large emitters to follow suit. Finally, it would generate revenue, which could be allocated to technologies that have the best chance of addressing emissions on a global scale, including carbon capture and storage (CCS). While policy tools in the United States such as renewable portfolio standards and production tax credits have added to the domestic stock of nonfossil energy sources, they will have a negligible impact on climate change as long as coal—soon to overtake oil as the world's leading energy source—continues to be burned in the developing world. Only by reducing the carbon emissions of coal (and, eventually, gas) in the global power sector or finding scalable alternatives for base-load power will it be possible to stabilize greenhouse gas emissions in time. Having commercialized CCS at scale, U.S. companies would be in a position to become the leader in the supply of the technology to the rest of the world. Using market mechanisms to correct market failures and acting to further its own economic and geopolitical interests, the United States could thus make meaningful progress on one of the most intractable governance challenges of the age.

Notes

1. International Energy Agency (IEA), *World Energy Outlook 2013* (Paris, 2013), p. 58.

2. Ibid.

3. BP, "BP Energy Outlook 2030" (January 2013), p. 11.

4. At the time of writing, there is some discussion about China and India joining the IEA as "observer" members, but this is still to be implemented.

5. For in-depth analysis of the challenge of human resource development in aspiring nuclear energy states, see John P. Banks and Kevin Massy, "Human Resource Development in New Nuclear Energy States: Case Studies from the Middle East," Policy Brief 12-02 (Brookings Institution, November 2012).

6. IEA, "Stakeholder Involvement in Nuclear Issues" (Paris, 2006), p. 13.

7. National Diet of Japan, "The Official Report of the Fukushima Nuclear Accident Independent Investigation Commission" (Tokyo, January 2012).

8. Geo-engineering taxonomy is sourced from Kelsi Bracmort and Richard Lattanzio, "Geo-Engineering: Governance and Technology Policy" (Washington: Congressional Research Service, January 2013).

9. Ibid.

10. Thanks to its abundant, relatively low-cost shale gas reserves, the United States will be able to play a similar role in the natural gas market, where it will be able to sell hub-linked gas that sets a price ceiling in Europe and a price floor in Asia.

Contributors

PAVEL K. BAEV
Peace Research Institute Oslo

KRISTIAN COATES ULRICHSEN
Department of Governance,
London School of Economics

JEFF D. COLGAN
Brown University

ALEX EVANS
New York University

ARUNABHA GHOSH
Council on Energy, Environment,
and Water

BRUCE JONES
Brookings Institution

ANDREW B. KENNEDY
Australian National University

CLAIRE LANGLEY
Climate Advisers

KEVIN MASSY
Brookings Institution

JOSHUA MELTZER
Brookings Institution

C. RAJA MOHAN
Observer Research Foundation,
New Delhi

EMILY O'BRIEN
New York University

LYDIA POWELL
Centre for Resources Management,
Observer Research Foundation,
New Delhi

ANTONIO JORGE RAMALHO
University of Brasília

ANGEL SAZ-CARRANZA
ESADEgeo Center for Global Economy
and Geopolitics, Barcelona

DAVID STEVEN
New York University

MARIE VANDENDRIESSCHE
ESADEgeo Center for Global Economy
and Geopolitics, Barcelona

MARK WESTON
Riverpath Associates

DANIEL KIM CHAI YEO
WaterAid

Index

Note: Page numbers followed by *t* and *f* refer to tables and figures respectively.

CPSIA information can be obtained at www.ICGtesting.com
Printed in the USA
LVOW08s0336250516

489841LV00001B/1/P